WITHDRAWN
HARVARD LIBRARY
WITHDRAWN

BEFORE INFALLIBILITY

BEFORE INFALLIBILITY

Liberal Catholicism in Biedermeier Vienna

Adam Bunnell

Rutherford • Madison • Teaneck
Fairleigh Dickinson University Press
London and Toronto: Associated University Presses

© 1990 by Associated University Presses, Inc.

All rights reserved. Authorization to photocopy items for internal or personal use, or the internal or personal use of specific clients, is granted by the copyright owner, provided that a base fee of $10.00, plus eight cents per page, per copy is paid directly to the Copyright Clearance Center, 27 Congress Street, Salem, Massachusetts 01970. [0-8386-3344-7/89 $10.00 + 8¢ pp, pc.]

Associated University Presses
440 Forsgate Drive
Cranbury, NJ 08512

Associated University Presses
25 Sicilian Avenue
London WC1A 2QH, England

Associated University Presses
P.O. Box 488, Port Credit
Mississauga, Ontario
Canada L5G 4M2

The paper used in this publication meets the requirements of the American National Standard for Permanence of Paper for Printed Library Materials Z39.48-1984.

Library of Congress Cataloging-in-Publication Data

Bunnell, Adam, 1946–
  Before infallibility.

  Bibliography: p.
  Includes index.
  1. Günther, Anton, 1783–1863. 2. Veith, Johann Emanuel, 1787–1876. 3. Vienna (Austria)—Church history—19th century. 4. Liberalism (Religion)—Catholic Church—History—19th century. 5. Catholic Church—Austria—Vienna—History—19th century. I. Title.
BX4705.G768B86 1989   282'.092'2   88-45618
ISBN 0-8386-3344-7 (alk. paper)

PRINTED IN THE UNITED STATES OF AMERICA

To Vienna, the City where I Came of Age

CONTENTS

Preface	9
Acknowledgments	11
1 The Search for Truth	15
2 Biedermeier Vienna	32
3 The Theologian and the Preacher	51
4 The World of Anton Günther	72
5 Johann Emanuel Veith as Güntherian and Preacher	95
6 1848	116
7 The Triumph of Infallibility	139
Epilogue	160
Appendix: The Güntherians and Their Friends	163
Notes	171
Bibliography	209
Index	235

PREFACE

The quest for the Holy Grail of Truth has brought much insight and much misunderstanding. Nowhere has that been more fully borne out than in the realm of religion. The human search for meaning in the face of contradiction and paradox has led many to claim divine revelation resting only on the insights accumulated in their traditions. Many angry words have been hurled, many a war has been fought, much hatred has poisoned the human community because individuals in their insecurity claimed absolute certainty, a certainty that precluded contradiction. Not surprisingly, fraternal disagreements have been the source of the most intense bitterness and the most intransigent refusals to compromise.

The past has often been called upon as evidence of the presence of Truth in a tradition that claims divine revelation must be preserved and protected. But the past is more often than not glorified: inconsistencies and insecurities are forgotten, and the past's "absolute Truth" dissolves under closer scrutiny. Thinkers in every age have given voice to their own sense of inadequacy in trying to capture Truth in words and doctrines and systems of thought. Only the incurably arrogant have claimed to have captured Truth within the confines of limited human thought, even if bolstered by appeals to divine intervention. More often, the conclusions of past generations are deified by a present unwilling to face honestly its own need to wrestle with meaning and Truth.

Through centuries of change and challenge, Christianity as an explanation of Truth has remained vital. At moments when it seemed about to succumb to enemies surrounding it or to the mediocrity attending its very success, it has shown surprising ability to recapture human hearts with a hope beyond the promise held in its own spotted history. To some that very fact speaks of divine protection and guidance. To others it is only a monument to superstition and the continuing need of humankind to escape more sober reality and to claim that history can be transcended.

Roman Catholicism has made more claims to Truth than most religions. Roman Catholic thought has relied less on demonstrable and necessary connections between a proposition and its principles (*scientia*, as Thomas Aquinas would define it) than on probable evidence pointing to Truth, evidence buttressed by the weight of authority (*opinio*, as the Thomas would have it).[1] Authority meant *church* authority, an authority that purported to teach eternal and unchangeable Truth as divinely delivered to it. It was Truth expressed in human language, but it was eternal Truth nonetheless.

When faced by those who doubted or found other authorities to follow, or when confronted with a changing situation it could not understand or control, Roman Catholicism in the modern world has reached into its past to find authoritative answers to present issues. After the Protestant Reformation, the scientific and industrial revolutions, the era of revolutionary democracy and the rise of national consciousness, Rome found it increasingly difficult to bring the world to heel. Rome began to insist on uniformity *within* the ranks to combat untruth in the increasing arena *outside* its control. Sincere attempts to express Truth in language that a contemporary world might understand were met with suspicion that the indifference of pluralism was creeping in. Integralists, those who felt called to protect and preserve the divine deposit of Truth, came to dominate the bureaucracy of the hierarchical Roman Church. Those who disagreed were discredited with labels that did no justice to the carefulness of their thought.

In the nineteenth century, Thomas Aquinas became the measuring rod of Truth, the judge of what was Roman Catholic and what was not. Sadly, Thomas was long dead and could not remind his posthumous followers of his own conviction that the words he had multiplied had ultimately been inadequate. Nor had the discipline of history invaded the Roman ranks enough to highlight the pluralism of Thomas's own era. Those who tried to introduce the perspective of history were accused of the error of historicism, of the belief that Truth is conditioned by time and place and the limits of human understanding.

This work is written with a great deal of love for Roman Catholicism and from a pluralist perspective. It is a study of two men, both priests, one a theologian and the other a preacher, in a German and Catholic world after Napoleon Bonaparte and Immanuel Kant. Anton Günther and Johann Emanuel Veith were convinced Roman Catholics; they had spent little time in the study of Thomas, but their thought was condemned by those who had. My intention in this study is not to excoriate the followers of Thomas Aquinas nor to vindicate Günther and Veith. I write in the conviction that the struggle for Truth and meaning demands humility and the willingness to listen with an openness to being changed, in the conviction that the study of any era with its struggles, conceits, and failures can move beyond quaint antiquarianism to valuable contemporary insight.

ACKNOWLEDGMENTS

I extend a simple, inadequate but heartfelt "Thank you" to my academic advisors, William Wright and Josef Altholz for their assistance, encouragement, and patience. I am grateful to Joseph Pritz and Erwin Mann for their help and suggestions. I am grateful for the assistance of the various archivists and librarians along the way, especially to the Frau Bishop in Bonn and to the Herr Oberdirektor of the Stadtarchiv in Vienna. The expert assistance of Steve and Marion Lassonde and Frances Estes as well as the skills of Jean Tasa deserve special mention.

Also, this work would not have been born without the support and understanding of many friends, most especially of the Levak and Lassonde families, of Jeffrey Luther, Timothy Nipper, Joel Tracy, Timothy Eberle, Richard Dorr, Roland Schwarz, and Anton Hrovath. Nor would the work have been so pleasurable without the delicate cuisine of Françoise Levak, Juliette Gallois and Franco Modica.

Finally, I am grateful for the hospitality and support of the Conventual Franciscans in Austria and middle America.

BEFORE INFALLIBILITY

1
THE SEARCH FOR TRUTH

In March of 1274, Thomas lay dying. He was fifty years old, grossly overweight and en route to France to the second church council of Lyons where he had been called as a consultant. Behind him lay a life of controversy and prolific writing—writings that the corpulent Thomas knew had not captured the essence of the God he was now about to confront face-to-face. Perhaps all those words were not simply straw—but they paled before the eternity that loomed. His work had gradually won acceptance in his lifetime in spite of the suspicion accorded to his use of Aristotle's rediscovered works with their Muslim commentaries. Thomas's thoughts at the moment of death are not recorded. Perhaps he gave some thought to his chief rival, the fifty-four-year-old Bonaventure who had also been called to the council, not as consultant but as the cardinal archbishop of Albano. Bonaventure too would die before the year was out, a victim of incurable constipation.

Thomas was from the small village of Roccasecca, not far from the Benedictine monastery of Montecassino in Italy; but his parents were from Aquino, and he was known to his contemporaries and to history as Thomas Aquinas. In his time, he was an innovator, subject to suspicion and investigation, begrudgingly given acceptance because of the sheer brilliance and scope of his works and the obvious sincerity and depth of his faith. Eventually, he would be declared a saint of the Roman Catholic Church and his works would eclipse those of Bonaventure in spite of Bonaventure's earlier canonization.

Both men belonged to new religious communities—also rivals. Thomas was a follower of Dominic and Bonaventure of Francis of Assisi. Both Thomas and Bonaventure were innovators in some ways, for both recognized the need for a *system* of philosophy and a *systematic* exposition of faith rather than the cumbersome *Sententiae* of Peter Lombard and their countless commentaries. But Thomas chose the rediscovered corpus of Aristotle to become the handmaiden of his theology. Bonaventure wrote out of the long tradition going back to Augustine of Hippo, and his knowledge of Plato filtered through Plotinus. But for all their apparent differences, Thomas and Bonaventure were very similar. They were both firmly convinced that faith and revelation came from God and contained absolute Truth. They further agreed on the principles of their Christian faith and that philosophy was "false" or "faulty" if it did not come to the conclusions of faith.

Thomas and Bonaventure, not unlike human thinkers in every age, were foundationalists. Their desire was to transcend their time and place and discover eternal Truth. Thomas, when he remarked that his works were so much straw, seemed to have caught a glimpse of the futility of such a project. His insight did not make an impression on either his contemporaries or those who would look to the "angelic doctor" or the "seraphic doctor" (as Thomas and Bonaventure came to be known respectively) for escape from their own place and time in history.

In the time of Thomas and Bonaventure, the Western world considered Truth in religious terms, theology building on revelation from God and his son. All knowledge had to conform to that Truth. Certainly, the thirteenth century was not as settled as some nostalgic thirteenth-century minds living in later centuries would have it. There were holy wars against the infidel and heretic to be convinced or burned. But there was also the presumption that Truth was attainable, indeed had already been attained.

Thomas, building on Aristotle, made a distinction between *scientia* and *opinio*. It was an essential distinction for Thomas and his time; each operation belonged to a different "faculty" of the soul. *Scientia*, usually translated as "science," demanded demonstration; it is the mode of reasoning which displays necessary connections between a proposition and its principles, as when a geometrical proposition is deduced from or reduced to the first principles of Euclidian geometry. *Scientia* is the science of essences; it provides absolute certainty and is Truth in its pure form.

Even for Thomas, the epistemological principle of *scientia* was rare, often caught in vicious circularity or infinite regress. *Opinio,* inadequately translated as "opinion," was the more common path to knowledge and Truth. In *opinion*, knowledge was not demonstrated; one's adherence to Truth so discovered is based on criteria other than strict demonstration. Opinions are judged more or less probable, but this is not statistical probability or a matter of evidence pointing to probable truth. For both Thomas and Bonaventure, *opinio* or probability was based on what *authority* approved.

Authority in the thirteenth century of the Western world meant church authority. The dream of an *Imperium Romanum* was represented most powerfully by the man by this time known as the Vicar of Christ, the Papa of Christendom, the Bishop of Roma Eterna. And by the thirteenth century the pope had a growing bureaucracy to legislate the dream.

In the world of thought, however, there were other and more ancient authorities. There was Augustine (354–430), the learned bishop of Hippo and defender of the faith. There was Peter Lombard (ca. 1095–1160) and Anselm of Canturbury (1033–1109) and Peter Abelard (1079–1142). Most especially there was Augustine. Truth came from the past. It might be commented upon in the language of dwarfs; but the writings of the giants of previous centuries were considered the authorities to be quoted and called upon as irrefutable proof. Thomas found his authority in Aristotle, but even when one used Aristotle to contradict Augustine, especially when one went beyond Augustine, the bow to Augustine's greatness had to be made. And it was made. Truth was that which was always and everywhere believed by everyone (*quod semper, quod ubique, quod ab omnibus creditum est*). Augustine *was* everyone.

From the perspective of later centuries, the understanding of *scientia* and *opinio*, especially of *opinio*, seemed quaint and naive. The irony is that "modern" humans, rejecting *opinion* as inadequate, became caught in a quest for the Absolute Truth of *scientia*, a quest that all too often ended on the horns of the dilemma structured by Aristotle and Thomas. It was the Roman pope who continued to stress *opinio* as the basis for the evaluation of Truth and whose supporters, paradoxically, would elevate the thought of Thomas to the level of the authority behind *opinio*. Most paradoxically, the pope insisted that he did not need to become "modern." The problem was that fewer and fewer educated people were listening. They were in search of *scientia*.

It did not take long after the deaths of Thomas and Bonaventure for the *opinio* that they relied upon so heavily to come under attack. It came from all sides, most powerfully from inside the Christian world. By the end of the thirteenth century, the authority of the pope was challenged by the authority of kings. They all relied on the church as the pillar of their realms, but the stress was on *their* realms and all were quick to protest interference from an "outsider" such as the pope in Rome was rapidly becoming, the ruler of a group of small states in the center of the Italian peninsula whose authority was more theoretical than real.

Then came the great western schism with two and then three popes, each with a set of cardinals and bishops and abbots. The Black Death brought a fear that reclaimed hearts for the mystery of Christianity, and especially for the example of the excruciating death of its founder, but it left in its wake inadequate, ill-educated and venial clergy and religious unable to inspire confidence in clerical authority. For survivors, neither this world nor the next held much fear. The official church continued to preach that this world had to be endured and authority obeyed until death brought heaven for those who had reached heroic sanctity, paid for the recitation of countless Masses, or somehow managed to sneak in at the last minute; hell for those who had "sinned boldly" but not been rich enough to have Masses said or lucky enough to die shriven; purgatory for those who had not been quite so bold in sinning or had been shriven before they could sin again; and limbo for the countless infants—infant mortality was very high—and an occasional "good" infidel who died without benefit of baptism. But "the immense appetite for the divine" was not satisfied with official church pronouncement, especially when official church lives seemed to contradict church words.

After Thomas and Bonaventure, the schools that claimed them as founders would fight and disagree, each claiming the Truth of the *opinio* that came from its own authority. Theologians who recognized the *mystery* of God seemed increasingly unable to allow opinions other than their own any validity. Nontheologians shook their heads. Schoolmen might quibble about angels on pinheads; others looked beyond mere words to mysticism and pious activity. Still others looked to a rebirth that was not the rebirth of Christian baptism.

Thomas himself had used Aristotle, even though he had "baptized" him. Others would look behind the baptism. Old and long-forgotten ruins would become silent witnesses to other and non-Christian civilizations, civilizations that somehow managed peace and unity and answer to life without the Christian message. Dusty monastery libraries yielded books of other philosophers, more skeptical of Truth then Aristotle or Plato. Adventurers began to return with tales of other lands, other peoples and other religions, not all primitive or entirely wrong simply because they were without Christianity. The sacred beliefs and traditions of Christianity itself came under scrutiny, and they did not always survive the light shed upon them. The hallowed Vulgate Bible, the only Bible generations had known (even if it was kept chained and beyond their reach), was found to have mistranslations of the original "sacred" languages. Some of the rights of the popes were found to have been based on forgeries—and the forgeries mattered more in an age of doubt than they had when it was presumed that bending facts to support what everyone knew to be true could do no harm. The *scientia* of Aristotle and Thomas had become the litmus test of the true.

And then came the sixteenth century, growing out of and turning on the Renaissance that preceded it. The Reformation was mistrustful of *scientia*. The reformers believed in *opinio* but were unable to agree on which authority was absolute, which had the right to judge other authorities. Was it pope or council or scripture or individual conscience? There was no more visible "church" but only churches, each claiming to have captured Truth within its own confines and condemning former brethren under labels of heretic or whore. How could anyone still claim authority in the midst of that irony, the bitter hatred of one follower of the man from Nazareth for another? There were many who found the notion that Truth is validated by religious authority to be doubtful at best. It was not the first time, nor would it be the last, that religious believers would advance the cause of unbelief.

Somewhere along the way, theology became the handmaiden of philosophy, reversing the relationship that Thomas and Bonaventure took for granted. The authority of community and tradition gave way to the individual, his inwardness, his discovery of authority within the autonomous principles of demonstrated truth. *Opinio* was no longer made probable by the witness of authority's approval; authority was rendered more or less probable by the individual's judgments and willingness to follow. *Scientia* became the judge of *opinio*. It was mathematics and geometry that remained the points of certainty, but they were not the mathematics and geometry of the time of Thomas and Bonaventure. Neither the probabilism of Jesuit moral principle nor the asceticism of Port Royal quenched the thirst for certitude.

A Frenchman named Descartes, taught by Jesuits and steeped in mathematics (although not in the theories of probability that were to be heard in the decades after his death), thought to find certitude by turning his attention to ideas as the objects of mental vision. He sought a foundational cognition that would be indubitable, self-evident, and logically independent from every other possible cognition. Without conscious admission, he called upon the influence of Plato and Aristotle to answer the problem of skepticism inevitable in the crisis of *opinio* and the difficulty of *scientia*. The crisis of authority made a break from tradition seem absolutely necessary. Methodological doubt sought to transcend the situation, to start over, to escape history. The escape failed, of course. Yet philosophers since Descartes, seldom able to think in historical terms, continued the search for certainty.

More tolerant voices emerged, tolerant of all but the intolerance of Christianity,—especially the infamous thing called Catholicism. Enlightened, they called themselves, in contrast to the darkness that had preceded them. They looked to *this* world and the magnificence of human potential based on the *scientia* of Copernicus, Galileo, and Newton. They excoriated the superstition and superficiality of past believers. They called for "reasonableness" in religion, and looked for clear and distinct ideas to which the mind may legitimately give consent. Vehemently antidogmatic and adamantly anti-enthusiastic, they pronounced revelation a humanly created fiction. Their pantheon included the goddesses Nature and Reason and, by implication, the goddess *Scientia*. If earthquakes destroyed, if life proved a desert, one could still transform one's corner of the world into a garden.

The "enlightened" looked to a world governed by common sense, unpreoccupied with the joys of heaven or the fear of hell. They believed in the omnicompetence of criticism and the ability of reason to mark its own limits. They did not understand sin or redemption, especially if spoken through some distant biblical myth. They found the laws of God and nature inscribed in the workings of the mind. They scorned *opinio* and claimed to search, to investigate, to proclaim the *scientia* of demonstrated and obvious truth. They dared to know and concluded that some truth remained forever beyond their grasp. They dreamed of Eldorado and met Robespierre.

This is a study located in the European world in the half century after Napoleon Bonaparte and Immanuel Kant, both of whom influenced the pursuit of *scientia* and *opinio* in ways that neither would have anticipated. One brought both the excitement of the new and a flight to *opinio*, a flight to authority based on fear; the other brought a flurry of metaphysical speculation that claimed *scientia* was indeed possible. Both completed the work that Martin

Luther's exercise of individual conscience had begun, and those dedicated to the principles of *scientia* or *opinio* rushed to object.

The bachelor Immanuel Kant (1724–1804) walked the streets of Königsberg in East Prussia, lost in the regularity of professorial existence and the intricacies of his own philosophical system. He stood at the crossroads of religious thought, representing the third generation of the Enlightenment and foreshadowing much of nineteenth-century theological thought. Kant represented the end of the Enlightenment's confidence in reason; in Kant, reason knew how to set its limits and be sure of its sureties, but only in the world of phenomena. The world of noumena (*Ding an sich*) was closed. Natural theology was impossible. Only in the realm of practical reason, the realm of morality, could immortality, freedom, and God be postulated.[1] After Kant, the issues of faith and reason, grace and nature took a different shape: for Kant, morality, not reason, became the ground of faith. Especially in the first decades of the nineteenth century, much ink would be devoted to discussions of the man whose name meant "God is with us." After Kant, the moral and the religious points of view began to diverge in an attempt to overcome the crisis of *opinio* that had troubled earlier centuries. But Kant, like most of those who preceded him, had a misleading picture of the past, a picture which obscured those features which had raised doubts about human autonomy and the limitations of modern morality.[2] Kantian notions of "duty" and "universal law of nature" might be sufficient principles of moral action in East Prussia in the late eighteenth century; other times and other places would not be so easily convinced. For a time, however, Kant dominated thought, and in the half century that is the focus of this study it was Kant who gave shape to the philosophical and theological debate that would extend well beyond the Protestant world of East Prussia.

Kant knew of the French Revolution from afar and could not feel the disruption that it meant in distant France. But the revolution spilled over into Kant's own immediate world, brought by the armies drafted by Napoleon Bonaparte to bring a new *imperium* to European lands. Theories of duty, moral principle, and freedom were reshaped by the man of action. It is moot to argue whether the changes would have come without Napoleon; whether cause or catalyst, Napoleon was the instrument of much change in the European world, and his conquerors, dedicated to restoration and legitimacy though they were, did not undo a great deal of what he had done. The Emperor of the French might be exiled to an island, but the Holy Roman Empire had totally disappeared from the face of the earth. The constitution of that ancient institution, once it had been questioned and changed, could not carry the weight of nineteenth-century conviction. Nations, and the dream of what nations should be, were changed. Prince-bishops, sustained by the inertia of tradition grown obsolete, disappeared and did not reappear even when the restorers returned to power. Only one prince-bishopric was to be restored (after

Napoleon had exiled two successive occupants of its throne and restructured its domains); its bishop, who ruled in central Italy, was the pope. In other lands, the deeds that Napoleon had done were deemed good and remained as seeds to shape the future: seeds of freedom, of liberty, of equality, and of nation. Even the Austrian chancellor, who represented he Old Regime through the first half of the nineteenth century, began to realize that he could only put off the dreams; he could not stop them.

Dreams remained after the death of Kant and the defeat of Napoleon: the dreams of romantics. The time after Kant and Napoleon became the era of Romanticism, a movement or a series of movements in religion, philosopy, politics, art, and music. In part, Romanticism was a reaction to the neoclassic art and rationalistic doctrines of the era that preceded it and ended in the French Revolution. It stressed the less rational aspects of life and a new vision of nature, vaguely pantheistic. Its soft focus looked on life as disordered, continuous, this-worldly. It was interested in organic and dynamic process and saw the individual in the context of his society and his society's past. Time was regarded as an important part of the social process, and history became an important discipline. In the searching and sifting, nostalgia sometimes obscured objectivity. Instinct, sentiment, and actual human experience were more important than logical argument or intellectual proposition. The medieval era seemed a simpler and more desirable time than the present.

The Romantics sought *opinio* in the authority of the past. *Scientia* was not empirical research (as its enlightened partisans had claimed) but philosophical speculation. By studying history, one could transcend it. Many intellectuals converted to Roman Catholicism, and cradle Catholics renewed their neglected heritage. If the Enlightenment was a time of the universality of criticism, the Romantic period was the time of the hero reveling in his uniqueness, the searcher for adventure and novelty. The hero took many and contradictory forms: the emperor, the pope, the nation. Many who lionized Bonaparte were also unwittingly influenced by Kant. The Enlightenment was not entirely dead. The revolt of the Romantics was too strong to let the opponent die. Not only did the world pulse with life (I sense; I feel; therefore I am) but, perhaps especially for the Romantics, the world was concatenated and teleological.

It was not only the ideas of Kant and the revolution of Bonaparte and the dreams of the Romantics that transformed nineteenth-century Europe. Other ideas and other revolutions were more quietly at work. In the space of a century, the population of Europe tripled, largely because of medical advances that brought a decline in the death rate of infants and children. Europeans colonized and emigrated, increasing their control of non-European territories by eight or nine fold;[3] the first major wave of European emigration happened between 1844 and 1854.[4] The resources of much of the earth were harnessed to serve Europe's needs.[5] Of those who remained in Europe, many, but not yet most, moved to larger cities. It was not so much an age of new technological discovery as of the resolute application of old technologies in new ways. The railroad and the steamship and the telegraph transformed the old relation between time and space, and the world came closer together. Literacy, building slowly, and a flood of newspapers written from every conceivable perspective, brought a sense of the relativity of all opinion, perhaps even a relativity of moral standards.[6] There was more wealth spread among more people, but it was no longer used to build pyramids or marble monuments; instead it was used to bring more wealth and to further the economic development of the world.

The old divisions of European society began to break down. The nobles and their clerical allies were threatened as land gave way to capital as the measure of wealth. Many called for a constitution—for freedom of the press and freedom of religion—not as rights granted by a monarch, but as inalienable rights. Anyone who favored freedom presumed himself to be a liberal.[7] More differentiation occurred as the liberals, mostly middle class, discovered that they were not so egalitarian as they had thought. The brief alliance of bourgeoisie and proletariat dissolved as self-interest and the issue of private property and the vote divided them. Socialists and Communists had more to say to a growing urban poor. Anarchists contributed to increased polarization.

Before the disappointments of 1848, bourgeois and proletarian wondered about, but did not yet totally abandon, a religion that seemed so allied to the past. Those who read the gospel, or listened carefully, thought it supported the principles for which they fought. Those who were not in power advocated reform until their own goals were achieved. Peasants fought for land reform and became conservative after it was won; entrepreneurs were happy to be left alone to make money. The nobility, long used to being in power, clung to their own rights and privileges and to those of the churches as if they were their own. The nobility looked to religion for justification of the power they had and the measures they took to protect it. The churches, by and large, provided that justification: the world they had once called a "vale of tears" became the place of "unlimited possibility and progress." The shadow-side was that those who did not share the growing wealth found suddenly that they were *poor*. The expansion and mobility of the population, the concentration in newer sections of cities that rapidly became slums, called for attention that only a growing state apparatus could provide. The institution of the hospital began to flourish; police departments blossomed and crime was defined. Even insanity took on a careful definition, a definition designed to protect the power that was.[8]

Christianity had proclaimed the doctrine of Christian universalism and human superiority to the world of nature, but the church was not pleased with what its doctrine had wrought. Eternal reward was hereafter and not to be bought in *this* time and *this* place. Christian leaders were disturbed when, instead of leaving the world, humans became committed to the process of transforming it; instead of waiting for the heavenly Jerusalem to descend on a cloud, they set about building it. The Reformation had baptized secular life, but the secularization of the European mind and heart found its stride in the nineteenth century. The irony was that the same century saw Christianity become a world religion. But success elsewhere did not make up for missed opportunities in Europe.

In the era after Immanuel Kant and Napoleon Bonaparte, the one hundred million Roman Catholics were still primarily European and concentrated in France, the Habsburg Empire, Spain, Portugal, Bavaria, and the Italian states. There were large Catholic populations in Prussia, the Netherlands, British Ireland, and Russian Poland.[9] When Napoleon was at the height of his power, it appeared that the structure, if not the being, of the Roman Church had been destroyed. Pius VI was even referred to as The Last Pope. But the tribulations of Pius VI and then of his successor, Pius VII at the hands of the Emperor of the French turned the pope into a martyr.[10] Romantics looked with nostalgia in the lost unity of a better age. New religious communities, following the call to proclaim the gospel to all nations, replaced those which had been suppressed by emperors and popes.

In the eighteenth century the Roman Church, and especially the position of its leader, was clearly suffering deterioration. In the beginning of that century the struggle over Jansenism had led many to question the pope's wisdom and his power. Toward the end of the third quarter of the that century the suppression of the Jesuits under pressure from Catholic monarchs, hailed by many as a sign of papal wisdom, marked a low point in papal power. Catholic monarchs did not hesitate to dictate to the churches in their territories. The coming of the French Revolution and Napoleon, both hostile to Roman Catholicism even while using it as a prop for their legitimacy, seemed to herald the end.

Before the revolution, there had been a surplus of clergy, but not of good clergy. A very large number of priests lived on church funds but without pastoral duties. There were too many monks and nuns for holiness to have been a way of life; comfort and the desire for security had invaded privileged monastic bands. The clerical hierarchy was simply incapable of differentiating between real requirements of faith and nonessential accessories.[11] The broad masses continued to perform religious duties, but whether out of conviction or habit or simply because the Mass was a spectacle is difficult to judge.[12] The Council of Trent (1545–63) had called for seminaries and visitations and synods; by the time of the French Revolution, even the meager attempts to fulfill the directives had ceased. Many who did not have the power or interest to change laws that had grown irrelevant simply found ways of getting around them.[13]

Eighteenth-century Catholicism cannot be dismissed so easily, however. It must be noted that there were movements of reform, as reform has been understood within Roman Catholicism. Saints and sinners lived side by side. Clerics were called to wear their collars and live regular lives, to stand on their pedestals and be examples to their flocks. There was a call for more simplicity and even attempts to reconcile Catholicism with the Enlightenment,[14] although the identification of reform with Jansenism would discredit the former when the latter fell into disrepute. There were movements to celebrate the Eucharist in the language of the people and to emphasize Eucharist as community and as the center of a Catholic's life. Some voices called for better sermons to be delivered *during* Mass; others opposed pilgrimages, processions, rosaries, and holy days as elements of a child's religion not suited for the adult Christian. Still others wanted to eliminate Mass stipends, the laws of fasting, and obligatory celibacy for priests.[15]

The concept of pastoral theology was born in the eighteenth century, but seminaries were not in agreement about what it meant. Napoleon did a favor for seminaries. Empty monasteries made ideal seminaries in a church that still considered the monastic model the best for those it wished to ordain. With the introduction of conscription, seminaries were full, even when numbers of ordinations declined.[16] Most seminaries, especially after the revolution, were under pressure to turn out new priests to overcome the shortage. Standards seemed high but actually declined. (What would one tell the bishop if candidates were turned away when so many places remained to be filled?) The records of visitations and documents now available suggest, however, that the clergy continued to be of the people and to be content to remain so, clerical collar or no.[17]

In Roman Catholicism, the importance of the sermon began to shift. It was not uncommon for Protestants to preach for an hour or more to their congregations. Roman Catholics began to do the same, although without a noticeable improvement in preaching. Catholicism still considered the confessional to be the most important place for a the priest, and, with long hours in the confessional, there was seldom time to prepare for a lengthy sermon. Still, one was expected to speak and, more and more, to speak on the Scriptures. From the end of the eighteenth century through and beyond the time of this study, the compromise was a flood of books of sermons, written by men with little qualification, easily published, and available to the busy pastor.

Of course, one could not simply *read* the sermon to one's flock. Notes were generally frowned upon, even when memory often failed. But sermons, even bad ones, were entertainment and the people came. In the time before the French Revolution, the emphasis shifted to short sentences, easy words, concrete ideas so that the "common people" might understand. Attempts at rhetorical embellishment were considered Ciceronian and therefore pagan. Energetic gestures were considered unnatural, although there are reports of many who got so caught up in their sermonizing that they were unable to do anything else on the days on which they preached. If acoustics were bad, the sermon was chanted. The doctrinal body of a sermon was seldom profound; simplicity and theological sophistication did not mix. The chief propounder of the simple sermon was Alphonsus Liguori, who founded an order whose main work was to go from parish to parish to preach revival missions.[18] North of the Alps, the sermon, along with morning prayer, actually threatened to take the place of Mass as the center of Catholic worship, as benediction, pilgrimages, processions, and the devotion to saints had done south of the Alps.[19] After Napoleon, most Catholics continued as they had before Napoleon; but this majority did not include those in power in the Roman Church.

The French Revolutionaries and Napoleon, believing as their opponents had that the best protection for throne was the altar, had taught the church to count on public funds even as they confiscated church properties and privileges. They also taught churchmen to fear. The Roman Curia was then, as now, notorious for its view that anything that happened outside of Rome was unimportant at best. It had been irritated by interference from Febronians and Gallicans, but that had been beyond the mountains. In the time of Napoleon, two popes had been kidnapped, ecclesiastical administration was a shambles, and church people and property, in Italy as elsewhere, were treated with disdain. For those who looked to Rome for leadership, the ideas of the revolution, even ideas that originated elsewhere but had been taken up by the revolution, and the destruction the revolution had done to the church was remembered in Rome long after nostalgia had set in in other quarters. After 1830, when a younger generation of Catholic clergy and laity thought to reconcile Catholicism and liberalism, their elders remembered the recent past. The elders were in power and, in a hierarchical structure, would choose those who would follow them.

In the Catholic Church, power, specifically authority, would remain the central issue. Theorists of papal, and hence curial, power had speculated differently through the centuries about how much power the pope indeed had.[20] After Napoleon, papal power was to become more absolute than it had ever been in anything but the most extreme theories, which then suddenly had new currency in the post-revolutionary church. It is one of the paradoxes of history that, after coming so close to extinction at the beginning of the century, the papacy would become more powerful than ever before.

Counterrevolutionary sentiment in the Catholic Church was not the same as political counterrevolutionary sentiment in governments of the Restoration. Pius VII, grateful for his release from house-arrest at the defeat of Napoleon, restored the Jesuits in spite of protests from restored governments. Throughout the century, the Zelanti, who advocated papal independence, were a force to be reckoned with in the election of a pope. The popes had maintained a heavy Italian majority in the College of Cardinals to offset the power of foreign cardinals, created to honor and maintain a balance of power among the kings and emperors who remained Catholic. France, Spain, and Austria still had a veto in conclaves,[21] and the Zelanti sought to elect candidates who were not under the influence of those nations but who were focused on Rome. In the eighteenth century they failed, although the popes of that time were acceptable enough. In the nineteenth century, they succeeded. The men elected, even when friendly to the modern world, were still convinced of the authority of their office over the state. And the Curia was there to maintain and enhance that position—and to remember.

Those in authority in Rome could not conceive of any situation in which the church did not occupy a central place in the state. Separation of church and state was demonic. They were displeased that so many Protestants and Jews had found tolerance in Roman Catholic lands even before Napoleon's time and equally displeased that so many Roman Catholics lived under Protestant sovereigns after Napoleon. The eighteenth and nineteenth centuries were the centuries of concordats, treaties between Rome and secular states, each acting as equal to the other, which sought to cement an alliance between throne and altar.[22] After the defeat of Napoleon, the Roman Church set out on a flurry of negotiations, even with Protestant states, in an attempt to regain lost position.[23] Catholic authorities could not think of toleration, for the Roman Church taught Truth and toleration would be of error. Freedom of the press to them was freedom to publish lies and immorality; any suggestion that clerical celibacy might be made optional was sheer republicanism. Democracy was a pagan concept, long since discredited by the divine church, whose hierarchical structure was to be a model for all other governments. Many conservatives seemed to forget that the church was based on a constitution of sorts and that the pope was selected by an election.

The conservative movement known as ultramontanism gained momentum throughout the period of this study. It was not a new idea to many in northern Europe who had looked "beyond the mountains" to the pope in Rome when dissent or oppression threatened. It was strongest in places where Roman Catholics were not themselves in power, in places like British Ireland or Russian Poland, where hope was kept alive by appeal to a far-off authority. Even in Catholic countries those who were dissatisfied with what their government was doing appealed to Rome for recourse, and the popes themselves began to insist on theories that justified their supremacy. As governments—even Catholic governments—became more secularized, and as the Roman Church lost more and more influence and land in the world outside the official church, the leaders began to demand absolute control within the churches of the various countries, especially control over what was considered Roman Catholic teaching. Just at the time when Roman Catholic theology was attempting to answer the questions raised by Kant and to come to terms with the European world created after Napoleon, Roman investigation became common. Appeal to Rome was a constant threat. Especially after 1830, Roman influence was spread by a growing number of mediocre Roman Catholic journals and periodicals that became readily available, by experts and informants who looked to the Congregation of the Index for the answers to theological debate, and by secularized governments' increasing indifference to church issues.

At the very time when the world was being transformed by new ideas, by an explosion of population, by an industrial revolution and the Europeanization of the world, Roman Catholics engaged in arcane debate and bitter fraternal condemnation. They condemned the modern world and proclaimed the Immaculate Conception. Their leader lost his sovereign lands in central Italy and proclaimed his infallibility in faith and morals. Catholics also built church buildings, apparently convinced that the only thing necessary to bring people to church was to erect edifices within easy reach. There were some attempts to reach out to the growing numbers of urban poor, who seemed invisible to a church that still thought all society was agrarian. Only at the end of the nineteenth century would the Roman Church speak with vigor to issues that touched the vast majority of human beings. By then it was very late.

Rome intervened in almost every serious theological controversy during the nineteenth century.[24] Its intellectual centralization was led by those who looked to the medieval era as the measure for Truth. In 1824, the Roman College was returned to the Jesuits and became a center for traditional scholastic theology. Still, it is generally conceded that scholarship in Rome was in a wretched state, and among "scholarly" institutions the Congregation of the Index was one of the most mediocre. It had been organized on the premise—common in most of Europe through the period in question—that censorship was necessary. Still, it was not an initiating body and only responded to complaints from outside. Most of the books condemned were either Latin or Italian books or Latin or Italian translations. Only after Jansenism had made the condemnation of a whole corpus of French books necessary was a broader scope established. Entire books, or all the works of a given author, were condemned. One could not expect a corps of mediocre scholars to sift through and separate the "false" from the "correct" in a work. As a result, authors or schools of thought were discredited more than they were refuted. Those who were condemned complained that they did not know why they were condemned and that they were misunderstood without being given a chance to explain.[26] Only as the nineteenth century wore on and as the Roman ranks of inquisitors were supplemented with German experts did the investigation and condemnation of works become more systematic and professional.

Our study focuses on the Roman Catholic Church in the area known as "Germania" in the time between the defeat of Napoleon and the Revolutions of 1848. Stereotypes gleaned from twentieth-century experience and the mythologizing of the mass media have to be disregarded when one looks at Germania at the beginning of the nineteenth century. It was a land of professors and poets and musicians. In fact, it was no land at all. Before Napoleon, Germania was divided into nearly three hundred individual states, loosely connected in a Holy Roman Empire which had been headed by Habsburgs for centuries (if one excepts one Wittelsbach at the time of Maria Theresa). After Napoleon, Germania was still composed of some thirty states, still loosely connected in a German Confederation that met at Frankfurt under the perpetual presidency of Austria.

After Napoleon, beyond the radical reduction in the number of governments, a perceptible shift occurred in Germania. The change was partly in response to the Frenchness of the conqueror and partly because of the writings of Johann Gottfried Herder (1744–1803), who championed a Germanic *Volksgeist* which he had found in the study of history. Originally, Herder's sense of the Germanic extended to Britain, the Netherlands, and even Scandinavia. After the defeat of Napoleon, the spirit of German nationalism became a significant force; at the same time, Prussia increased its position as a major German power. Roman Catholic Austria, with an expanded Habsburg hegemony over large Slavic, Magyar, and Italian as well as German areas, and with a mixture of minorities throughout its empire, could only espouse an internationalism or multinationalism; in Habsburg lands, therefore, German nationalism would be somewhat tempered and diffused. Protestant Prussia, in spite of its many Poles, appeared more clearly German.

The climate of German nationalism was strongly influenced by the spirit of Herder's *Volksgeist*. Again, it was not the rabid nationalism that would be associated with the later years of the nineteenth and the twentieth centuries. The Romantic movement in Germany was caught up in the dream of the German Nation. Johann Wolfgang von Goethe (1749–1832) was certainly not confined to narrow nationalism, but his literary talent breathed of universal human wisdom discovered in the particularity of the German professor Faust and the conviction that feeling is everything (*Gefühl ist alles*). Ludwig van Beethoven (1770–1827) captured the German soul in his movements of *appassionata*. Others followed in their own measure. Student organizations (*Burschenschaften*) formed around song and drink and dreams, and when they spilled over into demonstrations, a fear-struck government forbade them. But the government could not forbid what was growing in young hearts.

What was in the air affected religion, which was tired of Enlightenment austerity in any case. In the German world, Protestant and Roman Catholic had always rubbed elbows more closely than elsewhere. Even when differences were strong, rivals found a community in their language and their past. The strains of pietism that had been a part of German Lutheranism were reinforced by the Romantic movement. In the second third of the eighteenth century, German Catholicism also experienced a return of the heart.[27] Religious expression became more sentimental and less rigorous. Along with some emphasis on more frequent reception of the sacraments, there was an increasing stress on other, more external forms of piety. Devotion to the Sacred Heart, to Mary, to Joseph, and to Anthony of Padua experienced a revival. Popes, especially Pius IX, multiplied opportunities for indulgences, and once again pilgrimages became popular, encouraged by the peace that Europe enjoyed. The revival of the Jesuits brought renewed interest in their founder, and the Ignatian method was used in private retreats, which also came into popularity among those who had the leisure. Miracles, prophecies, and stigmatizations returned to vogue, with little concern for historical veracity. Insipid renditions of the Christmas crib not only showed bad taste but implied that religion was for children.

Even while more sentimental forms of piety were gaining ground, an intellectual revival in German Catholicism was taking place. In fact, the central issues in German Catholicism were intellectual. German-language universities, with the exception of those under Austrian control, were restructured. The dissolution of ecclesiastical centers of learning brought theological faculties to state universities where there was close contact with non-Catholic ideas. There were even ideas of academic freedom that more traditional authorities found unacceptable. Tübingen and Munich became centers of strong and independent Catholic theological thinking, and other university faculties followed their lead.

Theology in the German-speaking world during the first half of the nineteenth century was dominated by the desire to prove Kant wrong, and whole metaphysical systems were born whose scope and complexity could only have been conceived in the professorial leisure of a German university. Many attempted to reconcile revelation and faith with a philosophical system in such a way that Christian philosophy became, in essence, a philosophy of revelation. The theology was heavily dependent on the philosophy of the time, responding to Kant and Romanticism. It would take several lifetimes to untangle the intricacies of German thought during those early decades of the nineteenth century, but the man most important as background to the present study was Georg Wilhelm Friedrich Hegel (1770–1831).

Hegel viewed the French Revolution as a glorious dawn of freedom and Napoleon as an immense genius whom mediocrity destroyed. Hegel disagreed with Kant on the question of the knowability of the noumenal world of the thing-in-itself. According to Hegel, Kant had argued from the standpoint of understanding (*Verstand*), which was the type of thinking that prevailed in common sense, the natural sciences and mathematics, and in those philosophies that argued in quasi-scientific, quasi-mathematical ways. Reason (*Vernunft*) was the source of dialectical knowledge that distinguished conflicts and found synthesis.[28] Hegel's own project was to find a synthesis between Enlightenment and Romanticism.[29]

Reality, according to Hegel, is rational, and the rational is real. The world as we know it is the working out of the Absolute or World-Spirit realizing itself through the dialectic. The dialectic—thesis, antithesis, synthesis—is the movement of history, in which the synthesis both transcends and preserves the opposites. Humans are finite spirits, ultimately identical with the Infinite Spirit; in the development of the finite mind, the Infinite or Absolute or God rises to self-consciousness. Human history is the Infinite's or Absolute's or God's realization of himself through and in the process of human experience.

Hegel, in later life a frequent visitor to the Lutheran church in Berlin, was no ordinary theist. He was accused of pantheistic monism, although he insisted that God was more than the sum of his parts. His thought was dynamic and developmental and evolutionary, in sharp contrast to the static systems that had characterized much of eighteenth century thought, including the thought of Kant. Hegel's concept of trinity traced the movement of his dialectic and scandalized the pious. He believed religion, specifically Christianity, was the highest stage in the unfolding of the Spirit, the self-consciousness of the Absolute; but he argued that religion must be transposed into the key of metaphysics. Philosophy alone could penetrate to the Truth.

Hegel sought a logic that could bridge the chasm between the eternal Truth of reason and the accidental truths of history.[30] Hegel was convinced that the unfolding of that Truth was within history,[31] and he raised history to the dignity of philosophy. Hegel believed that the very foundations of the human condition could change from one historical era to another; history had meaning and significance in the progress of the consciousness of freedom.[32] Hegel saw the Protestant Reformation as the single key event of history since Roman times, as it freed humanity from the blind obedience of the medieval era and articulated the principles of the freedom of individual conscience.[33]

Hegel created as much controversy as he did light. In theology, he raised serious questions about the significance of Jesus as a unique person. His view of religion and its ability to come to Truth raised questions about the possibility of theology. Most immediately, and especially in the thirties and forties of the nineteenth century, Hegel raised serious questions about the relation of God and world, as he insisted that the world was the necessary unfolding of the life of God himself.[34] Hegel created a major crisis of faith in European religious thought, and his successors (Strauss, Baur, Feuerbach, Marx, Kierkegaard) would escalate the controversy over the Truth of Christianity.

This study treats of the search to make Christianity credible to intellectuals, who sat in libraries, and to simpler believers, who sat in pews. It is a story of the search for *scientia* and the resort to *opinio*. It is a story of small men who secretly issued reports of heresy and a paranoid Roman Curia that encouraged them, seeking not to understand but to defeat the modern world. Men who were reported never knew, in their innocence, how to respond to an attack from the very institution they had believed they were defending.

This is a study of the theologian Anton Günther and the preacher Johann Emanuel Veith, at home in Biedermeier Vienna and Roman Catholicism, who tried to guard Truth and found condemnation from the very church they sought to protect.

2
BIEDERMEIER VIENNA

To the late twentieth-century visitor to Vienna, the city on the Danube is an outpost of civilization, tucked in a narrow corner of the Western world and cut off by an Iron Curtain from lands that had once been an integral part of Habsburg sovereignty. It is a quaint city, living in the present and the past, an odd combination of socialiam and Roman Catholicism. In many ways still a vital center, Vienna in the twentieth century remains a city of the past. Nowhere is the presence of the past more visible than in the almost empty but nonetheless well-kept churches that one meets at every turn.

Vienna is the city of the Counter or Catholic Reformation. The baroque one meets everywhere stands in persistent testimony to the city's defiance of the purity of Protestant principle. Even the simple Gothic lines of St. Stephen's Cathedral have been interrupted by randomly placed baroque altars as silent but powerful proof that Vienna is the place of the Roman Catholic Church and none other. To the trained eye it appears almost as if the reforms of the Second Vatican Council had not taken place. The turned-around altars decreed by that council are barely noticeable in the sea of baroque magnificence that overwhelms the eye—and, theoretically, the heart—of the worshiper. The buildings, the fountains, the plaques on walls where heroes slept, the bells and towers that shape the skyline of the city, still proclaim the unabashed Roman Catholicism of Vienna. If the churches are now empty except for an occasional bent-over form, if the church's power is but a shadow of what it once was, Catholicism remains an integral part of the consciousness of this place. Viennese will pay the church tax year after year, not to visit the churches much more than on Christmas or Easter—and for baptism, marriage, or burial—but to preserve the tradition, to hold onto the past, to be able to show the children that here is still splendor and beauty and pomp. The new Vienna, with its bustling subways and burgeoning suburbs, with its businessmen and spies, still preserves the signs of the past. Vienna is Roman Catholic.

At the beginning of the nineteenth century, the past that is today so carefully preserved was the present. Napoleon had been defeated, in part, by the dogged determination of the Habsburg emperor and his pragmatic minister. It hardly seemed to matter that the French had twice occupied the city, had managed to blackmail the emperor into sending another of the daughters of the House of Habsburg to be the first empress of the French. What mattered was that

Napoleon had been twice defeated and the victors had gathered in Vienna to dance and drink and return Europe to old legitimacies. What mattered was that Vienna was the center of an empire that stretched across east central Europe and had one of the largest populations in the world. What mattered was that Vienna was the center of a continent, and her statesmen and her rulers were consulted by all of Europe. It was a heady time for the city on the Danube.

It was the time of Biedermeier,[1] everyone's idea of the "good old days." It was a time of peace and prosperity, and a growing middle class found respectability in the solid virtues of being Bürger.[2] Music set the tone. Beethoven, Schubert, Lanner, and Strauss the Father were there for those who could afford the coffeehouses and concert halls. The waltz saved dance from the rigid formalities of the eighteenth century and started traditionalists twittering about the morality of such rapid movement. It was an era of wasp waists, elephantine sleeves, and pigeonhole desks, when women and the home were joined in a hallowed (and virtually inescapable) union. Decoration was all the fad in everything from clothing to furniture. Long trousers and bright waistcoats told the tale of fashion and rank. The cloth and clothes of Vienna's Herr von Gunkel were world famous, and the furniture of Josef Danhauser was at once solid, useful, and beautiful.

Vienna was a city of parks and palaces. The long Congress held in the city after Napoleon's fall brought it fame as a place of graceful gardens and beautiful salons for dancing and parties. The old fortifications erected after the Turkish siege of 1683 (so ineffective against another, more recent invader) were still there; but the fifty-foot-high wall had become three miles of walkways and parks and coffeehouses, the famous Bastei and Glacis that have since been removed. Baroque architecture dominated in the center city, the home of the rich and powerful; but the bourgeois architecture in the growing first ring of suburbs gave testimony to the increasing value of solid functionalism.

Middle class standards set the tone of the time. Even the painters of the period were caught up in bourgeois idealism. It was a world comfortable with itself. Like most worlds comfortable with themselves, however, there was something about Biedermeier Vienna that contained the seeds of trouble. Historians concentrating on more political issues look back upon the period through the lens of the revolution that broke out in March of 1848 and call the time preceding it Pre-March (*Vormärz*). There were, however, few in *Vormärz* who saw revolution coming.

In the years between 1815 and 1848, the suburbs of Vienna remained semirural; but that was much less so at the end of the time than at the beginning. Growing numbers of peasants, made content for a time by the decrees of Maria Theresa and Joseph II but also made literate by the same monarchs,[3] were coming to Vienna in search of a new destiny. Their expectations were beginning to change. Roman Catholicism had taught them to do their duty in this world while expecting rewards in the next; it was an important shift in emphasis that everyone, from businessman to peasant, wanted to see rewards in *this* world and no longer felt content with the baroque promises for the beyond. By the end of the nineteenth century, peasants turned workers would be outside the institutional church structure. At the start of that century, they were only beginning to see the discrepancy between what the church, tied to the social order of monarchy and hierarchy, preached and what it actually did. In the beginning, the change was all but invisible except to playwrights (who were, after all, only artists) and to fanatics like Karl Marx. However, "poverty" was beginning to have a negative ring, especially to those who discovered themselves poor.[4] Metternich believed poor relief should come from private and not from state resources.[5] The "charity" provided by the church was only a minimum for the most destitute, and it was tied up in bureaucratic red tape and coupled with a lecture on obedience to patriarchal society.[6]

In 1800, the population of Vienna (including the suburbs) was about 230,000; by 1848 it had risen to approximately 430,000. The death rate continued to be higher than the birthrate. Even from the irregular statistical data issued, it is evident that the increase in population came mainly from the mass of workers (mostly non-German-speaking) flocking to the suburbs—and from their legitimate or illegitimate children. (It is estimated that, at the time of the Napoleonic invasions, two in every five births in Vienna were illegitimate. By 1850, this percentage increased to one illegitimate birth in every two births.)[7] Not even the outbreak of Europe's first epidemic of cholera in 1831 could do much to stop the steady increase of population in the city and suburbs of Vienna. This increase in population was accompanied by a corresponding shortage of housing and an official policy that made the building of new dwellings difficult.[8] Wages were low. Most families paid well over half their income for rent. There was some relief when work was to be had, for working class women did the same work as the men, carrying bricks and mortar on their backs when the need arose.[9] It was also customary to include children in the work schedule whenever that was possible. Both adults and children were expected to work from 4:00 A.M. until 8:00 P.M.[10] Long hours were softened, however, by a slow pace and the passive resistance of the workers.

It was the time of the Industrial Revolution. The boundaries between country and city began to dissolve, and the rhythm of daily life began to change radically. This was true all over Europe and was also true for Biedermeier Vienna, even if it was not perceived by the ruling classes of the time. While Vienna was parading its dandies and enjoying its influence, there was a growing contradiction in the suburbs, where thousands of farmhands, freed by law and changed agricultural methods, sought work in new industries. Vienna, like much of Europe, was faced with the contradiction of increasing productivity accompanied by increasing poverty.[11] With a reputation for pleasure-seeking greater than any city in German-speaking world, Vienna was also a city of growing poverty and destitution.[12] This was complicated by a rising inflation and a government that consistently spent more than it had.

The situation in the Biedermeier era was not yet critical. Vienna was still a rich city, and that wealth spilled over to the working classes. In the center of an empire there were both nobles and bureaucrats present who had enough wealth to keep those who worked for them content. Vienna consumed more meat (mostly beef) per citizen than any other city in Europe.[13] There was the famous grilled chicken as well and the beginnings of the sausage era. The consumption of grains and of the potato, introduced in the seventeenth century by the Franciscans, was down in prosperous times and up in difficult ones. Wine was giving way to beer as the drink of choice—a sign both that the lower class was gaining strength and that there was enough prosperity filtering down that alcohol, which made miserable working conditions a bit more tolerable, was available to most. Dairy products made little headway into the Viennese diet, perhaps owing to the difficulty of transport as much as to the preference of the Viennese. The health of the Viennese was improving. The child mortality rate, an index of the health of the general population, sank from 54.4% in 1800 to 46% in 1850. The birthrate, however, remained stable after a sharp increase (from 29.2 to 49.18 per thousand of population) in the last half of the eighteenth century.[14]

The time between the defeat of Napoleon and 1848 was a time for beginnings in the Habsburg lands. The increase in population, especially urban population, the evolution of agricultural production (which amounted to an agrarian revolution), and the improvement of means of communication and transportation all allowed for the development of a large-scale factory industry. There were showcase developments in the founding of the Danube steamship company (*Donaudampfschiffahrtsgesellschaft*) in 1829 and the opening of a horse-drawn railroad between Linz and Budweis in 1832. There was an attempt to get sound financing through the founding of the national bank in 1816 and one of the first savings institutions of Europe in 1819. Beyond the showcase, however, critical developments remained unperceived. Except for a bit of relief in rental prices in the 1830s, there was little recognition of the plight of the increasing population of workers and no action for their benefit.[15] Certainly the Roman Church did not recognize these developments, for churchmen were caught in the fight over Josephinism.

Generalizations frequently suffer from inaccuracy and need to be revised; but they are useful, sometimes even necessary instruments for historical discourse. Josephinism is the generalization used to refer to the Austrian brand of another generalization, Enlightened Despotism. Although the name comes from the emperor Joseph II, the phenomenon is recognizable back in the reign of his mother, Maria Theresa (1740–80) and survives well beyond Joseph's reign (1780–90) to the time of the revolutions of 1848. Josephinism was at once a paternalistic program of reform and a compromise with the baroque era that preceded and, in many ways, was entwined with it. It brought about economic, social, and intellectual changes. In the arena of religion, it was to make changes that would appear pagan or Protestant and would bring it into direct conflict with the Roman Catholicism that was an integral part of the empire of the Counter-Reformation.[16]

The sixteenth-century Protestantism that Roman Catholics feared had been heavily influenced by the revealed Word in its spoken and written forms. It had sought a purity in architecture and popular piety. In its more radical forms, it had attacked everything about Roman Catholicism, from its eucharistic doctrine to its ecclesiology. Vienna had flirted briefly with Protestantism but then, under the tutelage of the Habsburgs, who saw Roman Catholicism as essential to their ability to govern, returned to an exaggerated form of Roman Catholicism that "countered" Protestant understatement with baroque overstatement.

Tolerance was considered weakness (even if individual cases and private practice often allowed for some flexibility,[17] it was not a world in which pluralism could be officially accepted). Protestants, Jews, Orthodox, and Muslims all had to be wrong for Catholicism to be right. If those outsiders were tolerated for economic reasons, they were just barely tolerated and were hidden away in ghettos and taxed just for being who they were. They were to be used or abused as the opportunity dictated. But this was not a peculiarity of Catholic lands. Protestant princes treated their non-Protestant subjects with equal severity.

But the treatment of religious minorities was not the major issue at the time. Nor was much attention paid to issues surrounding an increasing population and increasing industrialization with their attendant crowding and poverty. The issue of the time was Truth and its expression, and truth came to be identified with power, the power of throne and the power of altar. Habsburg emperor and Roman pope were joined in a sometimes uneasy, but nonetheless essential, alliance that proclaimed the Truth. And the Truth was sustained and passed on by an army of religious—with the Jesuits, until they were suppressed, heading the list—by state and church woven together in a thousand different ways from feasts to finances. All of it is expressed in a popular piety that is still visible, if somewhat faded, in the churches of late twentieth-century Vienna.

Visible is the best description of baroque piety, which concentrates on sight and smell and elaborate sound—not the sound of the Word so much as that of music, almost visible in its richness, that could move the soul. Counter-Reformation Vienna was cluttered with candles and incense, pilgrimages and saints' days, and devotions to Mary and St. Anthony. There were long processions and forty-hours' eucharistic devotion to underscore Roman Catholic belief in the Real Presence. There were golden vestments and vessels.

Elaborate church music was written by world-famous composers and played on concert organs that are still polished and played with pride. The faithful at their prayers were lost in the rapture of overwhelmed senses, transported to heaven in spite of poverty and misery at home. Popular religion moved away from the *now* into an eternity the attainment of which demanded acceptance of the harsh realities of this world. The power of throne and altar was secure as long as all believed that therein lay Truth and inevitability.[18]

It was not a bad world—even in comparison to our own. The church provided protection and celebration. The church provided music for all when the concert hall was closed to all but the rich. The church provided pageantry for all when theater was scarcely born, still confined to the salons of the *literati*. The church provided meaning for all who would accept it, meaning in the midst of the chaos that was forever lapping, with its plagues and famines and high rates of mortality, at the edges of daily life. It is easy enough for critics from the twentieth century to laugh at vigil candles and Mass stipends and the popularity of preachers. It was another thing to search for meaning then, in the confines of a much smaller world. Even then, however, the world was not so smug or sealed as it sometimes seemed.

The emperor (or empress) did indeed embody the state and there was no one, least of all the rulers themselves, who could conceive of it any other way. The union of throne and altar was the linchpin that held the whole edifice together, the church bringing Truth and the state defending that Truth. Joseph II, after whom Josephinism was named, who traveled incognito through Europe as Count Falkenstein, was a man interested in his people and their welfare. It is not surprising that he was open to ideas that were planted during his education by men of the Enlightenment, or that he was open to those same ideas when he came into contact with them during his travels. It never occurred to him that these ideas could lead others to question his paternalism and indeed the very existence of the monarchy that brought him such power, but he did find many of the ideas of the Enlightenment fascinating. His mother, the pious Maria Theresa, was also instrumental in the introduction of the Enlightenment to Austria.[19] There can be no doubt that the empress, although deeply steeped in baroque piety, was also willing to promote ideas that were in conflict with the hierarchical Roman Catholicism that was the foundation of her power.

Much was to change in Habsburg lands under Maria Theresa and Joseph, changes whose consequences would not be apparent until the following century. It was not their modernity as much as their guarding of the long Habsburg tradition that motivated them. When Pius VI visited Joseph in 1782 to try to get him to reverse some of his plans, Joseph's polite reception of the pontiff and his staunch refusal to give in was not an attempt at disrespect or even an attempt to get more power than he already had.[20] It was the God-given duty of the monarch to care for the church and protect it, even against itself. Nowhere was the right more strongly claimed than by the head of the House of Habsburg—the Holy Roman Emperor who had saved the church from pagans and Turks, who had saved the church from a papacy caught in the grip of decadence and nepotism. The union of throne and altar would be important for the survival of the world of the Counter-Reformation, but it was not a world in which the altar would rule the throne. The union of throne and altar was never as peaceful as it seemed from the outside. When the emperor saw things differently from the pope, the emperor would prevail, even while the Holy Father would be revered and respected and heard and protected.

Maria Theresa was the mother of Josephinism, and not only because it was she who supervised her son's education. It was Maria Theresa who brought the Jansenist sympathizer Van Swieten[21] to court and gave him the power to reform the university as well as the practice of medicine in the empire. She stood under the power of her advisor Kaunitz,[22] whose hatred for the Jesuits and desire for a state church were main pillars of his policy. Kaunitz disposed of church property, levied taxes on clergy, and controlled contact between church hierarchy in the empire and Rome. Further, he abolished the right of citizens to seek sanctuary on church property. He restricted contact of members of Austrian religious orders with members (including heads) outside Austria. Maria Theresa also restricted religious communities in the acceptance of novices, and delayed the taking of religious vows until the age of twenty-four, not an early age then, with life expectancy still well under fifty. Maria Theresa did not hesitate to regulate the amount and the use of the religious communities' wealth; and she regretted but took advantage of the unavoidable suppression of the Jesuits.

Maria Theresa did not hesitate to decree reforms for the institutional church itself. Theology was concentrated in the universities, not in the hands of bishops and religious orders, and concentrated on church history, patrology, and pastoral theology.[23] Candidates for the priesthood had an austere life, so austere that there were protests from Rome that there were not enough servants to allow the students to study and not enough food and wine to allow them to concentrate.[24]

Maria Theresa was aided in her reforms by the cardinal archbishop of Vienna, Migazzi, whom she had appointed. The cardinal showed some austere if not Jansenist tendencies as he urged his priests to give up restaurants (*Gasthäuser*), theater, and the wearing of worldly clothes, threatening with suspension those who failed to comply. Each clergyman was to make a twice-yearly week-long retreat under the supervision of the cardinal himself.

The reforms of Maria Theresa are often forgotten because of the more radical nature of those initiated by her son Joseph in his ten-year reign. In those the years, Joseph published over six thousand decrees dealing with all the minutiae of daily life. More than six hundred of those decrees were directed at the church in an attempt to make it a part of the apparatus of a social state, run from the top.[25] Joseph knew what was best for his people, and he was determined that they should follow what he was convinced was their best interest. Such paternalism was, not surprisingly, destined to fail in many areas. What is surprising is how much it succeeded—without permission from Rome.[26]

Joseph sought to regulate everything from the number (fewer) of candles that could be burned during a service to the length (shorter) and content (this worldly) of sermons to be preached. He saw himself as the head of the church and, following the lead of his mother before him, insisted that all communication from the Habsburg church to Rome or vice versa go through himself or his government. As long as his own power remained, Joseph wanted to eliminate the wide gap that separated the rich from the poor in his lands. He wanted all to have a chance to be educated, to be enlightened Christians as he thought he and his circle were. Above all, he wanted to eliminate what many considered the lopsided status of the church and the preying of the church on the superstition of those who knew no better. He introduced tolerance for non-Catholics[27] and believed in bettering *this* world through education and reform.

Joseph continued the reform of the seminaries. He forbade study in foreign countries (especially Rome), ostensibly to make sure that seminarians were aware of the country that they would serve. He established general seminaries in Vienna, Pest, Pavia, and Louvain, which educated more in the principles of agriculture and medicine than in principles of theology. Daily Eucharist was considered too frequent, perhaps because of the Jansenist notion that no matter how good one was, one was not worthy of daily communion. The number of men joining the seminary declined. In 1779, before Joseph came to full power, 163 seminarians were ordained in Vienna; in 1792, shortly after Joseph's death and before the reinstitution of seminaries to church control by Joseph's brother Leopold could have an effect, two were ordained.[28]

It was not only seminaries that were affected. The life of the priest was controlled, from the sermons he preached to the funerals at which he presided. Marriage was brought totally under the control of the state, and the priest became the representative of the state in daily life. Maria Theresa had forbidden pilgrimages to Rome, Aachen, and Cologne. Joseph forbade all pilgrimages outside Habsburg lands and inside Habsburg lands when an overnight stay was necessary. (The one exception to this rule was a pilgrimage to Maria Zell, the most popular place of pilgrimage in Habsburg lands, then and now.) Statues and pictures could not be decorated with jewelry, gold, silver, wigs, or ordinary human clothing. (It had been customary to dress statues.) Only six candles could be burned during Mass—and only one Mass could take place at a time, except in St. Stephen's where the construction of the building created three churches. Bishops were admonished to teach their flocks the true meaning of indulgences; the Portiuncula indulgence of the Franciscans was to be discouraged.[29] Blessed candles, rosaries, medals, scapulars, and blessed belts were forbidden. Suggestions that Mass stipends be eliminated, that the Mass be celebrated in German (or the language of the people), and that it not be necessary for every priest to celebrate Mass every day were considered but not adopted. Consideration was also given to forbidding the collection of money during the Mass itself, especially during the sermon, but this suggestion was not implemented.

Religious communities in Habsburg lands were to come under heavy attack during this time, providing inspiration for the French of the following decade. Religious orders, founded throughout the centuries by idealistic people who wanted to live Christianity in a purer form than they saw in the world around them, had always been popular and had, in a sense, been corrupted by their own successes. A pledge of poverty combined with frugality and the good will of donors brought wealth, and the law of celibacy left the order itself as the only heir to the accumulated riches. It was clear that many orders were rich beyond need, and that they attracted a large number of people more interested in security than in sanctity.[30]

Religious houses to the number of 730 throughout the monarchy were suppressed during the time of Joseph. The hardest hit, not surprisingly, were the contemplative orders of both men and women. With emphasis on *this* world, there was little understanding for people who spent their entire day "uselessly" at prayer. The next hardest hit were the mendicant orders who seemed to many to be mere parasites on society. Only the orders that could prove themselves useful to Joseph's dream were allowed to survive, and new orders were not allowed to be founded. There was a great scramble. In Vienna, fifteen thousand religious were involved. Some left their communities and joined the secular world; these became teachers or governmental bureaucrats and seemed generally satisfied with the reforms of Joseph. Other communities attached themselves to schools or to hospitals, especially the General Hospital that was to be the pride of nineteenth-century Vienna.[31] Maria Theresa had forbidden new entries into the numerous third orders;[32] Joseph suppressed them entirely. The pruning that Joseph provided was to be a help to the religious revival that would be a part of the nineteenth century.

Joseph reorganized and founded dioceses and parishes.[33] His concern was not pomp but efficiency and convenience. No subject should have to go more than an hour by foot to reach his church. In the city, Masses should be coordinated so that there would be some choice available to people. No parish should be served by someone who simply came to celebrate Mass but should be served by someone whom the people knew and could trust. A parish should be built for every one thousand souls in the city, for every seven hundred in the country.

It is not at all surprising that Joseph came to be known as the emperor of the people and that his early death led many to believe that he had simply gone into hiding until the time should be more auspicious. Even Anton Günther was asked what he thought of Joseph and whether or not he thought he was still alive.[34] But, obviously, Joseph could not do the work of reform alone, despite his attention to duty and detail. Once again, building on his mother's example, Joseph was to place his trust in an army of bureaucrats who would process and approve or process and delay, who were adept at obfuscation or speed.[35] Joseph was to create a superstructure that would remain loyal to his principles and would defend the reality of a state church long after Joseph's death.

Many of the reforms of Joseph were reversed by his brother Leopold, and many were lost in the struggle with Napoleon. Many were also lost in the attempts of the Congress of Vienna to reestablish the papacy as a pillar of the old order. The position of Rome was further strengthened when Metternich married for the third time and appeared to find, through his third wife and new mother-in-law, conviction in Roman Catholicism.[36] Not even Metternich, however, was able totally to disarm the Josephinist bureaucracy, which would remain a force throughout the first half of nineteenth-century Vienna.

The French Revolution and Napoleon had shaken the Habsburgs to the core. Not only had one of Maria Theresa's daughters lost a throne and her life, but the Holy Roman Empire itself had been dissolved and the Habsburgs were now Austrian, not Holy Roman, emperors. A fear of revolution at home set in and created a sense of caution coupled with an increased affection for old traditions. When the enlightened Leopold (1790–1792) was succeeded by his less imaginative son (who eventually defeated Napoleon and continued to reign from 1792 through 1835), the task was one of holding together the pieces as long as possible. The man who became Francis I (Francis II as Holy Roman Emperor) was a complex man, attached to the wisdom of former Habsburgs. While the system of rearguard action—fearing change and fighting it whenever and wherever possible, allowing it only when absolutely necessary—was associated with Francis's astute foreign minister from the Rhineland,[37] the role of Francis himself should not be underestimated; he was raised with Josephinism and feared any outside influence—even from Rome.[38] After the emperor's death in 1835 (Johann Emanuel Veith preached the series of tributes to him at the week-long funeral ceremonies) that same minister continued to control Francis's retarded son Ferdinand until 1848, when both were driven from power. Metternich's power was, however, kept in check by his archrival, Kollowrath, who had also received his claim to legitimacy from the will of Francis I.[39]

In response to the shock that the disorder of the French Revolution had caused in Habsburg lands, a police state was set up.[40] Although sometimes referred to as "The China of Europe," the Metternichian system is not to be compared to twentieth-century versions of the police state. People were persecuted and ostracized, but there were also many loopholes, especially in the censorship which was to remain in place through the Revolution of 1848. There were ways of getting the written works are wanted.[41] The censors themselves often brought into the public arena the very ideas they censored. For example, during the twenty years in which Anton Günther was a censor of theological books, his review articles introduced much heterodoxy into the Austrian theological scene. A bit of official difficulty only created ingenuity. David Christian Strauss's *Leben Jesu* was popular in Austria even though it was officially forbidden.

One place in Biedermeier Vienna where dissatisfaction was developing was within the church. The toleration of Jews, Orthodox, and Protestants that had been granted under Joseph II was continued, and this form of the Enlightenment was a source of some concern for those who were convinced of the Truth of Roman Catholicism and uninterested in granting validity to various forms of error. It is interesting that even while an official policy of toleration was strong there was a wave of conversions, especially of Jews, to Roman Catholicism; but the conversions came through the more self-consciously *Roman* Catholic movement of what has come to be known as the Romantic Revival.

The bureaucracy of the church—the governmental agencies that dealt with church affairs and the church hierarchy that was appointed by the emperor and his government—was Josephinist throughout the period, loyal to the concept of the church as servant to the state. Francis I was very interested in preserving the ecclesiastical reforms of Joseph II, and he viewed the church along with the monarchy and the police as the pillars of his state.[42] Not even Metternich could convince him to allow a more powerful role to the pope and the Roman Curia within Austrian church affairs. The entrenched bureaucracy took on a power of its own. It was only when the bureaucracy overstepped its authority that Francis intervened. In 1816, Francis I seemed willing to consider a concordat with Rome, but he changed his mind. Not even the pleasant encounter with the pope in 1819, when Francis journeyed to Italy, could bring Francis to challenge the bureaucratic stranglehold on church affairs.[43]

The archbishops of Vienna during this time were all Josephinists: Hohenwart (1803–20), Firmian (1822–31), and Vinzenz Eduard Milde (1832–53). It was not that they were cowards or had capitulated to the state. They were not men who simply agreed whenever the emperor said something. They were churchmen who saw their proper role away from the arena of state politics, and they quietly went about their business of chiding their clergy and instructing their laity in the discipline and practice of Catholicism. The parish reforms of Joseph II had actually given Vienna a solid foundation for the care of souls during the Biedermeier epoch, even with the growing number of workers who came to the city and suburbs. There was a continued shortage of priests for traditional roles, but those who were there were well distributed in the new parish boundaries established under Joseph. There was a certain disdain in the church toward the growing working class. There was an implicit presumption that rural was better than urban, and since most of the priests came from farm or small handworker families, there was little empathy with the proletariat created by industrialization. The "new ways" brought in Protestants and created a shortage of domestic servants.[44]

Archbishops did not think larger thoughts than whether or not there were enough priests to celebrate Mass, to take care of the dying, to handle the baptisms and marriages, and to keep the houses of worship in good repair or build new ones when necessary. As the century progressed, the need for more and larger churches in the suburbs was a preoccupation of the Viennese ordinaries. If the bishops noticed the social problems that were developing, they did not mention them in reports that deal only with the Josephinist prescriptions.[45] The reports of archbishops suggested that the clergy were still "too worldly" and needed to be reminded that they should wear clerical dress and not conduct themselves as worldly lords. Bishops reminded priests of the scandal that could be caused if they were seen with women who were too young and shapely, or hired attractive women as cooks or housekeepers. Priests were also reminded to attend to their prayers and make their semiannual retreats.[46]

With respect to the laity, there was concern about the inclination to drink, although there was little insight into the problem of alcoholism as it is seen today. Workers (as well as monks) were to receive a daily allotment of wine or beer as a compensation in part for their long and difficult work and to make that work more tolerable. There was also concern about the "wild" dancing that was sweeping the city; the birth of the waltz was cause for some anxiety in clerical circles. There was, as one might expect, a clerical concern for the rising number of illegitimate births. All of these were topics for the Sunday sermon, preached only in parish churches and after the Mass was completed. Priests were also expected to preach on agriculture and health and other matters of interest to good subjects of the Habsburg rulers.[47]

During the Biedermeier era, the rules that Joseph had made remained mostly in effect. Emperor Francis, himself a pious man, was in no hurry to have the religious orders back, nor did he wish to restore their lands and riches, which had gone to support a growing bureaucracy and educational and hospital systems. Besides, there were reports that even those religious orders that had survived Joseph's suppressions were too worldly, more interested in prestige and honor than in the simple life of work and prayer that Joseph had had in mind for them. So, during the Biedermeier era religious communities were kept under tight control. New or restored communities found it difficult to establish or reestablish themselves in Habsburg lands, although if they were far enough from Vienna there was more tolerance. In fact, the bureaucracy used establishment in far corners of the empire as a way of removing problematic religious from Vienna.[48] The Josephinist bureaucracy, a haven for many former religious who had come to accept the view that the state should control the church, was the strongest fighter in the struggle to keep out international religious orders. For the most part, the bureaucrats had the support and cooperation of the emperor in this.

On the official level the church was docile to the state and cooperative with the Josephinist bureaucracy. Indeed, most of the hierarchy and clergy were Josephinist. For these men, the emperor embodied the state and no other form of government was conceivable. The recent foreign revolutions were aberrations: democracy was inconceivable in any form. The rumblings in Paris in 1830 and the death of Francis I in 1835 only caused such convictions to be stronger. There was work to be done and there was no time for philosophical speculation on liberties such as voting and freedom of the press. Much energy was given to the *Leopoldinenstiftung*, which supported missionaries to the large number of German-speaking emigrants to Protestant America, where the Catholic minority was dominated by Irish bishops hostile to German-speakers and their culture.[49]

Other than looking to America, Austrian churchmen gave little consideration to the international movements within Roman Catholicism. After 1835, there was a monarchy without a fit monarch, with an aging foreign minister who could only bring old solutions and methods. If Metternich saw what was coming, there is little indication that he knew how to do much other than hold the line. As the Biedermeier era progressed toward what would become its final catastrophe in 1848, Metternich offered only obfuscation and grudging compromise. He failed to grasp the Ultramontanist movement that was sweeping much of the Catholic world and would ultimately bring a papacy more centralized and more effective in claiming an independent role in Austrian church affairs.[50] There were, however, others within Austria who were convinced that a Roman Catholic revival was necessary. It was one of the bitterest defeats for the Josephinist bureaucracy that Clement Hofbauer, whom they knew to be subversive and whom they had watched constantly and tried to exile on several occasions, became the center of that revival, and that his order was given legitimacy by the emperor himself.

In summary, Vienna during the time of the Napoleonic occupations and then the congress was a city lukewarm to religion. Attending Mass was, to be sure, still the custom when it was obligatory; but the priest who could say the quickest Mass (about twelve minutes by some reports)[51] would attract the largest crowds, and it was customary to leave church before the sermon began unless the preacher was one of note. Josephinist regulation of the church had produced a functionary priesthood, controlled down to the topic and content of the sermons preached. In the process, the bureaucrats had underestimated human hunger for mystery and meaning, not only or primarily in *this* world, but in the beyond. In Vienna, where Habsburgs had entwined their rule and the Catholic religion so closely that one could not think of one without thinking of the other, nineteenth-century Romanticism had a special accent. Although a part of the movement that was growing in Europe during and after Napoleon, the Austrian Romantics espoused authoritarian beliefs that drew them into alliance with those interested in the restoration of papal influence in Habsburg lands.[52]

No movement can survive if there is but one person who gives it life, but it is often the case that one person will come to be identified with the movement and will give it direction and inspiration. Followers of that individual tend to ignore human weaknesses and frailties and to canonize the leader in their eagerness to present a saint of perfect proportions to the less-than-perfect world. Those who are not members of the movement will tend to ignore or to denigrate the leader. Great men and women have always transcended their times. But it takes an incredible arrogance or a thorough humility to do what one must, even when others would seduce by their adulation or their scorn.

Clement Maria Hofbauer[53] was such a leader. He arrived in Vienna at the end of September 1808, only after the special intervention of the archbishop of Vienna had managed to free him from the Prussian prison where he and the other Redemptorists[54] of St. Benno's in Warsaw had been taken on the fourteenth of June of the same year. Hofbauer, nearly fifty-seven, came to Vienna a beaten man. The twenty years of work at St. Benno's was completely destroyed by order of Napoleon himself. Only with extreme difficulty had the archbishop managed to get Hofbauer out of Poland, and the police in Vienna were not pleased with his sudden appearance in their city. The Redemptorists were suspected of being Jesuits—the Josephinists would never understand the differences—and, in any case, both orders were banned from Habsburg lands. The refugee from Poland who, after twenty years in Poland, spoke German with a thick Slavic accent was not welcome. When he was found to have brought church vessels and vestments, he was immediately suspected of being a thief—or perhaps it was only the beginning of the thousand excuses the police found to harass him until his death. At any rate, it took the archbishop, as influential as he was, three days to get Hofbauer cleared with the police and out of their custody. Then Hofbauer applied for a visa to Canada. He was convinced that the only way to get his order established in Austria was to leave for a place more hospitable, from which he could send missionaries when the time was riper. War broke out in 1809, and it became impossible for Hofbauer to leave; he spent the rest of his years in Vienna.

Clement Hofbauer was born on 26 November 1751, in the small village of Tasswitz in southern Moravia. He was baptized Johannes. In many ways, his life reflects the new world created by Maria Theresa and Joseph. His father was a butcher who changed his name to the Germanicized Hofbauer when he moved from Budwitz to Tasswitz to marry Maria Steer, a farmer's daughter.

There was no money to send the boy to school, but Maria Theresa's *Volkschule* gave him the taste that made him thirst for more. At age sixteen, Johannes became an apprentice in a local bakery and two years later was to take that trade to a local monastery (Klosterbruck)—but only after he had made his first pilgrimage to Rome, a two-month walk that led him to the many pilgrim places along the way. Using the influence of his richer cousin, who had actually joined the monastery where Johannes was working as a baker, Johannes was able to finish studies at the gymnasium by the age of twenty-five, when he made another pilgrimage to Rome.

Hagiographers claim that Johannes always burned with a desire for priesthood, but it was during the year he stayed in Rome that some sort of religious conversion was first evident. He spent time as a hermit and changed his name to Clement, in honor of another, earlier hermit from Alexandria in Egypt. When he returned home, he lived in a hut in the woods, dedicated to prayer and meditation and to leading in prayer and procession those who found their way to his place of refuge. The questions raised by those who sought him out made him realize that he needed more knowledge.

Clement moved to Vienna in 1780, the year in which Maria Theresa died and Joseph assumed the throne alone. He practiced his baker's trade and considered marrying the baker's daughter and taking over her father's business. God and a rainstorm intervened, however. While accompanying three spinster sisters in a carriage that he had gallantly ordered to save them from the downpour, he found wealthy sponsors who would support him through his studies for priesthood. This was precisely at the time when Joseph was changing the course of theological studies, and the teachers of theology were those who had accommodated to the new winds blowing in the monarchy. Clement was not impressed with the Enlightenment world view. Whether or not he actually charged his teachers publicly with not teaching Roman Catholicism, as hagiographers report, is uncertain. However, when Joseph II established his General Seminaries in 1784, Clement journeyed to Rome to continue his studies.

In Rome, Hofbauer and a friend joined the Redemptorists, ostensibly because the Redemptorists' was the first bell they heard for morning prayer when the two arrived in the Eternal City. More likely, Hofbauer had heard of Liguori and had already developed a deep respect for him. Like many a good religious before and after him, Clement added the name *Mary* to his own to proclaim his devotion to the Lord's mother and his disdain for Josephinist attempts to downplay the Virgin's role. Ordained on 29 March 1785, Hofbauer and his friend returned to Vienna in October of that year in the high hope of founding the Redemptorists in that city. They were not welcome; but they were befriended by Baron Penckler[55] who would be influential later.

The two unwelcome Redemptorists left the city for the Ukraine, where they had been promised they would be allowed to establish their order. After six months of travel, they had only reached Warsaw in Poland. Since the German national church of St. Benno was vacant, the Polish king Stanisaw II Poniatowski forbade them to leave the city. Seeing the will of God in necessity, the two began work in St. Benno's, where they would remain for the next twenty years. Hofbauer was to become very active at St. Benno's with those who spoke German and those who did not. He was successful in establishing a secret group of laity interested in following a life patterned on the Redemptorists. He even managed to gather together a group of young men who were interested in becoming Redemptorists, although the rule that they could not enter the novitiate before the age of twenty-four made it difficult to keep them. He taught the necessity of homiletic expertise and the conviction that the best way to Christ was through his mother.[56] His work displeased the authorities, who wanted a pliable priest, and with Napoleon's reorganization of Poland in 1808 Hofbauer was imprisoned. Hence, Hofbauer arrived in Vienna under a cloud of failure and suspicion.

After he was released from jail, and when it became clear that there would be no early chance of leaving Vienna, Hofbauer settled in. After several housing possibilities proved impossible, Baron Penckler arranged a room for him in the Minoritenkirche. Hofbauer had little visibility during the next three years until October of 1813, when he was appointed confessor and church director to the Ursulines, an order of teaching women. During the next seven years, the Ursuline chapel and Hofbauer's quarters were to become the center of the Roman Catholic revival in Vienna.

It was also through the influence of Baron Penckler that Hofbauer would be introduced to the salon of Caroline Pichler,[57] whose house had become the meeting place of many of Vienna's literati. Many of the circle were from other parts of the German world and many were converts to Roman Catholicism, people who had found the mystery and richness of Roman tradition more appealing than Protestantism. These converts showed a zeal and enthusiasm for their newfound faith that outdid the fervor of most of those who had been born to Catholicism. It was here that Hofbauer was to make the acquaintance of Friedrich and Dorothea von Schlegel,[58] at whose home he was to become an almost daily guest.

Friedrich and Dorothea von Schlegel had converted to Catholicism in April of 1808 in Cologne.[59] After he moved to Vienna, Friedrich von Schlegel became the intellectual leader of the Roman Catholic restoration movement. His lectures in the spring of 1812 were on history, a discipline that had found its champions mainly in Protestant circles. Schlegel lectured on Roman Catholic history—more than a little romanticized—and made claims for the validity of revelation (an anathema for the enlightened) and the importance of Tradition (an anathema for the Protestants). Schlegel collaborated with others in the writing of several periodicals that proclaimed the message of the Roman

Catholic revival; the Roman enthusiasts even founded a library to lend Catholic books to interested persons.

The most important members of the intellectual circle that surrounded Schlegel and found inspiration in Hofbauer included Clemens Brentano,[60] Laurenz Greif,[61] Leopold Horny,[62] Fredrich August Klinkowström,[63] Johann Madlener,[64] Adam Müller,[65] the Passy brothers,[66] Josef Anton von Pilat,[67] Joseph Othmar von Rauscher,[68] Johann Peter Silbert,[69] Franz Springer,[70] Franz Graf Szechenyi,[71] Zacharias Werner,[72] Roman Zängerle,[73] F. X. Zenner,[74] and Gregory Thomas Ziegler.[75] A large number of younger and aspiring intellectuals also moved in and out of this group. Hofbauer believed that the future was with the youth, and they had constant access to his attention and his quarters. Among the younger generation were Anton Günther and Johann Emanuel Veith.

The heart and soul of the Roman Catholic revival was Clement Maria Hofbauer. When he was appointed to the Ursulines, Hofbauer was sixty-two years old. He had been through success and failure, persecution and adulation. He sensed in himself a power and authority that could ignore bureaucrats and police alike. He despised the Josephinist regulations and hindrances as unjustifiable meddling by the state in the affairs of the church. It was not for him to use the passage on the prodigal son as an opportunity to educate the farmers on the raising of pigs and the preparation of sauerkraut. He was not interested in saying spiritual things in such a bland way that even a Freemason could accept what was supposed to be Roman Catholic doctrine. He did not agree with revolution and found the French model as unacceptable as Josephinism. The church had a role of its own that it must fulfill, and it was essential that the church remain true to its mission, in spite of any interference. Almost daily, Hofbauer would insist, "The gospel must be preached anew!"[76] In his life, he lived out that prescription.

Hofbauer created quite a stir in a city looking for something new and sensational. His enemies referred to him as a religious fanatic (*Schwärmer*); his friends flocked to his sermons. The majority of both were of the upper and middle classes. The lower class did not come to the first district, the major area of Hofbauer's efforts, except for an occasional street sweeper, hired to serve as a placeholder for some fashionable lady who did not want to appear early for church but still wanted a place where she could see the man who came to be known as the Apostle of Vienna.[77]

The police reports on Hofbauer indicate not only that he was watched, but that he had absolutely no art when he preached.[78] He had a foreign accent that made some complain that he was difficult to understand. His personal appearance was unkempt and, when he became excited, he looked almost fanatical. He followed no logical pattern and had no rhetorical flourishes to entice the listener. He did not pretend to know the secular literature of the time. He could become so emotional during a sermon that he himself would cry and bring his congregation to share in his tears. He could wave the gospel book at his congregation and call them to a rediscovery of the meaning of being Christian. He could be abusive of a congregation, sometimes using vulgarities from the common speech and sometimes even singling out a listener for a special rebuke. He believed that religion was in decline and therefore strictness was called for although his harshness from the pulpit was balanced by his mildness in the confessional. He wanted even children and women (*Weiber*) to understand what he preached, and he claimed to preach the pure, simple, and clear truth of salvation. He preached with the conviction that only the singleminded can muster.

Hofbauer was a busy man and it showed in his preaching. He spent six to eight hours daily in the confessional. Usually early in the week, he read the scripture passages for the following Sunday and made them the subject of his meditation during the week. Before he preached, he spent a quarter of an hour in silent reflection in his room—with a towel over his head if the ever-present youthful visitors were making too much noise. Then he would climb into the pulpit and preach. He spoke from the heart.

Perhaps it was the sheer audacity of it. More than anything, he flaunted his disdain for the Josephinist rules. Legally, he was not even supposed to preach in a convent church; preaching was reserved for parish churches and was to be from sermon outlines distributed by the government. But the constant harassment served only to make Hofbauer's convictions stronger and his sermons more popular. It was a sign of how weak Metternich's system had become that, except for constant surveillance and one brief period when he was forbidden to preach, Hofbauer went unchecked.

Claiming to preach true Catholic doctrine, Hofbauer concentrated on things forbidden by the Josephinist bureaucracy; for his was another world, and he believed firmly that he must obey God more than any human authority. His challenge to the throne's authority, which also claimed to be from God, was not a contradiction for him. He was not a man who espoused tolerance. Truth was truth, and there could be no compromise. And Truth was Roman Catholic with the Roman pontiff at the pinnacle of this world's authority because he so clearly pointed to another world.[79] The Josephinist doctrine of toleration was intolerable, but even more intolerable was the throne's interference with Roman Catholic doctrine. Josephinist tolerance wanted to make room for all, at least in not giving offense to any. Hofbauer took no cognizance of whether his sermons offended. For Hofbauer, whoever did not hear the Roman Church could not expect to find a place in heaven. It was as simple as that.

The men who were bishops at the time were personally pious men who lived comparatively austere lives. But they were governmental appointees who cooperated with the government. The church must be free, Hofbauer insisted, and he saw that freedom in an ardent papalism and in freedom to do and preach what he saw as church tradition. He preached the cross. He insisted on the other-worldly doctrines of hell and purgatory. He proclaimed the value of indulgences and pilgrimages, novenas, candles, and incense. Hofbauer brought back all of the baroque piety of the Counter-Reformation, and he found an echo in Biedermeier Vienna.

On 12 November 1818, Hofbauer's quarters were searched by the police. Later he was given an ultimatum either to leave Austria or to cease being a member of the Redemptorist order. It is difficult to say why the police made this test of strength at that time; perhaps they were convinced that the ailing Hofbauer would capitulate. He chose exile rather than leave his order, but was given permission to stay through the winter because of his delicate health and the difficulty of travel in the cold months. Emperor Francis signed the permission for Hofbauer to leave, remarking that he was sorry to see it happen, that he had never liked to see any of his children (*Landkinder*) go into voluntary exile. The emperor labored under the impression that Hofbauer had requested permission to leave.

This time, however, the Josephinist bureaucracy had overplayed its hand. Perhaps, had they denied the request to stay through the winter, the affair would have been over and Hofbauer would have been gone. As it was, the influential friends of Hofbauer had time to act. It was the emperor's own physician, Freiherr von Stifft, as well as the emperor's confessor, Vincenz Darnant, who approached the emperor and informed him of the truth of the matter. The emperor was not pleased with the duplicity of his bureaucracy. He had also been impressed by his visit to Rome in 1819, during which the pope himself had spoken highly of Hofbauer. Emperor Francis read a copy of the rule of the Redemptorists, then called Hofbauer for an audience in August of 1819. Francis informed Hofbauer that the Redemptorist order would be approved in Vienna and that the order would be given the Church of St. Mary's on the Bank (*Maria am Gestade*), a church abandoned since it had been used by the French for garrisoning troops. The plan of the Josephinists had backfired.

Hofbauer was not to see the final victory. The winter of 1819–20 had been very hard on his health, and he was confined to his bed where his friends and followers kept vigil. He died in the arms of his physician, Johann Emanuel Veith, on 15 March 1820. The patent approving the Redemptorists was delayed so as not to be lost in the excitement of the funeral. Much of Vienna, even many of the Josephinsts, turned out to honor the man who would later be canonized and made the official patron of the city of Vienna. On 19 April 1820, after their constitutions were rewritten to conform to Habsburg law, the Redemptorists became legal in Habsburg lands. The list of those who would enter the first Redemptorist novitiate included the names of Anton Günther[80] and Johann Emanuel Veith.

3
THE THEOLOGIAN AND THE PREACHER

Shortly after the death of Hofbauer, disagreements and difficulties among his followers began to surface. Adam Müller and Friedrich von Schlegel continued to stress unity; but they remembered the old days when the fight against the Josephinist bureaucracy had created the need for unity. The younger element, who had not known that struggle quite so personally, were beginning to split even as the old saint was dying. Two groups were forming that would come to hate each other as only brothers can hate. The split was concealed by the usual Roman Catholic and Habsburg civility and pious euphemism; but the trained ear could not help noticing the growing strain.

One group formed around Joseph Othmar von Rauscher, who later became the teacher of Francis Joseph and then the cardinal archbishop of Vienna. He emerged as a friend of the newly established Redemptorist order and was befriended by one of Metternich's conservative secretaries, Ernst Jarcke. For these successors of Hofbauer, church politics and practical questions were the major issues to be pursued. They were Ultramontanist, and eventually the signing of a concordat between Vienna and Rome became the goal that rallied them. Their strength was evident in the signing of the Concordat of 1855 and in the condemnation of the thought of another Hofbauer follower in 1857.

The second group of Hofbauer followers saw the main enemy of Catholicism (and of Truth) in pantheism, which they believed was present in all thought, past and present. This group saw the answer to the issues of the day in the defeat of that pantheism, whether in the thought of Hegel or Spinoza, Schelling or Thomas Aquinas. Their intellectual leader was Anton Günther, whom Hofbauer had called his "Augustinus." Günther's theological treatises strongly influenced German theological thinking in the Biedermeier era. The heart and soul and mouthpiece for popularization of the group, however, was Johann Emanuel Veith, whose preaching prowess was known throughout Habsburg lands and was carried even to America in the volumes of his published sermons. Had the thought of Günther not been condemned with the help of other former followers of Hofbauer, Günther's influence might have been measured with that of Tübingen.[1]

There were probably no two more unlikely friends than Günther and Veith. Although both grew up in Bohemia and both attended the University of Prague at the same time (they made each other's acquaintance during the Prague sojourn) they were totally unalike in background, temperament, and outlook. Günther was every bit the secluded scholar, content to live on little or nothing, hidden away in his book-lined study. The only people for whom he had much time were those who could comprehend his intellectual efforts. An ordained priest, Günther was content to celebrate a daily Mass without congregation and pray his breviary privately. A medical doctor and veterinarian as well as an ordained priest, Veith was one of the most lionized of preachers and one of the most sought-after of confidants.

Together, Günther and Veith attracted intellectuals and practitioners, clergy and laity, men and women, cradle Catholics and a surprising number of converts—especially Jewish converts like Veith himself. Their circle grew and flourished from the time of Günther's first book in 1828 through the fateful year 1848, when a revolution and its aftermath sharpened the differences between the two branches of the spiritual descendants of Clement Maria Hofbauer and intensified the lines of battle.

It is difficult, in the case of both Günther and Veith, to write about their private lives. Both were reluctant to talk of inner struggles, crises, turning points. Both expressed a fear that personal data would obscure intellectual objectivity—that too much autobiography would distort the thought being expressed.[2] Both men expressed acute embarrassment when praised.[3] The twentieth-century penchant for psychic exhibitionism was alien to the nineteenth century. There were no tales of sexual fantasy or dreams of power, and personal crises were mentioned only in passing, even in correspondence with personal friends. Günther wrote an autobiography of sorts,[4] but it is a chronology and an intellectual history that stops in 1828 with the publication of his first book, for, he insisted, anything else that would be of public interest was to be found in the various publications he had written.[5] Even Günther's brief autobiography is not totally to be trusted. Veith, in sending the manuscript to Knoodt, commented that there were many factual errors because of the failing memory of an old man.[6] What is known of Günther and Veith is from asides in letters and descriptions by contemporaries.

There is a portrait of Anton Günther by an unknown artist that hangs in the Old Catholic Seminar rooms in Bonn. It depicts Günther in middle age. His hair is nicely arranged, which, together with a high Roman collar that rides a little too close to the chin, gives him a stuffy air. His eyes are set a shade too close together and are looking off to the side. One has a sense of relief that it is so because, were he to turn his head, those piercing eyes would be too much for the stranger. His thin lips and long, pointed nose are set off by the slight roundness of his jowls. He does not look unpleasant by any means; but he does look proper. He looks as if he were about to speak, and his words would be a speech to set forth in professorial style some principle, some point of theology or philosophy. Although he was never a professor, Günther's portrait shows him every inch a learned man (*Gelehrter*).

Anton Günther was born on 17 November 1783 and lived until 24 February 1863. Günther presumed that his family was originally Protestant, living in Würtemberg until after the Thirty Years War, when they moved to Bohemia.[7] Anton was born in Lindenau in the region of Leitmeritz in Bohemia, the first of six boys to be born to Franz Günther and Anna Elizabeth Podlak Günther.[8] Both parents were from blacksmith families and had married not for romantic reasons but to carry on the family business. Franz was a bit of a dreamer who had an interest in watches and church organs. His smithy was a village center for gossip and talk of religion and politics. Franz, however, also insisted that what was begun should be finished, and he had no ambition for his son Anton other than that he continue work in the family smithy. Anna, at least in Günther's memory, was a gentle soul who defended her son's penchant for birdwatching and play and protested the long hours in the smithy for a son who was clearly of delicate constitution.[9] The family was aware of economic changes since the time of Joseph II and complained that farmers, grown rich with the changes, were unwilling to pay the prices for blacksmith work.[10]

Anton's horizons were expanded by a weaver godfather (who brought stories of the broader world back from regular trips to market)[11], by trips with his father to attend services (and hear the organs) at various churches within a day's journey, and by the conversations he overheard in the smithy. Franz, a Roman Catholic, was an avid reader of the Bible (considered a Protestant custom) and was known to criticize the sermons of the village priest when he did not agree.[12] The village preacher, again in the memory of the aging Anton Günther, was a man who preached a God of love and laughter and encouraged a questioning spirit.[13]

Perhaps because of the encouragement of his mother or the discouragement of his father, or a recognition of his hatred for the work of a blacksmith, or perhaps because of that indefinable "call of God," thirteen-year-old Anton Günther journeyed to Haida, where he lived with a step-uncle and began studies that were to lead him to the priesthood. The year was 1796: Emperor Francis was already on the throne, but Metternich had not yet become his closest advisor. Anton had grown a ponytail (*Zopf*), the badge of the student. He set off with a grey jacket, two pairs of leather pants (*Lederhosen*), a pair of woolen stockings, buckled shoes, a round hat, an extra pair of underwear wrapped neatly in a handkerchief, and two new pieces of featherbed tucked under his arm.[14]

Günther's first academic year was difficult and discouraging, and he had to repeat that year, but then things moved steadily forward for him in spite of occasional hunger and difficulty with Greek.[15] He lived in back rooms and in monasteries.[16] Between 1796 and 1800, he visited the Piarist middle school in Haida. From 1800 to 1803, he visited the Augustinian gymnasium in Leitmeritz, a transfer made possible because of his ability to sketch.[17] To the old man Günther looking back on his early years, it seemed that the voice of God had led him inexorably on the way to salvation. From another perspective, it was a long road made possible in a changing empire where upward mobility was beginning to be more of a possibility; and in a church where that upward mobility had always been there for any man willing to accept—or at least promise to accept—ecclesiastical restrictions.

In 1803 Anton Günther began his university study at the University of Prague, the oldest university in Habsburg lands. He began with the usual course in philosophy—a preparation for all fields of study but most especially for the study of theology. In the first three years in Prague, Günther was introduced to the heady world of German idealism.[18] He was a student of the priest-philosopher-mathematician-theologian Bernard Bolzano.[19] It was to the young Bolzano that Günther went to discuss his growing vocational crisis.[20]

It is precisely this Prague period that would be so interesting to psychological voyeurs if more of the tale could be told. Obviously, there was a major storm on the horizon; the young Günther was in deep crisis of vocation and faith. In his autobiography Günther spends much time discussing the people who employed him as a tutor for their children. His own story can be pieced together only through asides and conjecture.

Günther was becoming more and more convinced of the ability of science (*Wissenschaft*)[21] to unravel the mysteries of the universe. He was becoming a determinist.[22] The whole drama of world history seemed a necessity, with great leaders of a society essentially the train-bearers (*Schleppenträger*) of destiny and fate. Günther became enthralled by a dictionary of Kantian philosophy by J. Lossius.[23] He read Gotthilf Heinrich von Schubert's theories of positive Christianity.[24] He attended the lectures of Professor Villaume, whose logic was designed to destroy a naive belief in miracles.[25] Veith, still a practicing Jew, was also in Prague at this time and a casual acquaintance of Günther's. Veith remembered their student days in a letter to Knoodt shortly after Günther's death in 1863. He wrote: "We were poor as mice—but not church mice. Christianity was something for slaves."[26]

When Günther took his questions to Bolzano, they focused on Günther's inability to see the necessity for supernatural revelation when reason (*Vernunft*) and science (*Wissenschaft*) could come to the same conclusions. As Günther remembered it, Bolzano recommended a delay in beginning theological studies until things settled a bit. Günther took Bolzano's advice to avoid being ordained "in due course" rather than out of conviction; as an old man he still remembered the guilt he had felt in disappointing his parents.[27] In the fall of 1803, Günther began the study of law at the University of Prague.

Günther's interest remained in philosophy and he never went far with the study of law. The next years were occupied with finding support for himself by tutoring the children of various noblemen. His nursemaid stories present a humorous picture of a young intellectual dining and recreating with small children, trying to educate them in the intricacies of German idealism. In late

1809 he was given a position in the house of a Count Thun,[28] teaching the one son and two daughters of the Count's second marriage. Thun died shortly thereafter, before Günther could receive a guaranteed income; but the Count's widow invited Günther to accompany her to Vienna.

Anton Günther arrived in the capital of the Habsburg empire for the first time in 1810.[29] The year before, Napoleon had been defeated at Aspern but had managed to defeat Archduke Karl at Wagram. After the peace of Schönbrunn, Clement Lothar Metternich directed foreign policy and, in 1810, was steering a pro-French course. The plebian theater (*Theater an der Wien*) had reopened to the public and the young Günther, living in the Landstrasse on the suburban side of the Black Gate (*Schwarzes Tor*), enjoyed an occasional evening there, especially when the dramas of Schiller were on the program. He spent much time with friends in the local amusement park (*Prater*). He managed to make friends in Vienna in spite of popular prejudice against persons from the Czech provinces.[30]

At first, Vienna overwhelmed Günther, and his discouragement led him to consider returning to Prague to finish his law studies and bite the sour apple of marriage—a prospect sweetened by the thought that he could probably marry a rich nobleman's daughter and settle down to practice law and continue his private philosophical studies in a small country town.[31] Günther confided his quandary to a newly-found friend who introduced him to Joseph Milde, then a professor at the university. Milde introduced him to Prince Bretzenheim-Regetz,[32] who offered him a position as a tutor. Günther decided to remain in Vienna and never again mentioned the idea of marriage.[33] He worked just enough to keep body and soul together, dedicated to *Wissenschaft*.

His intellectual journey continued with a fascination for Franz von Baader and Adam Müller, both Roman Catholic Romanticists.[34] He also made the acquaintance of the two men who would influence him to return to a wholehearted Roman Catholicism, the study of theology, and ordination to the priesthood.

The first of these was Michael Korn, the pastor in a small rural parish in Brunn am Gebirge, where the prince was wont to take his family for vacation. As the children's tutor, Günther accompanied the family in the spring of 1811. Günther and Korn became intellectual friends: Günther talked about philosophy; Korn talked about theology. Korn was amazed that the young Günther, so hungry for knowledge of the meaning of life and the world, had never read the entire Bible. Korn had a considerable acquaintance with the Protestant exegetical schools of the time, which was most unusual for priests in Roman Catholic Austria. He recommended a commentary by the Swiss Kantian, Hess.[35]

The words of the old Günther reporting the event are almost matter-of-fact. Yet anyone who has solved a longstanding problem or has come to an intuition after long struggle can sense, even in the commonplace words of the tired old man, what was the considerable excitement of the young seeker-after-truth. The young man discovered that the *Wissenschaft* he had been following was not enough. Günther had what religious writers call a conversion-experience. "I came to understand," wrote Günther, "that the world was not redeemed by knowledge but by an act of love."[36] Günther spent the rest of his life explaining the insight of how science and revelation were to be reconciled. He shared his excitement with Korn but Korn seemed too rustic, too inexperienced. He was an excellent sparring partner; but Günther could not conceive of him as a Father Confessor.[37] That role would be filled by someone else whose reputation for holiness was growing in Vienna.

Just who introduced Anton Günther and Clement Maria Hofbauer is uncertain.[38] What is certain is that Günther was charmed and fascinated. He found Hofbauer's German difficult but the content exciting. It was one of the very few times that Günther was to leap into trust. Shortly after he met the man, Günther decided to make his first general confession.[39] What Günther confided to Hofbauer is not known, but one suspects that it dealt mostly with his doubts about the necessity of divine revelation in the face of the powers of *Wissenschaft*—the sin of pride, therefore. Nor is it known what Hofbauer said to Günther, except for the one remark Günther himself records in later years: "Be patient with yourself."[40] Whatever happened during that general confession, Günther continued unhesitatingly in the Hofbauer circle until Hofbauer's death in 1820.

The conversion and the contact with Hofbauer renewed Günther's interest in theology. He could not attend regular lectures because of his duties as tutor, but the university professors of the time were more than willing to encourage the eager young student in his private study.[41] He was most interested in the study of the history of dogma, although there were no specific classes in the history of dogma at the university, history being more a Protestant preoccupation. Günther received much encouragement in the Hofbauer circle, where he met Adam Müller and Friedrich von Schlegel and other Catholic intellectuals of the day.

It was also at this time that Günther made the acquaintance of the priest Lorenz Greif.[42] Greif interested Günther because he had done his theological studies in a university outside of direct Habsburg hegemony. Greif was from Würtemberg, which, although a part of the Holy Roman Empire, was Protestant—and the home of Günther's ancestors. When Greif was threatened with a return to Würtemberg, where the shortage of priests had made the pursuit of *Wissenschaft* difficult for clerics and work as a parish priest inevitable, Günther helped him to find a position in the house of the Schwarzenbergs as the tutor of the young Prince Ferdinand. Greif claimed to burn with the desire to pursue scholarship. The fire, however, seems never to have been lighted: there is no evidence that he wrote a single thing. But Greif, Günther, and Veith became lifelong friends, and Greif was a strong if silent support and sounding board for Günther in his work.

The Theologian and the Preacher 57

The next entry in Günther's autobiography is in 1819, when he moved to Raab in Hungary as the companion of the oldest son of Prince Bretzenheim-Regetz, who was to study law in the part of the empire where he would become a landholder. Initially, Günther was not pleased with the move, which was to last for two years; he was not enthusiastic about giving up his theological studies. It was Greif who came to the rescue by suggesting that Günther approach the Bishop of Raab, Prince Ernst von Schwarzenberg, the brother of the Schwarzenberg who had appointed Greif. It was agreed that Günther would continue his theological studies privately and then take examinations at the diocesan seminary in Raab. When Prince Bretzenheim-Regetz guaranteed Günther a lifetime pension, Günther, having passed the examinations, was ordained on the octave of the Ascension in May 1821, by the Bishop of Raab.[43] On All Saints Day, 1821, he celebrated in his home village of Lindenau. Both of his parents were overjoyed to have witnessed the day and Günther himself was deeply satisfied that he had "completed what he began."[44]

The journey ended in the priesthood after all. Günther discovered, as everyone who ends something after years of preparation and with a great deal of fanfare, that ordination was anticlimatic. He had a sense of uneasiness in the first year after ordination. He resisted pressure from Michael Korn to become his assistant in the country. After Hofbauer's death in 1820, Günther had lost interest in joining the Redemptorists.[45] Günther considered them too new and too untried. As an order, they had accomplished nothing important.[46] He wanted a home where greatness had already been proven by history.

It is not recorded when Günther met Pater Landes, S.J. The Jesuit order had been officially suppressed in 1773 but had managed to survived in a variety of unlikely and hidden places until they were allowed by Pope Pius VII to resurface in 1814. The Austrian Josephinists were not friends of the Society of Jesus, and the Josephinists still had considerable influence. Pater Landes was in Vienna to get permission to establish a Jesuit novitiate in the capital city. He met the young Günther, who was enchanted by the prospect of joining the order for "history teaches what the Jesuits have accomplished."[47] The Josephinists were not successful in banning the Jesuit novitiate completely; but they were successful in moving the German-speaking Jesuits to Polish Galicia, where there was already a flourishing community of Polish Jesuits. Pater Landes and four candidates—all priests—left Vienna for Poland in November 1822. Anton Günther was among them, thirty-nine and in delicate health.

In 1830, having left the Jesuit novitiate in 1824, Günther wrote a description of his concept of the ideal community.[48] It was very loosely structured togetherness rooted in common intellectual pursuit, each member of the community working at his own pace, keeping his own schedule. The gathering of the community was for intellectual discussion, usually around a meal or a coffee hour. If this was his ideal, it is no wonder that Günther had so little success in Poland.

The Jesuit novitiate, like so many novitiates the world over at that time, was designed for testing and shaping younger and more bendable souls than Günther's. The daily schedule called for being together from early in the morning until going to bed early at night. The extreme penances included kneeling for meals and kissing the shoes of the assembled brethren. The penances were voluntary, to be sure; but there was a not-so-subtle pressure to conform. Although he cooperated, Günther ridiculed the practices, whispering that the row of kneeling novices looked like a line of bears at Schönbrunn zoo.[49] He resisted the pressure to kiss everyone's shoes, but he could not resist speaking out in protest when someone claimed that the Jesuits were the "church within the church."[50] Nor could he help but be surprised when he was told that he would be expected to teach pastoral theology and liturgy at a Jesuit school to be opened in Galicia. When he wrote to the provincial and protested that he had no knowledge and no experience in either area, he was rebuffed with the reply that he should pay more attention to obedience and less to philosophy.[51] Pater Landes tried to protect him, to befriend him, to nourish him. But the disillusionment grew.

Günther's chronic health problems eventually made it necessary for him to leave the Jesuit novitiate in June 1824. The friendship with Pater Landes and the exceptions Landes allowed him were not enough to protect Günther's fragile constitution. His liver gave him problems, and he attributed a ringing in his ears to it. The doctors whom he consulted recommended a long stay in a health resort. Günther insisted that he be allowed to recover in Vienna, with the understanding that he would return to the novitiate when he had recovered sufficiently.

Once back in Vienna, Günther recovered quickly. He found pleasant lodgings with a friend who lived in Meidling near Schönbrunn palace and zoo. Dr. Glücker and his daughter nursed Günther back to health. Günther was eager to return to the novitiate and wrote the same to Pater Landes. It was Pater Landes who recognized that Günther should not return to the Jesuits. Landes sensed that the frail scholar would never do well in a community that demanded more conformity than Günther was capable of giving. "Everyone must sacrifice his Isaac,"[52] wrote Landes in reference to Abraham's call to sacrifice his only son.

Günther himself did not make the decision to leave the Jesuit novitiate, but he quickly accepted it without serious questioning. In later life, he lamented having left them because he had created enemies in so doing.[53] Others, especially his enemies, continued to call him Pater Günther or the Viennese Jesuit.[54] But in 1824 Günther needed a new direction. He had seriously considered both the Redemptorist and Jesuit communities, and it was clear that a religious order was not for him. Günther wanted nothing to do with the life of a parish priest. His parents were both dead. Hofbauer and Korn were also dead by then. At forty-one, Günther believed it was time to settle into something.

From 1824 to 1829, Günther lived in the rectory of the Church am Hof in Vienna. His duties were minimal—just enough to offset his room-and-board expenses. He chose the church over a return to the quarters of Prince Bretzenheim-Regetz because the salon life would be a distraction from scholarly pursuits. He agreed to take on Prince Ferdinand von Schwarzenberg as a philosophy student since the young prince had decided on a career in the church, but there was no question of moving into the Schwarzenberg palace: Günther needed quiet. He also accepted an appointment from Police Minister Sedlnitzky as a governmental censor in the areas of philosophy and law, which gave him access to works that others could not obtain and to connections that could help him when he was ready to publish.[55] Günther found his niche. From 1824 until his death in 1863, the city that had frightened him at first was to be Günther's home. He did not leave it except for an occasional outing to Baden or to Maria Zell or, at the farthest, the Salzkammergut near Salzburg. When invitations came to professorial chairs elsewhere, Günther could not bring himself to leave the city.[56] He stayed on even though Vienna never offered him a professorship; he stayed even when the leaders of that city became hostile to his thought.[57]

In Vienna after 1824, in a way that is hard for those who do not share the passion to imagine, Günther was to dedicate himself completely to his *Wissenschaft*. The indecision of youth was gone, replaced with the discipline of maturity. Günther had dabbled in reviews since his first years in Vienna,[58] but that was not the same as creating one's own works. It was only in 1828, four years after he returned to Vienna from Poland and at age forty-five, that Günther published his first volume. In the next twenty years, he published nine major volumes and numerous magazine articles and reviews. He remained a recluse, interested in only a few friends and these primarily because of their interest in the same life of the mind as was he. He remained a private scholar, earning a bit of money as a teacher, writer, and censor to supplement the pension he received from Prince Bretzenheim-Regetz.

In 1829, when a new pastor was appointed in the Church am Hof, Günther, with help from Veith, found an apartment in the Neustädlerhof in the Pressgasse.[59] His apartment had a small kitchen and two additional small rooms. His study faced a small, dark courtyard; his sleeping room–library faced a narrow and gloomy Pressgasse.[60] Here he lived out his remaining years, working long hours at his writing desk, taking short walks around the city. Each day he prayed the Roman breviary and celebrated daily Mass, with one acolyte in attendance, first in the Church am Hof and then in the St. Rupert's Church when he moved to the Pressgasse.[61] Günther lived in the church liturgical year completely; time was marked according to church seasons and festivals. He had an uncritical and simple devotion to Mary as the Mother of God, although he had no use for the doctrine of the Immaculate Conception that was being promoted at the time.[62] He lived and died a pious son of the Roman Church.

So Günther lived out his years. He cared little for money or personal comfort. He accepted the care and tenderness of friends, mostly students and mostly men. He suffered miserably from gout, already present in 1847 when he complained that the doctor had ordered him to do as little reading and writing as possible.[63] The gout eventually attacked his hands, feet, shoulders, hips, and face; still, he persisted in disobeying the doctor's orders and worked constantly. Günther, the intellectual recluse, could not let poor health stop his crusade to proclaim positive Christianity against the pantheism that, he was convinced, infected his age.

In his biography of Veith,[64] Johann Heinrich Löwe, Veith's nephew, included a photograph of Veith in his later years. The hair is rumpled and unruly, the eyes are set wide apart in the forehead and look straight into the lens of the camera, but they are not the piercing eyes of Günther. Rather, they seem to be inviting eyes, a bit of fire set below two uneven, bushy eyebrows and above a stubby broad nose. The lower lip and the jaw sag a bit but this effect is offset by the high cheekbones. The Roman collar is high but does not give the impression of scholarly distance. Even through the black and white of early picturetaking, Veith appears human, ready to smile. Here appears a man one could talk to about sin and fear and failure. A contemporary described him as short and slight of build, naive as a child of seven, clever as a snake and gentle as a dove; he liked to laugh and was genuinely interested in learning still, in spite of his immense knowledge, taking any instruction like a pious child.[65] Eduard Winter, writing in the first quarter of the twentieth century, called Veith "an unsightly, wizened little man with a repulsive, ugly, ape-like face."[66] But Winter was given to overstatement.

Even when allowances are made for the spirituality of the times, which made it seemly to denigrate oneself in order to praise God, Veith's constant self-disparaging remarks seem to be a bit of posturing. "I find myself detestable," he wrote in 1840. "I am an absurd monster with very sensitive feelings, a disastrous consequence of the eighteenth century. Often when I laugh, I feel in myself clearly the grimace of a hyena—a hyena who likes to gobble salad. People are entirely right who cannot stand me. I am so ridiculous that I occasionally am myself amazed."[67] Veith was shy[68] and private[69] and called himself a wallflower.[70] One time in a ship's restaurant he found that he could not speak up loud enough for the waiter to hear him because of his shyness; so he went without dinner. A brief flirtation with a young lady in his early years found him standing in front of a mirror wondering how anyone could prefer that face and that person.[71]

This lack of confidence carried over into Veith's priestly life. He felt that people listened to him less because he was a priest and that people could forgive a lay person almost anything but would allow a priest nothing.[72] He mistrusted his own effectiveness as a priest and preacher;[73] but there is no evidence that he lacked confidence in the medical profession, in which he was a pioneer, without the slightest hesitation. Perhaps it was simply a spirituality that would not allow Veith to take credit for accomplishments in the "spiritual" realm. That humility was accompanied by a discipline that denied all comfort. His indulgences were his morning and afternoon coffee and his inclination to have exotic green plants on his desk. He detested large social events, fancy dinners, soft beds, comfortable chairs, and animals kept as pets.[74]

Veith suffered from fragile health all his life. "My life sign is a migraine," he wrote.[75] He estimated that he spent one day in seven with a severe headache[76] and marked his calendar with an "M" for every migraine.[77] In later life he suffered from gout and from hallucinations—which he simply ignored until they went away. He had frequent nightmares and a peculiar habit of singing in his sleep.[78]

No matter how sick he was, however, Veith did not allow it to interfere with his work. He often said that a life of leisure was a dog's life.[79] In old age he felt guilty that he had given in to laziness and not worked more.[80] It was in his work that Veith found himself, and he was doggedly devoted to it. One can only see the wisdom in his decision to remain a celibate.

Veith was very generous with others. If he had no money to give to people in need, he would find something of worth, including his own writings, which he would give them to exchange for money. He was not the best judge of human character, often disappointed when people did not live up to his expectations.[81] He did not set office hours for himself because he knew that he would not keep them; he could not say "no" to anyone who sought him out as doctor or counselor, teacher or friend. In order to be unavailable, he found a secret room in a nearby house.

Veith was a complex man. Shy and reserved and always trying to "make nothing out of himself,"[82] he was known for his wit and quick comebacks in circles where he felt at home. Veith, who lacked self-confidence, was driven to write and speak, at once convinced of his own worthlessness and of the power of the message he had to proclaim. He was constantly working on something but never satisfied that he was productive enough.[83]

Mendel (Emanuel) Veith was born on 10 July 1787 in the village of Kuttenplan in northwestern Bohemia near the Bavarian border. Joseph II was the emperor, and Emanuel's father, Baruch, set a great deal of hope in him. A man of learning who was well read in Enlightenment writers, both Jewish and non-Jewish,[84] Baruch was a teacher of religion and enjoyed the respect of his fellow Jews not only because of his erudition but also because of his pleasant and winning manner. When an arbitrary tax collector[85] harassed the community, it was Baruch who was sent to Vienna to plead with the emperor. It is not clear whether it was because of his money or his charm—later events speak more strongly for the former—but Baruch was received by the emperor several times. The emperor was impressed enough that he not only took care of the matter of the tax collector but also offered Baruch the governmental tobacco monopoly in the district of Klattau, the major town in the area where the Veith family lived. At the time, the city was closed to Jews by imperial decree, accessible only to those able to pay the necessary bribes.[86] The Veith family moved to Klattau in 1793.

The second of four sons born to Baruch Veith and Bräundl Löwe Veith, Emanuel claimed that he did not rely on his father for anything—but the conflicts between them were real.[87] Baruch was not happy when Emanuel decided against rabbinical studies and turned to medicine. There were harsh words about Emanuel's move to Vienna and, later, about his encouragement of his brother Elias to move to the same city, even though the eldest Veith son, Joseph, had moved there in 1808. Ominous silence surrounds the conversions of both Emanuel and Elias to Christianity. (Joseph remained an active member of the Vienna Jewish community until his death in 1834.[88]) Emanuel was close to his brother Elias, seldom mentioned his brother Joseph, and never even named his youngest brother who remained at home. The death of his father in 1818 and of his mother in 1824 received only minor notice in Veith's correspondence.[89]

Veith had little good to say about Judaism. He was six when the family moved to Klattau, and it was there that he first encountered the Talmud. In 1866 he wrote, "Klattau is the place that I hate most. It was there that I lived my neglected, mishandled, and joyless childhood, troubled by atrocious examples. I did not even learn Czech, which would have been a thousand times better than the rotten Talmud."[90] When Emanuel was unable to pass the test his father gave him every four weeks, he was locked in a small room without food, sometimes for days at a time. The room in which he was locked had an entrance into his father's library, however. The resourceful Emanuel would climb through the transom over the door and plunder the library: it was in this manner that he first made acquaintance with the new philosophy and culture that became so important to him later. At the age of nine he wrote his first play, a comedy; but he could share it with no one but his brother Elias his partner in crime.[91] At the age of eleven, Emanuel began lessons at home in preparation for examinations at the end of each year in the gymnasium in Pilsen. At the age of fourteen, he moved to Prague to attend the Akademisches Gymnasium in the Altstadt. He resided with his mother's brother, Israel Löwe. In Prague, Veith distanced himself from his family, from his Jewish heritage, and from his father's wish that he become a rabbi.

The Prague Jewish community in 1801 had ten thousand members, one of the largest communities in the world. There was much movement for change among the Prague Jews: there were large numbers of Jewish followers of Jacob Frank[92] and many others who were influenced by the ideas of the Enlightenment. Although not able to agree on many things, the two groups did agree on the need for assimilation into society. It is probable that Veith was at least familiar with these circles during his time in Prague.[93]

In 1803, Veith began his philosophical studies along with the four-years-older Anton Günther. The two made each other's acquaintance but did not spend much time together. Veith was studying to be a rabbi at the time; Günther was studying to be a priest. They had little in common other than a growing interest in German Romanticism. Günther became passionately taken by German idealism, and Veith idolized Goethe, even taking the time to make a trip to Karlsbad to catch a glimpse of the poet.[94] Veith continued his passion for music, learning the violin and the bass; he also became adept in French and showed an increasing interest in botany.

In 1807 Veith decided against becoming a rabbi and began his study of medicine at the University of Prague. The casual acquaintance he had with Günther faded and would not be revived until they met again in Vienna, both by then different men. The reason for Veith's choice of medicine is not entirely clear, except perhaps that botany was closely connected with medicine in those days. In the faculty of medicine Veith was given the position of treasurer (*Fiscus*), which brought him enough income to be independent. His father was not pleased with his son's decision to stop studies toward the rabbinate.

One year later, in spite of the uncertainty connected with giving up his job as treasurer, Veith moved to Vienna where the faculty of medicine had a much better reputation than the one in Prague.[95] He moved into quarters in the Alservorstadt, near Joseph II's general hospital, and attended lectures in both human and veterinary medicine.[96] He continued his violin playing and poetry writing. He composed the libretto for the operatta *Der Augenarzt* by Gyrowetz that was well received in Vienna and Berlin.[97] Veith's command of French was an asset during the French occupation of Vienna, 12 May through 27 November 1809.[98]

Veith completed his medical studies in both animal and human medicines, both with distinction. He impressed his examiners and in 1811 had a position with the army. When veterinary medicine became part of the university's curriculum, Veith became assistant to the director of veterinary medicine. In 1813, Veith published a German version of his Latin doctoral dissertation, which dealt with medicinal plants in Austria; he also published an outline of the use of herbs by veterinarians and economists.[99]

Veith's literary talents were well exercised during this time. In 1814 he wrote the play "Die Rückfahrt des Kaisers" ("The Return of the Kaiser"), which was preformed at the Theater an der Wien. His works also appeared in several literary magazines of the time.[100] He had a free ticket to the court theater and the court opera and made frequent use of both; he was a special friend of the opera. He was known to the director of the court theater, I. F. Castelli.[101] Along with Castelli, Veith frequented a literary group that met regularly in one of the coffeehouses of Vienna.[102] Major literary figures of the time visited the group when they were in Vienna; regulars included Adam Müller and Friedrich von Schlegel as well as other friends of Hofbauer.

By all measures, Veith's accomplishments were admirable for anyone, but they were extraordinary for a Jewish immigrant from the Bohemian provinces. Veith, however, was not impressed by his own success. He wrote to his uncle in Prague, "I am everywhere rude, really rude in both written and verbal form. And since I have been that way, I am welcomed everywhere and everyone tells me beautiful things. I spread it on terribly thick—and, can you imagine, people listen to or read it!"[103] Veith was not so much ridiculing the superficiality of society as expressing disbelief at his own accomplishments. He wrote a hymn for the synagogue to commemorate the return of Emperor Francis from battle with Napoleon and was surprised that he had done it. He wrote to his uncle, "Would you believe it of me?!"[104]

After 1814, Veith was the assistant director of the institute for animal medicine at the university. His lectures were well attended and had to be moved to a larger classroom. When the director died of typhus, Veith took over as provisional director. Through the influence of Baron von Stifft, who had been Veith's examiner in human medicine and was the emperor's personal physician, Veith was appointed the actual director of the institute on 31 July 1819. Veith's career was well launched. He was a doctor of both animal and human medicine, the head of a large institute at the university; he had a comfortable, guaranteed salary and a large furnished apartment at state expense. He had that most important of Viennese commodities: connections (*Beziehungen*).[105] Yet, even at the time of his official appointment as head of a university institute, Veith had already moved beyond medicine. By the time he was appointed, he was ready to resign. The bureaucracy could not keep up with him. He held the post of director of the veterinary institute until September 1820.

On 4 May 1816,[106] Emanuel Veith was baptized a Roman Catholic in the Church of St. Charles Borromeo (*Karlskirche*) His Christian name was Johann, after John the Baptist. His godfathers were two professors from the university[107] who remain otherwise unmentioned in Veith's life. His journey from Judaism through agnosticism to Roman Catholicism is not well documented. Veith clearly was not at home in Judaism: he had little contact with the synagogue after he left home, and that fell to next to none when he arrived in Vienna. Yet there is a considerable difference between rejecting Judaism and becoming a passionate Roman Catholic. Some speculate that his conversion resulted from the influence of Bernard Bolzano from the Prague student days,[108] but Veith had little or no contact with Bolzano in the ten years prior to his conversion. More likely, Veith began the journey to Christianity in Counter-Reformation Roman Catholic Vienna. Concerning his conversion, Veith was intensely private. Most likely, an insecure Veith, dissatisfied with Jewish answers and in the midst of an environment where everyone who was not Roman Catholic was an outsider, found his call to Catholicism in the Vienna that lionized Hofbauer.

Shortly after his baptism, Veith wrote to his uncle in Prague. He apologized for the long lapse in communication and reported his conversion to Catholicism. He spoke of a new freedom from the inner labyrinth that had preoccupied him. He wrote of a "considerably confused row of inner and outer fears, joys, sorrows, madness, and struggles which have for such a time danced a strange but wonderful dance around and in me."[109] Later in life, Veith repeated again and again his conviction that he "came to belief in an entirely inner, clear, and precise manner. It was through no human that he was called from the dung heap to Christianity."[110]

Veith underestimated the influence exerted upon him by those around him. But, whatever their influence, it is clear that the decision for Catholicism was Veith's. It was a decision that would remain through the most difficult of times, through times when the very church Veith had committed himself to seemed to reject much of what he believed. A Jewish convert to Christianity had much prejudice to overcome, even among friends. Even Günther, fast friend and co-worker with Veith after 1830, often spoke in amazement about Veith's depth of insight and understanding when it came to Catholicism. Günther wrote of Veith's amazing ability to preach theology in depth, "since he is only a convert—and in the rule, converts only absorb Catholicism up to the neck and not any higher."[111] Not unlike Günther himself, Veith had journeyed through a great deal of doubt and uncertainty and had finally surfaced on what he believed to be the rock of Roman Catholicism. He had landed there not because of convenience or a desire for influence but out of personal conviction, and there he was to remain, no matter what storm winds would blow.

It is impossible to say whether or not Veith had decided to become a priest at the time of his conversion in 1816; however, he began the study of theology in October of 1817. There is a police report, with reference to Veith, complaining that the Jesuits had managed to corrupt the best young men into following their backward ways.[112] To become a Catholic was one thing. To become a priest was quite another. But there was a certain inevitability about it in the case of Veith, a certain logic that led him to the priesthood either concurrently with or shortly after his conversion to Christianity.

One can look for outside influences, and the name that immediately surfaces is that of Clement Maria Hofbauer. In old age Veith remembered daily visits to Hofbauer, the older man's fatherly love, and his own new enthusiasm. Veith himself commented that it was through Hofbauer that he first came to know the warmth of faith and not just its intellectual power. It was Hofbauer who criticized Veith for his intellectual pride.[113]

Outside influences notwithstanding, the decision to become a priest, like the decision to become a Christian, was Veith's. At this time, Veith wrote a letter to an unidentified Jewish friend who had obviously objected to Veith's whole Christian project, including the decision for the priesthood.[114] Veith's answer was short, even arrogant: he wrote that there really was no use in discussing the issue because obviously the receiver of the letter would be unable to understand the gospel. Beyond the arrogance, however, Veith tried to explain his decision, even though he did not expect his friend to understand. He mentioned Friedrich Schleiermacher, the Protestant preacher and theologian who was working in Berlin at the time.[115] Veith insisted that Schleiermacher had had no influence on him. The rest of the letter, however, sounded curiously Schleiermachian. Veith wrote of a small cathechism for children as the place to find the simple answers of faith. He wrote of how little others knew him—indeed, how little he knew himself. He prayed, "Lord, do not shove away your poor puppy that licks your feet."[116] Veith continued that he would "throw himself at the feet of the crucified and be content; even if he were to rot on the manure pile, he would give God praise and thanksgiving for that."[117] Veith's feelings of worthlessness and inadequacy could be analyzed from a variety of perspectives and could have led him in a variety of directions made understandable by twentieth-century psychology. Since Veith was a nineteenth-century Roman Catholic, his spirituality could only lead him to the priesthood and to religious life. Whatever role Hofbauer played in this was less important than the spirituality that was at the core of Johann Emanuel Veith himself.

And so the young Jewish convert—doctor of medicine, head of the veterinary institute at the university, literary critic and author, published authority in botany, popular lecturer—was to become a priest. His lectures at the university continued to grow in popularity. His bureaucratic tasks were multiplied by a growing university institute. He wrote in journals of medicine and journals of literature. He became a much sought-after medical doctor, especially among the poor, whom he served without charge. He made several trips to the far reaches of the empire to deal with animal plague and epidemic. Sometime between 1816 and 1817, he flirted briefly with the idea of marriage.[118] But after October 1817 his decision was firm. In the midst of all else that he did, he was a regular listener at the theological faculty and passed examinations in that discipline with his usual outstanding success.

On 15 March 1820, Hofbauer died in Veith's arms. On 19 April of that year the government finally gave its approval for the Redemptorists to be established in Vienna. On 26 August 1821, Veith was ordained a priest at age thirty-three.[119] By this time it was clear that the priesthood was not enough for Veith, and shortly after ordination he entered the Redemptorist novitiate. He remained a Redemptorist through the spring of 1830. Those years were some of the hardest of his life.

It is difficult to generalize about the type of person who joins a religious community. Almost always there is some inspiration from a strong leader, a father figure, alive or dead. Many who are attracted are seeking to be led, content to be passive in life and docile to the will of the superiors. Blind obedience is their key to eternal reward. But community life is also attractive to those who identify with the strong leader and are capable of becoming strong leaders themselves. They are unable to accept blind obedience as a way of life but need to follow what is in their own hearts. This works well if these people can be recognized as leaders within the community, but this usually requires a long period of silence on the part of potential leaders, long years of docility and obedience. More often such persons are the victims of petty jealousy and misunderstanding. Some stay in religious life, coming to grips with smallness and even managing to rise above it; others leave to found religious communities of their own. Others simply leave. The pettiness can be overwhelming and disillusioning. In 1848 Veith made disparaging remarks about blind obedience.[120] He was speaking to soldiers and created quite a stir. But he was also talking about himself and his difficulties as a Redemptorist. For all of his lack of self-confidence, Veith was a leader.

There is a common assumption in Roman Catholicism that one who is truly serious about holiness will join a religious community. Veith's appreciation for Hofbauer and his own conversion experience led him to think that he could find fulfillment in the style of religious life lived out by the Redemptorists. At first he followed the will of his superiors, whether that meant being sent to preach a mission in Styria[121] or taking on important persons as medical patients for the benefit of the order.[122] Veith continued to write in a religious vein; he published prayer books, meditation books, stories of pilgrims and their encounter with Mary. He continued to see patients, and not only rich ones who were of benefit to the order. He began to preach and found that his success in the classroom carried over into the pulpit. In later life he remembered a prophecy of Hofbauer's: "You will be a preacher who will draw large crowds and you will preach in a new way—but you will not convert many."[123] The truth of the last is difficult to ascertain, but Veith did draw large crowds. His public appearances brought more people to his door seeking advice and medical assistance.[124]

In many ways, as far as community life with the Redemptorists was concerned, Veith was the victim of his own success. The more people came to him he was unable to refuse either physical or spiritual help to those who sought him out the more he failed to appear for community prayer, community meals, community recreation. As a young man, Veith wrote to his uncle that the only order that he found authentic was disorder.[125] Religious life is built on a common order that brings people together for common prayer, meals, recreation, sometimes even common work or sleep. Disorder—everyone keeping separate schedules—is usually viewed as the work of the devil and of division, irrespective of what great things are being accomplished.

The jealousy of the Redemptorist brothers was growing. It was a matter of prestige to have such a popular and important man as part of the order, but there was little understanding for the exceptions he made for himself. There were complaints that Pater Veith had little or no time for the other Redemptorists and that he was weak when it came to the vow of obedience. Veith suffered mostly in silence. He tried to remain obedient and willing to go where sent. There was a brief rumor that he would go to Innsbruck to begin the order there; but Veith was neither consulted nor informed of either the plan or its cancellation. He wrote to his brother Elias that he was willing to go anywhere as long as people would stop toying with him. He wanted straight answers and straight reasons. He was tired of having all that he did considered nonsense (*Lapperei*), of being treated like a dancing bear (*Tanzbär*). But even while complaining, Veith did not think seriously of leaving the order. There was a strong conviction in him that he must stay, that this was his cross. The only glimmer of what would eventually happen is the final sentence in the letter to his brother Elias in which Veith wrote that the only thing that all of this led him to believe was that he must strive to discover God's will for him by looking inside himself.[126]

Veith's migraine headaches intensified. He continued his work under intense pain, attacks of dizziness, loss of appetite, and lethargy.[127] His friends, both inside the order and outside it, began advising him to think of leaving. They could see the contradictions, but Veith could not. It was becoming clear that Veith would have to give up his writing and preaching if he were to stay in the Redemptorists. Some of his friends even made their way to the cardinal archbishop of Vienna, Leopold Graf Firmian,[128] who told Veith that he would accept him as a priest of the diocese of Vienna were he to decide to leave the Redemptorists.[129] Still Veith was unable to leave. It was difficult for him to turn away from a decision he had freely made, a decision that was permanent when he made it. He still remembered Hofbauer with affection, and he still loved Hofbauer's Redemptorists.

Through a series of extraordinary incidents, Veith was forced to decide to leave the order. Günther, also drawn to religious life initially, had left the Jesuit novitiate and settled down to a life of writing. The first volume of his philosophical thought appeared in 1828, and he sent a copy to Veith, whom he had seen occasionally since his return to Vienna. Veith was deeply touched,[130] and it was not simply the gesture of a friend that touched him. As he began to read the volume, he became very excited. He was convinced that this was the theology for the time; this was the foundation of the new preaching of the gospel that Hofbauer had stressed so much. He took on the task of using the Güntherian philosophy, written for philosophers and academics, as the basis of his Lenten sermons in the spring of 1830.[131] His intention was to express Güntherian thought in a way that would make it available to all. It was reported that the series was well received and well visited. The Redemptorists, however, were not impressed. They were skeptical of this new philosophy from someone who had chosen the Jesuits over them and then had left even the Jesuits.[132] The excitement and the stress in Veith reached their greatest intensity during this time.

As he was returning to his room after the last sermon in the Lenten series, Veith collapsed. One of the brothers helped him to his room and onto his bed; the other Redemptorists gathered around him. Veith thought that he was dying. He was paralyzed but he could hear. One of the brothers blurted out that now the community would have the burden of taking care of a cripple, and Veith heard the remark. When he recovered, which he did in short order for he had suffered only a temporary collapse from exhaustion, he resolved to leave the Redemptorists. He would be a burden on no one. He went on a long vacation to the estate of Baron Christian Kinsky[133] in Hungary; from there he wrote to his superiors of his intention to leave the community. There was no resistance from the order: all had come to realize that Veith was not cut out to be a religious. He and the order were to remain friends, and in 1865 he was to receive a special notation from them for his long love and service. When Veith returned from Hungary, he went briefly to St. Mary's on the Bank to collect his things and then moved around the corner to the Church am Hof where he was made assistant pastor.[134]

It was a new life for the forty-three-year-old priest and doctor. Without the pressure of community life, without a superior to answer to or confreres whispering behind his back, Veith was able to dedicate himself to the loves of his life: preaching, writing, and practicing medicine. On 14 September 1831 he was appointed second cathedral preacher at St. Stephen's.[135] He was to preach all Sundays one year and all feast days the following year. The post brought with it an apartment in the archdiocesan residence on the south side of the cathedral, adjoining the diocesan seminary of the time. Veith's generosity continued. He became, for all practical purposes, the house-doctor for the seminarians; but this earned him the jealousy of the appointed house doctor. Veith was asked to avoid the seminary—until the cardinal himself fell sick and called Veith when the other doctor was unavailable. His bedside manner and his skill made such an impression on the cardinal that Veith was allowed to do as he saw fit when it came to medicine, even in the seminary.[136]

Veith continued his success as preacher in high circles and low. It was Veith who preached the funeral of Emperor Francis in April 1835.[137] From the time he began preaching shortly after his ordination in 1821 until his last Lenten sermon in 1863, there was scarcely a church in Vienna in which Veith had not preached. When Veith was to speak, the church was always full, and his published sermons circulated throughout the Roman Catholic world.[138] Honors followed. Veith became the first preacher of the cathedral in 1844. He was made honorary canon in Salzburg in 1846, honorary doctor of philosophy in Prague in 1847, and honorary doctor of philosophy in Vienna in 1851. Like Günther, he turned down calls to teach in various universities and to preach in various distant churches.[139]. Veith, too, had become Viennese.

Veith's health did not hold up. As early as 1839, he tried to resign his cathedral post because of ill health. The cardinal refused the resignation, however, commenting that Veith probably was exaggerating the problem and was doubtless a bit of a hypochondriac.[140] His resignation was finally accepted in March 1845.[141] Veith received a small yearly pension and continued to work feverishly. The fifty-seven-year-old man had been retired on his own request because of poor health; but he could not stop his own hectic pace. Once he said that he would love to settle down and write only novels,[142] but the closest he came was writing stories which were edited and published by the Conventual Franciscan Bruno Schön to be read by patients in the mental hospital.[143] After retirement, Veith continued to preach where and when he could. He preached even when he had to stay in bed until the time of the sermon and then hobble to the pulpit. At times he was in so much pain that the only position in which he found that he could write was the kneeling one, but it did not stop his productivity.[144]

Through all of the church activity, Veith remained a doctor of medicine, and his approach to medicine is a key to his religious understanding. As a doctor, Veith was totally dedicated to his patients, staying with them through the night, oblivious to the dangers to himself in the case of cholera or other plagues. He was also a theoretician when it came to medicine and, if one is to judge by the editions of his medical works and their wide circulation, was a much-respected theoretician. He was also a good diagnostician[145] and was conscientious about keeping abreast with developments in the medical field. He never became doctrinaire. He was one of the first to practice homeopathic medicine,[146] but he was also willing to abandon it when he found it no longer effective.[147] One of the unfinished works he left behind when he died was a medical handbook for the use of the lay person in medicine.[148]

This medical pragmatism influenced Veith's priestly ministry as well, setting him off from scholars like Günther who spent the majority of their time in book-lined studies working on systems of thought with internal consistency. Veith was a man who knew the ragged edges of life better than the theoreticians. He entered into the lives of many, and their influence on him is evident.

The friendship of Günther and Veith flourished in Vienna in the 1830s and 1840s. After his unpleasant experience in the Jesuit novitiate and much soul-searching, Günther had settled down to the life of a private scholar. Veith, soured by his Redemptorist experience, was a preacher and healer. They came together as often as they could. Neither had rooms for entertaining and so met at other places. For the most part, it was a weekly dinner for whoever could attend from the circle of old friends of the Hofbauer days and a growing circle of new friends. Most often the meeting was at the home of Dr. Michael Glücker and his adopted daughter, Notburga Piuma, in Meidling, where Günther had found hospitality when he returned from Poland. The food and wine and the cigars were plentiful. The conversation was lively, but it was not the idle chatter of society's salons nor the political intrigue of Metternich's famous parties: it was the burning passion of new ideas shaped and bent to defend old truths. Günther was almost always there; it was his theology that gave shape to most of the discussions. Veith attended when he could—more frequently after he had left the Redemptorists. When he was there, Veith provided a touch of lightness, as did Laurenz Greif, the old friend whom Günther had saved from a return to Würtemberg. Greif also had a talent for calming things, especially the intensity of Günthers. These three—Günther, Veith, and Greif—became the center of a widening circle of men and women who called themselves Christian Dualists.

4
THE WORLD OF ANTON GÜNTHER

In the mountains around Brünn, Anton Günther had discovered that salvation was through a deed and not through thought.[1] It was an experience that brought him through the doubt that had plagued him during his journey into non-Christian Western philosophical thought to firm belief in the truth of Roman Catholic Christianity, the religion of his youth. It came after he read, or while he was reading, the bible through for the first time, an experience which seemed to have been as close to a conversion experience as the intellectual Günther would ever come. Even after his "conversion," Günther remained a man of words, convinced somehow that the new preaching of the gospel that Hofbauer had encouraged so wholeheartedly would come through a new system of thought, a new way of looking at the universe, a system so convincing that even the most hardhearted of atheists would have to agree intellectually. Günther's would be a system of the mind, not the heart. In spite of his own "conversion," Günther would deny the mystical as little more than sentimental feeling. Living in an era of romanticism about Catholicism—indeed, considering himself a part of the Hofbauer movement—Günther was interested in a reasonable approach to the dogmas of faith.

Günther was a complex thinker, and those complexities defy generalization. He was condemned as a semirationalist who thought faith could be shown to be reasonable; but the title is too neat and does not do justice to the complexities of the man or his thought. Günther tried to preach the gospel anew—and from his small study in the Pressgasse, without traveling much and never occupying a chair of theology, he influenced, perhaps even dominated, the German-speaking Roman Catholic theological world for several decades. He fascinated and convinced one of the major preachers of Vienna, Johann Emanuel Veith, who remained a convinced Güntherian throughout his life.[2]

Günther's sense of history lacked the refined, rigorous discipline that he applied to his philosophical thought. He loved to forage through the history of Christianity but took much out of context in order to concentrate on pure thought: he did not hesitate to place Augustine of Hippo in the seventh century when he belonged in the fourth and fifth. Apparently Günther read no primary sources, but he was nonetheless more than willing to make generalizations about authors whom he had not read. As a result, a historically sensitive reader is often distracted from the core of Günther's argument by his inaccuracies in historical fact and his inability to place the thought in context.

Günther's view of the universe and his anthropology remained medieval; that is, the so-called scientific revolution had not had an impact on his world hypothesis. Columbus and Copernicus had proved that the world was round and orbited the sun. Galileo's telescope had begun the discovery of a universe much larger than ever before imagined. Newton and Leibniz had articulated laws that would seed the Enlightenment's fascination with a mechanical universe. Günther's focus on the human as the center of the mystery of creation was being challenged even in his own time, although the full import of the earth being tucked away in an obscure galaxy had not—indeed, has not yet—fully dawned on the consciousness of the average woman or man. Günther's perception of creation reaching its pinnacle in the human remains as operating principle for most of us. Both medieval and Enlightenment thought had strengthened this perception and had found human intelligence to be the true measure of reality in the world.

Günther had little sense for the world of the unconscious or the preconscious. His brush with Romanticism in the Hofbauer circle and his own experience of conversion gave him a sense of evolution and a sense of organism. His study of the Fathers of the church, especially Augustine, made him aware that humankind is joined at the genitals as well as at the head. But it was the world of rational thought that united humankind most effectively. Günther eschewed the term, but he very much defined humanness as the scholastics did: rational animal. As a celibate intellectual, Günther accented the rational.

Günther was firmly and thoroughly Roman Catholic and in no way a pluralist. He had some sympathy for Protestantism, perhaps born of his heavy reliance on Augustine. But Protestant Christianity was not an entirely legitimate heterodoxy for Günther.[3] Other perspectives were not "another way of looking at the Truth," but were near-truths or half-truths or falsehoods. The idealist philosophy of his day was his main enemy, and the Truth of Roman Catholicism was his weapon. In the final analysis, Günther was convinced that he was right and his opponents were simply wrong. Even within Roman Catholicism itself, where he was ultimately to fight his battles, one has the impression that had his enemies not succeeded in getting his works placed on the Index of Forbidden Books, he would have been happy to have seen *their* works placed there.

It is also important to note that the Roman Catholicism of Günther's time was becoming increasingly narrow in its perception of Truth—and to note that this Truth was not scripturally anchored. The accent was on Tradition, and that Tradition was becoming increasingly doctrinaire. The battles in Protestantism caused by decentralization and the growing use of the historical-critical method in scriptural scholarship were not unknown to Günther, but they were alien to him and to his church. It would be well into the twentieth century when the Roman Church would begin to accept the historical-critical method which post–Vatican II Catholics take so much for granted. Günther used the method that today is known as "proof texting," i.e., seeking isolated passage out of context to prove a certain point. Günther set out to find and prove Truth itself. For those who live in the post-Freudian, post-Einsteinian world of pluralism, in which the talk is of paradigms and hypothetical constructs, the task Günther set for himself seems a bit lofty, a bit too grand. If one is grounded in the acceptance of the contradictions of tolerant pluralism, one does not burn with the urgency of discovering the basis of all Truth, as one did in the nineteenth century. It is not possible to say which century has been more true to the scientific enterprise. Günther was never tempted by the agnosticism that is the reverse side of pluralism. Günther was a strange blend of Enlightenment and Romanticism, who could neither banish religion to the realm of superstition or to the museum of the early stages of human development, nor be content blithely to ignore the discoveries and principles of the science he so admired. Günther sought nothing less than a unified world view which would accomplish the medieval dream of the unity of all knowledge. The neoscholastics turned out to be his bitterest enemies. They could not see that their dream was also Günther's, just as Günther could not see that the very presuppositions that drove him came from the medieval world he despised.

A brief mention of Günther's style is necessary as a caution for those who would rush to read him in the original,[4] but also as a way of understanding the hindrances to an orderly exposition of his system. From 1828 until his death in 1863, Günther published a constant stream of books, articles, reviews, and expressed himself tirelessly in letters to friends, followers, and even enemies. The twentieth-century reader is comforted a bit by the fact that Günther was difficult for his own century to read. Friends were constantly pleading with him to write in a clearer fashion; enemies ridiculed his style as illiterate obfuscation. Throughout his life, Günther's writing was characterized by humor, a humor that could strike the uninitiated as out of place, as too strident, as cynical. In addition, Günther often wrote in letter form or in the form of a dinner dialogue, which makes it very difficult to decipher which position Günther himself actually is taking and which he is criticizing. He wanted opponents to have the opportunity to explain themselves from their own perspective. He wanted Protestantism and idealism, pantheism and semipantheism to express themselves through their own words.[5] The positions are not labeled, but simply appear in the mouths of one or the other character at the dinner table or in the letter of a nephew to his affectionate uncle. In Günther's writings, however, no matter who is speaking, humor is always the medium. It would be a mistake not to recognize that humor is an essential element of Günther's expression, not just a whim of style.[6]

Günther often cited, and indeed used as a model, the writings of Jean Paul.[7] For Jean Paul and for Günther, humor was an absolutely essential element of expression. It is this tenacious hold of humor on Günther—a hold that lasted through the years of trial and misunderstanding with his own church—that is one of the most important keys to understanding the contradictions of Günther's basic stance. It was in his humor that Gunther was most clearly influenced by Romanticism. It was the part of his writings that said, in spite of the quest for Truth in its purest form, that there were contradictions that could only be expressed in the back and forth of humor. Günther's wit, sarcasm, point-counterpoint was the medium for his message of dualism. It was the subjective side of his framework of objective ideas. Humor was not only a funny and witty mood, it was a metaphysical and ethical attitude. Humor grew out of the attempt to express contradictions, tensions, dissonances, dualisms in life that could be carried and balanced only in the freedom of the Spirit. For Günther, humor became the highest form of human wisdom.

The Christian was called by Günther to be a humorist precisely because to be Christian was to be a dualist. Günther borrowed the dynamic of the dialectic from Hegel. There was movement, there was point-counterpoint, thesis-antithesis. (This was one of the presumptions that seemed so obvious to Günther that he never bothered to try to prove that the world was actually so.) But Hegel had gone too far in accepting the inevitability of synthesis; for that inevitability led to the inevitability of monism, the inevitability of pantheism. For Günther, the diverse realms of reality were *contraposed* to one another. They manifested themselves as contradictions whose irreducible opposition to each other could never be overcome through Hegel's dialectical process of sublation and synthesis (*Aufhebung*). For Günther, the ideal system of the noumenal universe was a system of contrapositional dualism; that is, a system of irreducible opposition between contradictory principles.[8] The only way to express that adequately was through humor. In the sense that this exposition of Günther's thought is a sober prose presentation, it cannot totally capture Günther's system.

The final word of caution in this lengthy prolegomenon is to remember who Günther's enemy was. Günther saw the greatest danger to Truth in the rampant pantheism that he insisted surrounded him. Günther admitted that he himself had been infected by the disease in his youth and therefore had sympathy for those who fell prey to the sickness.[9] But if Günther had sympathy, he also had the arrogance of one who had conquered the disease and believed himself capable of discovering its roots better than others. In a paraphrase of his own description, Günther ate pantheists for breakfast (*Pantheistfresser*).[10] It was Molinari, an exiled Jesuit in the novitiate in Poland, who had first made Günther aware of the pantheist threat. In spite of a lifelong fear that he would end like Molinari, who retreated into the fantasy at the end of his life that he was God because he was unable to handle the church's displeasure, Günther engaged in a lifelong battle against pantheism within and outside the Roman

Church. With the arrogance of someone totally convinced of his own absolute rightness, he identified the enemy and threw down the gauntlet.

Günther was, for the most part, a self-taught man. His philosophical studies and his theological studies were done more on his own than in any formal setting. His field of vision was narrowed by his private exploration, without reliance on the breadth of knowledge of others. He attracted followers but was always the master. Beyond his relationship with Johann Pabst, who taught him to appreciate Descartes, Günther was a master who found it difficult to learn from his students, let alone from his enemies. There was an arrogance about this recluse who arose faithfully each morning to recite his Mass, then withdrew to spend the entire day in reading and writing. He found the enemy everywhere; one could almost conclude that he had a touch of paranoia. He was convinced that he had the key to Truth if only people would listen. The great tragedy of this man was that the philosophical world he sought to convert paid him little heed, and the church he sought to defend rejected his system.

The rest of this chapter is dedicated to explaining in twentieth-century English the insights of this nineteenth-century Austrian theological writer. The reader will, one hopes, understand the difficulty of the translation not only of German words into English but also of another world view into somewhat understandable conceptual prose. In violation of Günther's own preference, the chapter is divided into a section on philosophy and one on theology. The division is not meant to say that they are of necessity separate; it is merely a matter of convenience and intelligibilty.

The Two Realms

As Günther surveyed his own era and dabbled in the history of western thought, he detected a growing divergence between various ways of looking at that world, between faith and reason, between science and revelation. He was not alone in noticing this; the epistemological problem was seen as the key to metaphysics throughout the nineteenth century. Rather than seeing the separation as inevitable, as the coming of age of the human mind in shedding a need for myth and mystery, Günther sought to reunite the increasingly divergent worlds of science and religion. He accepted as true the fact that God was separate from creation (the ultimate dualism) but wondered why so many otherwise perceptive thinkers had fallen prey to pantheism—or would have had to become pantheist had they followed the logic of their thinking to its conclusion. Günther was sure that there must be some reason for this and that there must be some way back to a Christian view of the world.

From the German idealists, Günther borrowed and transformed a concept which he was convinced was the epistemological key to the problem. It was the difference between *Begriff* and *Idee*.[11] These two German concepts represented the results of two radically different processes of thought. They both had validity and both were necessary for Günther. The one (*Begriff*) led inevitably to pantheism or semipantheism; the other (*Idee*) provided the necessary counterpoint and the key to dualistic theism. When both were understood, the door that had slammed shut between science and religion was opened again. The difference, although perhaps a product of what Alfred North Whitehead would have called the fallacy of misplaced concreteness, is crucial to an understanding of Günther. A brief digression into the the history of philosophy should help to make that difference clear.

A question that has preoccupied the esoteric world of philosophical debate has been: what is real? In a statistical, quantifiable world, the question has been more implicitly than explicitly answered. The presumption has been made that the world that is measurable, quantifiable, visible, touchable, tasteable, hearable, *is* the real world. Indeed, even philosophers who might be convinced otherwise have had to act as if it were true when they have bought groceries, mowed the lawn, taken a trip. Through the centuries, however, the philosophical mind has always been plagued by the thought that the senses could only provide limited and perhaps skewed or even false data, no matter how far into the universe the physical senses might reach. Eastern thought (Hinduism, Buddhism, Zen) has always maintained that this world was illusion (*maya*); but even in Western thought there have been those who urged that the real world has little to do with the world of the senses, that the sense world is, at best, a shadow of the real world.

In the history of thought, there are seldom straight lines and oversimplification can be seductive. There are, nonetheless, some who would claim that the whole question about what is real is simply a footnote to the Greek thought of Plato and Aristotle. Plato found the physical world to be a shadow world—images projected on the wall of a cave with the human mind chained facing the wall and unable to see the real objects or the fire that cast the shadows. It was not surprising that the shadow was mistaken for the real itself. Only the few, the true philosophers, could break the shackles and see reality as it truly was. For Plato, reality was the world of ideas, and thought was the ground of being. In one of the early cases of student rebelling against teacher, Aristotle claimed that knowledge of the real world was available through the senses and that from the data acquired by sensory perception one could induce, generalize, conceptualize about the real world.

The debate continued with multiple variations down through the centuries. Some even saw Kant as another variation on Plato and Hegel as another variation on Aristotle.[12] Günther claimed to have transcended the debate and found the answer. He denied that he was a Platonist, although he was certainly in the Platonist line.[13] Günther claimed a validity to the position of Plato, even though he claims that Plato never got beyond the world of *Begriff*.[14]

Begriff is the result of a rational division of the essential elements of experience according to *a priori* constructs. It is born in the world of senses, the expression of the recognition of outward appearances. In its perfect form it is a complete schema of what Günther called the outer world, the world of senses. This is discovered by the human faculty of *Verstand*.[15] *Begriff* can be though of as a retort, to use the analogy of chemistry that Günther himself proposed.[16] *Verstand*, then, becomes a sieve, a place to sift through the data of sensation and come to generalizations and abstractions. These generalizations and abstractions are the closest *Begriff* can come to the kind of thinking that is interior. The *Begriff* is on a horizontal plane in the world of sense experience. It grasps that which can be experienced, the outer world, the world available through the senses, and simplifies the data into standardization (or statistical probability, in twentieth-century terms); but there is no *beyond* in this world. According to Günther, thought that is on this plane remains trapped in the conceptual and general, in the superficiality of appearances. It cannot grasp the essence of being. The world of *Begriff* is the real world, but it is only half the real world.

Günther insisted that the only real path for *Begriff* to take, if left on its own, would be the path to pantheism. No philosophy whose model of true being was a *Begriff* could avoid monism. Günther's logic concluded that, since true being in the world of *Begriff* would become an impersonal absolute in which thought and reality would become identified, the Absolute's metaphysical communication of reality to the finite world must take the form of a necessary emantion. This was true of the thought of all who had preceded Günther, whether Plato or Aristotle, Thomas Aquinas, Kant, or Hegel.[17]

If *Begriff* is the world of the logical, then *Idee* is the world of the ontological, the ground of all being. The world of *Begriff* cannot find the true inner meaning of reality; it cannot even be a bridge or a pointer to the world of *Idee*. *Begriff* occurs in the human faculty of *Verstand*. *Idee* occurs in the human faculty of *Vernunft*. There is a radical, uncrossable gap between these two. Each must maintain its own integrity, its own separateness if the total world is to be understood.

Idee is the thought of 'being'; it is the real ground of appearances. *Idee* is the dynamic, methodological principle that is the only place where pure categorical ideas are revealed.[18] *Idee* is the entry into the world of the timeless metaphysical reality. Günther never fully explored how one comes to this knowledge, but his discussion has a Platonic tinge that suggests a world open only to the philosopher—and then only to the philosopher who can move beyond the world of *Begriff*. Günther never used the word "intuition" to describe the process, but there is a temptation to infer it from his descriptions. *Idee* is the entrance into the world of the ground of being. It is the world of cause and effect and not just statistical correlation, a world closed to statisticians and experimenters. It is a world behind and beyond the world of *Begriff* (which is the world of appearances).[19] *Idee* is the world of ontological truth, the dynamically vertical, the world of 'being' itself. According to Günther, this is the world of the eternal thought (*Logos*) of God. The *Idee* explores the heights and depths of the divine thought. This is the metaphysical beyond, a world where appearances available to the human senses have no meaning, or at best a deceptive meaning. The *Idee* is both the "real objectivity" and the "subjective representation of reality."[20]

In summary, *Begriff* is the world of appearance, the world of things, the world of correlations. *Idee* is the ground of being, the world of idea, the world of cause. The world of *Begriff* and the world of *Idee* are antitheses, not gradual or quantitative differences. They remain dialectically opposed. Truth is found only in the opposition which respects the integrity and inviolability of each of these spheres. *Begriff* remains eternally and inevitably in the sphere of Nature; *Idee* remains eternally and inevitably in the sphere of Spirit.

Günther did his writing at the beginning of the nineteenth century and could not escape being influenced by the Romantic movement that was so much a part of the world around him. There is no place where this influence is more clear than in Günther's concept of Nature (*Natur*). Nature is the large, unified (monist), immense expanse of the universe that can be felt, smelled, seen, heard. It is not only the world of flowers to be plucked from crannied walls, of birds, rocks, sea, and sky; it is also the human world. Humankind is within Nature in all but one decisive point: the Spirit (*Geist*).[21]

Nature is dynamic, evolutionary, in process. There is a hierarchy in Nature, although Günther did not adequately explain how his discovery of hierarchy fit with the evolutionary principle he espoused. The evolution of the organic world of Nature is toward consciousness. The one principle (monad) that is Nature has become diverse in the multiplicity of appearances, shapes, and structures of the external world. Nature has become individualized, has expressed itself in the individuality of creation, and is only to be found as a generalization in the midst of the particularities; but it is a generalization that expresses itself in consciousness (*Seele*) that is a part of all Nature. Consciousness, which reaches through imagination to structured objective knowledge of phenomena in the human faculty of *Verstand*, is the highest form of Nature. This consciousness in the realm of Nature is an undifferentiated consciousness of 'being'. In the realm of Nature, there is no freedom; there is only necessity.[22] In the realm of Nature, there is only pantheism, the eternal principle of consciousness which emanates outward and seeks its way inward again. The human body and human consciousness (*Seele*) constitute the culmination of the world of Nature, and the human becomes the measure of all things of this world. The human is at once the individualized and personified world and at the same time a compendium of the reality of the world of *Begriff*.[23]

The world of Spirit (*Geist*) is the world of *Idee*. Once again, it is perhaps unfair to compare Günther with Plato and those who followed him, especially when Günther himself objects; but the world of Spirit is much like Plato's world of ideal forms. The world of Spirit contains not only Spirit but spirits. They are not extended in time and space but are rather 'being' itself. There is infinite possibility and therefore infinite inner freedom.

Spirit is 'being' without extension. It does not express itself in physicality or outwardness; Spirit remains inward and grasps itself as unity and as distinct from every other being. Spirit is independent of the outer world, free of division; this freedom and independence is the first key to the difference between the world of Nature and the world of Spirit. The other key is the self-consciousness of Spirit, which is radically different from the consciousness of Nature. There can be no emanation since there is no extension. Spirit remains self-contained. There are uncountable spirits, who are not dependent upon each other nor on Nature, but are self-sufficient.[24]

Through freedom, Spirit can reach for the realm of the Absolute. Through the strength of freedom, Spirit can understand itself as principle and lift itself to self-consciousness. In this radical freedom, Spirit is co-creator of the universe; Spirit moves, on the one hand, to self-consciousness and, on the other hand, to self-determination.[25]

Spirit achieves its actual self-consciousness through a dynamic process, a process that is achieved in relationship of one spirit to another spirit already self-realized. This process—through which undifferentiated substance determines itself into a subject—follows the three stages of the Hegelian dialectic. A spirit first exists in a state of undifferentiated substance (thesis). It then discovers, through the agency of another already self-conscious spirit, its own differentiation into two dynamic functions or faculties which are the dual faculties of free *Vernunft*: passive receptivity and spontaneous reactivity (the substance "passes over" into its faculties, which is the antithesis). Finally, the spirit reunites itself, returning from this opposition to a discovery of self as subject in an act of self-awareness, of intuitive self-possession (synthesis). Günther called this whole process "self-revelation" (*Selbstoffenbarung*) or the "objectification of subject" (*Subjectobjektivierung*).[26]

Another way of articulating the process, more in Cartesian and Kantian terminology, would be as follows: When the faculties of one spirit are stirred to action through contact with another spirit, *Vernunft* becomes aware of the noumenal spirits which it intuits and of the phenomenal objects brought to consciousness by *Verstand*. The spirit is thus enable to define itself as Ego, as knowing subject, over against the non-egos presented to it in its act of knowledge. In that very act *Vernunft* can intuit its own reality in the *cogito*. Consciousness of non-Ego gives rise to self-consciousness. Subject becomes object.

The unique differentiation in the process of self-consciousness when subject becomes object and hence knowable as subject is real, according to Günther, and not simply logical. It is ontological. The subject-object process is a relationship.[27] The spirit is not initially self-conscious but can be awakened to self-consciousness in relationship to another already self-conscious spirit. The perception of the inner relationship of faculties to each other and to self is self-consciousness.[28] In all of this, *to be* is equated with *to think*. Because of the spirit's ability to think, it can think of itself; therefore, it is Ego which is separate from non-ego. At the same time that the spirit discovers self, it discovers other. The process is contemporaneous.

In summary, there is the realm of Nature which struggles toward consciousness and the realm of Spirit which struggles toward self-consciousness. In both realms, thought is the key to existence. In Nature, *Begriff* leads to pantheism. In Spirit, *Idee* leads to a discovery of self and of other. The two are radically, essentially different. They remain in opposition and cannot come to a synthesis that melds the one into the other, but come only to a synthesis that continues and preserves the radical difference. The synthesis of Nature and Spirit transcends but does not totally transform: that synthesis, the key and cornerstone of creation, is none other than humanity (*Mensch*).

The Grand Synthesis

The keystone of Günther's system is his anthropology. As a part of Nature, *Mensch* (the German word for "man" and "woman") is an *animal cogitans*, a thinking animal, capable of going to the depth and height of the world of *Begriff*. As a part of Spirit, *Mensch* is capable of going to the heights and depths of the world of *Idee*. In recognizing herself or himself, *Mensch* recognizes the roots of every other form of being, recognizes the ground of all being. *Mensch* becomes the world sphinx: on the one hand facing the world of Nature and on the other the world of Spirit. *Mensch* is the crown of creation pointing to the Creator.[29]

Mensch is, on the one hand, an individual of a species and, on the other hand, a self-conscious, free person. In the arena of Nature, conception (*Zeugung*) is the rule. In the arena of Spirit, conviction (*Überzeugung*) is the rule. In *Mensch* the two meet and become one in form. They receive formal unity in the "marital union"[30] between spirit and animated body in the cognitive operations of the human knower. *Mensch* becomes a trinity of body-soul-spirit (*Leib-Seele-Geist*) unified by the form of striving toward consciousness.[31] *Mensch* becomes the key to the discovery of God. *Mensch* is the summit of creation and, as world compendium, the mirror image of the Trinity. As contrapositional dualism, *Mensch* reveals the absolute antithesis between God and world. As synthesis, *Mensch* sees himself or herself as reflex and created image of the absolute Trinity; indeed, *Mensch* is the masterpiece in the *Idee* of God, especially because he or she is able to think the God-thought.[32]

The crux of the whole exercise is, of course, the proof that God exists outside the world in order to give the lie to pantheism and to expose it, once and for all, as nothing other than masked atheism. For Günther, not only had the early Fathers of the church erred in this respect (although the dogmas that were eventually defined are, of course, accurate), but the major philosophers and theologians throughout Christian and secular history had erred along the same lines. Günther was harshest with the Thomists who, Günther claimed, had given the analogy of 'being' only quantitative difference: God is only the human written in capital letters. (Beyond the fact that Günther was poorly schooled in Scholastic thought and claimed he knew more than he actually did about the Schoolmen's systems, is the simple fact that some of Günther's own theories suffer from the same weakness he finds in others.) Günther was his most fiercely vitriolic when he was taking on other Roman Catholics; and when he was taking on Hegel. Günther accused Hegel of taking human spirit and writing it large as Absolute Spirit. Günther claimed to have escaped that folly. How did he manage?

Günther argues that *Mensch* is created in the image of God. But *Mensch* is the *mirror image*. This mirror image is found in the dialectical constitution of *Mensch* and in the dialectical process of self- or ego-consciousness. *Mensch* and God are radically different; but difference recognizes difference in the recognition of self.[33] As the *Mensch*, so in mirror image his God. As *Mensch* recognizes himself, he also recognizes God as God.[34]

Günther used a variation of the ontological argument, building on but going beyond Descartes. In the discovery of self there is also the discovery of limit, of dependence, of creatureliness. The very act of self-discovery is dependent on another self-conscious spirit who interacts and awakens one's self-knowledge as spirit. This recognition of the contingency of all relative being becomes the fundament of metaphysics, of the philosophy and theology of being, the beginning of ethics.[35] This sense of limitation brings with it a sense of something or someone that is unlimited, that is the ground of dependent being, that is creator. In the discovery of self there is also the discovery of non-self; and an integral part of that discovery of non-self is the discovery of God. The fact that this God is not simply non-self but a *Thou* to one's *I* is discovered in the world of *Idee*, but is not available to the world of *Begriff*. (Hence, Hegel missed it.)

The discovery of self has a double negative connected with it. It is clear that the discovery does not occur through the self itself but through another self-conscious spirit. It is also clear that the self comes to know itself not in itself but indirectly through its presence in appearances (*Erscheinungen*). These two negatives assure the discovery of the basic radical contingency of self.[36] As soon as the spirit discovers itself as a limited, finite being, it must transcend itself.[37] The thought of contingency, limit, and finiteness brings with it the realization of dependence on a higher, that is, independent, Being. As certain as the knowledge is of one's self-being, so certain is also one's knowledge of

The World of Anton Günther

God. If the *Idee* whose expression is the word *Ego* is reality, so also must the *Idee* of the unlimited Being be real in the word *God*. This reality must also be an objective reality (that is, outside one's subjectivity) because the idea of unlimitedness, although inherent in the thought of the spirit as self, must transcend itself and move from the thought of contingency to the thought of non-contingency. If the thought of unlimitedness did not transcend itself, then the spirit must think of itself as the unlimited and could never grasp itself as limited and contingent.[38] The spirit comes to the God *Idee* because it thinks of itself as dependent in being (that is, limited) in that it is dependent on appearances (*Erscheinungen*). Therefore, it must also think simultaneously of an unlimited Being and an unlimited Existence (*Sein* and *Dasein*).[39]

It is important to note that Günther, perhaps anticipating Feuerbach, does not see self-consciousness as the cause of the God *Idee*; but in self-consciousness, the God *Idee* is found analytically available. In the process of self-consciousness, the God *Idee* is the final moment. For all of his realization of self, the spirit remains a non-self because, in spite of its real position, it knows itself to be imprisoned by a negative which needs to be resolved if existence is to be real.[40] The resolution is God. The self-consciousness of the human realizes dependence and therefore the need for a ground of being that is beyond limit and beyond dependence, and discovers the reality of God.

Günther did not find a common substance in *Mensch* and in God, but he did find a common form: consciousness. In Nature that consciousness moves outward to recognize the fact of being. In Spirit the consciousness moves inward and returns to a self-awareness that brings insight into I and Thou, into one's own existence and the existence of being outside oneself. This self-consciousness is connected with a sense of freedom, an ontological freedom which is the ground for a moral freedom.[41] Epistemologically, the entire process is seen as moving from the human Ego to the Thou. Metaphysically, however, the human Ego is a relative and dependent Thou to the actual and absolute Ego of God.

Having established that an absolute and non-contingent being exists, Günther continued the argument and saw in the concept of Trinity the necessary manifestation of God *ad intra*, interiorly. Günther saw the Trinity that is God mirrored in the trinity that is *Mensch*. Both *Mensch* as synthesis of Nature and Spirit and the process of objectification of subject that is the discovery of self are keys to the triune God. As *Mensch* is one in thesis-antithesis-synthesis, so is God three in one. Being-as-absolute remains formless and is not yet called God because it is formless.[42] This *Idee* of the absolute makes itself into God—and indeed from eternity—because it has lifted the formlessness from itself, it has transcended its formlessness. This transcendence is effected in the subjectification of the object (*Objektivsubjektivierungprocess*) that is expressed symbolically in positive faith in the concept of Father, Son and Spirit.[43]

Father, Son, and Spirit are three stages in the divine self-consciousness. The process of self-consciousness, as transcendence of Being, is the basis for generation: before the generation of the Son ('before' is not a time concept here), the Father is potential Father, is Absolute Being. In the generation, Being enters into opposition to itself (thesis becomes antithesis). Since this process is accomplished in an absolutely perfect manner in the Absolute, it can only be thought of as total objectification.[44] This total objectification is *real* opposition, is actually doubling through emanation.[45] The Son is the absolute object of the Father; he is the objectified Father.[46] However, the process of the self-realization of God is not completed by the doubling of the divine being.[47] Since the opposition is perfect, the opposition builds an image which is also generated as such.[48] This exact image-in-opposition is such that Father and Son each finds himself totally. This exact image-in-opposition is Spirit. Such a product is the original real unity that is raised from potential to actual principle. Based on this repeated building of self (*Selbstsetzung*) of the Absolute, we receive a triplicated substance: the divine substance is present three times in three persons.[49] In the divine Being the process of consciousness is absolutely perfect, is the ideal form of personification (*Personenbildung*), and is therefore necessarily trinitarian.[50]

Thus God comes to know himself, not by knowing another being like contingent *Mensch*, but by knowing his own reality. God, as the unconditioned ground of universal intelligibility, must know himself as the prior epistemological correlate of his knowledge of other beings.[51] Along with this knowledge of himself as Trinity there comes the last moment in the process of the Absolute *ad intra*: the non-self thought of God, which is creation.

In Günther's system, the three divine persons are the result of the self-realization of the Absolute Being. This process of self-awareness in the Absolute Being is the manifestation of God intrinsically (*manifestatio Deo ad intra*[52]). In the life of the Absolute, negation also plays an important role. The negation in the opposition of the world of *Idee* to the world of *Begriff* possesses a being function. The negation is the thorn that pushes forward, the driving force in the life process of 'being'; it is the innermost contradiction that lives in every being, that gives it life, and that comes from the Absolute Being.[53] God's becoming is an absolute becoming, a becoming that is actually in 'being' (*Aseität*).[54] This becoming completes itself in time and space in the eternal sense of these words.[55] Time and space are necessary in God as a living after another (*Nacheinander*), which is time, and next to each other (*Nebenenander*), which is space. Time and space are not dead forms but manifestations (*Erscheinungen*) of a living being.[56] If time and space are totally negated, then the life process in the Absolute Principle is also necessarily negated.[57] So there is, next to the positive moments of identity, simultaneously a formal negativity, a formal exclusion of every other coefficient of the Absolute Life.[58] This excludes the possibility of other Absolute Being, of other God—but includes the idea of a contingent world as the non-self *Idee* in God. This *Idee* is the root of the world—a world which is created and not emanated. The non-self *Idee* of God cannot contain himself transmitted into the world. Only as creation is the world a Thou to God.[59]

The positive result of the process of self-consciousness in the Absolute is the Trinity—the three persons in which divine substance (*Wesenheit*) presents itself. The negative result of the process of self-consciousness of the Absolute is the divine *thought* of the non-self. As the negation of the Absolute Being, this thought of the non-self of God is the same as Absolute Nothingness. However, this nothing is based on something positive, that is, in the thought of God, and hence this nothing becomes the *Idee* of God for creation. Creation *ex nihilo* is nothing other than creation *ex Deo*. The Absolute Nothingness is the negation of the Absolute Ego.[60]

This thought of creation is the final step in the manifestation of God *ad intra* and is absolutely necessary revelation. The realization of the creation-thought is the manifestation of God *ad extra* (*Hypostasierung*) and is the absolutely free revelation or transcendent revelation of God. This *ad extra* manifestation of the non-self *Idee* of the Absolute Being is the first and primary revelation and manifests itself in the threefold mirror image of the Trinity that is Nature, Spirit, and *Mensch*. The non-self thought of God, the result of the process of self-consciousness of the Absolute, is born out of the Absolute and has life. As such, it has a claim to reality.[61] As a negation that which is Absolutely Not cannot *not* be and therefore is, it follows the law of logic that a double negative becomes a positive. In the world of *Idee* that positive becomes so in a metaphysical, that is real, sense.[62]

The Absolute Being stands opposite the non-absolute being. In the first, the Absolute Being exists in three persons but one substance. In the second, the one person, *Mensch*, exists as a synthesis of two substances which, while preserving the separateness and integrity of each of those two (thesis and antithesis) also becomes a new substance (synthesis) and thus combines three substances in one person. The difference between God and creation (*Urbild* and *Ebenbild*) is the contrapositional relationship (*umgekehrte Verhältnisse*) in which they find themselves. The difference is radical, essential. But in the mirror image of himself, *Mensch* is able to see the image of a creator.

Günther claimed that pantheism is a logical and therefore a metaphysical impossibility.[63] To plumb the reality of this, one has only to turn over the coin that is *Mensch* to see that God is creator and three. The two triangles of the Absolute and the non-self of the Absolute are the sum of revelation, because beyond these two triangles there can be no other being.[64] The turning point upon which the whole system rests is the self-consciousness of *Mensch*.[65] Revelation becomes a Jacob's ladder with human self-consciousness as the middle point: upward, the divine reality is recognized; downward, the fact of creation is recognized. Günther was fully anthropocentric, with the human as the middle and key to Truth.[66] But Truth needs to combine both faith and science (*Glaube* and *Wissen/Wissenschaft*) if it is to be all-embracing. It is the question of the relationship between faith and reason that brings us to a treatment of the theological thought of Anton Günther.

It should be obvious by now that Günther was attempting a grand synthesis, seeking the unitary principle that he sensed must exist behind and beyond all of the contradictory worlds that emerged at the beginning of the nineteenth century. He wanted to prove that there was no radical antagonism between Christianity (that is, its Roman Catholic manifestation) and science, between natural and supernatural, between grace and freedom, between the first revelation which is creation and the second revelation which is Christ. Günther was not attempting to collapse all of these into one, but he wanted to establish the fact that theology and philosophy were equals, both important, the children of one parent who should extend the hand of respect and friendship to each other.

Once again, Günther was a curious mixture of Enlightenment and Romanticism. He had a nostalgia for the certitude of belonging to a church that had always been right, but at the same time he saw himself as the "new revelation" that would correct past wrongs.[67] Günther accepted the dogmatic superstructure of Roman Catholicism but insisted that it be built and rebuilt in every era: every era had to speak out Truth in the language and categories of the time. The confrontation between revealed truth and contemporary thought could only occur in the language of the day, and that meant in the language of the German idealists who dominated in the days when Günther was writing. Günther spent much time denigrating the "Scholastics," but these were not so much the Scholastics of earlier centuries as those of his own time who would answer today's questions with yesterday's answers. Günther saw himself and his system as the culmination of much of Christian development, and he believed his insights opened a new era in Christian thought. Günther saw the present as the culmination of much of the past; he saw the mistakes of the past and attempted to correct them. One thing that Günther did not seem to grasp was that present will eventually be past and will eventually need correcting. Nowhere was this failure more clear than in his attempt to articulate the relationship between faith and reason.

Günther was not alone; this relationship of belief to knowledge occupied most of the thinkers of the early part of the nineteenth century. Does one go from the bottom up, from human reality to God? Or does one go from the top down, from God to the human? Günther's "Jacob's ladder" will attempt both. The secret is once more in the understanding of *Vernunft*, the world of *Idee*.

Günther maintained that faith and knowledge are but two moments in the process of life and therefore cannot be absolute opposites.[68] It is important to note that after his conversion-experience in younger years, Günther never doubted that Roman Catholicism was true. Even when he talked about his preaching the gospel anew in the Hofbauer tradition, he abandoned little of the body of faith that had been passed down through the ages. Günther himself had an explanation for it. Roman Catholicism contains the Truth; this Truth is revealed from above and is passed on intact in spite of the fact that humankind is not able to understand or grasp this Truth in its pure form. In those early years of Christianity one believed on authority, *credo ut intellegam*, as Augustine would put it: "I believe that I might understand." Here is a negative criterion of reason; reason and faith do not contradict each other if Truth is to be found. Of course, in those early days one relied on faith over reason (belief over knowledge). Revelation was a divine fiat that, although it did not contradict the thinking capacity of human understanding, was not open to human reason.

For Günther, a new age had dawned in which humankind could put aside the old *credo ut intellegam* for a more mature *intellige ut credas*: "I understand that I might believe." Christianity need not fear science. Günther had discovered a new positive criterion for reason (*Positives Vernunftskriterium*). Before, one could only grasp the fact that a dogma is true. With Günther's insights, one could also know *how* and *why* it is true. The positive criterion of reason is the ability of reason (*Vernunft*) to know faith not only as mystery (which, although not contradicting reason, is not open to reasonable understanding) but also in a positive sense, to know the why, the where from, and the where to. The facts of revelation are historical facts. The content of revelation can be known, not simply believed.

It is clear from earlier passages on Günther's philosophy that revelation is twofold. Creation itself is the first revelation, and that is known in the self-consciousness of the human as it reflects on the necessity of God as other. The second revelation is Christ. The important thing is that both revelations, creation and Christ, can be known in the human faculty of *Vernunft*. Further, in this human faculty, faith and knowledge become as one. For Günther, faith is anywhere the mind grasps something beyond or outside the senses; faith is *Idee*-knowing, the form of knowing that results from moving from *Begriff* to *Idee*. In *Begriff*-knowing, the subject and object stand face-to-face and become, in a certain sense, one in their direct presence and perceptibility. In *Idee*-knowing, the object of knowledge is not directly knowable but is knowable only indirectly through a recognition, through a knowledge of Spirit.[69]

Faith becomes *Vernunft's* passive reception of *Idee* intelligibilities. Knowledge (*Wissen*) or scientific knowledge is the result of *Vernunft's* active reflection on the intelligibility received in faith. Knowledge becomes nothing more (and nothing less) than a speculative reflection upon an intuited intelligibility (faith), which always preserved its cognitional priority to

Vernunft's act of self-reflective realization. Even in the philosophical order, reason or knowledge is always dependent upon a prior act of faith.[70] Günther's theology can best be described as a philosophy of revelation. Faith is a recognition of Being and recognition of Being is only possible as faith.

Faith is fundamental knowledge (*Grundwissen*) and has its sphere in the non-sensible but still reachable realm of *Idee*. The truths of faith are available to *Vernunft* in a formal way. The ground of the world of appearances (*Erscheinungen*) is God, who is absolute; and faith, because it is an intuitive grasp of the divine revelation, has absolute certainty. In human self-consciousness lies knowledge of the absolute objective principle that is God. Faith is a metaphysical reality, an act of knowing that goes beyond and behind the world of *Begriff* into the world of *Idee*. With God as the absolute fundament and the self-transcending reality that mirrors the objectification of self in human self-consciousness, faith and knowledge (*Glaube* and *Wissen*) are united, not extrinsically, but intrinsically. To go from the human to the divine, if only the right key is used, will bring the truths of faith (Roman Catholic) into clear and irrefutable light.

It is interesting to note that Günther convinced few people who were not already convinced. That is, those who already believed and were searching for a way to articulate their beliefs intelligently were fascinated by Günther's system, while those who did not believe were hardly interested in what Günther had to say. Thus Günther failed in his most urgent task. He claimed to be writing an apologetic that would lay bare the modern errors and bring thinkers alienated from Roman Catholicism back to the fold. With his system, he succeeded in fascinating or angering those already converted but not in bringing converts to Roman Catholicism. Johann Emanuel Veith was to have more success. Perhaps the crux of the matter is that, when all is said and done, Anton Günther moved from faith to knowledge and not from knowledge to faith as he claimed.[71]

Whether one believes that Günther was a philosopher and not a theologian at all[72] or that Günther was a theologian convinced that theology was speculative and therefore philosophical,[73] one has to accept the fact that Günther was much more at home in the speculative world than in the scriptural one. He accepted Scripture as revelation, but in a naive, fundamentalist fashion, in which God all but writes with his finger out of the clouds.[74] Günther admitted to a need for some interpretation of Scripture,[75] but this had little to do with the historical-critical method and more to do with the Roman Church's tendency to bend Scripture to its own purposes. When Günther spoke of faith and revelation, he spoke mostly of the doctrinal development founded in Scripture rather than of Scripture itself. Revelation is the manifestation of Trinity *ad extra*, the history of salvation in neat categories that cannot always accommodate the ragged edges and contradictions of Scripture. It has already been noted that Günther tended toward proof-texting, that is, selecting isolated scriptural passages for the justification of what he was claiming. In the Roman Catholic world of his time, he was certainly not alone in this.

In order to examine Günther's understanding of the second revelation in Christ, one must look again at the human, the anthropological center of creation. Günther believed in the unity of the human race. In part, this was based on his scriptural understanding, which insisted on a monogenism with Adam and Eve as the parents of the entire human population.[76] Because the human is the image of the divine, one of the most important parts of the human condition is freedom. This is an ontological freedom to say "yes" or "no" to the divine Thou. This freedom is in the Spirit (*Geist*) in the world of *Idee*. Pure spirits, who are without time or extension, have this freedom, but their choice is made once and for all. Pure spirits are able to decide at the moment of their creation "for" or "against" God, and in that moment they determine their personality and their fate.[77] The decision for or against God is the decision to love or not to love. Human freedom is based on this same principle; it calls for a decision to love or not to love God, for love, in order truly to be love, must be free. Since the human is an image of God, that image is most clearly seen in the freedom to love God as God loves creation. This freedom and capacity to love is an essential part of the human makeup and cannot be completely destroyed. This is a very Roman Catholic perception of the human *imago Dei*. God will not demand love, because that is not the nature of love.[78] Even after the so-called fall, freedom remains a part of the human makeup, a real freedom that can and does still move out of itself on its own to say "yes" to the love of God.[79]

Günther saw sinfulness as obvious in the world. In the world of paradise (a biblical fundamentalism) the human condition was one of justice, holiness, and integrity.[80] Günther presumed the biblical story of the fall, presumed that Adam had freely said "no" to God.[81] Had the Enlightenment thinkers spent time dealing with Günther, perhaps they would have pointed out to him the logical arbitrariness of this presumption. Günther found the obvious evil that surrounded him to be a result of the decision of *Mensch*. Evil is not something with a personality of its own that somehow fights with the good.[82] Evil had been brought into the world by the free decision of Adam, a decision which brought a darkening of the understanding, a weakening of the will, and a loss of control in the realm of Nature.[83] The image was damaged but not destroyed. Death had entered the world, but so had the promise of redemption.

The surest sign of the promise of redemption, of the fact that God had not abandoned his creation, is the voice of conscience (*Gewissen*), which is present in each human personality.[84] Conscience does not let loose; it pursues because it is the voice of God reminding of love. Conscience is the moral proof of the existence of God.[85] The fact of conscience is proof of the fact that there is an objective and not just subjective authority that both warns and threatens the human spirit. It is not the power of an inner law, but the power of a Person who is absolute, not contingent, and upon whom the human is dependent. The fact that conscience is present is proof of a personal, free, and living God and is the denial of an unknown and distant God.

Humankind is united because of the love of God present in conscience—but also because of the first parents who were the parents of all. This sexual interrelationship is the reason why the original sin of the original parents continues to live on. Original sin becomes inherited sin (*Erbsünde*), an inherited sinful condition of being in a state of guilt. It is not an individual's own sinful action, but it is a sinful condition without personal guilt.[86] The fact of this original sin, however, makes it impossible for the human to save himself. A redeemer was promised, and the promise is evident in the very fact that the human continues to exist.

The fact of Christ is as clear as the fact of sinfulness in the world and the fall of the first Adam. Adam did not pass his test of freedom. The guilt that he therefore bore for all of his descendants was not something that he personally could compensate for. According to divine justice, Adam's sin made him subject to death; indeed, he should have died before any descendants were born. That humanity exists and has a history even after and in spite of the sin of the first Adam (*Stammvater*) can only be because of the work of the savior. Human history is essentially the history of salvation. Without Christ there would have been no human history, for Adam would have died before any progeny could be born. Through Christ and only through Christ does the human race have history after the fall.[87] The savior was present even in the time before Christ: he was present in the promise. The promise came from God and therefore had absolute certainty in fulfillment. For Günther, that which certainly will come is already present. The historical God-Man is the sacrament (*Ursakrament*) of all of humanity.[88]

A son of Adam in the flesh became the second father (*Stammvater*) of the race and thereby the first Adam became a son of the second.[89] Only in an organic unity of the various parts of reality could such a double beginning be possible. Through his entry into human history, Christ was to be not only a part of the history of the race, but much more the middle point, the carrying element, and the dynamic subject. Without Christ, humanity would have had no history whatsoever because without the promise of Christ, there would have been no generation (*Fortpflanzung*). Everything good after the fall has its possibility in Christ, and in Christ only, because humanity is united in its sexuality, united as organism.[90]

The possibility of two founding fathers has its final ground in the *Idee* of God that *Mensch* is a being made of the union of two life-principles, both of which influence the human reality. In the natural descendants of the first Adam, the second Adam appeared. As the first Adam is the father in the natural sense, so is the second the father in the spiritual sense. Jesus Christ was perfect God united with perfect *Mensch*.

Neoscholastic theologians criticized Günther for the weakness of his understanding and explanation of this hypostatic union between God and the human that is Jesus Christ. Günther built on Anselm's *Cur Deus Homo*? to insist that a human savior could not satisfy divine justice, which needed a divine savior. The "no" of Adam was final, and only God could free him of the guilt and restore him to the good graces of his creator. The fact that Christ is the son of God is not simply one truth among many. It is the whole of Truth, the fundamental principle of the reality of God's presence in the world. It is *the* truth of faith (*die Glaubenswahrheit schlechthin*).[91]

While the fact of the hypostatic union is central to the thought of Günther, it must also be noted that he emphasized the humanity of Christ, emphasized Christ's being a part of the organic unity of the human universe. Christ is the redeemer of all the race because he is a part of the human generative history. Because of the flesh-taking of God, the harmony between Nature and Spirit that had been shattered has been restored. It could have been no mere human who did this. It had to be the *Logos*, the Son of God.[92] But it also had to be someone human who restored the harmony to preserve the organic unity of the race and of the revelation that is creation.

Salvation is not simply a repayment and wiping out of guilt and punishment. Salvation is a new creation, a new life with God. Humanity is saved as a result of the double repercussion (*Rückwirkung*) of the justice of Christ. That justice is first of all negative, in the sense that it removes the guilt and punishment; but then it is also positive in that it restores the original relationship, the real unity of the divine Spirit with the human spirit, which unity is in baptism in Christ.[93]

It was necessary for Christ to be human and divine. In Christ as a fact of world history a double good is apparent. The one is the work of God (*opus operatum als Setzung Gottes*), and the other is a work of the human race (*opus operantis als Setzung des Menschen*). Through his free act of love, Christ replaces the "no" of the first Adam with the "yes" of the God-Man, the second Adam.

In the human consciousness of Christ, Günther discovered the element in which the unity of humanity with the *Logos* would become conscious to Christ. Günther saw a distinction between the consciousness of the Son of man and of the *Logos*. However, there could have been no moment of Jesus' life when he was not aware of the fact that he was totally and completely (*ursprünglich und unzertrennlich*) united with the *Logos*; that is, Jesus always knew that he was God. The impossibility of not knowing was, for Günther, the basis for the reality of the unity of the formal consciousness of both substances (*in ihrer realen oder faktischen Vereinigung*).[94]

Günther also saw the miracles of Christ as intrinsic to this reality. The miracles, along with the teachings of Christ, are the two most important moments in the revelation of Christ. The divine strength and wisdom poured themselves from the *Logos* into the human consciousness and from there became the power of miracle in the outside world (*nach aussen*). The miracles are the necessary appearance and expression (*Äusserung*) of the God-Man Christ, not simply an additional confirmation (*Bestätigung*) of his teaching.[95]

The entire life of Christ was one act of free affirmation of the divine will; in contradistinction to the first Adam, the second Adam decided, with free human will, for the divine will.[96] Günther accented the free decision not to sin and to die on the cross as the act of complete forgiveness of sins. This free decision is apparent in the risen savior, who is restored to the original state with a balance between Nature and Spirit, between the human and the divine. Christ risen has a real body because in the realm of Nature there cannot be Spirit, but a true person is a dynamic union, although not destructive of the individuality, of the worlds of Nature and Spirit. In the Ascension, Nature and Spirit have left the world and remain a constant intercessor with the Father for the saved and the to-be-saved of the human race. The work continues through the church, the sacrament of Christ in this world.

Günther claimed that there is a difference between the essential and nonessential forms of the church.[97] The form that Christ gave the church is, of course, essential. Once again, Günther's understanding of Scripture (or his lack thereof) led him to make assertions that seem obvious to him but are not obvious to the historical-critical eye. It was clear to Günther that Christ gave a commission to the apostles, with Peter as the head, to go and make disciples of all nations. Each of the apostles was led by the Holy Spirit and hence had an aura of infallibility about him. The organic unity of the apostles with each other was assured through the headship of Peter as the Vicar of Christ. Günther was not advocating the infallibility of the papacy at this point, but rather insisted that each of the apostles enjoyed inspiration in his own right and that Peter's headship made the organism whole. Hence, when Günther claimed that the church was apostolic, he meant that it was founded on a real collegiality that respected the Spirit working in each of the apostles.[98] Christ chose the apostles; they did not choose him, at least not initially. The authority of the church comes from above and not from below, not from any sense of majority decision or opinion of all the baptized. Collegiality extends to bishops as direct successors of the apostles but not beyond that.

It is clear where Günther was headed; it was to the Roman Catholic Church as the one and only church founded by Christ upon the apostles. There is, however, no doctrine of damnation for those outside the Roman Catholic fold. There is no *massa damnata*; there is only a *massa redempta*.[99] Nor did Günther confine salvation to those who have been baptized in the Roman

Catholic fold. Church exists before the church in that even before Christ's historical entry, he was present in the promise. Günther's insistence on organic unity would not let him divide the world into the saved and unsaved along Roman Catholic, non–Roman Catholic lines.

For Günther, there were two foundational moments in the church: the one is the fact of the unity of the human race, which is deduced from the participation of the human in the sexual; the other moment is Christ's human presence in the world. The church, founded on the apostles, has to include all of the human race and is therefore missionary. Each human individual maintains the freedom of love to say "yes" or "no" to the invitation of Christ articulated by the church; but the church must proclaim that invitation to all.

It is apparent that in Günther there are already the roots of the concept of what later scholars of Scripture call the kingdom of God,[100] which will be much broader than the organizational structures of the Roman Catholic Church or indeed of all church bodies. But one should not push this too far. Günther's vision was limited. He saw some room for Protestant thought, if it recognized its mistakes and became more Roman. He extended an invitation to the "pagan" philosophers to see the limitations of their ways and discover Truth. However, Günther remained convinced,—in fact, he never questioned—that the Roman Church is the church of Christ. Whosoever sees the Roman Church sees Christ.

It is this Roman Church that has the necessary authority to teach and that is the necessary ground for the proclamation of the message of salvation. It is the Roman Church that is the necessary preserver of Tradition. Tradition is protected by a hierarchical authority that preserves and protects the message of Christ (which is present, to be sure, in the Christian consciousness of all believers, but is entrusted to those whom God had himself chosen to be leaders).

Günther spent little time discussing Eucharist as sacrament and much time on hierarchical priesthood. The visible organ of the message of Christ to the human race caught in time and space is the priesthood. Priests, bishops, and popes are the successors of Christ, and they have been chosen to hold in trust (*Verwalten*) the higher secrets of life in the Spirit, secrets that receive light and strength from above.[101] Not only is the work of Christ—salvation—continued in the church, but also the person of Christ is present in the church. This presence is primarily in the priesthood.[102] One of the powers that the priest has is the Mass, the Eucharist, which brings Christ present into the world through bread and wine. But the accent is on the hierarchical priesthood—and a total rejection of anything that might look like an affirmation of the priesthood of all believers so fundamental to Protestant belief. The church must develop, but it does so under the guidance of the hierarchy in whom a grace is infused that protects them from wrong. Again, Günther did not say that the pope or each individual bishop is infallible.

The church, as the presence of Christ in the world, is the place of the restoration of sinful humanity, the place of both justification and sanctification. If Christ is the first fact of Christianity, then the church (that is, of course, the Roman Catholic Church) is the second fact thereof. The Roman Church is *the* essential form of Christianity, without which Christianity itself would be formless. The church is an organic complex and has an inner unity that comes from the first Adam in a natural manner and from the second Adam in a supernatural manner. Church is the organism of Christ through which he works. There is an essential difference between clergy and laity, and there is an organically necessary hierarchy with a central head, the papacy. The hierarchical church is the will of Christ.

It is hard not to see that Günther would be attached to the hereditary and hierarchical monarchy as well as to the hierarchical church. In fact, he was against democracy as a form of paganism. It is not the purpose here to go into Günther's theory of government; that will be appropriate when the events of 1848 and Günther's role in them are examined for their influence on the thinking of this man.

After this view of the counterpositional dualism of Anton Günther, philosopher, theologian, recluse, and master of the mind, a next logical enterprise is to see how his philosophical-theological system was used and interpreted by a man of practice, Johann Emanuel Veith. As a convinced follower of Anton Günther, did Veith succeed in translating Günther's system into concepts and words that could be used from the pulpit?

5
JOHANN EMANUEL VEITH AS GÜNTHERIAN AND PREACHER

It is one thing to articulate a philosophical-theological system to those familiar with the arcane world of academic nuance; it is quite another thing to explain philosophy to those uninitiated into any form of philosophical thought, let alone into a particular system or into a disciplined and scientific approach to looking at the universe. In addition, it is all but impossible to attempt to do so within the framework of a sermon, during which one has limited time and in which there is no possibility of listener response. The pulpit is not the teacher's lectern, especially in Roman Catholicism, even if Josephinists tried to use it was such. The preacher faces an incredible challenge. It is presumed that he has understood the elaborate theological-philosophical thought that professors and mentors have so carefully thought through and elaborated in long lectures and discourses and in ponderous tomes with intricate footnoting. Beyond the presumption of personal understanding is the expectation that the preacher will be able to express complicated and sophisticated concepts accurately in language that will be understandable to an audience of mixed background. He cannot presume homogeneity in his listeners. They are young and old, educated and uneducated, conservative and liberal. Like any teacher or speaker, he cannot control what the individuals in the audience actually hear, for selective hearing is a reality in any attempt to communicate. Many a preacher or teacher has listened in examination or informal dialogue to what he is purported to have said, only to discover that he has either been sloppy in presentation or been grossly misunderstood. The art of communication depends on both speaker and listener.

Johann Emanuel Veith was teacher, doctor, priest, preacher, and writer. As a doctor, he worked tirelessly, especially during the cholera epidemic of 1831.[1] His sermons found few listeners among the growing number of workers from the countryside who crowded the Viennese suburbs; but he was known for his generosity in using his medical skills for all those who could find their way to his door. As an instructor in veterinary medicine, he had gained a reputation as a fine teacher.[2] Both as a priest and medical doctor, Veith was noted for gentleness and approachability. He was a great man who understood people.[3] As a preacher Veith had become popular as a Redemptorist[4] and reached a pinnacle of popularity as the preacher at the funeral of Emperor Francis I.[5] Veith's writings, mostly published editions of his sermons, but also short stories, poems, philosophical treatises, and works on botany and medicine, were nineteenth-century best sellers. Veith remained teacher, doctor, priest, preacher, and writer throughout his life. The focus here will be on his preaching and his printed volumes of sermons.

Johann Emanuel Veith's accomplishment as a preacher should not be underestimated. He preached in the center of Vienna to an audience of the educated of the time: members of the court, diplomats, state bureaucrats, students, artists, the literati, and the wealthier shop owners of the central city. An occasional servant would be in attendance.[6] His audience was comprised mostly of men.[7] The popularity his preaching gained while he was a Redemptorist was to continue when he became a diocesan priest and took up assignment, first as assistant pastor at the Church am Hof and then as second preacher at St. Stephen's Cathedral.

The art of the preacher is to be able to understand theology and to express it in language that those who do not know theology will understand. Even more, however, it is the task of the preacher to go beyond simple academic exposition to moral exhortation that will move his hearers, and himself, to a change in life. The cool reserve of the academician has little place in the pulpit, even when the fruit of academic discourse remains the basis for the preacher's work. Veith had not only a talent for explaining thought but also a talent for moving people. He was certainly not a preacher of the tent-revivalist type that swept much of the American West at the time when Veith was preaching in Vienna. Roman Catholicism would never have tolerated that. Flourish was reserved for architecture and music, candles and incense, which were designed to overwhelm while preserving a sense of awe and recollection. Nor could Veith compare with his mentor, Hofbauer,[8] who was an expert at reaching the common element of his audience with his enthusiasm and his personal conviction. For Hofbauer, the sermon was as much the man as what he said. Veith was known as a man of great generosity and personal conviction, but his sermons focused on content and reasoned thought. Veith, perhaps caught in his low self-image, always felt that he had little to offer and so relied on elaborate preparation.[9]

Vienna of the time between Napoleon and the Revolution of 1848, Biedermeier Vienna, was a city that looked for novelty. Part of that search for novelty focused on the church. Vienna flocked to the sermons of popular preachers, but it is difficult to assess the motivation. There was, to be sure, sincere conviction and hunger for the Word of God; but there was also the delight of tweaking the noses of the police, who had to stand helplessly by while their precious rules were often ignored. And there was a hunger for novelty: preachers became fads like the latest hat or the latest cut of coat. Veith was quite an attraction in that world. He was a former Jew, a medical and veterinary doctor, a former university professor who had given up position and wealth to become a simple priest who had little wealth and gave away that which he had. Veith was an odd mixture of self-deprecation and self-confidence. Even those without interest in the content of his preaching were interested in the phenomenon of a man who had changed so much.

People — at least upper and middle class people—did attend church frequently in Biedermeier Vienna. The Habsburgs themselves were often to be seen, and the churches of the inner city and the near suburbs had special boxes for high members of the court who might come by to hear Mass. The most popular times were the high holy days and Lent. The high holy days—Christmas, Easter, Corpus Christi—and even the regular Sunday attendance were times when festive sermons were held after Mass. But it was the Lenten sermons, held during a time when social activities in Roman Catholic Vienna were at a minimum, that attracted the largest number of hearers.

Lent was a time for fire and brimstone, and that has always been a part of Roman Catholicism as well as of evangelical Protestantism, even if it has been expressed differently. Lent is a time to go to the desert and discover guilt and repentance and redemption. Whether in a revivalist tent or a baroque church, the preacher of sin and repentance has an easy time moving his audience, for the Christian seems always to have a large strain of guilt waiting to be tapped. It is not the purpose of this present work to analyze guilt as a phenomenon in Christianity (although a later citizen of Vienna and former Jew would have much to say about that); suffice it to say that the Lenten season, then as now, continued to bring more people to church and produced the most memorable sermons if not the most lasting conversions. Veith's Lenten sermons are among his best. His own conviction that his listeners would tend to minimize or explain away sinfulness in order to be "modern" lent intensity to his usual eloquence. His festive sermons were preached after Mass, usually from 8:00 A.M. to 9:00 A.M. His Lenten sermons were more freestanding, at most with a Benediction or prayer service attached. They were from 4:00 P.M. to 5:00 P.M. They were packed; one report indicated a crowd of three thousand with over one hundred clergy and an auxiliary bishop in attendance.[10] Veith's first Lenten series was in 1826 while he was still a Redemptorist. They were held in St. Mary's on the Bank in Vienna. His last Lenten series was preached in 1863 in the Capuchin Church in Vienna.[11] The years in between are a significant period in a man's life but also in the life of the Roman Catholic Church in the German-speaking world.

For the superficially curious who came to see and hear this man preach, there was disappointment. He was not an imposing presence in the pulpit. He took little care with personal appearance and so seemed shabby in dress, which only accentuated his short stature and ape-like visage. He spoke with his eyes half closed, and he used few gestures. His voice was not one that overwhelmed; if anything it was weak and hard to hear, almost a monotone. It was Veith's natural voice, however, and even when monotonous was also calm; and, for those who listened intently, the words buried themselves in the heart.[12] Veith himself complained that it would be easier to preach at a retreat or to prepare lectures for a class because then people would be there because of an interest in the material. An interest in the material would spare the speaker the "emotion, intensity, empty rhetoric, explosion, rage, sweetness, cursing and swearing (scolding), and praisings demanded by the Philistines"[13] who came to sermons. Veith claimed that he could not imitate "this spiritual casualness" but had to risk preaching in his own way. Eventually, Veith gave up trying to include speculative theology in his preaching, but that was not until late in life, after many years of attempting to include it.[14] Veith's popularity continued throughout his life. His sermons always found crowded churches long after the novelty had faded. The published editions of his sermons reached the second, third, fourth, and even fifth editions, and some were translated into French and English. Perhaps Veith did not pander to the whims of his hearers, but something he said or perhaps something he unconsciously tapped kept them returning again and again. There were many who considered Veith to be the most popular preacher in the German world of the 1830s and 1840s.[15] Even when he was old, all but blind and hardly able to be heard, wherever Veith preached the churches were full to overflowing.[16] Why the popularity?

In the introductions to the various volumes of sermons that he published, Veith often took time to give advice to fellow preachers on the art of preaching. His most constant piece of advice focused beyond the sermon itself. The preacher, unlike the actor, who uses many of the same skills, must actually *live* what he preaches, wrote Veith.[17] Although plagued with the conviction of his own worthlessness and constant failure, Veith was a man who exemplified that axiom to Biedermeier Vienna. His name was a commonplace even in the suburbs, where the workers lived, because Veith attempted to be present to all.

The second rule of preaching that Veith practiced without failure was preparation, for misunderstanding was easily spread. He was known for having an excellent memory and for being extremely well-read in science, literature, and politics, as well as in the religious disciplines that included scripture, Roman Catholic philosophy and theology, and Protestant and non-Christian thought. He avoided any extemporizing because, as he said, when he was not prepared he heard himself babbling on and on.[18] Veith did not read his sermons, but he always had them written in some form before he entered the pulpit. The notes that have survived time and war were written and rewritten, with words scratched out and others added. The rough draft was on a piece of paper divided into fours, each section having a brief outline and room on the left side for revisions and additions. He reworked the sermons before publication, expanding and correcting. But a study of the manuscripts left behind by Josef Bermann, who had the habit of writing out what he had heard whenever he attended one of Veith's sermons,[19] shows remarkable similarity between what Veith preached and what he later published.

The organization was classical: introduction, major part, and conclusion.[20] The introduction, usually quite long, was a story or a series of general thoughts designed to catch listener interest by creating a tension. More often than not, Veith began with a quotation from scripture; he made his own translations from the Greek or Hebrew texts. His favorite passages were from Psalms (especially Psalm 36:10, "In your light we see light"), or from wisdom literature, or from Paul. The main part began with a brief overview of the content and division of the topic or question to be treated. Calling on the guidance of the Holy Spirit, Veith proceeded to move from basic knowledge that he presumed would be familiar to his listeners to more complex knowledge. He would build to a single major point and then would repeat that from several different perspectives, both positive and negative. Then he attempted to bring the point home to his listeners by a clever story or turn toward daily life so that applications could be made. He often spoke out against ideas and people, although he seldom mentioned those people by name, leaving the identity clear from the allusions he made. The story or anecdote was the transition to the conclusion, which would usually be a repetition of the introductory story, a poem, another citation from the Bible, or a spontaneous prayer. References to Mary were frequent in the conclusions to Veith's sermons.

The sermons were carefully constructed and demanded intense attention from someone who was attempting to understand them through listening. Veith usually preached a series of sermons in Lent, preaching on Wednesdays and Fridays, the traditional monastic days of penance. In these series of sermons Veith would attempt to write each sermon so that it would stand alone as well as fit into the series. There were seldom repetitions, dull filler, or extraneous excursions. Every word was weighed carefully by Veith. The stories, the humor, the choice of Scripture, all were carefully chosen and had a pointed place in the sermon. A listener who had come to be challenged would not be disappointed.

Veith's major source of quotation was Scripture; but he did not hesitate to use other sources. After 1830 there are frequent direct and indirect references to Günther. Veith was well-read in the Fathers of the church, and he often quoted from Augustine, Jerome, Ambrose, Leo the Great, Basil, Athanasius, Cyril of Alexandria or Cyril of Jerusalem, Clement of Rome, Ireneus, Gregory the Great, John Chrysologus, or Tertullian. He also quoted Origen, Gregory of Tours, Peter of Ravenna, Cajetan, Bellarmine, Dominic, Francis of Assisi, Benedict, Peter Damian, Anthony of Padua, Francis de Sales, Francis Xavier, Peter Canisius, Teresa of Avila, Vincent Ferrer, Anselm of Canterbury, and Suarez. He was not above citing Albert the Great and Thomas Aquinas, although his citations of these men frequently lacked special reference to the specific source. Veith also quoted many of the pagan authors, including Plato, Plutarch, Euripides, Homer, Tacitus, Livy, Cicero, Pliny, Juvenal, and Seneca. Secular authors who were read and cited by Veith included Kepler, Bacon, Goethe, Montesquieu, Pascal, de Maistre, and writers in comparative religion.

Veith was well-read in the literature and politics of his own time, and there are many references to contemporary events in his sermons, a fact that makes them a bit difficult to read for those unfamiliar with the people and events of Biedermeier Vienna. In all the quotations, Veith took to heart Hofbauer's dictum of the importance of preaching the gospel anew. He often admonished fellow preachers to be careful about lifting thought from writers of the past without reworking it to make sense to the present.[21]

Like Günther, Veith was a believer in the importance of humor. He was fond of Jean Paul, who was a favorite of many of the younger clergy in Biedermeier Vienna. When Veith treated topics toward which he was favorable, the humor was mild and gentle. When he preached against someone or something, Veith could be derisive, mocking, and bitterly sarcastic. His favorite enemy was, not surprisingly, the pantheist; but he also found harsh words for the communist, the materialist, and, in later years, a special condemnation for Darwin. Veith had strong words about the deplorable state of the modern world and even for the state of affairs within the church. Needless to say, Veith had little good to say about the "lukewarmness" of the Josephinists; nor did he hesitate to criticize the youth of his age, whom he accused of not knowing anything other than sleeping and dreaming, eating, digesting, growing, putting clothes on and taking them off, reading frivolous and shallow periodicals, worrying about what they would do, and silly intrigues.[22]

Veith was a master storyteller. He had a gift for creating suspense in unwinding what he had to say. The crispness of his language and the precision of his choice of words made contemporaries compare him favorably with famous preachers of the eighteenth century. His experience as a doctor and his love of nature filled his sermons with anecdotes from the sickbed as well as stories from the flower and animal worlds. His sermons were alive, contemporary, and true to life. He had an exceptional capacity to empathize with sinners and those in pain.

But how was Johann Emanuel Veith a Güntherian? Certainly, as a preacher and practical man, he was more interested in ideas and issues that would reach the man and woman in the pew than he was in speculative theology. His main goal was to bring the gospel closer to his hearers, to enable them to sense a transcendent and trinitarian God. He wanted them to recognize their sin in ignoring a relationship to a God who promised a true freedom in the redemption. His exhortations to moral and spiritual authenticity could never have been subsumed under a theoretical system. He, like Günther, was an odd combination of Enlightenment and Romantic. He built his whole preaching career on the classical form and seemed to speak out again and again against a religion of feeling; but at the same time he preached a new vision of God, a new vision of the human, a vision of the world that was a far distance from anything that Enlightenment thought would have tolerated. With vigor he preached Christ as Lord and Redeemer and not simply the bringer of a new ethic. Veith seemed to believe in and to be immersed in the fire of the Holy Spirit, a man of deep feeling even while he condemned a religion of feeling. He used the theological thought of Anton Günther as the skeleton upon which to hang his moral exhortation for a better world. As a man of action, he was not the critical thinker that the careful academic of the Sterngasse was, but he found in the thought of Günther a system upon which he based much of his own thought. He never denied Günther's influence on his thought and his preaching. No one familiar with Veith's writings from the publication of Günther's *Vorschule* in the late 1820s through the time of Veith's death could doubt that Veith was a Güntherian, not only before Günther's condemnation but also after it.[23]

The first volume of Anton Günther's *Vorschule der Spekulativen Theologie* appeared in 1828. It is not surprising that Günther gave a copy of his *Vorschule* to his friend from his student days in Prague and the Hofbauer days in Vienna, with whom he still regularly met for discussion and dinner. Johann Emanuel Veith was rapidly becoming one of the major preachers of Vienna at this time. In his Lenten sermons of 1830, Veith took great pains to articulate the Güntherian system in a manner that was understandable to his audience. The first published edition of those sermons appeared in 1831, the second in 1833, and the third, a revised edition, in 1842. All three editions, and the translations and reprints that were to follow, were Güntherian.[24]

The Lenten sermons of 1830 were neither philosophical lectures nor theological discourses. Veith protested that he had to leave those tasks to the theologians and referred his readers to the works of Anton Günther for further study.[25] Veith was not interested in a systematic exposition of a system. Rather, he found an organizing theme for his lectures in the common Christian prayer, the *Our Father* (*Vater Unser*), which supplied the title of his series in both pulpit and print. Each sermon had a unity of its own and each fit into the larger cycle.

Some general characteristics are worth noting. The most obvious is the way that Veith seldom directly mentioned but nonetheless built on the thought of Günther. There were few directly epistemological or metaphysical discussions in Veith's sermons. Veith did not spend time articulating the difference between *Begriff* and *Idee* nor even between *Natur* and *Geist*. These were the philosopical underpinnings that inspired the sermons, but they were never highlighted. Güntherianism was insinuated into the text by indirect references, by the subtle presumption that the listener certainly agreed that "reality was indeed that way."

Another characteristic of Veith's sermonizing is readily apparent to the twentieth-century eye, which has a democratic bias and finds constant references to the nobility a bit quaint: the vast majority of Veith's anecdotes are connected somehow with the nobility who, he said, were a class that transcended the limits of locality and nation.[26] Even the canonized saints chosen as examples are more often than not canonized nobility. There could be several explanations for this. Veith could simply have followed the presumptions of the age in citing the nobility as the only class that counted (although his firsthand knowledge of the less noble segments of city and country would suggest that this was not the case). More likely, Veith was speaking to the majority of his audience who came from the the center of Vienna and were somehow connected with court and bureaucracy, for whom such examples would be most powerful. The nobility mentioned were drawn from all times and from all nations and were much more likely to be examples of what should be than of what should not be.

The printed sermons (no manuscripts are now available), are entitled *Vater Unser* and are divided into nineteen chapters, suggesting either some alteration in the transcription from pulpit to print or more actual sermons than the thirteen that would be required for the Wednesdays and Fridays between Ash Wednesday and the beginning of the Triduum on Holy Thursday. It is likely that Veith preached more frequently during Holy Week itself. Each of the sections in the book is approximately twenty pages long, short enough to have been included in its entirety in an hour-long sermon.

Veith's Vater Unser

Veith's introductory sermon (*Eingang*) was on prayer: "Lord, teach us to pray." He cited both the disciples, who observed Christ praying, and Brother Leo, who watched as Francis of Assisi was transported in ecstasy. Prayer is the yearning of the created ego to discover itself in the uncreated Ego; the *Geist* that in its very discovery of self-consciousness has also discovered the unendurable fact of its limitedness and dependence and yearns for a deep knowledge of the uncreated and unlimited other who is God. "Who are you, Lord, and who am I?" "If I know who I am, then I know who You are as well." Christ is the perfect example; he united the human and the divine in himself and, consequently, he was able to teach prayer in a perfect way. The *Our Father* is, as Cyprian claimed, the quintessential gospel message, a summary of all else that the gospel contains. The human heart, even when it empties itself of all the evil of this world that clutters it and bows in humility to the God who does not need human prayer, is too small to receive all the gifts that the God of love (love seen as the combination of justice and mercy) wants to shower on it. It is only God (i.e., Christ) who can teach prayer, and we must learn to pray constantly, to live always in the presence of God, and to know of our own worthlessness in his sight, and his boundless generosity. Words are not to be multiplied, for the Father knows what is needed even before we speak. There is a strong sense of emptying so that God can fill us, a strong stress on the cross of Christ. The prayer for light and life suggests that knowledge comes only through accepting ourselves as creature and making way for the gifts God will shower upon us.[27] Veith concluded the first sermon with a suggestion that there was an appropriate part of the *Our Father* for each day of the week: Sunday, "hallowed be thy name"; Blue Monday,[28] "thy kingdom come"; Tuesday, "thy will be done on earth as in heaven"; Wednesday, "give us this day our daily bread"; Thursday, "forgive us our trespasses as we forgive those who trespass against us"; Friday, "lead us not into temptation"; Saturday, "Amen."

With the second sermon (*Unser Vater, der du bist*), Veith launched into the middle of Güntherian thought. When someone is addressed, it is important to know titles, rank, place of residence, and, above all, that that person exists. The existence of God is a mystery, but a mystery that does not exclude thinking. "The light of divine revelation does not obscure, but rather it enlightens *Verstand*."[29] Veith, like Günther, looked at the human as a mirror of the divine. One could not say "you" unless one knew an "I". The self-knowledge of the human led to the discovery of dependence and limit and demanded an absolute and limitless "you" to sustain existence. But that absolute and limitless "you" is called 'Father,' and in the concept of 'Father', which is the source of all, is also the necessity of 'Trinity', the mirror image of the revelation of God *ad extra*, which is *Mensch*. Veith presumed that all of this would be self-evident to his Roman Catholic audience taught to believe in God as Trinity. He presented the Güntherian dualism of *Geist* and *Natur* with their non-dissolving synthesis in *Mensch* as the key to trinitarian reality, presuming the actual subjectification of the subject-objectification in the self-knowledge of God. Veith did not discuss the necessity of creation in the inner workings of the Trinity as did Günther, who found creation a necessary part of the intrinsic reality of God as the non-ego *Idee* of God. Instead Veith stressed the fact that God's love wants to express itself in the giving of the clarity and sanctity of itself. God does not *need* human praise and prayer, but that praise and prayer are an absolutely necessary part of the human identity and are part of the recognition that God exists. Veith waxed eloquent about the reality of God (and against pantheism):

> If this absolute power is the source of our ego, what is it itself? Could it be the soul of the world, the hidden inner gears of all power and movement, itself blind and impersonal and unconscious? What, asks the Psalmist, he who formed the ear should not hear? He who formed eye should not see? He who taught *Wissenschaft* should be without it? He who planted and awakened self-awareness in us should be thought of as having no self-consciousness of his own?[30]

The third sermon (*Unser Vater*), expanded the second and had the same title. Just as the disciple did not ask for the Lord to teach *him* to pray but rather *us* to pray, so too it is not *my* father but *our* Father to whom we pray.

But we do not possess the right to call God "Father" because sin has alienated us from him. Rather, when one considers what is right, we are slaves. The love of God has been violated and only perfect love can restore it. Veith, like most Christian writers before and after him, was convinced that God had to become human in order to redeem *Mensch* from sin which, on his own, *Mensch* could never escape. Christ is the Second Adam and the restorer of all creation. The incredible scandal of the incarnation is that God should deign to empty himself, to become like a slave so that we might call God "Father." Although the planet earth, with *Mensch* at the center, is incredibly small and insignificant when one begins to contemplate the universe (Veith was familiar with the astronomy of his time), God sent his Son to redeem the world lost through the sin of Adam. For those who accept the definition of *Mensch* as the union of *Geist* and *Natur*, the union of God and man is not so very difficult. The love of God that is mirrored in *Mensch* could not ignore human need. Christ became the firstborn among many children whom he brings to rebirth and reunion with the love of God, he himself being both human and divine with God as Father of both the human and the divine. (Veith presumes the virgin birth, that Mary conceived without sexual intercourse and that God is therefore Father of the human Jesus as well as of the divine *Logos*.) Because of Christ we are adopted children, and when we pray "Our Father" we are in fact proclaiming the two greatest commandments: to love God with heart and soul and whole being (a love for a father implies a total love) and to love our neighbor as ourselves (since we are children of the same Father).

With his next sermon (*Unser Vater, der du bist im Himmel*), Veith turned an analysis of "who art in heaven" into a rout of the pantheists and an exposition of Güntherian cosmology. Heaven is not the place where the Greek gods and goddesses cavort, nor is heaven this world with God as the unknowing, unconscious soul. God is his own time and place, and this is clear from Güntherian thought. He is everywhere, but not everywhere in the sense understood in the world of *Begriff*. No one can flee his presence, but it is a presence in the world of *Geist*. The *Idee* of Absolute Being is not spatial or temporal; God is everywhere and nowhere. Anywhere God is is heaven. Paul the Apostle ascended into the third heaven (2 Corinthians 12), and this, according to Veith, indicated a created and visible heaven (the place of the stars and planets), a created and invisible heaven (the domain of pure *Geist*), and an uncreated and invisible heaven (the absolute being and existence of God in himself in trinity and unity). Although the world cannot be thought of without God, God can be thought of without the world. (Günther found creation as such a necessity for God to be God, but *this* particular creation is rooted in the freedom of God.) Therefore, God is not simply an emanation in creation, but is an ineffable and eternal existence who lives in inaccessible light. The Son of God came *from heaven* because he is from all eternity in the essentiality of God. Time and space in God are eternity and limitlessness. God is not *in* the world but over or beyond the world; that is, God is *up*. This is obvious in the fact that *Mensch*, the mirror image of God, stands upright and can look up. It is further proven by the fact of the Ascension, in which Christ was taken up into heaven to be an intercessor for his many brothers and sisters. To call out "Our Father who art in heaven" is to make an act of faith, faith that goes beyond the *Begriff* to the world of *Idee*.

> Our Father, you are in heaven; we, however, are on earth. You are in your eternal Being; we, however, in time and in becoming. You are in absolute bliss; we, however, in a state of vacillation and choice and testing. To whom should we, who are on earth, cry out if not to you who are in heaven?[31]

The next sermon in the series treated God's name (*Geheiligt werde dein Name*). Since God is, in himself, holy and complete, how can we presume to add to holiness of his name? How can we pray "hallowed be Thy name"? For Veith, the most important form of prayer is the prayer that sings the praises of God, that is the language of the angels, who simply sing the glory of God. Although it is clear that prayer for our needs and for the needs of others is a reality, what of this highest form of prayer? Can we pray to God for God? Is not his holiness eternal and complete? For Veith and Günther (and here they are one with most of Christian spiritual history), creation itself has the purpose, by its very existence, of praising God. Humankind's disobedience was in falling into self-aggrandizement and ignoring the wonder of God. Consequently, the prayer "hallowed be thy name" is a prayer that God will receive from all his rational creation the honor and homage rightfully his, for it is properly a part of his outward (*ad extra*) possession. No one is essentially good but God, and all goodness has its root in him. The glory of God is not dependent on human free will; nor is God's love conditional upon the fulfillment of his interests by his creatures, for that would pollute the purity of God's love. The pure love of God manifests itself inwardly in the love of Father for Son and their love for the Spirit, and outwardly first in the creation and then in the redemption. Neither the creation nor the redemption adds or subtracts from the inner love of God that is Trinity. "Hallowed be Thy name" is a cry for the pure and simple love of creature for creator, a creator whose love is ever present whether the creature notices or thanks the creator for it or not. The sinful creature can only gain when he praises the name of the God who loves him simply and completely.

> I hope in you. I adore you. I praise you as my God because, on my side, I am totally defined by you and am dependent upon you. You, however, have need of neither me nor my possessions; because you are marvelous and holy in yourself. No creature is capable of taking or giving you anything, whether inwardly or outwardly.[32]

The *Our Father* is a prayer that is like a golden chain from heaven to earth, praising God and asking for those things most necessary to creation. Each link of the chain builds on, overlaps with, is dependent upon the other. To pray "Thy kingdom come" (*Herzu comme dein Reich*) is to pray all of the *Our Father*, just as every other link also includes the other petitions implicitly. "Thy kingdom come" implies the struggle between the world of *Natur* and the world of *Geist*, implies other kingdoms that are not God's, and implies the mission to bring the message to all that Christ's kingdom is not of this world. The kingdom of God is, to be sure, within; and each person is called upon to pray that Spirit will rule Nature. The Son of God was born human that he could be a part of all humans from the beginning of time to its end. The presence of Christ continues in the church, which is the kingdom of God on earth. The church is neither simply a visible gathering of believers nor an invisible spiritual band among God-seeking upright souls. The church is the continuous living relationship between Christ and humanity whose task it is to proclaim to all the message of unity through a visible living organism built on unity. The unity of the church is most visible in the institution of hierarchical presbytery — priest, bishop, pope — which represents the priesthood of Christ and presents a visible head, a Vicar of Christ, upon earth. For this reason there can be only one church, which teaches and leads and decides. To pray "Thy kingdom come" is to pray that the kingdom of grace, founded with the second Adam, will be spread throughout the entire world. It is to pray that all will become Roman Catholic. It is also to pray that it will be strengthened in those who have been baptized, for there are many officially within the Roman Church who, by their lives and their indifference, are in fact enemies of the one church.

It is impossible to pray "Thy kingdom come" without also praying "Thy will be done" (*Dein Wille geschehe*). There is too much distracting sinfulness, and that sinfulness shows itself in the lukewarm and imperfect search for happiness in *this* world. Veith saw the clinging to this life in the fear of death, even though death is the entry into the glory of the *other* world where true freedom is to be found. Death is a punishment for sin and a punishment that one does not long for; but death, as uncertain as the hour is, remains the entry into the promise. (Veith had a very individualistic and other-worldly view of the promise. He often preached about what needs to be done on this side of death to build the kingdom and bring about the will of God; but it was all conditioned by an understanding of this world as struggle and test for the next world.) Not everyone who cries "Lord, Lord" will enter the kingdom of heaven but only those who do the will of the Father in this life. True freedom is doing the will of God, and that freedom is discovered in *Geist*, which is still able to choose, rather than in *Natur*, which is not free. Spirit is not bound by the flesh or fleshly copulation, which is the transmission of sin. The spirit is created directly by God and is endowed with the freedom and dignity of its creator.

(Veith built on the Roman Catholic belief in the individual creation of each human soul that is contemporaneous with but not caused by the creation of the human body in sexual intercourse.) The spirit has the free choice of saying "yes" or "no" to its creator because it is a reflection of that creator who himself is free. Although we are dependent upon the creator for our existence, our salvation is only through our free decision to cooperate. God has freely chosen to be unfree (*ad extra*) by giving the freedom to say "yes" or "no" to his invitation to salvation. *Natur* remains slavery, and the human composed of *Natur* and *Geist* who chooses that slavery chooses death, not the death that is the door to life but the real death to the spirit that denies the will of God.

> Your will, O Father, be done in us, through us, and to us. In and through us in that we fulfill in free obedience the divinely revealed divine law which we could resist through disobedience. To us in that the divine will reveals itself in such overwhelming providence that we cannot resist it although we could rebel and resist.[33]

Heaven represents perfection, and to pray that "Thy will be done on earth as it is in heaven" (*Dein Wille geschehe, wie im Himmel, also auch auf Erden*) is to pray that perfection will be a possibility in this life. It is to pray with St. Teresa of Avila that one will have the courage, when choosing between two good things, always to choose the better and never to be satisfied with "just enough". Created by God, we are also co-creators of our own destiny; it is not God alone who determines or we alone who determine what we shall become. And the challenge is to bring the life of *Natur* under the leadership of *Geist*. For the celibate Veith, this often meant bringing the drives of the flesh under control. Wisdom and morality are inseparable sisters and both dwell in the world of *Geist*. The whole world of *Natur* strives towards progeny, which is the only way *Natur* knows how to find eternity. When God's will is done on earth as it is in heaven there will be no need for marrying and all the urges that go with that state of life. *Geist*, created directly and individually by God, is the place where true perfection and right order can take place. When the *Mensch* is perfect, he will be like the angels, free from the slavery of sexual love and ruled by the pure and spiritual love that gives the strength to overcome the sensual and dishonest inclinations of the flesh. (For Veith, there was no venial sin against the sixth and ninth commandments, which deal with sexuality.) It is only Christian marriage that makes possible the fulfillment of God's plan for creation, that makes the sinful impulses of *Natur* the occasion of new creation.

It is symbolic of how difficult things are on this earth that the last four links in the golden chain are requests for specific favors for us from God. The first of these, "Give us this day our daily bread" (*Unser tägliches Brod* gib uns heute), is a plea for life itself, a plea for food, clothing, and shelter. It is not a plea for a social revolution, although Veith recognized the vast differences between rich and poor. Veith was convinced that the poor will always be present, for God allows poverty as a test for the poor. He was equally convinced that the rich will always be present and will be tested in whether or not they give alms to the poor. Veith's was a static view of society, unaware of deeper issues of justice. He did spend time warning about "conspicuous consumption," especially in the matter of food.[34] Our need for bread is a symbol of the dependence and woes of this world, a world that has not and will not reach the perfection of the kingdom of God, which is only the other side of death when no "bread" will be necessary. Since sin has entered the picture, *Natur* and *Geist* are out of synchronization, and that shows itself strongly in the need for work and the temptation to accumulate the goods of this world. Our need for bread reminds us of the fragility of today and the promise of death tomorrow. It calls us to dependence on God and on each other, and it calls us to a poverty of the spirit that sees beyond this world to the next. Veith gave numerous examples of saints who had chosen poverty and found spiritual happiness. "O happy poverty," he prayed, "O greatest of all treasures which accompanied Christ on the cross, which was buried with him, and which ascended to heaven with him." With Francis of Assisi, Veith proclaimed, "Thank you, Lord, for sister Poverty."

Veith used his knowledge of languages to analyze several possible translations for "daily bread"; he found merit in all of them but liked most especially St. Jerome's translation of the *Our Father* section of the Gospel of Matthew. Veith found the concept of "give us this day our daily supernatural bread" (*Unser tägliches, überwesentliches Brod gib uns heute*)[35] in the Vulgate. Not surprisingly, Veith then launched into a discourse on the Eucharist as the daily supernatural bread that is a gift from God. Just as eating and drinking are necessary for the life of the body, so too is the Eucharist necessary for supernatural life. The Eucharist is the real body and blood of Christ and is real food, not symbol or commemoration, not a pantheistic presence in all creation. When *Natur* is properly subjected to *Geist*, then physical eating, like the Eucharist, is done to the honor and glory of God; it is, in short, prayer. The *Geist* hungers and thirsts for Truth and justice, for *Wissenschaft* from God and for the will of God. It is in communion with the Truth that is the church that *Geist* is able to find these. In the beginning was the Word, and in the fullness of time the Word was made flesh and lived among us to bring us light and Truth. That Word is Christ, who is food in the Eucharist, the daily supernatural food that Jerome and Veith prayed for. It is that bread that sustains us on our pilgrimage to the kingdom of God.

Sinful *Mensch* must pray "Forgive us our trespasses" (*Und vergib uns unsere Schulden*). Although Veith began this chapter with a reference to the parable of the prodigal son and peppered it with constant references to the limitless love of God, the major theme remained how sin can be an insult to a God who is, in himself, complete and perfect, from whom nothing can be taken, to whom nothing can be added. Sin is creature denying creatureliness and limitedness, attempting to *become* God and thereby insulting God. It is not an insult as normally understood but rather an insult in the logical (and also real) order. One's attempt to be God cannot make God less, just as one's praise cannot make him more, but one's attempt to be God is a contradiction to the *Idee* of God and consequently calls forth a judgment from God. It is not the vengeance of the human but rather the vengeance of a loving and merciful God who sends his own Son, the *Logos*, to reestablish the proper order between creator and creature. The anger of God is not essentially different from his holiness or his pure love, and that love is incarnate in the redeemer. Whoever hates Christ, then, hates the Father also, a not-so-subtle assertion of Christianity (and ultimately Roman Catholicism) as the keystone to right order. Further proof that the anger or mercy of God is in the Roman Church is the sacrament of penance, where the power of God is dispensed to the generations, all of whom are sinners by the very fact of being descendants of the first Adam, but are also offered forgiveness by virtue of being descendants of the second Adam. When we pray "forgive us our trespasses" we are aware of the valley of death in which we find ourselves, but we are also aware of the boundless mercy of God. We need to ask for that forgiveness daily (as we ask for daily bread) because most of us also sin daily in some greater or lesser manner. Even if we do not sin daily, we have a Christian duty to pray for our fellow human beings, that all may experience the forgiveness of God. No one is without sin (except Jesus and Mary), but no one stands alone. We need only to admit that we have sinned, that we are sinners, to experience the healing mercy of God.

For Veith the key to having our sins forgiven was "*just as* we forgive those who sin against us" (*Gleichwie auch wir vergeben unsren Schuldigern*). It is a question of humility and of attempting to be perfect as the heavenly Father is perfect: the creature should imitate the creator. Although revenge and hatred are a part of the human heart (from the examples Veith cited one would assume that venality was only a characteristic of the middle and lower classes, not of noblemen), it is the challenge of Christianity to accompany anger and outrage with love and forgiveness. Veith admitted that it is a very narrow path between "the steep cliffs of arrogant pride and the bottomless depths of fainthearted timidity." However, if God's kingdom is to come to earth *just as* it is in heaven, then that is what must occur. Veith did not rely on the human ability to do this, but rather on God; no one would have returned to God if God himself, in his endless love, had not turned to us and re-established the link between heaven and earth. But God did turn to sinners, first of all in their consciences, then through the prophts, and finally through the sending of his Son. If we want to be like God, then we must forgive those who sin against us: not conditionally upon their accepting the forgiveness, but irrespective of how they respond to us. Christ died for *all* and not just those who were his friends. Whoever does not forgive will not be forgiven and will remain condemned.

Veith did a bit of an about-face when it came to discerning the meaning of "lead us not into temptation" (*Und führe uns nicht in Versuchung*). In early passages of his sermons he had spent considerable time insisting that the words meant what they said and not something different from the literal meaning. Here Veith tried to insist that the literal passage said one thing but meant something else. Veith saw temptation as both inevitable and something that would test one's mettle. The soldier does not ask his commander not to go to war; neither does the Christian pray to be freed from all temptation. Rather, said Veith, the Christian prays that he will not be swallowed up by, nor succumb to, temptation. Temptation is the necessary condition of freedom, for temptation is the situation in which one can choose in total consciousness and in one's total being to say "yes" or "no" to God. Temptation, so defined, whether it be temptation of the flesh, of the spirit, or of the devil, is not something to be delivered from, but something that is a necessary corollary of freedom. It is, to be sure, a contradiction; but as high as the heavens are above the earth, so high are God's ways above human ways. Veith also made a short digression in this sermon on who would be saved. Faith is necessary for salvation, and that faith is found in the Roman Church. Veith did not, however, espouse an ecclesiology that said "outside the Roman church there is no salvation." Rather, he relied on the concept of baptism by desire and insisted that no one knows what happens between an individual and God in that last moment of death, and consequently no one could know who is saved.

Veith prayed, "And lead us not into temptation but deliver us from evil" (*Und führe uns nicht in Versuchung: sondern erlöse uns von dem Übel*), the evil which Veith held to be the temptation to replace creator with creature. Veith cited various religions[36] which he claimed had missed the point. He deliberately threw down the gauntlet to the "enlightened" who believed in progress through education. Veith reminded his hearers of the fact that their age was no less bloody than any other and, for those inclined to romanticize the past, that every century had its cruelties. Storms and temptations are present in every age. Is not life itself, asked Veith, with all of its limitedness and its physical and spiritual suffering and its ultimate death, a string of evils?[37] Some have become fatalists, some have fallen into a dualism between a limited principle of good and one of evil, some have become pantheists, some have become cynics, some have simply become indifferent to thought and are content to quaff a beer and live in ignorance. But the Christian prays, "Lead us not into temptation, but deliver us from evil."

Veith was convinced that the seventh petition of the *Our* Father, "but deliver us from evil" (*Sondern erlöse uns von dem Übel*), contains the entire truth of positive Christianity within it: the doctrine of guilt and punishment for sin and the doctrine of salvation, which is the redemption from sin and punishment through justification and salvation.[38] In addition to a sermon on "lead us not into temptation but deliver us from evil" treated in the previous section, Veith devoted three more sermons to the topic of "deliver us from evil." These three sermons are filled with quotations from Christian writers and numerous examples from Christian history, all marshaled as illustration of (or perhaps proof for) a Güntherian anthropology and soteriology. Veith took great pains to express the Güntherian dualism of *Geist* and *Natur*. The latter could not be free, and the former had abused the freedom intrinsic to it and had brought sin into the world. Veith separated guilt from punishment, and claimed that all suffer punishment (sickness, death, injustice); therefore, all are guilty. As life has come through the loins of Adam, so too do guilt and punishment. *Geist* has lost its proper role and *Natur* has become unruly. The knowledge of good and evil (which, it is interesting to note, Veith claimed would have had to come simply from the essence of freedom[39]) had ended in disobedience. In 1830 Veith was a strong promoter of blind obedience, giving several examples of nobles and saints who had profited through blind trust in the apparently insignificant wishes of a sovereign.[40] The failure to follow blindly what a greater power has commanded results in necessary punishment. In the case of the sin of the first Adam, the sin was committed in the freedom of *Geist*, but the punishment was to fall upon both *Geist* and *Natur*, most especially in their union, which was *Mensch*. Veith saw *Natur* as subject to change and death, even without sin; it was in sinning that *Mensch*, who is a union of *Geist* and *Natur* and as such will not die, comes to know change and death. Even now, however, without a knowledge of God, there is no knowledge of guilt. It is in God's revelation that human guilt becomes visible, a guilt that presents a wide gap for the creature that ultimately only the creator can bridge. God's justice is God's anger; but God is love, and so every test of freedom that ends in failure is also a trial of God's love. That love was clearly expressed in the coming of the Son of God who, through his free obedience, removed the old disobedience of the first Adam. Christ, like us in all things but sin, was born of a virgin, the new creation who made all things new. O happy fault of Adam to merit such a redeemer! But the freedom remains, and the *Mensch* still has the choice to say "yes" or "no" to the call of God, who continues to speak through conscience even to those who do not listen to his Son or his church. It is neither *Mensch* alone nor God alone who brings about salvation. Rather, it is *Mensch* cooperating with the grace of God.[41]

Although Veith was aware of the ending "for Thine is the kingdom and the power and the glory" and mentions it as a possibility, he opted to omit it and end wih the more Roman Catholic simple "amen," dismissing the other ending as "man made." Veith claimed that Tertullian, Jerome, Augustine, Ambrose, and others knew nothing of it. The "amen" signifies acclamation: "let it be so" or "so it is" and consequently signifies Truth and certainty. Consequently, the "amen" at the end of the prayer is as significant as the "Our Father" at the beginning. The "amen" has the same force as "through Christ our Lord" and consequently provides a unity to the prayer. Christ began many of his teachings with "Amen, amen, I say to you"; therefore, the "amen" takes on a divine authority. Christ, who is divine, uses it at the beginning of his discourses; we humans use it at the end to affirm the divine Truth, to say "yes" to God. Veith gave the "amen" of the *Our Father* particular theological significance because of the rubrics of the Tridentine Mass in which the "amen" is recited quietly by the priest alone to symbolize the role of the priest as mediator between God and *Mensch*. This is another indication of the central role of the presbytery in bringing God's Word to earth and human response to God.[42]

Veith's final sermon in the series was on the "ave." Although Veith was not pleased by the formal declaration in 1854 of the doctrine of the Immaculate Conception of Mary, it would be a mistake to consider him anti-Marian. In his series of sermons on the *Our Father*, as in so many of his sermons, Veith ended with an unrelated tribute to Mary, the Mother of God. The "ave" was the greeting of her cousin Elizabeth when Mary came to visit her, Elizabeth pregnant with John the Baptist and Mary pregnant with Jesus. The one simple word conveyed peace, joy, and good wishes to the second Eve, whose "yes" brought redemption to the world. Veith compared Mary to the wife of the first Adam. But he also compared her to Pandora (Mary brought not evil but good of all kinds into the world), and he compared her to Juno, whose beauty paled beside that of Mary. Mary seemed more human than Christ, and her example inspired even the humblest to aspire to being "handmaid of the Lord." Mary most perfectly prayed the *Our Father* with her entire life.

Veith was remarkably well read; but he read all through Roman Catholic eyes. That meant that Veith's critical eye searched constantly for error to be corrected or for a position that might lead to Catholicism. Yet Veith, for all his insistence on using his Roman Catholicism as *the* criterion, took a more openminded approach than most. In one volume, *Die heiligen Berge* (*The Holy Mountains*),[43] he did an impressive beginning study on comparative religion. He analyzed the flood stories found in various religions and saw them as proof of the flood experience in human history. The flood was, for Veith, also proof of original sin; the flood was obviously a punishment for something *Mensch* had done, for God did not punish unless there was guilt.[44] But Veith went beyond simply comparing the fact of flood stories in other religions: he quoted Greek and Roman mythology, Confucius and Buddha, the Upanishads and the Koran. He talked of the unity of religions as evidenced in various stories of the flood. He even managed to consider religions such as Saint

Simonianism.⁴⁵ In the end, he found them all wanting, but the evidence is that he had done considerable reading, especially when one bears in mind his overloaded pastoral schedule. In other volumes, Veith described the Near East and Africa, life on the Ganges and on the Mississippi — all places he had not been. His inaccuracy can be traced less to Veith's active imagination and more to the state of the contemporary works on those subjects. The man brought a rich background of reading to his sermons and made them interesting to his contemporaries, even if they seem a bit quaint today.

Veith as Güntherian

The *Vater Unser* was Veith's first attempt to use Güntherian philosophy and theology as the backdrop for his sermons, but it was not to be the last. Once he had discovered the thought of Anton Günther as a framework that helped him articulate his own thought, he was remarkably consistent throughout the rest of his long career. Even after the Roman condemnation of what were assumed to be Güntherian propositions, Veith remained influenced by Günther's thought. There were few direct attempts to articulate that system, and none after the controversy with Rome had ended in defeat. Yet the influence remained in a subtle but nonetheless real manner. Veith believed firmly that salvation in its fullness was to be found in the Roman Catholic Church;⁴⁶ but the Roman Catholicism of Johann Emanuel Veith was the Roman Catholicism of Anton Günther.

There are some who claim that Veith was not a Güntherian. Most pointedly, there is the argument made by Cardinal Schwarzenberg, when Rome began investigating Veith, which suggested that Veith was a preacher and not a theologian and that, if there were a few traces of the Güntherian heterodoxy, they should be taken lightly. Although politically wise, and effective in stopping the Roman investigation, it was an argument that both patronized the importance of preaching and understated Veith's own philosophical-theological expertise. Veith's sermons were based on his theology, which influenced his choice of subject as well as the way the presented that subject. That theology, by Veith's own admission, was Güntherian.

Some claim that Veith did not clearly understand Günther even though he purported to use his theology. Again, this is simply not true. Günther himself presumed not only that Veith understood him, but that Veith could express the Güntherian system in language and imagery that communicated it better than Günther himself. When a clear and concise exposition of the position of Günther was needed for argument in Rome, it was not Günther but Veith who wrote the deposition. In some ways it would have made more sense to condemn Veith rather than Günther, although Rome was interested in the thought of the theologian, not the sermons of the preacher.

Epistemology is the one area where the label of "Güntherian" is attached to Veith with difficulty. In none of his actual sermons did Veith articulate the semirationalism for which Günther was to be condemned. Yet the tone of what he said indicated that he was convinced that *Wissenschaft* and faith not only supported one another but also that *Wissenschaft* should lead to faith. He did phrase it differently than Günther. Veith stressed the element of "love" more than the intellectual Günther, and he made his point by quoting an unknown source who said that "human things must be known in order to be loved whereas divine things must be loved in order to be known."[47] However, Veith did write and publish works which were, in fact, an exposition of Güntherian epistemology. The most direct outline was not a sermon but a paraphrase of some sermons that he had given. One section was almost a word-for-word reproduction of Günther's discussion of the difference between *Begriff* and *Idee* and the certainty of knowledge that came through *Wissenschaft* which was guided by revelation.[48] If Günther was to be considered a semirationalist, Veith also should be so considered.

The metaphysics and anthropology throughout Veith's works were clearly Güntherian. Veith was a dualist both in seeing God as separate from the world (an acceptable Roman Catholic position) and in seeing a difference between *Geist* and *Natur* in *Mensch* (a position unacceptable to the Roman Catholic hierarchy). Developed from the second dualism was Veith's definition of original sin as the free choice of *Geist* in saying "no" to God, and thereafter the lack of harmony between the two realms. Veith shared Günther's vision of the world of *Natur*, with its pinnacle of consciousness in human reality, as a world that was unfree and blind and only able to reach beyond itself through the realm of *Geist*. For Veith as for Günther, *Mensch* was the mirror image of God and, therefore, the measure of all things.[49] Veith was constantly talking about this world as a vale of tears, as a test and a challenge, as a time of pain and suffering. Certainly that reflected some of Veith's own self-image and his life's experience. But it also reflected Günther's thought that true freedom comes only in the world of *Geist* and that *Mensch* can bring unity back to creation if that freedom is exercised correctly.[50] Knowledge should turn to conscience (*Wissen* to *Gewissen*)[51] and the gospel should become a real part of the world of *Natur* ruled by *Geist* freely choosing the love of God.

Veith was Güntherian and did not change throughout his long life. Veith's works between 1830 and 1848 were all directly influenced by the philosophy of his friend and intellectual mentor. Some of the volumes of sermons are more obviously Güntherian; these include *Die Samariten*,[52] *Die Erweckung des Lazarus*[53] *Mater Dolorosa*,[54] *Die Heilung des Blindgeborenen*.[55] The series of Sunday sermons that Veith published in the pre-1848 period also were heavily Güntherian.[56]

Labels are difficult, especially labels that stem from Roman condemnations. Not to see that Günther had a profound influence on Veith is, however, to be blinded to the fact that Güntherian words, phrases, and concepts run throughout Veith's sermons. Anyone familiar with the writings of Günther could not fail to recognize a follower in Veith, albeit a follower who was not simply a carbon copy of the master. It is fitting to conclude a discussion of Veith's sermons by quoting a prayer composed by Veith himself and published in 1833, when Veith's fervor for Günther's thought was at its peak. It is a paraphrase of the *Our Father*.

> Our Father — not a father of Nature, not a father of the mountains or the trees or the animals; but a father of light, a father of the spiritual [*geistige*] creatures to whom alone you have given the freedom of will, the light of consciousness so that they might be blessed with clarity. O how blessed that creature, which you have blessed with the seal of your image so that it might call out "Father" to you![57]

6
1848

Before 1848, both Günther and Veith published extensively, but neither directed much attention to discussion of the constitution of the state. They accepted the hereditary monarchy as God-given; and they accepted the important role of the monarch within the church. The battle that Hofbauer had fought with the Josephinist bureaucracy had focused on liturgical and homiletic freedom and had, for the most part, been won. The hierarchy, especially the archbishop of Vienna, continued to be appointees of the government, but neither Günther nor Veith, nor anyone else for that matter, questioned the monarch's right to make those appointments. The American concept of separation of church and state was a distant and repugnant idea. Perhaps because Roman Catholicism was *the* religion of the Habsburg lands and Roman Catholicism was, for Veith and Günther and other Roman Catholic thinkers, the epitome of divine revelation, the thought that throne and alter should have totally separate and distinct spheres of influence was simply not entertainable. The spheres were at once different and very much intertwined, as different and intertwined as were the realms of *Geist* and *Natur*.

Günther's and Veith's writings before 1848 reflected their presuppositions about the relationship of state and church. In the dualsim of *Geist* and *Natur*, the state exercised leadership in the realm of *Natur*. The function of the state flowed from an undertanding of the sinfulness of humankind. The task of the state was to work on the redemption of *Mensch* in *Natur*.[1] Sinful *Mensch* needed authority. Günther and Veith spoke of freedom in both of the realms of human existence (*Geist* and *Natur*), but freedom in and through the state was a limited freedom. True freedom came only in the realm of *Geist*, where *Mensch* could choose perfection. Since original sin, that perfection had been lost; through Christ, the second Adam, that perfection was once again possible but must still be freely chosen. Freedom in the state was grounded in this possibility of freedom in choosing perfection in the realm of *Geist*.[2] In practical terms of power, it was the state's prerogative to use force when necessary to enforce the principles of Christian (i.e., Roman Catholic) polity. That force included censorship, which protected society from corrupting ideas, and the right to incarcerate as well as execute enemies of the state, who were also *ipso facto* enemies of the church.[3] The state also had the right and obligation to provide education for its subjects, an education that inculcated truth but did not teach freedom of thought.

Günther and Veith perceived divine agency in the monarchical and hierarchical structure of the Roman Catholic Church, and before 1848 they considered that structure the only model for state government as well. Authority came from above, from Christ, and not from below. There was no room for democracy in church or state, although the role of the monarch in nominating church hierarchy was acceptable to both Günther and Veith. Christianity was all but equated with ordained priesthood.[4] The ordained priesthood was the place of the pastorate of Christ, and error was not possible because of the selection and guidance by Christ of his ministers. Priesthood did not confer privilege on the ordained nor rob the baptized of the dignity of being chosen by Christ,[5] but the service of priesthood (hierarchy) in the Church was to define Truth and to guide the flock on the right path. As the hierarchy was an essential part of the chruch, so was the aristocracy an essential part of the state. In relation to each other, the church was higher than, but not over, the state.[6] The Papal States were a model, based on the Donation of Constantine as a legitimate document.[7] The Roman pontiff, as head of the universal church, should have jurisdiction over the church in every country. The role of the state was legitimate, but subordinate.

The nineteenth-century theologian's affinity for the images of the body of Christ legitimized hierarchy and difference. While a fledgling Unites States was grappling with a system that was based on the principle that all are created equal, but which ignored women and allowed slavery to continue,[8] Veith and Günther were proud of the compassion of a system based on the concept that there is not equality of creation. For Günther and Veith, democracy was a regression, a pagan principle of dangerous pride and individualism. Monarchy was clearly the higher principle because it brought peace and progress through obedience and service. The subject was to obey; the monarch was to serve by promoting and protecting the welfare of his people. The monarch was predestined by God to have those qualities which made him ruler just as the head is that part of the body with capacity to rule. Günther and Veith joined other Viennese of their time in the conviction that a hereditary monarchy was a reflection of divine providence. Like the majority of the Viennese, neither Günther nor Veith was able to blame, dislike, or protest the monarch even when there was evidence of his inadequacies.[9] This was not in any sense an endoresement of absolute monarchy, which implied that the divine right of kings placed them over the church. Rather, it was the centruies-old position that both church and monarch received their authority from above, that each had a proper "sphere of influence," and that both had the mission to make and keep the world Roman Catholic.

Although insisting on the constitutional rights of the Roman Catholic Church within the monarchical principle of state, Veith and Günther were not advocates of a liberal call for constitutional monarchy. To have called Anton Günther or Johann Emanuel Veith liberals before 1848 would have severely stretched the meaing of that word, even in its nineteenth-century clothing.[10] The question can be debated as to whether the events of 1848 in Vienna turned them into Catholic liberals or not.

Revolution and Response

The reforms of Maria Theresa and Joseph II would have unexpected results in the middle of the nineteenth century, long after the august monarchs were buried — one in magnificence and the other in simplicity in the crypt of the Capuchin church in Vienna. Maria Theresa had decreed that her subjects, male and female, between the ages of five and thirteen learn to read. Her churchmen had warned her of the dangers of demagoguery but had been overruled by her instinctive trust in the loyalty of her subjects. Both were right. In the Viennese revolution of 1848, those who had learned the fundamentals of reading without being encouraged to think were indeed susceptible to the blandishments of pamphlets and placards. Yet the Viennese remained loyal to the Habsburgs and convinced of the good will of the monarch. Except for a few extreme radicals, the call for reform in the Habsburg lands was a call for a constitution with a strong monarch. Republicanism was deeply mistrusted.[11] When the sense of being not only Habsburg subjects but Czechs, Poles, Magyars, Slovenes, Croats, or Serbs was beginning to inspire political passion elsewhere, the majority of the Viennese remained fond of Emperor Ferdinand.

Population explosion and Industrial Revolution were slow in coming to Habsburg lands, which remained seventy percent agricultural; but beginnings were made. The growing cities felt the changes the most and were the most vulnerable, with their housing shortages and cries of hunger when the harvest was not large enough to bring adequate foodstuffs. The Viennese, well fed in times of plenty, were uneasy when a poor harvest heralded a very long winter. The 1840s had seen a series of bad harvests, the worst of which was in the fall of 1847. Provincial assemblies might discuss and decide about licenses and tariffs, but it was all in vain if there was not enough food or goods to be shipped.

The government in Vienna did not even seem to recognize the problems that were growing as 1847 turned to 1848. The Metternichian system was still intact: the seventy-three-year-old man was still powerful, although becoming a bit talkative and living more and more in the past. His skill at staying in power was based on playing one faction off against the other, and no successor to him was able or allowed to emerge. The other major power in the state was the minister of finance. Metternich was not on speaking terms with Kolowrat. Communication they deemed neccessary was through written correspondence or through subordinates. Both had access to the emperor, the ebullient Ferdinand, whose mental state made him agreeable to whoever happened to have his ear or whoever might put a paper before him to sign. "It was easy to govern," he was said to have remarked; "the hard job was writing one's name." There were those who thought that the only "man" at court was the Archduchess Sophie, sister-in-law to the reigning emperor and mother to an eighteen-year-old son for whom she had many dreams.[12]

The nobility remained jealous of prerogative and privilege and persisited in their belief that the human race only began with the rank of baron.[13] There was a growing number of wealthy capitalists who were pushing at the gates of power and who were not above buying their way into the ranks of the nobility. There was also a growing number of small business people, the shopkeepers and restaurateurs and owners of small hotels who serviced the growing population. There were the poor but proud intellectuals, the students and their professors and chaplains.[14] The ranks of the intellectuals were being invaded by the sons of blacksmiths and farmers and the sons of Protestant and Jewish mercants, proof to the powers that were that it had been a mistake to educate all those peasants and give liberty to those Protestants and Jews.

And there were all of those former peasants who had wandered to the city in the hope of finding a handsome income — or at least enough to feed themselves and their families. The factories were not much better than the farms they had left behind and in bad years were much worse. In 1848 unemployment was high among the estimated ten thousand factory workers who lived in Vienna. Prostitution, robbery, drunkenness, and murder were not uncommon in these areas of Biedermeier Vienna.[15] The workers were not themselves revolutionaries, in spite of the call of writers like Karl Marx for them to throw off their chains. But they listened to the students, most of whom had not forgotten whence they had come and could speak the language of the hungry.

The few who recognized the explosiveness of the situation and hoped for reform did not look to the church for leadership or inspiration. The church — even the church influenced by the Hofbauer reform, the theology of Günther, and the sermons of Veith — was viewed as the main prop of the old system. Church leaders, appointed through the emperor and his government, did little to contradict that perception. Their intellectual and economic stake in the prevailing order of the day did not allow them to rethink the gospel in any terms that would have radical implications in *this* world.

The year 1848 did not begin with more danger signals than other years. The bad harvest, the unemployment, the search to be free of Habsburg rule had all taken place many times before. If anything, there was reason for optimsim. The outbreak of violence in Poland in 1846 had been contained and promised not to flare up again. There was a revolution brewing in France, but press censorship was still firmly in place in the empire and the "China of Europe" felt safe from that influene. When revolution actually broke out in France in February, there was no great sense of alarm. The French were forever revolting, and the bourgeois king had only limited claim to legitimacy.

News of the revolution in France leaked into Vienna on 29 February. On 3 March, the fiery speech of Kossuth to the Magyar Diet, meeting in Pressburg, denounced the policies of the Habsburg regime and advocated Hungarian nationalism; Pressburg was just over twenty miles from Vienna. For centuries, the Habsburgs had played one part of their empire off against another. The people of Germanic origin had been the settling influence as they found their way to distant parts of the empire to govern or start new homes. In 1848, those Germans themselves looked for freedom from the censorship and control that no longer seemed to be the care of a parent watching out for his children, but a system of oppression and degradation.

On 13 March there was a scuffle in the Herrngasse, where the Diet of Lower Austria was meeting. A policeman was shot and the revolution began. That same day the government issued a proclamation of appeasement with a view to establishing a constitution. The floodgates were opened: poems, pamphlets, and newspapers deluged the city. Ferdinand the Good was exalted as the liberal monarch who would lead the Austrian people out of the wilderness of despair into a constitutional utopia.[16] On 20 March the students published demands in the *Wiener Zeitung*: they wanted freedom of the press and of speech; they wanted academic and religious freedom; they wanted public procedures and universal representation of the people. Those demands were anathema to court and church, but their time had come in other quarters. The focus of the revolution was not the emperor. Rather the cry was to liberate the good Ferdinand from the bonds of his enemies, the bureaucrats, governmental ministers, and, above all, Metternich. The government was weak and unprepared. On 25 April the emperor bestowed a constitution that granted suffrage to the middle class but not to the workers. Metternich quietly slipped away from Vienna.

In the excitement, unemployment increased. Workers used freedom of speech and the press to demand higher wages, a ten-hour day, a restricted number of apprentices assigned to any employer, reduction in the number of women in industry, and more humane treatment. A vacillating and timid government was slow in implementing reforms and slow in putting down dissent; the result was more and louder demands. Students joined with workers, and both joined with the lower middle class in seeking reforms that would be to their benefit.

The church was perceived as a part of the government. On 5 April the mob "serenaded" Archbishop Milde outside his residence. On 6 April the Redemptorists, the order that Clement Maria Hofbauer had brought to the city, were driven from their church, St. Mary's on the Bank. That same night, the Sisters of Penitence were also driven from the city. On 8 April mobs in front of the home of the papal nuncio and the Benedictine monastery demanded that "unuseful" religious houses be suppressed. On 2 May some fifty thousand demonstrated in front of the archbishop's palace, shouting insults and breaking windows. The clergy were attacked for not joinng the national guard, which had been formed to protect the people. There were cries against celibacy, against monasticism, against the privilege of a church that was an integral part of the state.

Demonstrations continued in May and brought more governmental concessions;[17] the radicals seemed to be winning, but Ferdinand's departure from Vienna turned many against them. The peasants lost interest after their dues and services were abolished on 11 April. The more liberal nobility and the conservative professionals, who had originally welcomed the revolution, became increasingly alienated by working-class riots. Karl Marx, who visited Vienna in early September, left convinced of the immaturity of the revolutionary leaders.[18]

It is not our intention to tell the whole story of the Revolution of 1848 in Vienna[19] It is important to note that it brought some reform: freedom to the peasants, freedom of the press, freedom of assembly, freedom of religion. All but the abolition of peasant serfdom werre relatively short-lived as the revolution took a more radical turn by October, when one of the emperor's ministers, Latour, minister of war, was lynched outside his office. By the end of October forces of the military, loyal to the emperor, had surrounded Vienna; they brought law and order and, eventually, a new emperor on 2 December, when Archduchess Sophie's son, Francis Joseph, replaced Ferdinand as the emperor of Austria. The new emperor seemed sympathetic to the demands of his people and granted them a constitution in March 1849, a centralist document which guaranteed a measure of personal freedom and communal emancipation. The constitution recognized freedom of religion and the right to practice it in private (in public if the religion had been recognized by the state).[20] Of course, what had been granted could be rescinded.

The revolutionaries, by and large, despised the church; churchmen, by and large, mistrusted the revolution. Both created straw men to criticize, hate, and fear; as usual with those who seek scapegoats, both despised those of the enemy who challenged their stereotypes even more than the ones who conformed to them. The revolutionaries were unwilling to admit that clerics (*Pfaffen*) could be allies in any sense; the church was an enemy, and it was inconceivable that any churchman might want to help in revolutionary activity. When help was offered, the revolutionaries responded with an intensified anticlerical campaign consisting of slanderous pamphlets, heckling at sermons, and simple ridicule.

The response of the church to the revolution of 1848 was not uniform. the revolution brought fear to some and hope to others, even within the ranks of the Roman hierarchy and clergy. Although one is aware of the limitation of generalization, it is helpful to divide the various responses into four[21] major categories. It is not surprising that the clergy dominate in all four categories, although their attitudes toward the laity's role varied. In all but one group, the clergy were in no way revolting *against* their church, but were interested in assuring freedom *for* their church.[22] This was all the more difficult because the major portion of the Viennese citizenry were mistrustful of the church, which seemed to them a part of the state and therefore in need of reform as well.

The first group was composed of the majority of the bishops in the empire, including the archbishop of Vienna, and the older clergy. Remembering who had selected, trained, and placed them, it is not surprising that they were Josephinist in their view of the state's role in the church. Nor is it surprising that they were mistrusted by the middle and lower classes.[23] To be sure, Archbishop Milde had been the first man of the lower classes to be raised to the episcopate, but his sympathies were not with the class from which he had risen. The Viennese Josephinists were not as radical as their Bohemian counterparts, who wanted the liturgy in the vernacular, the removal of obligatory celibacy from the clergy, and lay administration of church properties.[24] The Josephinist clergy of Vienna took for granted that the legitimate government would take care of all larger matters, including dealing with Rome, and that the role of the church was to support and obey the state while providing people with the opportunity to go to confession and communion, to be baptised, married, and buried according to the rites and rituals established by the Josephinist bureaucracy. For this group the vision of the church was clearly functionary. Church officials were to confine themselves to concern about the clerical dress and recreational habits of priests and religious.[25] Although this group of Viennese clergy could not be accused of ultramontanism, they were in full agreement with the Roman distaste for democracy within or outside the church, and they certainly had no use for freedom of religion, of the press, or of assembly. Therefore, within the church there was to be no compromise with the revolutionary principles. Even should freedoms be allowed by the monarch, those freedoms had no place within the church itself, where Truth and authority came from divine revelation funneled through a hierarchy.[26] Authority knew best and subjects needed to be protected from polluting doctrines, as they were obviously not mature enough to be able accurately to distinguish between right and wrong.[27] These people found the revolution distasteful and retreated into silence, sometimes leaving Vienna for country estates to wait out the storm.

The second clerical response to the revolution came from a group of younger clergy influenced by Clement Maria Hofbauer. They were clearly ultramontane and wanted nothing to do with the revolutionary freedoms except freedom of the church from the state. This did not translate into freedom *inside* the church. These people did not want to destroy the monarchy or even establish a constituitonal one. They looked to a partnership with the monarchy. This was the group that eventually gained the most from the events of 1848.[28] This group spearheaded the move to a concordat with Rome which recognized the pope as head of the Catholic Church in Austria and as having the right to negotiate as an equal to the emperor.[29] Their major spokesman was Joseph Rauscher, who had been the tutor of the young Francis Joseph and was to become archbishop of Vienna in 1853. The group included most of the Redemptorist congregation, which claimed direct descent from Hofbauer and which received the brunt of the anti-Catholicism of the revolutionary forces.

The third group was a radical element, led by clergy who were suspended by their bishops. They formed the core of the movement known as German Catholicism. The movement appealed strongly to the working class, which was largely ignored by the other groups.[30] The German Catholics wanted a democratic church, including the election of bishops and pastors by the people and freedom from any Roman control. Their program included the suppression of obligatory celibacy, the abolition of monasticism in all its forms, and the end of Latin in the liturgy. They opposed auricular confession and indulgences for the remission of sin. Their numbers were never large, although the suspended Silesian priest Johannes Ronge[31] was able to draw a large crowd when he spoke in Vienna in August and September of 1848. Most of the convinced German Catholics eventually became Protestants, many joining the Old Catholics after the first Vatican Council. There was a strong emphasis on lay participation at the upper levels in this group.

Needless to say, the first two groups were alarmed by any tendency toward German Catholicism and were unfavorably disposed to anyone whom they suspected of this tendency. Their attitude, however, was to ignore the German Catholics as much as possible, in the conviction that any attention would only serve to make them more important than they were. It was Johann Emanuel Veith who, in August and September 1848, took on the German Catholics in a series of sermons expounding the Roman Catholic faith.[32]

The fourth response of the Roman Catholic Church to the revolution came from the group who came later to be called Güntherians.[33] Günther's *Mensch*-centered thought made this group more open to the ideas of the revolution, even while condemning many of the revolution's principles. This group of young clergy and laity saw the principles of the revolution, albeit in modified form, as a possibility both for freedom of the church from state control and for freedom within the church itself. It was this group that had some credibility with the revolutionaries; Güntherians tried to walk a very thin line between the autocracy hated by the revolutionaries and the democracy that was anathema to other churchmen and the crown.

Revolutionary disdain was tolerable; one simply used the revolutionaries' own arguments for freedom to demand a voice for the church's position.

Dealing with the other churchmen proved much more difficult. The Güntherians lost credibility with the church and state authorities who returned to power after the Revolution of 1848 ended.[34] They lost credibility because they had attempted to come to terms with the principles of the revolution and the revolutionaries.

Güntherian epistemology was optimistc about the ability of free discussion and consideration to grasp and affirm the truths of Roman Catholicism. Although not enthusiastic supporters, they were not intimidated by the concepts of freedom of religion, conscience, and press, for they were convinced that Truth would conquer. The Güntherians were interested in using the freedoms espoused by the revolution, not only for the advantage of the church structure but also for the Truth that they were convinced would shine through. They feared the chaos democracy seemed to threaten, but rolled up their sleeves and worked with the world that presented itself to them. They did not retreat to country estates to wait out the storm. Their conviction that the gospel had to be preached anew extended to entering into the world of the revolution and harnessing it for the beliefs that they held. Their political activities were to take two directions: an organization of the clergy and an organization of the laity. The presence of Günther and Veith were essential to these activities.

Güntherians and the Revolution

Archbishop Milde of Vienna was not interested in an organization of his priests, even if the climate indicated that such an organization could do much to combat the rampant anticlericalism. Priests should not mix in politics, opined the aging archbishop, and a gathering of clergy looked suspiciously like politics to him. In spite of his disapproval, and claiming the right and duty to be responsible citizens as well as obedient clergy, a small group of younger clergy did come together on 17 April in the lecture room of the Pastoral Theological Institute at the University of Vienna under the leadership of William Gärtner.[35] The younger clergy affirmed their right to meet and claimed that the church could only profit from freedom, for the truth of Catholicism would become self evident.[36] Also in April, Sebastian Brunner began publishing his newspaper for faith, knowledge, freedom and law in the Catholic Church (*Wiener Kirchenzeitung für Glauben, Wissen, Freiheit, und Gesetz in der Katholischen Kirche*)[37] which was to be a Catholic voice in the flood of newspapers and handbills that had sprung up since freedom of the press had been granted. Co-operation from Milde was not forthcoming. Answering the request from younger clergy to form groups to read and discuss, Milde granted permission to read but not to discuss. Answering the request for the establishment of a Catholic journal, Milde agreed, but he wanted to see the articles three years in advance. Priests, according to Milde, were to pray to God and not presume to judge, praise, or blame in earthly affairs, which would exceed the limits of the priestly calling. A priest was not to mix in the affairs of this world but was to concentrate on the next.[38] Milde did not understand that his own subservience to Josephinist principles and the status quo, even though proclaimed only by silence, could be construed as a political statement even more powerful than the literary and hortative efforts of his younger clergy.

The Güntherians were not to be deterred, however. Brunner's newspaper was a constant thorn in the side of the slower-moving bishops and clergy as well as of the revolutionaries. The Güntherians found voice in Brunner's paper, and Brunner himself was the most vocal. He called for nothing less than the dismantling of Josephinism. He insisted that the church administer itself and its properties, enjoy freedom to communicate and to organize, and be free from state services; and he demanded the protection of the revolution in exercising those freedoms.[39] But Brunner did not stop there. He called for diocesan synods, meetings of priests to discuss with their bishop the issues of the times and the affairs of the church. These diocesan synods had a long history in the Western church and had only fallen into disuse with the centralization of church and state government and state or Roman control of local dioceses.[40] When the younger clergy called for a plenary session of all the clergy of the archdiocese on 25 May, Milde forbade the meeting as against church law.[41] Brunner continued to make demands. He required some voice, at least by the clergy, in the selection if not in the actual election of bishops. Brunner wanted ecclesiastical trials of clerics to be public, demanded a legalization of the situation of assistant pastors, insisted that there was a difference between the allegiance a priest owed his bishop in church affairs (where he had sworn obedience) and situations that concerned issues for the citizen (in which the bishop had no right to expect obedience).

Milde again reminded his clergy to pray, to wear clerical garb,[42] and to stay out of politics; and then he left for his country estate at Kranichberg. Brunner might have accepted the revolution's definition of citizen and the separation of church membership from citizenship, but Milde could see in these ideas only rebellion against legitimate authority. Brunner was tolerated because the situation was too explosive to move against him, but his fiery and polemical style won him few converts and created a situation in which the one sure way to insure episcopal opposition to a position was to have Sebastian Brunner espouse it. Eventually there were meetings of the German bishops in Würzburg and of the Austrian bishops is Vienna. Brunner had the satisfaction of having his newspaper declared the official organ of the assembly of the Vienna clergy, but the assembly never met.

The organization of the laity was another matter. The clerical church had always seen a proper sphere for laity as involvement in the politics of this world, although they might be constantly urged not to become tainted by that involvement. There were numerous precedents for organizations of the laity in church history, the most immediate example being the organization of the Pius Union (*Piusverein*) in Mainz during March of 1848.[43] Perhaps because of their *Mensch*-centered theology and perhaps simply because of their pragmatic instincts, the Güntherians became active in an attempt to include the laity. Johann Emanuel Veith was one of the first to see the possibilities offered by the new freedoms, particularly the freedom of assembly. Veith did not want to step back and let the vacuum of power, left by the exit of the emperor's government and the archbishop of Vienna, be filled by anti-Catholics.

An active writer and popular preacher and a known presence among the educated Catholic laity of his day, Veith joined with several other Jewish converts to Catholicism in founding the Catholic Union for Faith, Freedom, and Correct Behavior (*Katholikenverein für Glaube, Freiheit, und Gesittung*) during late May and early June 1848. The union was led by laity, although clergy (not more than three at a time) could play an official role in the lower levels of the organization. The head of the organization was I. G. Schwarz.[44] The founding of the Catholic Union was not noticed immediately by the secular press, but it was soon excoriated as an insidious work of the clergy (*Pfaffen*) trying to return the revolution to the days of the old empire. Perhaps owing to a pragmatic attempt to counter these accusations, perhaps owing to genuine conviction, perhaps owing to the American influence of Schwarz, the leadership of the union protested that their church could live under any form of government.[45] Reading that, church hierarchical leadership was strengthened in its conviction that the Güntherians and the Catholic Union could only have been founded to support the revolution. Not even the fact that Cardinal Schwarzenberg joined as an ordinary member of the Catholic Union could dissuade the hierarchy from that conviction.[46]

There could be no doubt that the Catholic Union was Güntherian. Membership was heavily from those who were at least familiar with and favorable to the positions of Günther. At one of the first meetings, an attempt was made to warn of the dangers of philosophy to religion. A Güntherian replied by defending philosophy, whose task it was to prove the truth of Christianity from the depths of human consciousness. The assembly erupted in applause.[47]

The constitution of the Catholic Union concentrated on religious, political, and humane goals. Religiously, it was a Roman Catholic organization, open only to Roman Catholics[48] and founded to make certain that their belief in the rightness of the Roman Catholic Church would not be lost in indifferentism that could result from the freedom of religion. They explicitly stated, however, their own respect for those who believed differently. Politically, the organization was to work for the realization of Roman Catholic priniples in the public sphere, for they wanted their convictions to be mirrored in the laws of the land. The humane goals of the Catholic Union were to express gospel love in social works, especially in helping those who were neglected, young, or proletarian. Members would try to be available when their neighbors were in need; the wealthier members promised to establish small savings banks for workers and apprentices.

In practice, membership in the Catholic Union was mostly from the middle class who accepted the constitutional monarchy decreed by the government. Decisions were by majority vote. The union supported the biweekly publication entitled *Aufwärts* (*Upwards!*), which began publication on 5 July, 1848, and appeared under Veith's editorship in thirty editions until 14 October, when it ceased publication.[49] *Aufwärts* was not to speak out directy in political matters or espouse a certain political party, but it was to discuss the broader social and religious context in which political decisions should be made.[50] When *Aufwärts* proved a bit too intellectual for the majority of the union members, a second publication was added, *Der österreichische Volksfreund*, which appeared only once in 1848, resumed a weekly publication in January 1849, and continued to appear until 1875. But the Catholic Union had changed by then, and the *Volksfreund* concentrated on personal piety.

When the emperor's troops invaded Vienna and brought an end to freedom of assembly, there were some two thousand members of the Catholic Union in ten branches.[51] There were also affiliate groups in Styria, Salzburg, Tirol, Bohemia, and Moravia.[52] Members of the union had sent petitions to Milde to return to Vienna, had protested the taking of church goods and the closing of cloisters, and had demanded a free church within a constitutional state. In a church in which lay organization was viewed skeptically, it was a significant beginning.

From the brief description of the Catholic Union, it is clear that Johann Emanuel Veith was very active during the time of the revolution. In fact, he was so visible that Milde was afraid that others would follow his example and sent him a letter of fraternal warning in June of 1848.[53] He was one of the founding fathers of the union and became the editor of both the publications that were organs of the Catholic Union (*Aufwärts* and *Der österreichische Volksfreund*). Veith was present in Vienna throughout 1848 and appeared here and there as a minor character in the greater drama. Veith is the preacher who antagonized some of the far left and on occasion needed the protection of the National Guard when he ascended the pulpit.[54] He was a witness to the lynching of Latour and preached at the minister's memorial service on 28 March, 1849.[55] On 16 November, the night before he died, the condemned leader of the October revolution, Wenzel Messenhauser, sent for Veith to discuss the meaning of life and death and the existence of God.[56]

Since Veith and the other Güntherians remained active during the revolution and attempted to use the revolutionary principles to their own advantage, there is the temptation among historians to consider them friendly, or at least neutral, to the revolution. Some, partly because of events after the revolution was suppressed, have even called the Güntherians, and especially Günther and Veith, liberals.[57] Although the simple fact that they remained active in Vienna throughout the revolution might convey the impression that they were liberals, and one could then search their writings for proof of such a label, a close examination of Veith's preaching and writing and Günther's writing will not allow such an appraisal to stand.

On 10 March 1848, Veith began a series of Lenten sermons on Psalm 51[58] in the Church Am Hof, where he had lived when he first left the Redemptorists and where he was a frequent preacher. Veith used the same psalm as the basis for the Lenten sermons in Prague in 1852.[59] The Prague sermons were published in 1853, and in the preface Veith mentioned that it was a completely new consideration of that psalm and that the notes on the first series of sermons had been lost. That was just as well, wrote Veith, for the events in Vienna at that time led to so great a confusion of minds and created the need for so many digressions to comment on the moods and aberrations that the treatment of the subject matter itself was scarcely possible.[60]

Veith's notes on those 1848 sermons have not surfaced to date. A series of handwritten copies of the sermons, however, written either while Veith preached or shortly thereafter, have surfaced.[61] These sermons and a transcript of the sermon preached at the memorial service for Latour[62] provide clear insight into Veith's views on the revolution. The hearer of these sermons would have been hard put to label Veith a liberal.

The first sermon was delivered on 10 March, the second on 12 March, both before any revolutionary activity had taken place in Vienna but after the events in Paris and Pressburg. Veith showed a knowledge of what happened in Paris[63] but did not seem to know of the events in Pressburg. He was familiar with the principles of the Enlightenment and began his series with an attack on those principles. Preaching on the verse, "Have mercy on me, O God, in your great mercy," Veith went right to the heart of what he thought was wrong with the revolutionary creed. Veith saw *Mensch* as sinful creature and criticized the Enlightenment's blindness to that simple fact. The business of human life was, for Veith, the business of salvation; and salvation had to do with sin and forgiveness and the attainment of heaven, not with heaven on earth. Veith was, as always, Güntherian, presuming the enemy was pantheism. Self-knowledge led to knowledge of oneself as sinful creature and God as redeeming other. In order to believe in oneself, one had to believe in God.

It is not times that change, but *we* change, claimed Veith. One generation follows the next, and before the one exits a new one enters with other thoughts and perceptions. And every age has a dark side (*faulen Fleck*), a touch of hubris. Pointing to his own time, Veith claimed that many accused it of being preoccupied with cotton and iron and steel, farming and manufacturing, in short, with materialism. But said Veith, that was pure slander. Were not such things as "National Spirit," and "Freedom from Superstition," and "Common Kingdom and Progress" expressions that were spiritual?[65] Veith was at his sarcastic best as he compared the suppression of processions with the cross to the lines of men parading with flags to political worship services. It was, said Veith, a time when everything was stirred up and questioned and no firm ground was left. He bemoaned the fact that so much of the past was viewed simply as old furniture to be broken up and thrown in the fire.

In the opening words of his first Lenten sermon for 1848, Veith threw down the gauntlet to those who welcomed the revolution. The hearer of those first words expected a political treaties (which, in fact, he did get). But Veith quickly issued a disclaimer that he was to issue time and again, but which he never succeeded in following.[65] Veith never perceived his position as political; he did not consider a flight to the "salvation of the soul" as itself a political position. The preacher, said Veith, is the voice of one crying in the desert, "Make straight the way of the Lord!" Veith sought spiritual reality that was outside the realm of cotton and iron and steel.

That which was worse than human death was sin, and sin meant living outside the pleasure of God, not recognizing that one is a sinful creature. Veith joined with Luther[66] in proclaiming an awful God of love who could only love his creatures, but who demanded that they recognize that *He* was God and not they. Veith's Lenten sermons for 1848 were clearly intended to be an exposition of Güntherian thought which saw pantheism as the main enemy. Veith planned a philosophic exposition of sin and redemption with examples from the contemporary situation as support for his Güntherian thought. The vehicle for discussion was to be the psalms of David, and the great king was to be an example of God's demand and God's mercy. David, who sinned more boldly than most when he seduced Bathsheba and arranged that her husband, Uriah, and his men be killed so his sin would go undetected, was also brought to a knowledge of his sinfulness through the prophet Nathan. David was redeemed not through his own power but through his recognizing his sin and throwing himself on the mercy of God. The sinner must want mercy, not justice, and therefore must admit, "against you alone, O God, have I sinned."

In the two sermons before the revolution spread to Vienna, Veith showed his ridicule and disdain through sarcasm: David was a real king who did not have to worry about representatives in government or constitutions (*Kammern und Constitution*). Nor was Veith above direct contradiction of revolutionary principles. Veith did not favor freedom of the press, believing that those who sought it could not truly know *Mensch*.[67] He compared the press censor to human conscience, which was a necessary element and, indeed, the voice of God within. Freedom is empty if it allowed all things; indeed, it is poison, and the poison of Jean Jacques Rousseau had spread throughout humanity— the most recent outbreak of the fever having occurred on 23 February in

Paris.[68] There is hope if only the contemporary world will admit its sinfulness, yet that is one of the most difficult things for anyone to do. Witness David, who hid from his own sin for so long and did not recognize it until the prophet Nathan appeared. Even then, David could not recognize it until Nathan abandoned all subtlety and directly accused David of sinning. Veith, aware that prophets are more often beheaded than believed, still felt the call to be a prophet to his age. But his prophecy was not a liberal one, either for the church or for the state.

By the time of his third sermon, on 17 March, the pace of events in Vienna had begun to escalate. Students and working class had rioted on 13 and 14 March. Veith mentioned "such events that have not taken place in many years" but once again insisted that "that does not belong here—it is not my task to discourse on political events."[69] Veith simply told the story of a Spanish professor who, after long years of political imprisonment, returned to the exact place where he had left off in his lectures, not once mentioning the events of the intervening years. Veith continued his sermons on the *Miserere*, but was not successful in ignoring outside events.

Veith's sermons reveal a man who was deeply involved with the times and events around him. He was a product of the old society and still preferred the old order, but he began to realize that the old order was passing. In the midst of all the events that created confusion in his life, he never abandoned his belief that the old values were the best. But he did recognize that one could not simply sit back. His major concern was for the Catholic Church, which he equated with the kingdom of God.[70] His skepticism about the state's ability to preserve and protect that kingdom was colored by his experience of Josephinism as seen through the eyes of Hofbauer. He hated the revolution and the principles for which it stood, but he saw a chance for true freedom in using the principles of the revolution (freedom of press, freedom of religion, representative government) as a means of securing the position of the Roman Church. Since Truth is to be found in the Catholic Church, the prerogatives of that church need to be preserved. The church is the "upholder of humanity, of morals and human rights, the support of the inner life which has to go through the Red Sea but whose Truth is eternal."[71] The form of the church has been established by Christ and will not change. "We are all brothers until we approach the foot of the altar."[72] Pope, bishops, and priests are the teaching and ruling church; the laity, even when organized in the Catholic Union, are the listening and following part of the church. Revelation and authority are from God and given to the *head*, not to the feet. There are, said Veith, too many feet trying to be rulers these days.[73]

After the announcement that the emperor's government was ready to grant a constitution, Veith's position on the form of state government softened. The church could exist in any form of state government as long as freedom (i.e., for the church) was protected. In fact, Veith actually announced that the best form for the church was the constitutional government, and the worst was absolutism.[74] Veith also admitted that everyone who was influenced by what a state did should have some say in how that state was governed, but he hastened to add that the experts should have the final say. The state should be Christian; anything less would have been unthinkable to any preacher in nineteenth-century Vienna. Consequently, the state is to protect Christian marriage and family, to ensure true freedom (which is not freedom from law but freedom to say "yes" to God and the gospel), to protect the rights guaranteed in the gospel, and to promote art, science, and education. In general, the state is to safeguard the welfare of its citizens so they can live through this life which is a valley of tears and achieve heaven.[75] It is the state and not the church that has the duty to use force when necessary for the preservation of Christian order on *this* side of heaven.[76] Of course, it is the church that defines the Christian order.

One should not expect consistency from the pulpit even in the best of times. The preacher often contradicts himself by different emphases or issues and, in a short space of time, is unable fully to clarify. Veith's positive comments about constitutionalism need balance from his basic skepticism about the ability of a people to govern itself with representatives selected from below. "In my stupidity, I did not realize that the highest good is the constitutional state!" commented Veith in what must have been very thinly veiled sarcasm.[77] Veith was not pleased with all of the celebration about constitution that he witnessed in 1848, but he did not dare criticize too loudly. He feared the pagan republicans and atheistic socialists and communists, and he attempted to salvage as much as possible from the situation. Therefore, he threw in his lot with the constitutional monarchists, in part because the monarchy itself seemed to agree, but even more to prevent the chaos he was convinced would overwhelm the state if more radical revolutionaries should win the day. David was directly responsible to Jehovah; by implication so was Ferdinand. Both ruler and ruled, in a truly Christian state, had their positions from God. "Three times woe to that people who laid hands on its sovereign!"[78]

The crucial issue for Veith was sin, and he saw sin most potent in the denial of God. He did not perceive poverty or wealth in themselves as sinful unless they hampered the ability of the church to proclaim the gospel, a gospel that accepted the present order of the world and did not preach revolution. Veith needed little in life beyond his books and his writing materials. It was hard for him to understand why others could not be content where they were. Although personally not interested in "this world's goods," Veith saw no gospel prohibition of luxury; "without it where would the workers be?" From there he proceeded to talk about the true freedom found in self-control and self-denial.[79] Veith's was a prime example of the attitude of most Roman Catholic churchmen until the time of Leo XIII.[80] It was, in part, a romantic yearning for the medieval world in which "everyone had a place in society—when the various estates of society were organically divided; when it was not so much majority rule as the following of Truth; when obedience came not because the people (*das Volk*) were enslaved or gagged but because they choose to obey in freedom and joy and love."[81]

On the other hand, Veith criticized those who only wanted *useful* information, pointing to the contemporary ridicule of Copernicus and Columbus as examples of why the mind should be allowed to soar.[82] Life, according to Veith, should not be all *Tabakhandel* (tobacco-selling or shopkeeping) but should also be poetry and music and the worship of God, although for the worship of God one should be sure to select worthy German music and not the frivolous tones of a Donizetti.[83]

Veith was no friend of capitalism. The best state is the true Christian state. Veith's vision of knights and chivalry and joyful serfs could be disputed, but it was how he saw the world of the past. He contrasted that with the world he lived in and his contemporaries came up short: "Today's knights are capitalists and their serfs are factory workers. The fight for life and death is competition based on luck or fashion. When a capitalist falls, so do thousands of workers."[84] The railroad had created devastation both for the towns near it and far from it; all this production and transportaiton of goods had made a hundred thousand times more goods than humankind could possibly use.[85] However, Veith did not criticize capitalism on economic as much as on spiritual grounds. What he bemoaned was that the workers were abandoning the simple life. "Why even as little as thirty years ago, the workers had a simple life and a simple faith. They went with Christ and Mary to Calvary and prepared for paradise after death and lived peacefully and quietly here." The family was being destroyed by the removal of work to factories away from the home. The ideas of freedom and equality were making people unhappy and discontent. "Where freedom is, is joy; where joy is, is peace."[87] The message is that the truly spiritual person does not need to rebel. Humankind needs a heaven and hell on the other side of death; otherwise it would be intolerable for the poor workers[88] who cannot expect to find more than spiritual consolation in the midst of his vale of tears. Veith was no friend of the revolution. True freedom and true joy were only possible in the realm of self-consciousness, in the realm of *Geist*.

Like every preacher, Veith tried to explain the events of his day in a way that would make his hearers more aware of what he was convinced the gospel meant. Like every preacher, those attempts at relevance could be easily misunderstood, especially when taken out of context. No one escaped Veith's praise—but no one escaped his blame either. At one point, Veith seemed to support public trials and open courtrooms; then he went on to a discourse on the importance of God's law and to assert that if fear of God disappears, none of the constitutional rights will have any meaning. If one does not believe in God, there is no foundation for oath or marriage or holiness. Veith criticized humanism and communism and could see no value in any system that did not include God. Veith often used asides that seemed to approve of what was happening in Vienna, but the asides were only that. If he referred to Uriah as a "courageous, steadfast man, a real member of the National Guard,"[90] he also warned against a generation that believed only *now* could humankind begin to live. "What is a people without history? A people without the nobility had none of the radiance of history."[91] If Veith insisted that the encouragement of nationalism was good and that, after all, "Christianity had its actual seat among the Germans as the preservers of civilization."[92] it must also be remembered that it was not only a national German kingdom (*Reich*), but also a *holy* German kingdom, founded on Christianity. Veith greeted the black, red, and gold tricolor of the German nation that flew from the tower of St. Stephan's Cathedral, but he also reminded his listeners that black represented guilt, death, sorrow, and the old Adam, as well as faith that cannot see; that red represented life, joy, and hope as well as bloodshed in battle; that gold represented true indestructibility, which is rooted in the new Adam and is eternal love more than human happiness.

Veith, in the final analysis, was a church man with a spiritual message that he was convinced transcended all of the worry and rhetoric about freedom of the press, of religion, or of political system. The man who did not care a thing for this world's possessions could not be sympathetic with workers or students who wanted to better their this-worldly lot. It was not only irrelevant; it was dangerous, for it ran the risk of republicanism or socialism or communism, all of which denied the divine existence and the divine order and gave witness to the sinfulness of *Mensch*, who would not let God be God. Veith told a long story about a professor who could not resist wine and whose students, having found out his weakness, cluttered his way with filled wine glasses. The professor never made it to class until he was drunk and once there was unable to lecture. "Many cannot pass up a glass of wine; they give in to every temptation; they no longer search for God— that is the sad truth that every preacher should proclaim but dares not because he would heap the hatred of the world on himself."[93]

It was only in the Roman Catholic Church that one could still find the "taste [*Geschmack*] for the divine" as it should truly be discovered. The Byzantine Empire's absolutism (could Veith have been thinking of the Josephinists when he spoke of Constantinople?) and the Protestant priesthood of all believers, which was dangerously close to communism, were inadequate. The Roman Catholic Church is constitutional, democratic, and monarchical. It is constitutional in that there is a law of God that all must follow, even popes, bishops, and priests; in that truths and dogmas could only be declared with all the bishops gathered in council;[94] and in that the pope was freely elected. The Roman Catholic Church is democratic in that all are alike before the throne of God; therefore, in the church there are no nobility nor beggars, but only one rebirth in Jesus Christ through the Holy Spirit. The Roman Catholic Church is also monarchical because there is but one faith, one hope, one grace, one spirit and one love, and one head; therefore there is one head as absolute ruler who is rightly called "Holy Father."[95]

It is not surprising that Veith contradicted himself in the midst of very difficult and confusing times. What is clear from reading all of Veith's sermons is that he was not a friend of the revolution. He did accept a constitutional monarchy, but that was less out of conviction that it was the best form of state and more out of a conviction that the form of the state did not concern him. If the monarch wished to grant a constitution, then Veith would work within it and work against those who were a threat to that which he believed to be of real importance: the Roman Catholic Church as the protector and proclaimer of the spiritual message of sin and punishment, reconciliation and resurrection, not in this world but in the world where the corruption of sin and death would be no more. As long as the rights of the Roman Catholic Church were guaranteed and protected (and to this extent Veith was a constitutionalist), the form of the state did not matter. Veith would remain an obedient subject.[96]

The only other works of Veith from 1848 are preserved in the journals of the Catholic Union. With the very first issue of *Aufwärts*, the clearest picture of the concerns of Veith at the time surfaced. There were articles on "The State and the Catholic Church," "The Meaning of Freedom of Religion and of Education," "The Political Principles of the Catholic Church," "The Catholic in Relationship to Authority and Freedom," and several articles about the rising sense of German nationalism, espousing the position that Vienna should become the capital of a greater Germany (*Grossdeutschland*). *Aufwärts* was also filled with small quotations and anecdotes designed to bring home to the reader points and perspectives on the events of the time. One such vignette was a supposed quotation from Goethe on "The True Liberal"[97] who never resorted to violence (*Feuer und Schwert*) because violence will spoil the good that is being espoused; the liberal is satisfied, in this imperfect world, to continue patiently the peaceful struggle until times and conditions are more favorable.

In the Saturday, 15 July, issue of *Aufwärts* appeared the first in a series of articles by Veith that were essentially a paraphrase of the Acts of the Apostles in the New Testament. Amidst the stories of faith and bravery, the theme of obedience is the dominant motif behind the points Veith made. Paul, the great apostle to the Gentiles who recognized that the gospel must be preached not only to Jews but also to Gentiles, found legitimacy in his mission through the approval of Peter. "In fact," wrote Veith, "without the agreement of Peter, even the faith of a Paul would have been denied to the church. It is the true faith of Christ from above, protected by the successors of the Peter who was also chosen from above, that is the Truth that humankind must seek and obey."[98] Again, Veith rejected any thought of a democratic majority when it came to the church or to *Glaube*. He found particularly repugnant the idea that a new humanitarianism should arise from the struggles of Roman Catholics against Protestants, replacing even Roman Catholicism with a higher synthesis.[99] The Truth of Christ is eternal and absolute and Roman Catholic. In anecdote and humor, in stories of saints and sinners, Veith hammered home the conviction that real freedom comes in the discovery of the Unseen and Eternal and *not* in this visible world which is passing away.[100]

What of Anton Günther during the eventful days of 1848? Did the revolution affect him and his thought? There are those who claim that Günther helped establish the basis for democracy with its principle of majority rule, the basis for the enfranchisement of all voters, the basis for the separation of church and state, and the theoretical framework for the involvement of the laity in the workings of the church. Günther, for some, was the great nineteenth-century prophet who foresaw the theology of Vatican Council II.[101]

In fact, Günther was all but oblivious to events around him. There is little evidence that his daily schedule varied much, that the great debates of those days had any influence on his plodding academic existence. He stayed in Vienna, except for a brief vacation to Rodann in the country home of Greif, where he wrote the one article that he published in *Aufwärts* in a six-part series. In fact, even his friends and followers were a little peevish about the academic distance of their leader. In a letter to Peter Knoodt, Ludwig Croy commented on Günther during the October bombing of Vienna. "Günther did not even know that the city was being bombed, but thought that it was outside the city near the Danube. He sat in his academic chair, as naive as always."[102] When he did respond to the issues of the times, Günther was convinced that if all sides would recognize his contrapositional dualism, then all would be well.

The six-part article by Günther in *Aufwärts* was the only writing of Günther from 1848 that even purported to deal with the issues of the revolution.[103] Although it has been interpreted as a dramatic affirmation of revolutionary principles, a close reading makes it hard to believe that it is much more than a short restatement of Günther's system. The basic question is: What is man? The basic answer is a synthesis of *Geist* and *Natur*, and the synthesis does not dissolve the opposites but rather somehow unites them in a bipolar entity that is the mirror image of God. Both realms have sovereignty in their spheres of influence, and one cannot dominate the other without peril to true humanness. Günther's anthropology, with its dualism and mutualism, provided the basis for Günther's view of the church and state.

Much of the *Aufwärts* article was refutation of wrong ideas, most of which had pantheism as the root of their evil. Hegel was wrong[104] in seeing the state as the general principle which included religion, art, and science as subordinate particulars. Such thought had led to Protestant subservience of church to state as well as to royal absolutism even in Roman Catholic lands. However, to talk of the separation of church and state was as nonsensical as to speak of the separation of *Natur* and *Geist*.[105] The church and the state are both empowered by God in their spheres of influence: the state in the realm of *Natur*, where freedom must be created, and the church in the realm of *Geist*, where grace from above brought Truth.

Günther was clear that his concept of freedom was *not* the freedom advocated by the revolution. Günther's use of the word "freedom" did not imply anything more than the conservative Christian conviction that *Mensch* must remain free for the glory of God and that the freedom was to say "yes" or "no" to God as creator and other. Günther admitted that there was no power on earth or in heaven that could force *Mensch* to say either the "yes" or the "no" to God.[106] The state could, and indeed should, use force to create an environment where that freedom would be encouraged toward the "yes." The church could, and indeed should, preach the Truth of the gospel to all the peoples of the world who, if they listened to the conscience that is the voice of God within them, would also be moved to say that "yes" to God.

Church and state are not *independent* but *interdependent*. They are set by God, not only next to each other but also interwined with each other[107] Like the marriage of true Christian man and woman, they become two in one flesh; neither is ruler and neither is slave.[108] The monarchical-hierarchical form of government in the church comes from above and will not change. Under Peter and only under Peter is the one and true church of Christ to be found. As all humankind is descendant from the one Adam, so all of humankind can find salvation in the one church that preaches the one redemption for the entire human race through the second Adam.[109]

There was only one hint of development in Günther's thought in the *Aufwärts* article: there was a hedged statement that, even though it is clear that the hierarchical-monarchical form of government is the will of Christ for his church, it does not therefore follow that it is necessarily the ideal or only form for every other construction in society.[110] Günther admitted that it is the prerogative of humankind as individuals (i.e., in the realm of *Begriff* and *Natur*) to decide the shape of their earthly life or the form of their society, and to allow voting about the conditions of the common life and business practices.[111] Yet, majority rule can never have a place in the realm of *Idee*. Truth is truth whether the majority says so or not. Copernicus was right even though all of his contemporaries thought him wrong.[112] In short, what did it matter if the herring dealer decided to sell his fish in this manner or that?[113] It would not affect *true* freedom one way or the other.

To fellow Roman Catholic clergy, Anton Günther and Johann Emanuel Veith were identified with the revolutionary movement of 1848 and were labeled with the hated term "liberal." Later historians, more positively inclined to the liberal label, concurred with that epithet applied to the group of men who found their inspiration in the thought of Anton Günther. It is a matter of definition. The Güntherians, including Veith, stayed in Vienna during the difficult days of 1848. If the liberal label refers to the simple fact of dealing with "the enemy," then Günther, Veith, and the other men of their circle were indeed deserving of that title. And for the churchmen who gained control in Vienna and in Rome after the death of the revolution, this was enough.

The main body of the revolutionaries, however, never considered the Güntherians liberals. If anything, they considered them reactionaries because of their avid insistence on obedience to lawful authority within church and state. The Güntherians entered into dialogue with their opponents and in so doing adopted the language and categories of those whom they wished to convince. That seemed to be liberalism to churchmen unwilling to admit that any dialogue was either possible or desirable. But if they and the revolutionaries used a similar vocabulary, the words took on a different meaning on the lips of a Veith or a Günther. "Freedom" could only mean the possibility of a "yes" or "no" to God. "Constitution" could only mean the God-given balance between church and state that had, in the minds of the Hofbauer followers, been compromised by Josephinism as well as by the principles of the French Revolution. This was not a liberalism that would be recognized as such by any but the most reactionary. Only Sebastian Brunner, who was a close friend of Veith's but who knew little Güntherian theology, called for reforms within the church beyond the anti-Josephinism of the Hofbauer circle.

Yet there was a another side to the writing and preaching of Günther and Veith, a side that could be interpreted differently from the way Veith or Günther might have interpreted it. There were conclusions implicit in their thought that Günther and Veith did not reach, but which others, especially those looking backwards, might choose to pursue. Veith, more than Günther, is open to a variety of interpretations. He criticized a liberalism that included pluralism because then everyone would be right, including the one who was an absolutist.[114] He meant to preach an absolute obedience to Christ and the church as the representative of Christ, but his talk of freedom, even a spiritual freedom, led others to hear support for the revolution itself. Veith admitted that "the times are changing and we are moving forward; it could not remain the same and I will not claim that it should remain the same."[115] But the distance Veith was willing to go in changing was much shorter than the distance revolutionaries of any stripe would go and much longer than the distance ecclesiastical authority would go. Veith preached that one could honor the pope and attend all the sacraments and still not be Roman Catholic: he was articulating the need for a living faith based on an interior obedience. There were others who heard those words and thought he was encouraging insubordination. Veith and Günther both encouraged people to think. Whoever does not think cannot believe, said Veith; he only believes that he believes.[116] However, both Veith and Günther were convinced that thought and questioning must bring the searcher to Roman Catholicism. Veith said that a Christian state must allow pagans to be pagans without forcing them to be Christian.[117] He claimed that religion is a matter of free choice and that only children have to be educated through force.[118] But Veith would not hear a call for pluralism in those statements, only the recognition of the very conservative spiritual truth that not even God can make someone holy if that person does not wish to be made holy.

Neither Veith nor Günther were liberals. They believed that people must help themselves and not sit back and wait for a *deus ex machina* ending to this world's trials. Again and again they complained of the Viennese as comfortable (*gemütlich*) Catholics who would be content to be comfortable pantheists, of the Viennese who could only shrug their shoulders and complain that it was a sad time in which to live.[119] But the message of Günther and Veith was not a call to revolution either within or outside the church. Rather, it was the deep conviction they shared that God is not manipulated by burnt offerings or lip service but by an obedient, humble, and contrite heart.

In October of 1848, Veith was given an engraved chalice by the clergy of Vienna.[120] It was a token of appreciation to Veith, the proclaimer of the Word of God. It was not a gift from those who had left Vienna to wait out the storm; it was given by those who appreciated the presence and the leadership of a man who had not cowered in the face of threats but had continued to preach in season and out of season. Veith was the man of the hour, and Veith was a Güntherian. In the storm that came for the Güntherians after 1848, Veith was left untouched by official condemnation. It was Günther who suffered that. Yet Veith lived through his own form of condemnation as he assisted his friend in his defense and lived with the unspoken condemnation of the men in power in the church in Vienna after the guns of Windischgrätz and Jellacich had roared their verdict. Veith's activism had angered more than had Günther's arcane scholarship, but Günther remained more vulnerable to the plots and proceedings of the bureaucracies of Vienna and Rome.

7
THE TRIUMPH OF INFALLIBILITY

The revolution in Vienna ended on 31 October 1848, to the sound of cannon and Johann Strauss the Elder's *Radetzky Marsch*.[1] It was clear that, although it had not accomplished all of its ends, the revolution had made a difference. The Biedermeier era was over. In 1848 the new emperor was young and impressionable. He would continue on the throne until 1916, and each year he grew a little more experienced, a little more bent by the tragedies that the years after the excitement of 2 December 1848 brought. His death in 1916 was in the midst of a world war that had been started to defend the dignity of his by-then doomed empire.

One suspects that the years must have seemed one constant retreat for the longest-reigning Habsburg. His empire was torn by nationalism that could never hold still for any compromise. Contending with various peoples, languages and religions, he seemed able to find no way to please one group without displeasing another, and even those whom he tried to please only seemed to come back with more demands. And as if the internal strife were not enough, there were constant crises from the outside. The Crimean War had brought loss of face for Austria. Francis Joseph lost most of northern Italy in 1859, was pushed out of the German Bund by Prussia in 1866, and watched helplessly as a new German state was born in 1870 and as the old Papal States disappeared in the same year. The pope and council might proclaim papal infallibility in faith and morals, but the then middle-aged emperor of Austria heard the declaration without enthusiasm.[2] He knew that it would only feed anticlerical sentiment in his own land and could only work against the Roman Church in Habsburg lands, the church which he had tried to protect but which refused to be content with any compromise, refused to give any quarter to the pluralism that had to be accepted whether one was a federalist or a centralist in Habsburg politics.[3]

The Concordat and Its Collapse

When the guns fell silent in late October 1848, it was not clear who had won the long war over religion. Windischgrätz had immediately suspended the right of assembly and freedom of the press when he entered Vienna. Moderate men and women knew that those freedoms had brought much abuse during the months of turmoil, and it would be hard to convince authorities (who had never favored them) that the abuse did not negate the intrinsic value of those freedoms. The constitutional congress which had been called to revise the constitution of 25 April 1848—which needed revision from the beginning—had been transferred to Kremsier when the October violence had broken out. It looked as if the liberals had won disestablishment of the Roman Church and freedom of religion and religious practice.[4] But the emperor's troops dismissed the Kremsier representatives and the emperor himself issued a constitution. That constitution granted freedom of religious choice and expression (nonapproved religious were to be expressed privately). The constitution also allowed religious groups to control their own resources, education, and charity. Roman Catholicism retained a privileged position, but it was unclear exactly what that meant or just how long it would be maintained. No one who knew those troubled times believed that the constitution was the last world. What the emperor had granted, he could also retract.[5] The forces who favored Roman Catholicism as the established religion vied with those who insisted that the state should encourage religious pluralism under the state.

A meeting of the bishops of the Habsburg lands was called for April 1849. Reports vary on who intended to call it. Certainly the cardinal archbishop of Salzburg, Ferdinand von Schwarzenberg, who had held a meeting of the bishops in his church province and who had been the only Habsburg bishop to attend the German bishops' conference in Würzburg in October and November of 1848, wanted the meeting.[6] And Schwarzenberg was the brother of the minister president. But it is also clear the the archbishop of Vienna—still the aging Josephinist Milde—wanted nothing to do with such a conference. In the end, it was the government's Count Thun who actually called the conference, maintaining the impression that the church was under the state.[7] The new bishop of Seckau, Joseph Othmar Rauscher, tutor of Francis Joseph since 1844,[8] did the major preparing and was the chief force during the bishops' meeting in Vienna. The bishops called for self-determination by the church in all ecclesiastical matters under episcopal control. They stressed the right of the church to administer church justice and the education of clerics.[9] They also wanted continuation of state protection of the Roman Church and the special status of the Roman Church in all Habsburg lands. They supported the idea of a concordat with the papacy as the best means to guarantee the rights, privileges, and protections they required.[10] Francis Joseph accepted the basic thrust of the bishops' requests. By April 1950, communication with Rome was without government interference, and the bishops controlled church education and justice.[11] Negotiations for a concordat began in seriousness when Rauscher was appointed the emperor's representative.

The appeal of a concordat was not new and had been the papacy's way of dealing with the increased power of national monarchs. Popes were convinced that, as the Vicars of Christ and Peter, they had the right to a say in the life of the churches that still called themselves Roman Catholic. For Rome, a concordat was necessary to protect their rights in countries where Roman Catholicism was still the established religion but where the monarch was infringing on church rights. It was often a rearguard action to defend an eroding position. But papal theorists maintained the fiction that a concordat was granted by Rome as a special concession to Catholic monarchs. The monarchs, on the other hand, often needed to defend their position of power and looked to the Roman Church as a pillar of their stability. Not always sincere Catholics, they made a concession—often only temporary, until their power could be consolidated—to a powerful and usually established church within their jurisdiction. Lawyers maintained the conviction that it was a contract between two separate but equal partners; in reality, the concordat with any country was more a series of temporary compromises.[12]

The Josephinists had not been particularly interested in a concordat, although there had been some rumblings in that direction, especially after the European revolutions of 1830. But the conviction that religion was a department of state—or should take care of saving souls and leave the governing to the legitimately constituted authority of the state—did not encourage dialogue with Roman officials who seemed to want to preserve their place in the internal business of the empire. The old Josephinist archbishop of Vienna, Milde, who would live through 14 March 1853, did not favor a concordat.[13] Milde even took the extraordinary step of sending a letter to the *Wiener Zeitung* of 10 May 1850 that assured the populace that the church in Vienna would not plot with the church in Rome.[14]

After the events of 1848, there was no return to the pre-March complacence of the Josephinist bureaucrats. The new emperor was aware that he had come to the throne in the most unusual of circumstances and that he now had little time to consolidate his position. He was strongly influenced by his mother, Sophie, and by his former tutor Rauscher, whom Francis Joseph nominated as the archbishop of Vienna. Rauscher was convinced that a concordat was entirely in the spirit of his great mentor, Clement Hofbauer.[15] Pius IX, who had come to power in 1846 and had been noted as a liberal on his election, was shocked into the reactionary camp by the events of 1848 in Rome, when he was forced to flee the city and to witness the murder of his prime minister. Pius could not comprehend that minor reform with timing and content from above would not be enough to satisfy those who had deeper yearnings.

The constitution granted after the dissolution of the Kremsier convention had, in fact, disestablished Roman Catholicism and had recognized pluralism of religions. The state remained neutral and above the various religious confessions. But the constitution had been put together hastily and had been granted under the pressure of the days following the end of the revolution. There were many issues that remained undecided and the position of the Roman

Church remained dominant, a situation which led to discontent among liberals who wanted clearer acceptance of pluralism and among Roman Catholics who wanted a clearer definition of Roman Catholicism as the established religion of the entire empire. The empire of fifty million remained seventy-four percent Roman Catholic;[16] but the areas where Protestantism was concentrated resented Roman predominance as much as did the old Josephinists and the new political liberals in Vienna.

After 1848, Rauscher represented the emperor at discussions with Rome concerning a concordat. Rome was was not sure whether he was the emperor's man or theirs. In fact, Rauscher was convinced that Roman Catholicism should have a predominant role in Habsburg lands but also knew that there were some areas where compromise would be essential. The Romans came to trust him after his stay in Rome. He had come in December 1854 to lend legitimacy to the declaration of the Immaculate Conception[17] and had stayed on through June of 1855. The concordat was initialed by the two negotiators, Rauscher for the emperor and Viale-Prela for the pope, on 18 August 1855, and it was signed by the pope and emperor at the beginning of November that year. It was a temporary victory for Rome.

It is not the interest of the present work to tell the story of the intricate negotiations leading up to the concordat nor of the opposition that would eventually nullify it.[18] It is important, however, to note the major issues that were the focus of the debate. First in importance and first to be granted (even before the concordat itself was approved) was the right of Austrian bishops to communicate directly with Rome and not be forced to communicate through the government. This issue also applied to international religious communities, who were allowed to communicate freely with their foreign headquarters. The freedom of communication was also connected with the jurisdiction of the church over its own clergy and its own affairs. The second issue was that of marriage. The family was considered by both state and church to be the basic unit of society, and both struggled to control laws governing marriage. The concordat granted the church the right to rule in all marriages that involved anyone who had ever been a Roman Catholic. When there was a conflict between civil and canon law, canon law took precedence. This was bitterly resented by non-Roman religious groups (Protestants and Jews) as well as by those who considered marriage to be a secular and not a religious affair. The third issue was education; the Roman Church insisted on its right to determine curricula and to approve teachers both in theological schools (seminaries) and in the religious education of Roman Catholics. For the more radical religionists, this meant the control of all school subjects. Needless to say, the education of children was considered a state issue by those who wished to remove the influence of clerical "superstition." The concordat granted the church the right to control education for Roman Catholics and even promised state cooperation in a form of censorship of books critical of the church. The final issue was the position of the Roman Church in relation to other religious confessions. The concordat recognized the primary position of the Roman Church and guaranteed it state protection. But other religions were tolerated as they had been since Joseph II. This did not sit well with Roman Catholics, and Pius IX actually complained to the emperor of the privileges being granted Protestants and Jews. The concordat granted the Roman Church all the rights and privileges assigned to it in church (canon) law, but there was never complete acceptance of that principle in the empire. The emperor maintained his prerogative in nominating bishops in his lands, a prerogative which would continue to be exercised until 1918, even after the concordat had been abrogated by Austrian (but not Roman) decision after the 1870 declaration of papal infallibility (Francis Joseph agreeing with his liberal ministers that the pope had thereby changed his own and therefore the concordat's character).

The liberals were convinced that the concordat made the emperor subject to a foreign power and fought tirelessly to keep the church out of marriage and education. In fact, the thirty-six articles of the concordat did presume a Roman Catholic state, which, in many respects, Austria was no more. Pluralism and tolerance in religious practice had become a fact of life, and the industrialization of the empire was creating a different value system. It is difficult to say what the mind of the emperor was, though it is clear that his primary loyalty was to his house as the ruling house of the empire. He was personally a sincere Roman Catholic and a pious man, who attended Mass daily. But he was also a realist, something that few in Rome seemed to be. The more the clerics were given, the more they seemed to demand, and they were incensed when the emperor was forced to make concessions to liberals and non-Catholics after the string of defeats that the empire had faced on the military and economic battlefields. After the *Ausgleich* that created the Austro-Hungarian empire in 1867, there was even more pressure to accept toleration and pluralism as the Protestant Magyars made it increasingly clear that a pluralist state could not accept one religion's laws as law of the entire land. But the Roman Church showed no understanding and gave no quarter: they wanted the entire empire. The pope was only narrowly convinced not to condemn the emperor himself when Pius wrote objecting to concessions being made to Protestants.[19] Rauscher dismissed the liberal opposition as men of fifty or sixty pat phrases to be used interchangeably according to the need of the moment. He would not credit them with the ability to think, nor would he even listen to their programs and policies.[20] Rauscher even complained that Protestants were being buried in consecrated Roman Catholic ground.[21] Bishop Rudiger of Linz claimed the liberals wanted to eliminate the monarchy and establish hedonism as the state religion.[22] To many it seemed that the church was claiming to be above the state.

It was the definition of papal infallibility—although protested in Rome by

Rauscher and Schwarzenberg as inopportune in its timing if not in its content[23]—that would be the final argument that the opponents of the concordat needed. Their argument that it created a state within a state seemed justified even as the Papal States were being dissolved. By May of 1874, the churches were placed *under* the state although with freedom to control their own affairs. Marriage was recognized as a civil possibility even if the church refused to marry a couple. Education came under state control. Anyone fourteen or older could change religious confession without difficulty. Pluralism and secularism had won. The old Josephinists would have rejoiced.[24] It was only the tempering influence of Francis Joseph himself that insisted on a mild interpretation of the anti-church laws and thereby avoided an Austrian *Kulturkampf*.[25] Rauscher died on 24 November 1875, the same year that Vogelsang came to Vienna to be the new editor of *Das Vaterland*, the conservative Catholic paper that was to become the voice of Christian Socialism in the latter half of the century.[26]

The Habsburg bishops wanted no political activity at any but the highest level. Their conviction was supported by a government who found it easier to negotiate concordats than to comprehend and respond to a changing religious environment. In the years from November 1848 through the signing and then abrogating of the Condordat of 1855 in 1870, the bishops had clear control of church affairs. It would be unfair to conclude that their excellencies were only interested in preserving their own power; even were that the case, it would be impossible to deny their sincerity in believing that they were the voice of God in their land. Industrialization and urbanization were changing even the static Habsburg lands and Vienna was undergoing more transformation than most areas of the empire through immigration and industrial and urban expansion. The Austrian bishops, like the Austrian government, did not comprehend the dimensions of the shift but did allow some new developments. A new field of priestly endeavor was created to minister to the needs of the workers who were building the Semmering railroad.[27] The bishops, concerned about the *religious* education of youth working in factories, noted in passing that no one under ten years of age should be hired.[28] The priest Anton Gruscha was allowed to re-establish his journeyman's union.[29] An annual "Catholic Day" (*Katholikentag*) when the people would gather to celebrate their Catholicity under the leadership of their bishops was established in Linz in 1850 and in Vienna in 1853.[30]

The "Exile" of J. E. Veith

Neither church nor state trusted those who had been active in the days of the Revolution of 1848. It was as if any activity during that time was like a disease that made any further contribution suspect. The Güntherians, to no one's surprise, were most suspect; but the suspicion extended to the entire middle class of Vienna.[31] The one most unpopular was Sebastian Brunner, but his high profile and the power of his pen made any direct movement against him difficult. He was treated mostly with benign neglect. He continued to write that the priests should have some say in the selection of their bishops, but he also insisted that decision-making in the church could not and should not be democratic. He wrote that the liberty of the church was a right and not a privilege to be granted or taken away when it was no longer convenient. He opposed the concordat as too little, as nothing more than a patchwork of defenses against the encroachment of the state. In the absence of response from those whom he wished to influence, Brunner's voice became increasingly strident, his tone increasingly negative. In 1852 he was elected to the post of university preacher, which gave him security and the leisure to continue his writing. But he lost momentum and turned to writing memoirs and reflections on 1848. He supported Anton Günther and Johann Emanuel Veith against their attackers, but even that turned increasingly difficult as the Güntherians lost favor.[32]

The Catholic Union was affected by the decrees denying public assembly, as were other "political" groups. The leadership of the union was allowed to meet privately once a month in the presence of a commissioner from the archdiocese. Milde still smarted from the public challenge the union had issued to him in demanding his return to Vienna during the days of the revolution (some eight hundred members of the Catholic Union had signed a letter in July 1848 requesting Milde's return to Vienna), but he did not feel strong enough to eliminate the union. He acquiesced when Veith, along with Hock and Bondi, was delegated to rewrite the constitution of the union to limit its activities to the purely religious, educational, and charitable. Milde was even agreeable to the resumption of publication of *Der österreichische Volksfreund* in January 1849, under the editorship of Veith, Hock, and Häusle. But that was as far as Milde would go; these concessions were granted only temporarily, until he was able to establish his own control. It was the military governor of Vienna who made decisions—but he did not make them in Catholic affairs without consulting and following Milde.[33]

Veith's energy and productivity were high after the events of 1848. He wrote a good portion of the articles in the *Österreichischer Volksfreund*, major articles and filler articles. He reported "events in France" in a way that suggested he was actually commenting on events closer to home. He told homespun stories about a land where the oxen were banned because cattle would produce more cheese, and he ended by criticizing republicans who preferred meat to cheese.[34] He condemned those who were against private property,[35] and he claimed that the concept of the right to work was a communist discovery—that Christ had talked of having the poor always with us.[36] Commenting on the ceremony of departure for Gethsemane, Kentucky, of a group of Trappist monks, Veith called his readers to remember that we all have our own cross to bear.[37] He spoke of 1848 as the year of the chameleon[38] and warned about the seriousness of taking an oath[39] and being careful about whom one believed.[40] He preached against rumors,[41] tattoos,[42] the California gold rush,[43] and the drabness of socialist funerals.[44] He was against the atheism of the Enlightenment[45] and against women who tried to usurp the husband's role as the head of the house.[46] He defended the celebration of the Lord's Day against socialist encroachment[47] and claimed the bishop (and especially the bishop of Rome) was at the head of the fight for God.[48] Occasionally Veith spoke of how church and science might dispute with one another, but he insisted that they also needed each other.[49] Mostly, his articles were filled with warnings about the indifference (*Wurstigkeitsgefühl*)[50] and the lack of belief[51] that he saw around him, more in the city than in the country, but in the country as well.[52]

On 28 March 1849, Veith preached at the memorial service for Latour, the man whose death he had witnessed at the beginning of October 1848.[53] It was not recorded who was present for the occasion, but most probably the dignitaries of the court came together to pay tribute to the man who was looked upon as a martyr for his emperor. It is also likely that Milde would have been in attendance, or at least would have been informed of the content of Veith's preaching.

The eulogy for Latour is nothing short of a canonization of the man who has not fared so well with historians more sympathetic to the revolutionary cause.[54] Veith used the opportunity to plead for reconciliation between the military and the middle class;[55] he produced a vivid and detailed description of the death that he had witnessed and offered a bombastic interpretation of Latour as the warrior who in dying has actually won victory. Veith prayed that the name of Theodor Baillet de Latour would be honored in the Austrian army and by the Austrian people, by all Christian nations, and would shine in world history with unfading brilliance.[56] Veith did not spare the enemies of the empire: the democrats such as Kossuth and Mazzini, who wanted the destruction of the imperial houses of Europe along with Christianity and the Roman Church. "These were the handful of people in the know about the goals of the revolution who deceived the many with their magical powers to wilt opposition. There was nothing more dangerous than boldness and power mixed with ignorance and the insane fury of the aroused mob; aroused by the rattlesnakes and vipers of the daily newspapers who poured out their most dangerous poison against Latour. The paper heroes of the left raised their wolf's howling against him."[57] Yet, even in his death, he conquered, for even while he was being brutally murdered the saviors of the emperor and empire were gathering. God took up the righteous fight of Latour and brought it to victory through the "magnanimous commanders with their admirable forbearance and mildness."[58] Brotherhood was well and good, but, as the apostle Peter insisted, it must be combined with reverence for God and respect for the constitutional emperor.[59] It was a blatant and perhaps sycophantic plea for acceptance into the returned order. Whether or not he heard it, Milde was not impressed. Perhaps the problem was the world *constitutional* that Veith connected, but only once, to the emperor's office. The emperor had indeed issued a constitution that made him a constitutional monarch, and most who followed Hofbauer would insist that there was a constitutionality about this world that came, not from an emperor but from God and that guaranteed certain things to individuals and to the church. The Güntherians, also followers of Hofbauer, had fought to defeat both democracy and absolutism. They thought they had won, or at least that they had prepared the way. But appreciation was not to come; the opposition was to grow.

On the Sundays of Lent, 1849, Veith preached six sermons in the Church Am Hof.[60] His disappointment with the revolution was clear and poignant, but his distaste for the Josephinism that produced Milde was only thinly veiled. At a time when public meetings were still banned—and more especially the public meeting of the Catholic Union—Veith's sermons were daring.

The words he had for the revolutionaries would have been most acceptable to the authorities, but one has to wonder about the response of his audience, many of whom had at least passively supported the revolution. Veith offered them a way out, however, by identifying himself with the ones who had been seduced by the fine ideas and eloquent language of those who sought reform. "We hoped for and sought an entirely new salvation and found, for the time being, disaster. We find the cross wherever we turn; but on this cross there is no Christ. All the political revolutionizing has only accomplished the destruction of the old, true thoughts of faith: respect, modesty, patience, and self-control. On the other hand, efforts towards egoism, vanity, and the unbridled reign of lesser passions ring out with much greater power."[61] Communism is the culprit. Communism hides its murderous face behind the seductive name of the democracy that claims to be an essential element of the constitutional monarchy. (Again, the two words "constitutional" and "monarchy" come together in a manner that would be understood differently by different hearers.) Communism seduces the poor and weaponless proletariat with many promises and few demands, but it only waits to trample on the authority of conscience, church, state, and on divine and human order to place itself on the throne. Do not rejoice, you upper classes and petty bourgeois, that the power of the mighty has been broken. The storm that leveled the cedar can even more easily bring down the pine![62]

Veith compared the revolutionaries with Judas Iscariot. Judas complained to Jesus that the woman who was pouring expensive oil all over his feet was wasting money that should be given to the poor; in fact he wanted the money for himself.[63] Veith was appalled that so many were so ready to betray emperor and country and place their own and others' lives in danger for filthy lucre (*schnödes Geld*).[64] Although Veith never retracted his support for the pride in heritage that each nation should have in its language and literature, he was appalled by the nationalism that was no more than national egoism, resulting in a pagan and murderous fight among peoples who would not be reconciled.[65] Anarchy and national hatred had become virtues![66] The people (*Das Volk*) had come to be ruled by the mob (*Der Pöbel*),[67] a mob that even looked to Istanbul and the Turks for rescue from its own legitimate Christian monarch.[68]

Communism preached an equality that was unacceptable to someone convinced of the hierarchy of being in the universe and the organisms of church and state in human society. The animal and vegetable worlds were the only places where the communist call for absolute equality could have any possibility.[69] Veith protested that this false call for equality would destroy the treasures of art as well as the treasures of a society that was grounded in God. One of those treasures that would be lost would be the symmetry of the priestly hierarchy, which Veith viewed as the God-willed teacher, lawgiver, and ruler of the laity.[70] The call for liberty, equality, and fraternity had replaced the call for faith, hope, and love and had become the self-centered and greedy call for anarchy, pride, and terrorism.[71]

In the end, Veith blamed the excesses of the revolution on the failure of people to see beyond *now* into life after death; Christ's promise to the good thief (Dismas) on the cross as well as Christ's own resurrection and ascension were proof that there was life after death.[72] The only true socialism would come in heaven.[73] In the meantime, there were entirely too many people who did not know anything about it who were mixing in politics, and the result was not freedom but anarchy.[74] Veith traced the problem back to the Protestants who, having deserted the church, found in their secular leader the head of both church and state, and to the absolutists, whose insistence that the king was the state brought about the response that insisted that the people were the state and had power invested in them[75] Democrats and absolutists (Febronianists) had brought on this anarchy; it was time to return to the old values and not simply throw them out unexamined.

The old values were the values of the middle class: marriage, family, private property, the right of inheritance. The old values were those which espoused a state that understood its role as protector and promoter but not ruler of the church. The people (*Das Volk*) was an organically divided whole which operated most effectively when its head and its heart were working strongly. Humankind had sunken into the animal world of *Natur* and must find its way back to the world of *Geist*.[76] The form of government was not important, but the role of the government was important and must be Christian.[77] Instead of trying to establish heaven on earth, humankind should be attempting to establish order, law, and custom (*Ordnung, Gesetz, und Sitte*) to focus the attention of society not on unseemly personal greed but on the cross. Whoever humbles himself will be exalted; whoever exalts himself will be humbled. The work of the Christian in *this* world is to embrace the sick, the infirm, the oppressed, and the needy.[78]

Veith's social gospel was acceptable to the church leaders of his time: it was a social gospel that looked to the healing of downtrodden individuals but not to a reform of structures that may have created or might be continuing the problems. It was Veith's blind spot. There were others who recognized the structural problems, if only in a crude way. The rhetoric on both communist and Christian sides was not conciliatory. They could not hear each other and consequently could not learn from each other. Veith was only one example of that deafness. But it was not his condemnation by the this-worldly communists that would be the most painful for Veith. It was the Roman Church itself that proved the most relentless in its shabby treatment of Veith and the other churchmen who had tried to make sense out of the revolutionary ideas.

Veith and the Güntherians who were active with him supported the monarchy and its values but insisted on a constitutional right to have a say in state matters. Veith never directly claimed that clerics should or should not themselves be involved with politics, but it was clear that Catholics should somehow be heard. Veith was confusing in his stands—and it is sometimes difficult to discern his exact position in the midst of rhetoric and sarcasm—but the ambiguity was enough for Milde, the Josephinist, who simply could not comprehend the church's having any place in government decisions. Milde wanted nothing to do with Veith or any of the Güntherians.

Along with Häusle and Hock, Veith had been allowed to resume publication of the *Österreichischer Volksfreund* in January of 1849. Public meetings of the Catholic Union were not allowed, however, pending a rewriting of the constitutions of the organization to eliminate any possibility of political action by the group. In July 1849 Milde was asked to allow public meetings of the union. Whether he remembered the embarrassment the union had caused him in 1848 by calling for his return to Vienna was not mentioned, but Milde refused. Hock and Häusle, authors of articles that could have been interpreted as critical of Milde, resigned in the hopes that their departure from the organization might convince the archbishop to allow public meetings. In August of 1849 Veith, now the lone editor of the *Österreichischer Volksfreund*, again requested permission for public meetings of the Catholic Union. Milde again refused. In January of 1850 Milde was presented with the revised constitutions of the Catholic Union, statutes that followed his directives closely. He rejected the revisions. In February of 1850 Milde submitted an article highly critical of any Catholic union movement for publication in the *Österreichischer Volksfreund*. The paper was forced to publish the article. Later in the same month, Milde presented his own version of the constitutions for the Catholic Union. On 27 February, Veith resigned the editorship of the paper and membership in the union; his excuse was that he was moving to Prague to accept the invitation of Cardinal Schwarzenberg, who in 1850 had become the cardinal archbishop of that city at the request of the emperor.[79] There must have been some debate in the union itself, although it remains unrecorded. One can only guess that the Güntherians remaining in the group were outraged by the power play, but the Güntherians were a minority. In August of 1850 the union approved Milde's constitutions and the union was approved by the government. By the end of 1850 there were no Güntherians left in the Catholic Union; it would not be until 10 November 1851, however, that public meetings of the Catholic Union were approved. By then, the name of the union had been changed to the Severinus Union (*Severinusverein*), and Bishop Rauscher had been elected as their honorary head and protector.[80] The major activity of the Severinus Union was works of charity. They strenuously avoided anything that looked like political opinion.[81]

Veith did not leave for Prague immediately. He stayed on as editor of the *Österreichischer Volksfreund* until March of 1850 and he again preached a series of Lenten sermons in the Church am Hof.[82] The sermons were very similar to those preached the previous year, but the tone was calmer. Veith still believed that the suggestion of the communists that humankind could be perfected (*Vervollkommnungsfähigkeit*) in this world was an illusion,[83] but he spent more of his time in 1850 looking at the church. He began with Güntherian anthropology[84] but quickly shifted to a historical analysis. Veith seemed to suggest that the church should be judged by its history and that the judgment is favorable. The church will continue, but whether in Europe or not Veith found impossible to predict.[85]

According to Veith, the church has preached God, educated the people (German and Slav), worked with several forms of state, and continued to proclaim the unity of all peoples, the holiness of family life, the need for order in the community, and to insist that all earthly possessions were a gift from God. It was only indirectly an attack on the communists, who saw the world in much harsher terms and the church as an agent of class oppression. Veith admitted that there had been mistakes, an admission that was rare in his times (and remains unusual); but he attributed these mistakes to the high-handedness, blindness, and the moral perversity of the hypocrites, traitors, and priests of Baal in the church's own bosom even more than to enemies from without.[86] Veith admitted that there were scandals enough to point to in church history: the striving of rulers for the absolute power that belonged only to God, the jealousy of pope for emperor and vice versa, the Great Western Schism that set three popes wandering about looking for supporters.

But the church was not the abuses. The church—the visible church in general—was the kingdom of Christ on earth. It was protected by the Holy Spirit even in the midst of inadequate human leaders. In equating the church with the kingdom of Christ, Veith was aware of the historical developments that had taken place in the church. He mentions the increased awareness of crusaders returned home from the East with unthought-of luxuries, the rediscovery of pagan Greek and Roman art in Italy, the discovery of America, the meaning of the printing press, the horror of gunpowder, the discoveries of Newton.[87] He ridiculed those who thought that the Bible should be viewed as a textbook of astronomy or physics,[88] and he claimed that the church had already recognized and integrated those changes and would do the same for changes in the future.[89]

Freedom of religion could not be denied because the *Mensch* had been created with free will. But freedom did not allow the individual to choose to ignore all positive religion or to disrupt the public security or the moral order. It was not a freedom between two equal choices but the freedom to say "yes" or "no" to Christ. The church was there to point the way to Christ's kingdom. The state was there to protect and preserve the social order that would create a Christian atmosphere so that citizens could say "yes," for a "no" meant eternal damnation. Freedom of the press was the freedom to witness to the Truth in all areas. There was not a need for the church to exercise absolute censorship as long as people were willing to listen to what the church taught. The problem was the sort of censorship that developed among literate people who refused to read the "drab and dull" religious literature that was good for their souls but not very titillating to their imaginations.[90] In the end, he who submits to the teachings of the pope in the areas of positive religion and moral truth is Catholic and remains a part of the body of the church. Disobedience is a denial of the organism that is the church.[91] Equality is to be found in the reality that we have all sinned and all been saved by Christ if we say "yes" to the divine forgiveness and become a part of the kingdom of Christ.[92] As long as we are in this life, the opportunity to say "yes" is there. Those who have said the "yes" in this life must recognize that many have not done likewise. The church and the state will exercise their true freedom when they accept the law of God, but one should always be mindful of the wheat and weeds that will grow together until the time of harvest.[93]

One can but wonder what thoughts filled the mind of the doctor, priest, and preacher as he made his way to the capital of the Bohemia he had left so many years before as a Jew and a student. How the years had changed his life! Now he was not only a Christian but a priest of the Roman Church who viewed the fate of the Jews as an extension of the fate they had called down on themselves at the death of the man Veith now accepted as savior. But the officials of the church he had joined had not been overly enthusiastic about his ministry. The return to Prague was entry into exile—even if it was at the invitation of the cardinal archbishop of the city. Veith remained in Prague until the summer of 1855, when ill health was his excuse for a return to Vienna. In Prague he continued to preach,[94] to work with the Catholic Union, to give priests' retreats, and to advise Cardinal Schwarzenberg on the Günther trial.

The Trial of Anton Günther

Anton Günther continued his work right through the bombardment and occupation of Vienna by the imperial troops. He was all but oblivious to events, for he had found the way to resolve the questions of the day through his beloved *Wissenschaft*. He saw the solution to the problems that plagued the city in the acceptance of his positive Christianity with its dualist anthropology. If only people would understand the world of *Geist*, then the world of *Natur* would not be so topsy-turvy.[95] Once the revolution had ended, Günther opined that he was not excited by democracy anyway and that one would have to make do with a constitutional monarchy.[96] When he was made aware of the controversy about the place of *Wissenschaft* in the Catholic Union, he resolved to write an article about the hatred of *Vernunft* among Catholics.[97]

Günther was excited by two new projects in the time immediately after the end of the revolution. One was the establishment of a journal for theology (*Zeitschrift für die gesamte katholische Theologie*) that was founded at the University of Vienna by Häusle and Scheiner. The journal was published twice yearly and the first years were dominated by articles from Güntherians.[98] Günther himself wrote two articles for the journal, both expositions of Güntherian anthropology as the basis for theology, one on civil marriage and the other the promised article on the hatred of *Vernunft* among Catholics.[99] The second project that warmed Günther's heart was a joint venture with Veith: the publication of the journal *Lydia*.[100] The articles in the journal were unsigned, but the vast majority were wrtten by Günther himself. *Lydia* was a continuation of Güntherian thought;[101] as such, its articles were repetitions of Günther's earlier works. The attacks on those who disagreed, especially those within Roman Catholicism, remained relentless and biting.

Like Veith, Günther had no time for communism, which he viewed as an atheistic philosophical movement responding to the perverted social circumstances of the time.[102] Communism denied the distinction between *Natur* and *Geist* and consequently emphasized the rule of the collective (*Natur*) over the free spiritual personality (*Geist*).[103] Günther saw communism as the understandable but erroneous conviction, growing from the sordid conditions of the working classes, that private property was theft.[104] Only Christianity—more specifically, Güntherian positive Christianity—could bring the insight that inequality (hierarchy) was a necessary part of the world of God's creation.[105]

Günther was hard on those within Roman Catholicism who seemed unable or unwilling to understand. Most of his attacks were simply *ad hominem* dismissals. One enemy he called a graduate of a school for train engineers (*graduierter Lokomotivführer*).[106] Günther continued a hard line of ridicule for Scholastics.[107] What he failed to notice was that the winds were changing and the followers of his old whipping boy, Thomas Aquinas, were moving in for revenge. There was outrage when Günther appeared to attack the Council of Trent, the beacon for those who believed they were called to protect orthodox Catholicism.[108] Günther had given other thought systems, especially those of the Thomists, no quarter: it could be no surprise when they returned in kind.

The revolution left Günther without finances. He lost his position as censor when censorship was abolished, and his old protector, Ferdinand Bretzenheim-Regetz, lost his lands to his peasants and was no longer able to support Günther with a monthly stipend. Cardinal Schwarzenberg took up the responsibility of making sure that Günther had a monthly income—not princely, but adequate if Günther watched what he ate and drank. The cardinal invited Günther and Greif to come to Prague with Veith. Greif complained that he was too old, and Günther said that he feared the Hussites in the city.[109]

Günther discovered that Vienna was not a very friendly city either. Milde had been one thing. The old Josephinist had caused Günther and his followers plenty of trouble. There was much more to come when Rauscher, an old acquaintance from the Hofbauer days, became the cardinal archbishop of Vienna.

By 1848 Günther and Veith were at the center of a large circle of followers who made up one of the largest theological schools in the nineteenth-century German theological world.[110] They perceived the enemy as pantheism in its many forms, and dared to accuse much Catholic thought that preceded them as being guilty of semi-pantheism. In the spirit of German academic debate, they were merciless when attacking their enemies and loyal to each other when they were in turn attacked. Within their own system, the Güntherians were as convinced of their discovery of Truth as any and more arrogant than most theologians. Convinced of the overpowering logic of their own system, the Güntherians were confident of success. Before 1848, that success was impressive.

When a process was introduced in Rome against the theology of Günther, those who introduced the case were well aware that they were not simply attacking an aging and impoverished eccentric in Vienna. Those who looked to Günther for a mentor were located throughout the German-speaking world. The main academic centers were in Vienna, Bonn, and Breslau. The protection of Cardinals Schwarzenberg and Diepenbrock, Archbishops Förster and Tarnoczy, Bishops Arnoldi and Müller, as well as connections in Rome with Pappalettere, Hohenlohe, and Flir made the Güntherians confident of their survival.

Günther's influence went far beyond cardinals and government officials, however. There were other people, less visible to a history that concentrates on the struggles for power. There was Bruno Schön, the Conventual Franciscan who worked with those confined to the insane section of the General Hospital and who claimed that Günther had given meaning to his life.[111] There were large numbers of educated laity, even beyond Veith's Catholic Union. There were women who not only cared for Günther and Veith in old age but who also were invited to write articles of substance in Güntherian publications.[112] Perhaps through Veith's influence, there were a large number of Jewish converts—even though Günther himself expressed his doubts about a convert's ability to understand his system (all but Veith, of course).[113] There were also several medical doctors—perhaps explainable by the fact that medicine was a philosophical discipline in those days as much as by Veith's influence. To be sure, Güntherianism was a home for many, and the stories about the exchange of mustards and wines and small knit caps as well as visits and letters and outings made together suggest an intense community spirit.

Yet it was the intellectual power of Günther's thought that did most to draw the group together. Günther's thought attracted a large and diverse group of Roman Catholics of one background or another who were interested the revival of the gospel in new terms that would answer the questions of the times. The thirties and forties of the nineteenth century were dominated by the German idealists, and the Güntherians rushed to answer the questions raised by those "pantheists" in language that would defeat the enemy, the language of positive Christianity built on modern *Wissenschaft*. Günther remained a private scholar—but not because he was not offered opportunity to enter the university world. Because of the theological writings of Günther and the homiletic works of Veith, it would have been difficult to find an educated Roman Catholic in the German world who had not heard of Christian Dualism.

So the fight that surrounded Günther's thought was not simply the investigation of a system of a single German thinker, a private scholar. It was not just the investigation of an old priest living out his final days in a changing world. The fight affected many beyond the clerical circles where the battle was fought, and those who fought on both sides were aware of that. But the battle—the term is accurate even though no weapons were drawn other than the pen—was to be fought in Rome and ultimately to be decided by Pius IX, who was never known for theological acumen. Although fought on Roman soil, the battle was a peculiarly German battle: fought by German academics, ecclesiastics, and diplomats on the turf of Italian bureaucrats.[114]

In the spring of 1853, in a letter to Cardinal Schwarzenberg, Veith complained peevishly that Günther could not wash his hands in innocence—and even less in ink. Günther, opined Veith, had created and provoked these enemies himself.[115] Indeed, the controversy had begun years before and Günther's incendiary language had been a part of the problem. Calling one's enemies "apes"[116] did not entice them to cool academic debate. Another problem was Günther's limited and often inaccurate knowledge of the Scholasticism that he ridiculed at the very time when the Catholic academic world was finding the writings of medieval Scholastics, especially Thomas Aquinas, to be of particular value.[117] As early as 1836, the papal nuncio wrote a letter to Cardinal Schwarzenberg complaining that, although not uncatholic, Günther's works were useless and dangerous.[118] Günther even managed to alienate members of the Tübingen school who were favorable to his work and who wanted a Güntherian replacement for Drey.[119] Günther's followers were not always more circumspect than their mentor.

There were also the usual rivalries between religious communities and between religious and secular clergy. In the midst of the process, Günther expressed regrets that he had ever had anything to do with the Jesuits, whom he now considered his enemies.[120] And it was clear that an unusually strong criticism came from the Redemptorists, whose voices were raised ever stronger after the departure of Veith from the community in 1830.[121]

Politics most assuredly played a role. The Prussian government was influential in calling several Güntherians to chairs within Prussian jurisdiction. It was clearly an attempt to aggravate church authorities, especially the cardinal archbishop of Cologne, Johann von Geissel.[122] Peter Knoodt, a second generation Güntherian, became a professor in Bonn and, in spite of the efforts of the papal nuncio,[123] was never able to establish anything more than a temporary and uneasy truce with Geissel.[124] Two of the most vocal anti-Güntherians were men passed over for the appointment that Knoodt received in Bonn.[125] The neoscholastics joined the old enemies of Hermes[126] in opposition to Günther's thought.

Although enemies were common since the publication of the *Vorschule* in 1828, it was only after the events of 1848 that there was any seriousness in the attempts to have the Güntherians condemned. It was then that the enemies on the Rhine would be joined by enemies in Vienna and one important former Güntherian[127] to apply the pressure necessary for the condemnation that came in early 1857. On 2 May 1849 Ludwig Croy wrote to Peter Knoodt that the lay support for Günther seemed at a high point at the very time that his clerical support seemed to be decreasing. In Croy's opinion, the problems before 1848 were not the issue; the involvement of Güntherians in 1848 became the factor that was unpardonable.[128] It did not matter that Günther's system might have died on its own as idealism and rationalism declined.[129]

As is the custom of the Roman Curia, the process against Anton Günther began quietly and in secrecy.[130] It began unofficially in 1851 at the request of Cardinal Geissel of Cologne.[131] The fact that there was an investigation leaked through rumor, not official communication—it was not Rome's custom to inform those under scrutiny until well along in the process. The leaks brought inquiries from Günther's friends and denials from the Roman authorities, (whether in good faith or as a deceptive move is not ascertainable). Schwarzenberg and Diepenbrock were assured by Pius IX that Günther had nothing to fear. That was in 1852.[132] Hohenlohe, the Austrian government's representative in Rome, claimed in the same year that his information indicated no action had been taken. Also at the beginning of 1852, the papel nuncio in Vienna insisted that he knew nothing of any process and that he would be surpised if there were one.[133]

The case against Günther gained momentum when Rauscher began applying pressure. In the empire, Rauscher's star was rising and Schwarzenberg's was falling. As Bishop of Seckau, Rauscher had appointed a Güntherian (Ehrlich) to a professorship at Graz; but by the time he became the archbishop of Vienna, he was alarmed by what he perceived to be the Güntherian support for more democracy within the church.[134] Four days before the death of Milde, Rauscher sent to Rome a comparison of Günther's thought with official church teachings. Six weeks after Rauscher became the archbishop of Vienna, the same papal nuncio who claimed there was nothing in the air against Günther wrote to Rauscher of his conviction that the works of Günther needed to be condemned.[135]

The battle was joined. The Güntherians certainly had enough backing—but as it turned out, only enough to delay, not to prevent, a condemnation. An article in *Deutsche Volkshalle* in May 1853 reported Günther's condemnation.[136] It was premature; but the process probably had concluded by then, and it was only the influence of Günther's protectors that prevented its earlier publication. Günther himself did not even know what steps were being taken in his defense.[137] He took comfort in the conviction that Rome would wait to decide until he was dead and that he could die in the good graces of the church without having to recant his writings.[138] The defense was organized by Veith and orchestrated by Schwarzenberg—both of whom thought Günther too speculative to be able to answer the questions raised in a manner that would satisfy the investigators.[139] Greif remained in the background but was the major personal support of Günther in Vienna. Neither Günther nor Veith traveled to Rome, and the representation there was probably the worst possible.[140] Perhaps the most naive mistake that the Güntherians made was in presuming that Pius IX was favorable to them because of his sympathetic tears at the letters of Günther.[141]

Despite protests that their enemies did not really understand the dualist system,[142] the works of Günther were condemned on 8 January 1857 by unanimous decision of the Congregation of the Index.[143] The actual decree is dated 17 February 1857. Pius IX wanted Günther to have a chance to submit— and the final decree included the sentence indicating Günther's submission (*autor ingenue, religiose ac laudabiliter se subjecit*). Several months later, at the request of Cardinal Geissel, the major points of the condemnation were listed. Further explanations were given by Rome to the archbishop of Breslau in 1860 and to the archbishop of Munich in 1863. Günther is mentioned in the Syllabus of Errors published in 1864. His works were also discussed at the provincial synod of Vienna in 1858 and of Cologne in 1860.[144] The main points of the condemnation focused on Günther's epistemology, which was considered semirationalist, and on Günther's dualist anthropology,[145] which did not coincide with the Thomist concept of the infused soul.[146]

Veith and Greif wrote Günther's submission.[147] It is a masterful work of both submitting and defending. Pius IX was impressed by the humility of its tone; others also were amazed that Günther seemed to be so resigned to the will of the Roman congregation. His private letters suggest that it was much more difficult than his public stand suggested. In a letter to Schwarzenberg right after Günther had received the letter asking for his submission to Rome, one of Günther's Viennese friends (Hock) commented that Günther was very upset and that it would take a great deal of effort to get him to agree to the unconditional submission demanded by the Romans.[148] In a letter dated 2 February 1857 Günther wrote Schwarzenberg in a bitter tone that his enemies had waited until the concordat was signed to pounce. Günther also showed an uncommon trust in Pius IX, apparently believing that he was, after all, on Günther's side. "I will write the Holy Father," Günther wrote Schwarzenberg, "and tell him that I have been handled worse than the worst heretic."[149] By 11 February 1857, however, Günther was writing to Schwarzenberg to inform him of his willingness to submit and that Veith and Greif had agreed to write the submission, which was too difficult for Günther himself.[150]

By 1860, Günther was writing to a friend (J. N. Hubner) that his submission was not so difficult because not one specific dogmatic thesis of his had been directly condemned; there had only been a statement that his works deviated from the accepted manner of theological discourse and were a stumbling block for seminary students.[151] In 1861 Günther wrote to another friend (Frohschammer) that he was working on his autobiography so that it could come to light after his death. "The only revenge I have taken," continued Günther, "is that I have remained silent." But Günther could not resist an aside to his friend that his own theory of creation had more substance than the Mariology that made all of creation dependent on the "Be it done unto me" (*fiat mihi*) of Mary.[152] Günther said again and again, however, that "everyone had to offer up his Isaac" (*suus cuique Isaak*), which he had learned in the Jesuit novitiate and which he applied to his own fallible conscience, which had to bow to a larger, infallible one.[153]

All in all, the decree of the Congregation of the Index defeated the man Günther. He had written a work against one of his critics that was already printed when the condemnation came.[154] Cardinal Schwarzenberg bought the entire printing and had it destroyed so there would be no more trouble for the aging theologian. One last work was published posthumously from the notes of Günther, but Knoodt was the editor and by the time the work appeared had become a member of the Old Catholic movement and was in schism from Rome.[155] Günther's only public act was to join the Viennese Academy of Science—an honor he had refused before because of the then-president's public statement that he would allow no one into the academy who believed in purgatory. Even the anticlerical Grillparzer rejoiced at Günther's membership.[156]

After 1857, Günther lived the life of a defeated recluse. He took his daily walks and muttered about the changes that were taking place in the landscape since the decision in 1857 to tear down the old town walls and build the Ringstrasse. As long as he could get around, he prayed his breviary and said his private Mass daily. Finances were tight, and he rejoiced over each small gift. (He had not been able to afford wine since 1852, but did not complain, for this made a nap in the afternoon unnecessary and he could get more work done and sleep better at night.)[157]

Günther died at 7:00 P.M. on 24 February 1863. His friend Veith had been attending him but was away preaching at the time of his death. It was said that the old Veith preached about creation with all his heart that night.[158] Veith later claimed that he was awakened from sleep that night by a vision of his friend Günther as he had been as a young man.[159] The funeral procession was led by Veith and Greif, who later joined Günther in the same crypt in the Matzleinsdorfer cemetery.[160]

Veith returned from Prague to Vienna in the summer of 1855. His health was bad and he had a growing sense that Günther's works would be condemned. Prague, with its increasing Czech nationalism, was not a place where he felt at home, and he had never spoken Czech. In early 1856, he had moved into a third-floor apartment at Franziskanerplatz 5 where he remained until his death.

Günther's condemnation in 1857 was hard for Veith, and a deep pessimism about the immediate future of the church clouded his work, but he continued working feverishly. The more the church seemed to ignore him and the other Güntherians, the more he seemed to preach the church and its rights.[161] Veith himself came under investigation for unorthodoxy. Cardinal Rauscher, who had encouraged Veith to preach in spite of the cloud that hung over Günther's thought, was rumored to have also been the one who wrote to the Congregation of the Index about Veith's possible unorthodoxy. In December 1858 Rauscher protested to Cardinal Schwarzenberg that he knew nothing of any process against Veith, but by March 1859 he was writing to Schwarzenberg that there were errors in Veith's works.[162] Although it is not clear who started the proceedings, it is clear that Cardinal d'Andrea of the Congregation of the Index was looking into Veith's works. It was a letter of Cardinal Schwarzenberg that seemed to end the investigation.[163] On 3 September 1871 Veith celebrated the fiftieth anniversary of his ordination to the priesthood. The emperor conferred the Francis Joseph Order on him; the Vienna city council conferred honors; the Empress Caroline (wife of Ferdinand) and Cardinal Schwarzenberg wrote notes of congratulations and praise from Prague. Only Rauscher, who once had called Veith an artist of speech (*Sprachkünstler*), was silent.[164]

Veith continued his feverish pace into old age. When asked if he was prepared for his eternal rest (*ewige Ruhe*) he responded cheekily that he presumed heaven would be not rest but a higher activity (*höhere Tätigkeit*)[165] Veith preached his last series of Lenten sermons in 1863.[166] His eyes were giving him increasing difficulty until he was totally blind. Still he kept working. In the last thirteen years of his life he published eleven new works—dictating to the two women who dedicated themselves to serving him in his last years, or writing with a pencil between two rulers positioned on a page of paper, or using the typewriter that he had been given to make his work easier.[167]

Veith remained hopeful that Günther would eventually be vindicated. Although he ceased any direct references to Günther and his ideas, his works show the clear influence of Günther's view of the world, and he remained

Güntherian to the end.[168] Veith was one of the main witnesses in the canonization of Clement Maria Hofbauer, although he felt that he had to conceal Hofbauer's occasional statements against Rome. Veith advised Cardinal Schwarzenberg on his stance at the first Vatican Council against the definition of papal infallibility. However, when the dogma was defined, Veith resisted the invitations of many of the Güntherians to join them as Old Catholics.[169] Veith protested that he was too old to leave that which he had loved and served so long.

Veith became increasingly cantankerous in his old age. He even became disillusioned with Cardinal Schwarzenberg, whom he blamed for not being vigorous enough in leadership in the church. The cardinal continued to send financial support and to be genuinely concerned for the aging preacher.[170] Anna von Hoffinger and Antonie Hönig continued to wait on him hand and foot.

Johann Emanuel Veith died on 6 November 1876. He was eighty-nine years old. The cause of death was listed as old age. The funeral was attented by those who remembered him as an excellent preacher and a tireless servant of the church. He was buried with his friend Anton Günther and their friend Laurenz Greif, who had died ten years earlier. A tombstone was placed over the graves which read: "One in life, one in death, here rest in God Anton Günther, Laurenz Greif, Johann Emanuel Veith. Christ is my life and death is my gain. O Lord, give them eternal rest."[171] Veith would not have been pleased with the "eternal rest."

EPILOGUE

On 4 August 1879, Leo XIII published the papal encyclical *Aeterni Patris*, addressed to theological faculties and concerning the education of future priests as well as the basis of theological training for Roman Catholic laity. The disciplinary document was written by a group of anonymous Vatican bureaucrats and issued under the reigning pontiff's name, as is Roman custom. The probable main author of the document was Joseph Kleutgen, an early Güntherian enthusiast and later a rabid Güntherian foe. The *persona grata* of the document was one Thomas Aquinas, Angelic Doctor, sage of the thirteenth century. Thomas was proclaimed to be the most Catholic of thinkers. His system of thought expressed the Truth most coherently. The words Thomas himself had finally considered so much straw were the words that nineteenth century Roman Catholicism turned to in the growing confusion of pluralism in the modern world.

The *personae non gratae* of *Aeterni Patris* were all whose systems of thought, in whatever century, diverged too radically from the Thomistic measuring stick. Truth was eternal and Truth was Thomistic, or neo-Thomistic, to be more precise, for there was much that Thomas himself would not have recognized or agreed with had he recognized it. The *personae non gratae* were, among others, the Güntherians: the theologian and the preacher and their followers. By then the pen of Günther had long been at rest and the voice of Veith long been silent. Those that remained of their circle had ceased to care much for Roman labels and pronouncements. Most had joined the Old Catholics, who would hear nothing of papal infallibility.

The academic debate on Günther has continued, fueled by the passion of the erudite to conclude and contradict. Günther's writings, usually poorly read and selectively quoted and without a deeper understanding of the German and Roman Catholic worlds between Napoleon and 1848, have been the focus of many doctoral and professorial treatises. The aim of each study has been academic objectivity, the pursuit of Truth. Some have written to prove that the Roman label of "rationalist" does indeed apply. Others have written to claim to have found a "liberal" in the midst of reaction. Still others have written to proclaim a "Viennese prophet," decades ahead of his time.

Veith, perhaps because a popular preacher is seldom taken seriously by scholars, perhaps because the march of time betrays the limitedness of his pronouncements to contemporaries, has escaped much notice. There have been only occasional reminiscences by those who wished to celebrate the man and his service and protest that the labels applied to Günther did not apply to Veith, and there has been an occasional article or dissertation by students of homiletics or the history of medicine.

At the end of this study, there is a temptation to *conclude* as well, to be definitive and final, to have the last word. Living so long with Günther and Veith, gaining sympathy for their hopes and their struggles, having empathy with their banishment by Roman disparagement and disdain, looking from the perspective of the decades that have intervened, all invite dogmatic denouement. The labels, however, whether favorable or unfavorable, are too small, too confining. Dogma, of whatever stripe, fails to do justice to the richness of any age and the complexity of those who pursue Truth in time.

In the nineteenth century, when the authority that underpinned *opinio* had dissolved in Kantian critique and Napoleonic bravado, the search for *scientia* was strong. Truth was still looked for; pluralism was still eschewed. Günther and Veith found certainty for themselves and thought that others could not help but see Truth through their eyes as well. Günther and Veith were as much convinced that they had found Truth as those who condemned them. They thought they had discovered irrefutable Truth, that with them a new age had dawned when *opinio* and *scientia* were joined. They were Roman Catholics to the core and, in the end, it would be the Roman pontiff who would do them in. Perhaps that is the only lesson to be learned: the hubris of too much certainty this side of death.

And there is one other lesson. Biedermeier Vienna was a city triumphant. The defeat of Napoleon brought a sense of security that made the Viennese blind to less obvious events around them. Religion was losing its grip because the hope of reward or fear of punishment in the world after death had a lesser hold on those who sought cotton and iron and steel. The lessening was partly because of the sense of well-being in so many. But it was also a growing sense of despair and disillusionment in many others who perceived this world's injustice and were no longer content to wait for the promises of a better world after death. Churchmen spent their time on esoteric theological debate. Thinkers were convinced that the enemy was the one who denied their particular Truth. But there was a revolution being born in the hearts of many because of issues the churchmen did not want to see or were unable to see. Middle and upper class clerics were blind to the growing size and increasing misery of the lower class laborers. It was not until May of 1891 that the same Leo XIII who had declared Thomas the Catholic theologian par excellence would discover the importance of the workers. By then, the wisdom of Marx and his followers had long since sounded the call for the workers of the world to unite. And unite they did — but outside the circle of religion which they viewed as the bastion of the Old Order, of privilege and oppression. And, in most respects, the workers were right. The churchmen were late, too late, in recognizing that injustice done in this world was also their concern. One cannot but wonder what the world would have been like if the churchmen had seen and spoken earlier.

Each age struggles to discover the truths that give meaning and life. Each age butts against the limits of its own ability to know, usually and unfortunately only in retrospect. Every age, but our age especially, is in need of humility. Everyone in power, but especially church people in power, need to know the limits of their own "inspired" knowledge. In the study of the limits of another age, there is hope of discovery of the limits of one's own. Thomas Aquinas died in the knowledge of his own frailty, humbly ready to meet his God. Will we die with as much grace?

APPENDIX:
THE GÜNTHERIANS AND THEIR FRIENDS

ARNOLDI, WILHELM (1798–1864). Bishop of Trier, although favorable to Günther, bowed to Roman pressure and forbade the use of Günther in his seminary in 1852; as late as 1856 wrote favorably of Günther's thought, but accepted the Roman condemnation.

BALTZER, JOHANN BAPTIST (1803–71). Professor of dogmatic theology in Breslau who introduced Günther and J.H. Pabst; was a follower of Hermes until the latter's condemnation in 1835 and was considered a Güntherian after 1837, even though Günther rejected the Hermesian treatment of Kant. Defended Günther in Rome, but his abrasive approach won Günther no friends, became an Old Catholic after the Vatican Council.

BERMANN, MORITZ (1823–95). Art dealer, Viennese-born convert from Judaism to Roman Catholicism; along with Veith and Bondi wrote the original constitution of the Catholic Union. Editor of the *Wiener Courier* after 1856.

BONDI, IGNAZ: Born in Prague, probably influenced by the Frankists. Convert to Roman Catholicism from Judaism; director of unnamed institute at the University of Vienna. One of the leaders of the Catholic Union who, with Veith and Bermann, wrote its original constitution; elected to the municipal council of Vienna in 1848 and headed it during and immediately after the reconquest of Vienna.

BRAUN, JOHANN WILHELM JOSEPH (1801–63). Professor of church history in Bonn. A follower of Hermes and, in 1831, co-founded *Zeitschrift für Philosophie und katholische Theologie* with Achterfeldt, a periodical in which several Güntherians, especially J. H. Pabst, published.

BRÜGGEMANN, TH. (1803–71). Official in the Prussian ministry of culture, influential in getting Güntherians appointed to various theology positions. A special friend of Peter Knoodt.

BRUNNER, SEBASTIAN (1814–93). Priest and author who defended Veith against verbal attackers, active in Vienna during the 1848 revolution. Editor of the *Wiener Kirchenzeitung* and author of several volumes on the events of the times.

CATERGIAN, J. (1820–82). Priest of the Mecharisten community who defended Günther in Rome.

CROY, L. (d. 1855). Priest, friend of Sebastian Brunner; a feisty defender of Günther who retired in 1851 to devote himself entirely to Günther's defense.

DIEPENBROCK, MELCHIOR VON (1798–1853). Poet, cardinal of Breslau and protector of Günther who spoke against the definition of the Immaculate Conception.

EGERER, FRANZ (1830–1918). Parish priest, student of Carl Werner, wrote in defense of Günther.

EGGER, A. (1833–1906). Bishop of St. Gall who was a convinced Güntherian in his seminary years.

EHRLICH, JOHANN NEPOMUK (1810–64). Member of the Piarist order, priest and professor of moral theology in Krems, then Graz, and then Prague. One of the founders of fundamental theology (apologetics). Met Günther in 1835, probably through Hock, and remained a lifelong friend and a convinced Güntherian who went beyond Günther in later years.

ELVENICH, JOSEPH PETER (1796–1886). Professor of philosophy in Breslau. A former Hermesian, became a friend of Baltzer and Reinkens and a Güntherian. Joined the Old Catholics after 1870.

FLIR, ALOIS (1805–59). Priest and professor of philosophy and aesthetics in Innsbruck. After 1853, rector of the German National Church in Rome and consultor to the Index Congregation. Disgusted by the tactics of the Güntherians in Rome, he nonetheless was sympathetic to their science and attempted to prevent the indexing of Knoodt, a close friend of Leopold Trebisch.

FÖRSTER, HEINRICH (1799–1881). Bishop of Breslau after 1853. Was favorable to Güntherians until 1857, when he hoped they would quietly accept the church condemnation.

FÜHRICH, JOSEF (1800–76). Artist and friend of J. E. Veith who put texts to many of his works.

GÄRTNER, WILHELM (1811–75). Native of Bohemia, poet and priest, preacher at the University Church in Vienna, Professor of German Language and Literature in Pest.

GANGAUF, THEODOR (1809–75). Benedictine abbot in Augsburg. Defended Günther in 1853, but submitted after 1857, although his private correspondence suggests that he continued to believe in Günther's insights.

GASSER, VINZENZ (1809–75). Professor of Old Testament in Brixen and later bishop of the same city. Tried to prevent Günther's condemnation although he thought Günther had made some philosophical errors.

GERKRATH, L. (1832–64). Student of Knoodt, professor of philosophy in Braunsberg. Supported Günther, but was unwilling to get involved in the fight against condemnation.

GLÜCKER, MICHAEL (1773–1855). Medical doctor and host (with his daughter Notbura Piuma) of many of the Güntherian dinners, where much philosophy was discussed.

GREIF, LAURENZ (1785–1866). Priest of Würtemberg who moved to Vienna in 1811 with Baron Hake and remained after the Baron's return as tutor to Ferdinand von Schwarzenberg. A lifelong friend of both Günther and Veith and eventually buried with both. His own ambitions as a scholar never flourished, but he was a calming influence on Günther and Veith.

HÄUSLE, JOHANN MICHAEL (1809–67). Priest, professor of church history in Brixen. After 1838 director of students in the Frintaneum. Founder (along with J. Scheiner) of *Zeitschrift für die gesamte katholische Theologie*, which initially published many Güntherians.

HILGERS, J. (1803–1874). Student of Knoodt. Assistant professor of church history in Bonn who became an Old Catholic in 1870.

HOCK, CARL FERDINAND VON (1808–69). Native of Prague. Convert from Judaism through Veith's influence. Poet, economist, politician, editor of *Constitutionelle Donau-Zeitung*, and enthusiastic Güntherian.

HÖRFARTER, M. (1817–96). Güntherian through the influence of Tarnoczy. Friend of Hohenlohe in Rome.

HOFFINGER, ANNA VON. Took care of Veith in his sickness and helped him to continue his *Wissenschaft*.

HOFFINGER, JOHANN BAPTIST VON (1825–79). High official in the government bureaucracy. Active in the Catholic Union.

HOFFINGER, JOSEFA VON (1820–68). Post and translator of Dante. Contributed to all the Güntherian periodicals.

HOHENLOHE, GUSTAV ADOLPH FÜRST ZU (1823–96). Most prominent German in Rome, anti-Jesuit, favored Günther, obtained private audience with Pius IX for Günther's defenders. Later named cardinal.

ISFORDINK, JOHANN NEPOMUK (1776–1841). Medical doctor and professor of pathology in Vienna. A convinced Güntherian.

KALMUS, FRANZ (d. 1862). Native of Prague, Jewish convert, priest, teacher of religion at the Vienna Engineering Academy.

KAULICH, W. (1833–81). Student of Löwe and Ehrlich in Prague. Taught philosophy in Prague and Graz. Frequent visitor to Günther in Vienna.

KAYSER, J. B. (1826–95). Student of Knoodt. Taught philosophy in Paderborn. Remained Güntherian even after the condemnation.

KNAUER, VINZENZ (1828–94). Benedictine who taught philosophy in Vienna and Innsbruck. Wrote for *Wiener Kirchenzeitung*. Friend of Croy, Brunner, Egerer.

KNOODT, PETER (1811–89). Student with Günther in Vienna 1841–44 and then with Baltzer; professor of philosophy in Bonn. Ineptly defended Günther in Rome. Became an Old Catholic after 1870. Published biography of Günther.

LASAULX, ERNST VON (1805–61). Friend more than follower, taught philosophy at Munich and then Würzburg. Often visited Günther in Vienna, even after Günther attacked his father-in-law, Franz von Baader.

LEWISCH, J. C. (1805–84). Member of the Piarist order, priest, friend even after the condemnation, philosophy teacher at the military academy in Wiener Neustadt.

LÖWE, JOHANN HEINRICH (1808–92). Veith's nephew who converted to Catholicism under Veith's influence. Studied law and then philosophy after meeting Günther, taught philosophy in Salzburg and Prague. Began teaching Scholasticism after Günther's condemnation. Wrote biography of Veith.

LÖWE, JOSEF (d. 1861). Veith's newphew, a businessman who contributed support to Veith. Worked to keep Veith's writings off the Index.

MARX, J. (1803–76). Professor of church history and church law in Trier.

MAYER, GEORG KARL (1814–68). Professor of dogmatics and of exegetics in Bamberg who wrote in defense of Günther.

MELZER, ERNST (1835–98). Convert from Protestantism, student of Baltzer. Became an Old Catholic after 1870 and continued to espouse Günther's thought.

MERTEN, JACOB (1809–72). Professor of philosophy at the seminary in Trier whom Arnoldi forbade to use Günther's writings.

MÜLLER, GEORG (d. 1870). Bishop of Münster considered to be entirely favorable to the Güntherians.

NICKES, JOHANN PETER (1825–66). Student of Knoodt who became Benedictine to dedicate himself to scholarship. Moved to Rome and became active in defending Günther.

PABST, JOHANN HEINRICH (1785–1838). Medical doctor and one of Günther's closest friends who was an enthusiast for works of Descartes and Schelling.

PAPALETTERE, DOM SIMPLICIO (1815–83). Benedictine abbot of St. Paul's Outside the Walls in Rome. As consultor to the Congregation of the Index, active in Günther's defense.

POGAZAR, JOHANN CHRYSOSTOM (1811–84). Student of Pabst, professor of dogmatics at the seminary in Laibach and later bishop of the same city. Defended Veith as not a Güntherian.

REINKENS, JOSEPH HUBERT (1821–96). Priest and professor of church history in Breslau. Became the first Old Catholic bishop in 1873.

REINKENS, WILHELM (1811–89). Pastor in Bonn. A Romantic who was upset by Günther's condemnation and later became an Old Catholic.

SCHEINER, JOSEF (1798–1867). Native of Bohemia who worked as censor with Günther. Priest and professor of Old Testament in Vienna. Founder (with Häusle) of *Zeitschrift für die gesamte katholische Theologie*.

SCHLÖR, A. (1801–84). Priest and spiritual director of the seminary in Graz who published articles in defense of Günther.

SCHLÜTER, C. B. (1801–84). Professor of the history of philosophy in Münster who introduced Kleutgen to Günther's thought. Remained friend of Günther after condemnation.

SCHMID, FRANZ XAVIER (1819–83). Professor of philosophy in Salzburg and follower of Günther who became a Protestant in 1853 and became professor in Erlangen. Criticized Günther for submitting to Rome.

SCHNORR, LUDWIG VON CAROLSFELD (1788–1853). Painter and professor of art in Vienna who frequented Günther's dinner parties.

SCHÖN, BRUNO (1809–81). Conventual Franciscan, priest and pastor of the parish serving the General Hospital. Worked with the mentally disturbed. A convinced Güntherian and a close friend of Veith. (He was never provincial of the Conventual Franciscans as claimed by Pritz, et al.)

SCHÜLTER, BERNHARD (1801–84). Taught the history of philosophy in Münster and corresponded with Knoodt.

SCHWARZENBERG, FERDINAND VON (1809–85). Cardinal of Salzburg and then Prague and one of the most faithful protectors and supporters of Günther and Veith.

SCHWINGENSCHLÖGL, JULIUS (1826–98). Student of Carl Werner, priest and pastor who published in defense of Günther under the pseudonym J. Justus.

SMITH, BERNARD. Benedictine, vice rector of the Irish College in Rome. Defended Günther as consultor to the Congregation of the Index.

SPÖRLEIN, JOHANNES (1814–73). Professor of dogmatics and exegesis in Bamberg who published defense of Günther in which he claimed that a condemnation of Günther is a condemnation of Truth.

STAUDENMAIER, FRANZ (1800–56). Professor of dogmatics in Giessen and Freiburg. Praised Günther's work but suggested that his style alienated. Remained in written contact with Günther, dedicated his *Philosophie des Christentums* to Günther.

STEINRINGER, F. (1796–1866). Benedictine abbot of St. Paul's Abbey in Carinthia who supported Günther materially and spiritually. Willing to go to Rome to defend him. Ready to undertake a revision after the condemnation.

TARNOCZY, JOSEF MAXIMILLIAN (1806–76). Professor of dogma in Salzburg and later (1850) bishop there. Supported Günther but accepted condemnation.

THIEL, ANDREAS (1826–1908). Studied church history with Reinkens. Taught philosophy in Braunsberg. Became bishop of Ermland (1885). Friendly to Günther although not Güntherian.

TREBISH, LEOPOLD: Convert from Judaism who studied medicine in Paris and theology in Vienna. Unable to become priest because of a deformity. Wrote *Die christliche Weltanschauung*, in which he claimed Thomas Aquinas was the origin of monism in Christianity. More interested in secular politics after Günther's condemnation although he remained friends and was with Günther when he died.

TRÜTSCHEL, MAXIMILIAN. Taught philosophy in Braunsberg, defended Günther against Kleutgen.

WATTERICH, JOHANNES M. (1826–1904). Student of Knoodt, Benedictine, priest and professor of history in Braunsberg. Studied the papacy, became Old Catholic, then returned to Catholicism although afraid of his Old Catholic wife. Became Old Catholic once again, but returned to Roman Catholicism before he died.

WEBER, THEODOR (1836–1906). Favorite student of Knoodt, priest, professor of philosophy in Breslau. Joined Old Catholics and became their bishop in 1896. Tried to make Güntherianism a part of Old Catholicism.

WERNER, CARL (1821–88). Priest and professor of moral theology in St. Pölten and Vienna. Wrote in defense of Günther, but his study of the Scholastics brought him to appreciate them.

WERNER, FRANZ (1810–66). Priest and teacher who wrote for the Güntherian periodicals. Agreed with Günther's starting point of consciousness.

WOLTER, ERNST (1828–1908) and GUSTAV RUDOLF (1825–90). Brothers, both Benedictines, students of Knoodt. Lived in Rome during Günther's trial. Favorable to Günther but not willing to fight for him. Later helped found Beuron Abbey.

ZUKRIGL, JAKOB (1807–76). Priest and philosopher and Güntherian who followed J. S. Drey in Tübingen (1848).

NOTES

Preface

1. Jeffrey Stout, *The Flight from Authority: Religion, Morality, and the Quest for Autonomy* (Notre Dame, Ind.: University of Notre Dame Press, 1981), 37–40.

Chapter 1. The Search for Truth

1. Claude Welch, *Protestant Thought in the Nineteenth Century, Volume I: 1799–1870* (New Haven: Yale University Press, 1972), 45.
2. Stout, *Flight from Authority*, 234.
3. William Woodruff, "The Emergence of an International Economy," in *Fontana Economic History of Europe, Volume 4-2: The Emergence of Industrial Societies*, ed. Carlo M. Cipolla (London: Collins/Fontana Books, 1973), 656.
4. Ibid., 703.
5. Ibid., 714.
6. Owen Chadwick, *The Secularization of the European Mind in the Nineteenth Century* (New York: Cambridge University Press, 1975), 40.
7. For a description of the many definitions of "Liberalism" in the nineteenth century, see Thomas P. Neill, *The Rise and Decline of Liberalism* (Milwaukee: Bruce, 1953), the introductory chapter.
8. Michael Foucault, *Power/Knowledge: Selected Interviews and Other Writings, 1972–1977*, ed. Colin Gordon, trans. Colin Gordon, Leo Marshall, John Mepham, Kate Soper (New York: Pantheon Books, 1980), 47, 105.
9. Roger Aubert, *The Church Between Revolution and Restoration*, Vol. 7 of *History of the Church*, ed. Hubert Jedin and John Dolan, trans. Peter Becker (New York: Crossroad, 1981), 86.
10. Owen Chadwick, *The Popes and Europe an Revolution* (Oxford: Oxford University Press, 1981), 481.
11. Ibid., 7.
12. Ibid., 4.
13. Ibid., 108.
14. Ibid., 406.
15. For further development on liturgical reforms see Leonard Swidler, *Aufklärung Catholicism 1780–1850, Liturgical and Other Reforms in the Catholic Aufklärung* (Missoula, Mont.: Scholars Press, 1978). The weakness of the work is that Swidler viewed the period with the eyes of the Second Vatican Council and is looking for precedents. Hence it is a series of isolated examples of individuals who thought as Vatican II thought rather than a search for understanding of the period.
16. Chadwick, *Popes and European Revolution*, 518.
17. Ibid., 196.
18. Ibid., 165–71.
19. Ibid., 159.

20. Ibid., 254–56.
21. Ibid., 266–67.
22. Ibid., 297.
23. Ibid., 538.
24. Gerald A. McCool, *Catholic Theology in the Nineteenth Century; The Quest for Unitary Method* (New York: Seabury, 1977), 26.
25. Roger Aubert, *The Church in the Age of Liberalism*, vol. 8 of *History of the Church*, ed. Hubert Jedin and John Dolan, trans. Peter Becker (New York: Crossroad, 1981), 228.
26. Chadwick, *Popes and European Revolution*, 324–29.
27. Aubert, *Church in the Age of Liberalism*, 218–20.
28. Stout, *Flight from Authority*, 137.
29. James Collins, *Interpreting Modern Philosophy* (Princeton: Princeton University Press, 1972), 12.
30. Welch, *Protestant Thought*, 89.
31. Ibid., 93.
32. Peter Singer, *Hegel* (New York: Oxford University Press, 1983) 9–11.
33. Ibid., 19; Welch, *Protestant Thought*, 100.
34. Welch, Protestant Thought, 104–6.

Chapter 2. Biedermeier Vienna

1. *Biedermeier* is a term applied to all of the German world between the defeat of Napoleon and the revolutions of 1848. It is a combination of the names of two of Victor von Scheffel's characters, Biedermann and Bummelmaier. Biedermeier was reputed to have been a small-town schoolmaster in Swabia.

The term *Biedermeier* usually applies to cultural divisions. The term *Vormärz* refers to the political periodization and treats as a unit the time between the Congress of Vienna and the Revolution of 1848. The difficulty of the labels and the dates is discussed in Peter Stein, *Epochenproblem "Vormärz" 1815–1848* (Stuttgart: J. B. Metzlersche Verlagsbuchhandlung, 1974).

There are numerous general works on this period—the majority of the picture-book sort. The best scholarly introduction is found in Felix Czeike's *Geschichte der Stadt Wien* (Vienna: Fritz Molden, 1981) in which the Biedermeier era is treated on pages 157 to 186. A good treatment in English is Stella Musulin's *Vienna in the Age of Metternich from Napoleon to Revolution 1805–1848* (London: Faber and Faber, 1975), although the book does not follow most scholarly conventions. The best of the picture books with text is Franz Endler's *Wien im Biedermeier* (Vienna: Ueberreuter, 1978). Antal Madl has a short article entitled "Wien im Literarischen und Kulturellen Spannungsfeld zwischen Ost und West Europa" in *Wien zwischen den Revolutionen 1789–1848*, ed. Reinhard Urbach, (Vienna: Jugend und Volk, 1978), 167–180, in which he documents the proposition that the Biedermeier era was not all as pleasant as presumed in retrospect.

2. The German word *Bürger* is similar to the French word *bourgeois*. It refers to solid, middle-class respectability. At this time in Vienna, the bureaucracy had attained the status of *bürgerlich*. Throughout the Biedermeier period, this class remained comparatively small. Cf. Winfried Bammer, "Beiträge zur Sozialstruktur der Bevölkerung Wiens auf Grund der Verlassenschaftakten des Jahres 1830" (Ph.D. diss., University of Vienna, 1968), 363–64.

3. Maria Theresa and Joseph II both recognized the importance of the peasants as allies against the nobility but neither made extensive or obvious use of this natural

alliance. However, the reforms put in place by the two monarchs made the peasants a major factor in the early decades of the nineteenth century. These included a school program that sent first young boys and then young girls to school to learn the elements of reading and writing. The church opposed this measure, fearing that literacy would make the peasants susceptible to demagogic manipulation. Later land reforms were also to work to the advantage of the peasants.

    4. Bertram M. Gordon, "Catholic Social Thought in Austria, 1815–1848" (New Brunswick, N. J.: Rutgers University, unpublished dissertation, 1969), 29.

    5. Ibid., 172–74.

    6. Ibid., 193.

    7. The statistics for the population of the city of Vienna are taken from Erwin Schmidt, *Wiener Stadtgeschichte* (Vienna: Jugend und Volk, 1978). The 1848 figures find general agreement. The 1800 figures vary slightly from work to work. Erika Silber in her "Beiträge zur Sozialstruktur Wiens im Vormärz. Eine sozial-und wirtschaftsqeschictliche Arbeit auf Grund der magistratischen Verlassenschaftsakten des Jahres 1840" Ph. D. diss., University of Vienna, 1977) outlines a 32.8% increase in population between 1815 and 1840, with the most important increase coming from immigrants from Bohemia and Lower Austria. It was only in the 1830s that the birthrate began to exceed the death rate and also became a contributing factor to the increase. Silber refers to the high percentage of illegitimate births at the time (p. 252). Silber also carries some indices of wealth: over half the population died without mentionable possessions, and the majority of those who had anything had under one hundred Gulden. Only 3% of the population could be considered rich with possessions worth more than 10,000 Gulden. The middle class was actually very small (p. 252).

    8. Musulin, *Vienna in the Age of Metternich*, 60.

    9. Ibid., 131.

    10. Wolfgang Häusler, "Von der Manufaktur zum Machinensturm," in Felix Czeike, ed., *Wien im Vormärz* (Vienna: Verein für Geschichte der Stadt Wien, Kommissionsverlag Jugend und Volk, 1980), 32–56.

    11. Roman Sandgruber, "Indikatoren des Lebenstandards in Wien in der ersten Hälfte des 19. Jahrhunderts," in Felix Czeike, ibid., 57–74.

    12. "Wien galt zu Ende des 18. Jahrhunderts als genusssüchtigste Stadt Deutschlands, wenn nicht ganz Mitteleuropas," Ibid., 65.

    13. Ibid., 68.

    14. Josef Ehmer, "Produktion und Reproduktion in der Wiener Manufakturperiode," in Felix Czeike, *Wien im Vormaerz*, 107–32.

    15. Renate Banik-Schweitzer and Wolfgang Pircher, "Zur Wohnsituation der Massen im Wien des Vormärz," in Felix Czeike, ibid, 133–74.

    16. The reform ideas of Joseph II in the area of church and religion have been much described and much debated. A general introduction to those reforms, although a bit dated, is Georgine Holzknecht's *Ursprung und Herkunft der Reformideen kaiser Josephs auf kirchlichen Gebiete* (Innsbruck: Verlag der Wagnerischen k.k. Universitätsbuchhandlung, 1914). There has been much debate over whether Joseph's policies concerning religion and the church represent a reform of Catholicism or whether they were an attempt to make the church a branch of the state. The major proponents of the idea that it was a legitimate reform movement include Holzknecht herself, Eduard Winter (*Der Josephinismus und seine Geschichte: Beiträge zur Geschichte Österreichs 1740–1848* (2d ed. Vienna: 1962) and Fritz Valjavec, *Der Josephinismus: Zur Geistigen Entwicklung Österreichs im 18. und 19. Jahrhundert* (Munich: Oldenbourg, 1945). The major defenders of the concept of Josephinism as a state church are Ferdinand Maass, *Der Josephinismus* (Vienna: Herold, 1951) and Herbert Reiser, *Der Geist des Josephinismus und seine Fortleben* (Vienna: Herder, 1962). For review articles

on the issue, see Roger Bauer, "Le Josephinisme," in *Critique* 134 (1958): 622–39 and Erich Zöllner, "Bemerkungen zum Problem der Beziehung zwischen Aufklärung und Josephinismus," in *Österreich und Europa: Festgabe für Hugo Hantsch zum 70. Geburtstag* (Vienna: Styria Verlag, 1965), 203–19. A detailed description of religious practices before and during Josephinism is Klaus Gottschall, *Dokumente sum Wandel im religiösen Leben Wiens während des Josephinismus* (Vienna: Institut für Volkskunde der Universität, 1979).

17. Economic and political reasons prompted even the pious Maria Theresa to allow certain Protestants in her most Roman Catholic domain. Cf. Gordon, *Catholic Social Thought*, 5.

18. Anna Coreth summed up Habsburg baroque piety as emphasizing the Eucharist, the cross, and Mary (*Pietas Austriaca: Österreichische Frömmigkeit im Barock*, 2d rev. ed. [Vienna: Verlag für Geschichte und Politik, 1982]. Klaus Gottschall spoke of the major festivals of Habsburg piety being the Christmas midnight Mass, the Corpus Christi procession, the Rogation days, and the cult of Mary (*Dokumente Zum Wandel*, 47).

19. Franz Loidl quotes Ferdinand Maass as calling Maria Theresa the "Mutter des Josephinismus" in *Geschichte des Erzbistums Wien* (Vienna: Herold, 1983), 143.

20. Eduard Winter, *Josef II von den geistigen Quellen und letzten Beweggründen seiner Reformideen* (Vienna: Bindenschild Verlag, 1946), 6. See also, Loidl, *Geschichte des Erzbistums Wien*, 185–89.

21. Gerhard van Swieten (1700–72) was born in Leiden and brought to Vienna to be the personal physician of Maria Theresa. Along with his medical skills, he brought the ideas of the Enlightenment and of Freemasonry to the Habsburg court.

22. Wenzel Anton von Kaunitz-Rietberg (1711–94) was a soldier and advisor under both the Emperor Charles VI and his daughter Maria Theresa. He is reputed to have been a Protestant.

23. The discipline of church history is one that received most of its impetus in Protestant circles. The discipline of patristics was, next to the study of Scripture, the most important discipline for the foundation of Protestant theology and reforms. It was generally eschewed by Roman Catholics, who stressed dogma and doctrine. Joseph added insult to injury when he decreed that church history and canon law would be taught by the secular departments of the university and not by clerics. Pastoral theology was also introduced at the time of Maria Theresa. Cf. Owen Chadwick, *The Popes and European Revolution* (Oxford: Oxford University Press, 1981), 129.

24. Loidl, *Geschichte des Erzbistums Wien*, 141–49.

25. Franz Sissulak, "Das Christentum des Josephinismus. Die Josephinische Pastoralliturgie in dogmatischer Sicht," *Zeitschrift für katholische Theologie* 71 (1949): 54–89.

26. Chadwick, *Popes and European Revolution*, 412.

27. Ibid., 434 suggests that Joseph's toleration was not prompted by generosity on his part.

28. The shortage of clergy has been a problem throughout the history of Roman Catholicism. It is always difficult to assess exactly why some times and some places have more or fewer clergy. The celibate question seems to surface through the ages; Joseph himself thought of doing away with obligatory clerical celibacy, but decided against it because of his belief that a celibate would make a better servant of the state (Hans Hollerweger, *Zwischen Kaiser und Volk. Bemerkungen zur Situation des Priesters in der josephinischen Zeit* [Linz: Oberösterreichischer Landesverlag, 1972] 100–103). Joseph also seems to have considered a *simplex sacerdos* concept where there would be two levels of priesthood: the fully trained who would be able to perform the traditional priestly functions; and those who were not so well-prepared (*simplex*) and

could say Mass and perform most other ritual functions, but could not hear confessions or preach. (Gottschall, *Dokumente zum Wandel*, 34). See also Gordon, *Catholic Social Thought*, 219.

29. An indulgence was a remission of the temporal punishment due to sin. One could earn a number of days' or years' indulgence through certain prayers or practices. The plenary indulgence took away all the temporal punishment due because of sin. One of the most popular of the plenary indulgences was the Portiuncula, a privilege granted the Franciscans on the feast of the church of the Portiuncula on 2 August. One could gain the indulgence by visiting a Franciscan church and reciting six Our Fathers, Hail Marys, and Glory Bes; provided one had been recently shriven and was in the state of grace.

30. Rupert Winkler, *Der Zustand der Klöster in der Wiener Erzdiözese um 1828 nach den Visitationsberichten des Wiener Erzbishofs Leopold Maximilian Graf Firmian* (Vienna: Miscellanea aus dem Kirchenhistorischen Instituts der katholisch-theologischen Fakultät 22, 1972), cites numerous examples.

31. Gerhard Winner, *Die Klosteraufhebungen in Niederösterreich und Wien* (Vienna: Herold, 1967), gives a lengthy account.

32. It was not uncommon for founders of religious communities to found a first order, usually for celibate men who wanted to live in community; a second order, usually for celibate women who wanted to live a cloistered life; and a third order, for lay men and women, usually married, who wanted to live "in the world" but still participate in the specialness and grace of belonging to a religious community. The religious life has commonly been considered to be a "higher" form of life than the secular life, whether one is married or simply living as a single person. This attitude shows a certain gnostic tendency.

33. Chadwick, *Popes and European Revolution*, 414.

34. In his school years Günther was asked to respond to the question on whether or not he thought Joseph was still alive. Cf. Peter Knoodt, *Anton Günther* (Vienna: Braumüller, 1881), 1:43.

35. Gordon, *Catholic Social Thought*, 2.

36. Metternich has evoked any number of studies. The most recent attempt in English to give a summary of other works is Andrew Milne's *Metternich* (Totowa, New Jersey: Rowman and Littlefield, 1975). There is also an account of the foreign minister in Egon Caesar Conte Corti's *Metternich und die Frauen* (Vienna: Kremayr and Scherian, 1977), but there is little evidence of scholarship in the work. Metternich was, after all, *foreign* minister and not minister of the interior. His influence on internal Austrian policy is still debated. A good introduction to his work in this area remains R. W. Seton-Watson's "Metternich and Internal Austrian Policy" in *Slavonic and East European Review* 17 (1939): 539–555, and 18 (1940): 129–41.

37. Alan Sked, "The Metternich System, 1815–1848" in *Europe's Balance of Power, 1815–1848*, ed. Alan Sked (London: Macmillan, 1979) 98–121.

38. Eduard Winter, *Frühliberalismus in der Donaumonarchie: Religiöse, Nationale und Wissenschaftliche Strömmungen von 1790–1868* (Berlin: Akademie Verlag, 1968), 69.

39. Gordon, *Catholic Social Thought*, 2.

40. The idea for the police state was a pet project of Francis I himself. It was he who suggested the possibility to his father, Leopold II, and developed the first guidelines. It was against Freemasonry and Jacobinism, but the language was so elastic that it could be easily applied to anyone the state found suspect. Musulin, *Vienna in the Age of Metternich*, 21–22.

41. Censorship was never completely effective. The large private libraries containing

many forbidden volumes are proof of this. It seems that luxury editions of works or collections would have more chance of being approved than cheaper editions. Musulin, *Vienna in the Age of Metternich*, 256.

42. E. Winter, *Frühliberalismus*, 19.

43. Francis I went to Rome in 1819. It was considered a defeat for the Josephinists, who did not want their emperor to be influenced by the magnificence of Rome. Cf. E. Winter, *Frühliberalismus*, 72, 87–88.

44. Gordon, *Catholic Social Thought*, 151.

45. Ibid., iii.

46. Rupert Winckler, "Erzbischöflicher Visitationsbericht von Jahre 1830," *Beiträge zur Wiener Diozesangeschichte 14 (1973): 23*–24.

47. In 1804 the clergy were asked to preach on the value of the smallpox vaccination. There was much resistance from priest and people because the vaccine was thought to contain the Antichrist. Gordon, *Catholic Social Thought*, 233.

48. The Jesuits were suppressed in 1773. Most found their way into the diocesan clergy, the teaching or governmental bureaucracy, or into Russia or Prussia. The Jesuits were re-established by Pope Pius VII in 1814. They were allowed to found a novitiate, but only in Galicia, far removed from the seat of power in Vienna. It was only after the death of Francis I in 1835 that they regained a presence and renewed influence in Vienna itself. It was after 1835 that they came to have charge of the University in Innsbruck. It is commonly thought that Jesuit influence was behind the expulsion of the Protestants from, the Zillertal in 1837, the last exile of Protestants in Habsburg lands. See Alan Reinermann, "The Return of the Jesuits to the Austrian Empire and the Decline of Josephinism, 1820–1822," *Catholic Historical Review* 52 (1966): 372–90.

49. Johannes Thauren, *Die Leopoldinen-Stiftung zur Unterstützung der amerikanischen Mission. Ihr Werden und Wirken* (Vienna: Missionsdruckerei St. Gabriel, 1940); and Gertrude Kummer, *Die Leopoldinenstiftung 1829–1914. Der älteste österreichische Missionsverein* (Vienna: Dom Verlag, 1966).

50. Andreas Posch ("Kirchenpolitische Einstellung Metternichs," *Religion, Wissenschaft, und Kultur* 13 [1962]: 119–127) disagrees with the ideas developed by Ernst Widmann in *Die religiöse Ansichten des Fürsten Metternich* (Darmstadt: Wintersche Buchdruckerei, 1914). Posch suggests that although Metternich had little use for *Schwärmerei*, he did learn to tolerate it and actually was influenced by his third wife to a more convinced backing of Roman Catholicism. Metternich did help in the re-establishment of the Jesuits in Habsburg lands, but there is no evidence that he encouraged the "state within a state" for which the Jesuits were sometimes known. Widmann admits that Metternich became more pious with his third marriage and as he grew older, but insists that Metternich remained a son of the Enlightenment and an opponent of the Jesuits. Alan Reinerman (*Austria and the Papacy in the Age of Metternich*, vol. 1, *The Union of Throne and Altar, 1809–1830* [washington, D.C.: Catholic University of America Press, 1979], 46) is convinced that Metternich wanted to dismantle the remaining religious orders, but came up against the attachment of Francis I for all that his ancestors had set in place.

51. Musulim, *Vienna in the Age of Metternich*, 272–73.

52. Gordon, *Catholic Social Thought*, 283.

53. Most of the many lives of Hofbauer run to the pious, typical of hagiography. The facts are there, but they are usually embellished with accent on the Finger of God. The saint becomes superhuman in an attempt to show how close he was to God. One notable exception is a work by Karl Richard Ganzer, *Der heilige Hofbauer, Träger der Gegenreformation im 19. Jahrhundert* (Hamburg: Hanseat Verlag, 1939). Ganzer's

seventy-two pages, written in the era of National Socialism, have all the facts correct. The interpretation is, however, much different from the usual pious fare. He excoriates Hofbauer as lazy, asocial, pro-Jewish and against the superior nation of Aryans. Ganzer sees a direct line between Hofbauer and Kurt von Schuschnigg, the last chancellor of Austria before Hitler took over. The connection is not meant to flatter either man. The only truly balanced and reasonably objective account is Rudolf Till's *Hofbauer und sein Kreis* (Vienna: Herold, 1951).

54. Redemptorists, or the Congregation of the Most Holy Redeemer (CSSR) were founded by Alphonsus Liguori in 1732 in a small town near Naples. Their major work was the preaching of parish missions, retreats, and novenas.

55. Josef Freiherr von Penckler (1751–1830) was the son of an Austrian diplomat and himself a politician. After 1802, he was also the prefect of the Minoritenkirche which was (and still remains) the Italian national church in Vienna.

56. The Polish people seem to have had (and to continue to have) a special devotion to the Mother of God. Hofbauer was not the first, nor would he be the last, to use this form of devotion as a point of attraction.

57. Caroline Pichler (1769–1843), a poet and author who grew up in court and was in contact with the great literary men of her time. Her maternal grandfather was a Protestant officer.

58. Friedrich (1772–1829) and Dorothea (Ca. 1760–1839) von Schlegel hosted Hofbauer almost daily. Friedrich was the son of a Protestant minister from Hanover, a philosopher and diplomat. Dorothea was from the Jewish family of Mendelsohn, and had two sons by a first marriage (Philipp and Johann Veit). All four converted to Catholicism in 1810 and later Friedrich and Dorothea moved to Vienna. Friedrich's writings are of the romantic genre and glorify the papacy as the legitimate head of the church in every nation. The medieval period of history was normative for both Schlegels.

59. Friedrich's older brother August Wilhelm von Schlegel (1767–1845) also converted to Catholicism. He visited Vienna occasionally; but he continued to work in northern Germany. In later life he became a rationalist, interested in eastern civilizations.

60. Clemens Brentano (1778–1842), poet and playwright whose collected works fill seven volumes, was a friend of the Schlegels from their German years. He spent the year beginning in July 1813 with the Schlegels in Vienna and was known to the members of Hofbauer's circle.

61. Laurenz Greif (1785–1866) was born in Würtemberg and moved to Vienna in 1811 with Baron Hake. He became a part of the circle of young clerics who lionized Hofbauer. When the baron returned to Würtemberg, Greif stayed on in Vienna as the tutor of a banker's children and then in the service of the Schwarzenberg family. He became close friends with Anton Günther and Johann Emanuel Veith, and eventually all three were buried in the same crypt. Greif was a calming influence in the theological and philosophical discussions, staying in the background and providing humor.

62. Leopold Horny, priest, was a member of the Hofbauer circle—and was the one who introduced Hofbauer and Günther. After Hofbauer's death, he remained a friend of Günther.

63. The Klinkowström family had strong ties to Hofbauer. The father of the family, Friedrich August (1778–1835) was a painter and teacher from Pomerania. He converted from Protestantism to Catholicism under the influence of Hofbauer and started a school for the children of the nobility in the Alsergrund. Friedrich August's wife Luise was the sister of Josef Pilat, also in the Hofbauer circle. Hofbauer became the godfather of their first son, who eventually became a Jesuit and one of the more

famous preachers in Vienna. Friedrich and Luise considered it an honor to be buried near Hofbauer. They were in the same cemetery, a few graves down, until Hofbauer's remains were moved to the church of St. Mary on the Banks.

64. Johann Madlener (1787–1868) was a priest, philosopher, and preacher. He joined the Redemptorists and went to Innsbruck to help found the order there. He returned to Vienna in 1830 and wrote against Hermes, Günther, and Veith, whom he considered to have become rationalists and pantheists in the process of refuting Kant and Schelling.

65. Adam Müller (1779–1829) was born in Berlin and secretly became Catholic in Vienna in 1805. He was involved in Prussian politics and in 1811 was sent to Vienna by Hardenburg, who preferred to have him at a distance. He delivered a series of lectures in Vienna in the spring of 1813 which created a stir because they were strongly anti-Napoleonic at a time when Vienna was pro-French. He was a friend and rival of Friedrich Schlegel. His writings romanticize the state and originally suggested a synthesis of Roman Catholicism and Protestantism as the basis for government. He believed that freedom was the freedom to obey God and not the freedom to leave one's social state. In later years he became increasingly ultramontane.

66. Georg (1788–1847) and Johann (1788–1847) Passy were both members of the Hofbauer circle. Georg became a lay brother in the Redemptorist order and carried on a literary career that included editing a periodical (*Ölzweige*), establishing a loan library, and becoming the librarian for the Redemptorists in Vienna. Johann became a priest and Redemptorist. Johann preached the first Mass of Johann Emanuel Veith.

67. Josef Anton von Pilat (1782–1865) was a civil servant and a publisher. He edited the *Österreichischer Beobachter* and became Metternich's private secretary in 1801 when Metternich was the Austrian ambassador in Berlin. He followed Metternich to Paris and then back to Vienna. In Vienna, he left his Freemasonry and indifferentism through the influence of Hofbauer and his circle. He became a major protector of Hofbauer.

68. Joseph Othmar Rauscher (1797–1875) was one of the youngest members of the Hofbauer circle. He was ordained a diocesan priest and eventually became the Bishop of Graz (1849) through the influence of Cardinal Schwarzenberg, and the Archbishop of Vienna (1853) through the influence of his former pupil and then Emperor Francis Joseph. His early years in Hofbauer's group are not well documented; but after Hofbauer's death, he was increasingly opposed to Günther and Veith and played a large role in their troubles with the church authorities.

69. Johann Peter Silbert (1777–1844) was a prolific author and priest. He was born in the French border area of Alsace, moved to Vienna in 1817, and found his way into the Hofbauer circle. He became a friend of Veith and worked with him on *Der Bote von Jericho* in 1828.

70. Franz Springer (1791–1827) was a painter who joined the Hofbauer circle and became a Redemptorist and a priest. He was in the first group of novices to join the order after it was made legal in Habsburg lands.

71. Franz Szechenyi (1754–1820), a baron from Hungary, befriended Hofbauer and hosted many of the meetings of the group. His daughters Sophie and Franziska made Hofbauer their confessor. His son Stephan became a great warrior and patriot.

72. Zacharias Werner (1768–1823) was a Prussian Protestant who turned Roman Catholic after a conversion experience in 1810. He was ordained a priest four years later and then moved to Vienna. He had known of Hofbauer in Warsaw but had hated what he stood for. In Vienna, he found a home in the Hofbauer circle although his decision to become a Redemptorist did not last. He was a popular preacher in Vienna, both because of his eloquence and because of the curiosity caused by a Protestant, thrice-married, who had become priest and preacher.

73. Roman Zängerle (1771–1848) was born in Ulm, became a Benedictine, took a doctorate in theology and philosophy, became a professor of Scripture first in Salzburg and then in Vienna, where he became a friend of Hofbauer. He became a secular priest when his monastery was dissolved. In 1824 he was appointed the Bishop of Seckau (Graz) and was responsible for bringing Veith and the Redemptorists to that diocese.

74. Franz Xavier Zenner (1794–1861) was a friend of Hofbauer's and from 1826 to 1833 the director of the Vienna seminary. He was the confessor of Johann Pabst and introduced him to Anton Günther. He later was against Günther and, as the Auxiliary Bishop of Vienna from 1851 to 1861, did much to increase Günther's tribulations.

75. Gregorius Thomas Ziegler (1800–52) was a Benedictine and a professor of dogmatic theology at Vienna. He was a friend of Hofbauer's and doubtless met Günther and Veith. His theory of self-consciousness is very similiar to the one later developed by Günther. Ziegler was made a bishop in later life.

76. "Das Evangelium muss neu gepredigt werden."

77. "Sagten die Wiener: 'Willst du einen berühmten Redner hören, dann geh' in diese oder diese Kirche; willst du aber einen Apostel hören, dann geh' zu Pater Hofbauer.'" Adolf Innerkofler, *Der Heilige Klemens Maria Hofbauer, Ein Österreichischer Reformator*, 2d rev. ed. (Regensburg: Pustet, 1913), 116.

78. Till, *Hofbauer und sein Kreis*, 163.

79. There was much controversy over Hofbauer's position on the issue of papal infallibility during the years when that was being debated and Hofbauer was being considered for canonization. Veith was of the opinion that Hofbauer had little use for a papacy that claimed to be infallible. Many Güntherians who became Old Catholics after the proclamation of papal infallibility by Vatican Council I stressed this very much. Most of the hearers of Hofbauer would not have heard him either denounce the pope or claim that he was infallible. The arguments of other generations should not be read backward into the mouths of those who did not consider those issues. (See Innerkofler, *Der Heilige Klemens*, 125.

80. Anton Günther was never to enter the Redemptorist novitiate, although it is likely that he seriously considered doing so, which would account for his name on the list. Johann Emanuel Veith actually joined and remained a Redemptorist until 1830.

Chapter 3. The Theologian and the Preacher

1. The University of Tübingen was founded in 1477 and included a theology faculty which became Protestant in 1534. A second, Roman Catholic, theology faculty was added in 1817. Both the Protestant and Roman Catholic faculties were influential in nineteenth-century thought.

2. Peter Knoodt, *Anton Günther* (Vienna: Braumüller, 1881), 1: 360; and Karl Pleyer, "Johann Emanuel Veith und sein Kreis" (Ph.D. diss., University of Vienna, 1934), 74–75.

3. Knoodt, *Günther*, 1:382 and Pleyer, "Veith," 74–75.

4. Günther decided to write his autobiography after his seventy-second birthday in 1855. It was not completed until 1859 and was not published until eighteen years after his death. The publisher was Knoodt, who had received the materials from Veith shortly after Günther's death in 1863 (Knoodt, *Günther*, 2:246). The publication came after Knoodt had joined the Old Catholic movement in protest against the declaration of papal infallibility by the first Vatican Council. Günther's autobiography occupies the first 165 pages of the two-volume work and runs through 1828, the date of publication of Günther's first book. Knoodt continued beyond 1828, mostly with a

series of introductions to lengthy quotations from letters and documents. Knoodt's stance is, not surprisingly, anti-Roman.

5. Knoodt, *Günther*, 1:165.
6. Ibid., iii–iv.
7. Ibid., 274. Günther was not clear on when and why his family became Roman Catholic.
8. Three of the six children were not to live past the age of four, a fact which Günther attributes to the failing health of his mother (Knoodt, *Günther*, 1:12), but which was certainly well within the prevailing mortality rate for young children.
9. Ibid., 8.
10. Ibid., 9–10.
11. Günther was named after his godfather, Anton Groh, and St. Anthony of Padua.
12. Knoodt, *Günther*, 1:11.
13. Günther referred to the Piarist at the local church, Pater Nickels, who preached in sharp contrast to the diocesan pastor and, indeed, to the majority of preachers of the time who stressed a God of judgment before whom one came in fear and trembling (Knoodt, *Günther*, 1:15–16).
14. Ibid., 22.
15. Ibid., 53.
16. In Haida, Günther lived first with the Trauscke family (Knoodt, *Günther*, 1.24) and then as the chamber servant of Pater Nepomuk Janke, where he lived in Pater's room and waited on him when needed. (Ibid., 39.) When Günther moved to Leitmeritz, he lived with the Platzer family (Ibid., 50) and then with the village mayor (Ibid., 56). Living arrangements were always such that Günther had little privacy. His most agreeable lodging was in the monastery, where he slept in the corner of the room of Pater Jarcke. Since the Pater was gone a great deal, Günther had the needed quiet for study.
17. Ibid., 40.
18. Ibid., 66–79.
19. In 1805, Bernard Bolzano (1781–1848) was given the newly created chair of the philosophy of religion at Prague. In 1819, he lost his position on charges that he was not orthodox. His orthodoxy has been much debated; but one thing is certain: he offended the Emperor by some of his theories on freedom. He taught both Günther and Veith.
20. Knoodt, *Günther*, 1:76.
21. Günther was not to outgrow his belief that the structures of reality are visible to the correct method applied systematically. His theology is very much influenced by this presumption. See the next chapter.
22. Günther claimed some influence from Abbe Millot's *Universalgeschichte* and Herder's *Ideen zur Philosophie der Geschichte* as the basis for his own growing disillusionment (Knoodt, *Günther*, 1:72–73).
23. Günther mentioned the book by Lossius as *Wörterbuch der Kantischen Philosophie* (Knoodt, *Günther*, 1:84). The actual title of the work is *Neues philosophisches allgemeines Reflexion*, published in Erfurt in 1806, (Eduard Winter, *Die Geistige Entwicklung Anton Günthers und seine Schule* [Paderborn: Schöningh, 1931], 258).
24. Schubert's book is entitled *Ansichten von der Nachtseite der Naturwissenschaften*. Günther mentioned the works by Lossius and Schubert along with Adam Müller's *Staatskunst machen Epochen* as the most influential in his young years.
25. Knoodt, *Günther*, 1:74. Theo Schäfer (*Die erkenntnistheoretische Kontroverse Kleutgen Günther* [Paderborn: Schöningh, 1961], 28) gave these lectures more

importance than seems merited. Villaume's approach is common even today in shocking people from "childhood" into "adulthood" in matters of belief as well as other of life's belief structures.

26. "Arme Mäuse waren wir, aber keine Kirchenmäuse. Das Christenthum war nur Sache der Heloten." Knoodt, *Günther*, 1:93.

27. Ibid., 76-78, 94.

28. Ibid., 88.

29. Donald Dietrich ("German Idealism and the German Catholic Theological Response—Hermes, Möhler, Staudenmaier, and Günther" [Ph. D. diss., University of Minnesota; 1969], 377) wrongly listed the date of Günther's arrival as 1812. In fact, he contradicted himself by putting the date for Günther's meeting with Hofbauer in 1811-12, which would have been impossible if Günther had arrived in 1812.

30. Knoodt, *Günther*, 1:92.

31. Ibid., 94-95. The expression "in den saueren Apfel der Heirath zu beissen" is Günther's own.

32. Ibid., 97.

33. It is interesting to note that Günther was not unusual in not talking about the rigors of celibacy; one just did not discuss those things in any public forum. When Günther did consider marriage it was for money and position but not for love; it is only in the twentieth century that marriage based on romantic love became common.

34. Günther met Müller through Hofbauer. Franz von Baader (1765-1841) was a Romantic theologian and philosopher in Munich, where Günther's writings were well received.

35. Knoodt, *Günther*, 1:97.

36. "Kein Wissen sonder eine Tat habe die Welt erlöst." Knoodt, *Günther*, 1:104-105.

37. Ibid., 112. Günther continued to visit Korn until Korn's death in 1824. He modeled Peregrinus Niger, the affable and intelligent country pastor in his *Vorschule*, after Korn.

38. Günther himself was imprecise about the date he met Hofbauer, putting the meeting at the beginning of the chapter on the years 1815-21 (Knoodt, *Günther*, 1:113). Günther was introduced to Hofbauer as Veith's friend and Veith was not known to be a member of Hofbauer's circle until 1817. Karl Pleyer ("Veith," 63) concluded that Günther could not have known Hofbauer before then. Hermann Mayer's conclusion ("Anton Günther: Peregrins Gastmahl" [Ph.D. diss., University of Vienna; 1951], 10) that Veith would have been known to Hofbauer in any case is plausible and the earlier date (1815) is probable.

39. A general confession is the practice within Roman Catholicism of telling, not just the sins since one's last confession, but all the sins of one's past life. It is common among those entering religious life at the time of final profession of vows and is generally considered of value at the time of any conversion experience.

40. Knoodt, *Günther*, 1:114.

41. Günther studied privately with the following university professors: Old Testament, Ackermann; church history, Rutterstock; moral theology, Fritz; dogma, Ziegler; New Testament, Zengerle (Knoodt, *Günther*, 1:117).

42. Ibid., 119.

43. Günther was ordained because he had a guaranteed income from a nobleman. The more usual situation for ordination was to be ordained for a particular bishop to work in his diocese or for a religious community to work in the various places staffed by that community. There was, however, a long tradition of lay ownership of various churches and chapels and these laymen had the privilege of selecting their own clergy

with ecclesiastical approval. In Günther's case, that lay prerogative is interpreted simply in monetary terms. Ordination meant that the church would not be responsible for the individual. With a guarantee that that would be taken care of, the church was willing to ordain one who had passed the proper exams, even without approval from his bishop or from a religious superior.

44. Knoodt, *Günther*, 1:122.

45. Günther must have been considering entering the Redemptorist novitiate in 1819–20 because his name appeared on the list of possible candidates submitted to the government in 1820 when the erection of a novitiate in Vienna was finally granted. But Günther must have changed his mind by the time of his journey to Raab (Thomas W. Simons, Jr., "Unveröffentliches über den Aufenthalt des Wiener Philosophen und Theologen A. Günther in Galizien" in *Wiener Geschichtsblätter* 30 [1975], 147).

46. Knoodt, *Günther*, 1.125.

47. Ibid., 125.

48. Anton Günther, *Peregrins Gastmahl: Eine Idylle* (Vienna: Mechitaristen, 1830).

49. Knoodt, *Günther*, 1:144.

50. Ibid., 142.

51. Ibid., 145–46.

52. "Suus cuique Isaak." Ibid., 100. Landes remained in contact with Günther until the former's death in 1844. He did not stay in Poland much longer than Günther but was transferred to Rome. Günther was convinced that the Polish party had won.

53. Ibid., 2:57.

54. Ibid., 1:100. "Pater" is the Latin-German title for a priest who also belongs to a religious order. Simons ("Unveröffentliches," 146) suggests that Günther's having snubbed the Redemptorists and then having left the Jesuits to remain a private scholar was part of the reason that he created so much hostility with his writings. There could be some truth in the argument. History knows many stories of rivalries between religious orders and between religious communities and diocesan priests. That sort of rivalry is usually couched in polite language, but did have an effect on politics.

55. Knoodt, *Günther*, 1:159.

56. Günther received invitations to chairs at the Universities of Munich (1831), Bonn (to replace Hermes after his condemnation in 1835), Breslau (1844), Munich again (1844), and Tübingen to replace Drey after his retirement in 1847. Although Günther accepted none of the posts, they were filled by Güntherians (except Munich). Günther was also offered the position of canon in the cathedral at Breslau in 1847, a position he also turned down (Knoodt, *Günther*, 1:366).

57. Günther did not receive a call to a university chair in Vienna, at least in part, because of the enemies he had made who were influential—especially after 1848 when Rauscher's power was on the rise. Part of the reason may also have been that Günther had no doctoral degree from an Austrian university. He received an honorary doctorate in theology form the University of Munich in 1833 and another honorary degree in law and philosophy from the University of Prague in 1848. He also received an honorary degree from the University of Giessen in 1848 and was made an "auswärtiger Mitglied der philosophisch-philologischen Klasse" in Munich in 1853 at the suggestion of Lasaulx (Paul Wenzel, *Das wissenschaftliche Anliegen des Güntherianismus* [Essen: Ludgerus, 1961], 10). Günther had acquired the Viennese love-hate for the city, which was expressed in constant complaint about life there coupled with the inability to leave it. It was not even, as Pleyer ("Veith," 66) suggests, that his friends were in Vienna. Even when his closest friends—Veith, Schwarzenberg, Ehrlich—were in Prague, Günther was unable to leave Vienna.

58. Günther's first reviews appeared in the *Wiener Allgemeine Literaturzeitung*

(1812), the *Theaterzeitung* (a reveiw of Grillparzer's *Ahnfrau* in 1817), and the *Wiener Jahrbücher für Literatur* (1818/1819—edited by Buchholz of the Hofbauer circle).

59. The present-day Sterngasse 3 in the First District of Vienna. The Neustädlerhof was built in 1734 as a residence for monks visiting Vienna from Wiener Neustadt.

60. Knoodt, *Günther*, 1:508.

61. St. Ruprecht's, in the First District of Vienna, is the oldest church in Vienna; parts of the structure date from the eleventh century. It is currently used as the French national church.

62. Knoodt, *Günther*, 2:45.

63. Ibid., 1:371–372.

64. Johann Heinrich Löwe, *Johann Emanuel Veith: Eine Biographie* (Vienna: Braumüller, 1879). This remains the standard work on Veith. Löwe referred to an autobiography that Veith supposedly wrote; since none has been found, one presumes Löwe meant Veith's extensive correspondence.

65. Pleyer, "Veith," 48.

66. ". . . das unansehnliche verhützelte Männlein Veith mit dem abstossenden, hässlichen affenartigen Gesicht . . ." (Eduard and Maria Winter, *Domprediger Johann Emmanuel Veith und Kardinal Friedrich Schwarzenberg: Der Güntherprozess in unveröffentlichten Briefen und Akten* [Vienna: Böhlau, 1972], 9).

67. "Ich bin mir selbst zu wider. Ich bin ein lächerliches Ungeheuer mit sehr feinen Fühlfäden, und eine verunglücktes Ergebniss des achtzehnten Jahrhunderts. Oft wenn ich lächle, fühle ich in mir deutlich die Grimasse einer Hyäne, einer solchen nämlich, die gern Salat frisst. Die Leute haben ganz recht, dass sie mich nicht leiden können, und ich bin sehr albern, dass ich zuweilen noch darüber mich wundere." Löwe, *Johann Emanuel Veith*, 339–340.

68. Ibid., 225.

69. Ibid., 51.

70. Ibid., 340. Veith called himself a "Winkelhocker," which literally means someone who cowers in the corner.

71. Ibid., 48, 341–42.

72. Ibid., 239–40.

73. Ibid., 199.

74. Ibid., 344–45.

75. Ibid., 200.

76. Pleyer, "Veith," 76.

77. Johann Heinrich Löwe, "Der hundertste Jahrestag der Geburt J. E. Veiths am 10 Juli 1887" in *Österreichishes Jahrbuch*, ed. J. Helfert, vol. 11 (1887), 181.

78. Löwe, *Johann Emanuel Veith*, 349–51.

79. "Ein müssiges Leben ist ein Hundeleben." Ibid., 230.

80. Ibid., 308.

81. Ibid., 352–53.

82. ". . . nichts aus sich." Ibid., 345.

83. Sigmund Freud was twenty years old when Veith died. One cannot help wondering what the younger man of Jewish background would have had to say about the older man who converted from Judaism to Christianity, never married, and never felt that he measured up.

84. In Prague at the time when Veith was studying there, the movement called Haskalah was very popular among Jews who looked to German culture. Following the lead of Moses Mendelssohn (1729–86), the Haskalah advocated assimilation into the culture in which the Jews found themselves. When Joseph II issued patents of toleration, even though on a limited basis, it looked as if assimilation could work.

85. Jewish citizens of the Habsburg empire were expected to pay a tax simply because they were Jewish. There were also other taxes levied on Jews, such as a tax to entertain guests. Taxes were collected by a tax-farmer who was allowed to keep a percentage of what he managed to collect.

86. Thomas W. Simons, Jr., "The Prague Origins of the Güntherian Converts, 1800–1850," in *Leo Baeck Institute Yearbook* 20 (1977), 249.

87. Löwe, *Johann Emanuel Veith*, 23, 117, 201.

88. Simons, "The Prague Origins," 249. Constantin Vidmar (*Johann Emmanuel Veith: Ein Gedenkblatt zu seinem hundertsten Geburtstag* [Vienna: Mayer, 1887], 10) claimed that Joseph was baptized and also wanted to become a priest. Perhaps Vidmar confused Joseph with Elias, who became a Catholic and a doctor, but seemed never to have considered priesthood.

89. Löwe, *Johann Emanuel Veith*, 89.

90. "Klattau, dieser mir allerverhasstest Ort, wo ich meine vernachlässigt, gemisshandelte, freudlose und von abscheulichen Exempeln geärgert Kindheit zubrachte, ohne wenigstens als einzigen Nutzen Böhmisch zu lernen, was tausend mal besser gewesen wäre, als das verrottete Talmud. Ibid., 9.

91. Ibid., 4.

92. Jacob Frank (1726–91) believed that the messianic era would be ushered in, but only after a conversion to Catholicism. His belief in himself was not shaken even when he was imprisoned for thirteen years as an insincere convert. There were reports of licentiousness in the Frankist camp and the movement seemed to fade with Jacob's death, although his daughter Eve assumed leadership.

93. Simons ("Unveröffentlichtes," 247–51) noted that the Löwe (Löwy) family had Frankists in their ranks and that, although not all tobacco monopolists were Frankist, many Frankists were tobacco monopolists. Both Frankist and Enlightenment segments were drawn from the elite of better-educated and wealthy Jews. Veith would have had access to both these circles in Prague. When he moved to Vienna, he wrote poems to the glory of Bernhard von Eskeles and Fanny von Arnstein, both members of Jewish banking families and members of the Jewish Enlightenment. Simons concluded that Veith rejected both the Frankist and Enlightenment tendencies and that the poems were mere pleas for patronage.

94. Pleyer ("Veith," 10) claimed that this trip had to have taken place in 1806 or 1807 since Goethe was not in Karlsbad between 1795 and 1805.

95. In 1808 Vienna did indeed have a reputation for medicine. The reign of Maria Theresa had brought Gerhard van Swieten to Vienna. The reign of Joseph II had brought the building of the general hospital (*Allgemeines Krankenhaus*) which is still in use today and only slowly being replaced by newer facilities. The progressive ideas of Johann Peter Frank had influenced policies at the hospital at the time Veith moved to Vienna.

96. Knoodt, *Günther*, 1:93. Pleyer ("Veith," 127) noted that some have questioned whether or not the veterinarian Veith was the same as the medical doctor Veith. Pleyer proved that they were.

97. Pleyer, "Veith," 13.

98. A popular story about Veith was the courage he showed in intervening in a hostile situation between French troops and Viennese citizens. It was simply a misunderstanding, but the inability to communicate threatened major blows. Veith's role as interpreter saved the day (Löwe, *Johann Emanuel Veith*, 23).

99. Veith's dissertation ("Dissertatio inauguralis medicobotanica sistens plantarum officinalium in Austria sponte crescentium aut in hortis cultaram enumerationem systematicam") was published by Geistinger in Vienna under the title: *Systematische Beschreibung der vorzüglichsten in Österreich wildwachsenden oder in Gärten*

gewöhnlichen Arzneigewächse. His outline of herbs was issued by the same publisher under the title *Abriss der Kräuterkunde für Tierärzte und Ökonomen*.

100. Pleyer ("Veith") discussed the writings of Veith in *Thalia* (13–14), *Selam* (18), and *Friedensblätter* (23).

101. Ibid., 13.

102. Pleyer ("Veith," 22) claimed that this was the Strobelhofgesellschaft which met in the Wollzeile from 1815 to 1818. He connects this with Georg Passy also, a brother of Joseph Passy who had connections to Hofbauer. Winter (*Geistige Entwicklung*, 12), on the other hand, referred to a coffeehouse in the Essiggasse. The Strobelgasse and the Essiggasse meet at the Wollzeile.

103. "Ich bin überall grob—ordentlich grob, mündlich wie schriftlich, und seitdem ich's so hatte, mag man mich überall gern dulden und sage mir viel schönes . . . ich schmiere ganz entsetzlich viel, und stellen Sie sich vor, die Leute lesen's oder hören's an." Quoted from a letter of April 1814, Veith to his uncle, in Pleyer, "Veith," 21–22.

104. Ibid.

105. Löwe, *Johann Emanuel Veith*, 31–32.

106. Winter and Winter (*Veith und Schwarzenberg*, 12) claim that the year was 1814.

107. Professor of zoology Franz Ritter von Scherer and professor of pathology Carl Philipp Hartman.

108. Pleyer ("Veith," 9) stressed Bolzano's influence.

109. "eine ziemlich verwirrte Reihe von inneren und äusseren Ängsten, Freuden, Leiden, Tollheiten und Kämpfen eine Zeit lang einen so wunderlichen Tanz um mich her und in mir herum aufgeführt hat" (quoted in Löwe, *Johann Emanuel Veith*, 45).

110. "Ich bin durch keinen Menschen zum Glauben und zum Priesterstande vom Misthaufen her berufen worden, sondern in ganz innerlicher, aber klarer und präziser Weise," quoted in ibid., 43. Veith often spoke badly of his Jewish heritage—could, in fact, be considered anti-Semitic. Pleyer ("Veith," 110–111) found this attractive and comments that Veith had all the good but none of the bad qualities common to Jews. Pleyer pointed to the friendship between Veith and the antisemite Sebastian Brunner as proof thereof, since Pleyer assumed Brunner would not have befriended Veith otherwise. It should be remembered that Pleyer wrote in 1934.

111. ". . . da er eben Convertite ist, bey denen in der Regel der Katholizismus nur bis in den Hals, aber nicht höher hinauf vorgedrungen ist" (quoted in Joseph Pritz, *Wegweisung zur Theologie: Briefe A. Günthers an J. N. Ehrlich mit einer Einleitung* [Vienna: Domverlag, 1971], 96).

112. Pleyer, "Veith," 26. The police and bureaucracy did not make distinctions between various religious communities. All groups whom they considered to be reactionary and superstitious were labeled "Jesuit."

113. Ibid., 27–29.

114. Löwe, *Johann Emanuel Veith*, 80–84.

115. Friedrich Schleiermacher (1768–1834) was a theologian and preacher in Berlin. The core of his religious insight was that God can be discovered in a feeling of total dependence (*Schlechthinige Abhängigkeit*).

116. "Herr, stosse das arme Hundlein nicht von dir!" (quoted in Löwe, *Johann Emanuel Veith*, 82). This reminds one of Hegel's remark about Schleiermacher's theology when he says that if Schleiermacher is correct, then the most religious of all creatures is the dog.

117. "Wenn ich auf einen Misthaufen verfaulen müsste, so weiss ich dass ich ihm auch dafür Dank und Lob werde bringen müssen." Quoted in Löwe, *Johann Emanuel Veith*. 81.

118. Ibid., 47–48.
119. Dates for Veith's ordination vary; the 20 April 1820 date is from the Vienna Archdiocesan Archive.
120. Pleyer, "Veith," 77.
121. Löwe, *Johann Emanuel Veith*, 90.
122. Ibid., 103. Among others were Landgrafen von Fürstenberg, Fürst Collato, and Fürst Kinsky. Although he was encouraged by the order to be the doctor for these people, Veith's Redemptorist brothers later complained that he was too friendly with the rich and took advantage of them.
123. "Du wirst einst als Prediger gewaltig ziehen und predigen in einer ganz neuen Art, freilich bekehren wirst du nicht viele." Quoted in Pleyer, "Veith," 29.
124. Ibid., 29. Cardinal Schwarzenberg, an old friend and ally of Veith, is one of the few who wrote that he would not want Veith for a confessor: "Ich ehre ihn unendlich, schätze ihn als Prediger und Schriftsteller, liebe seine belehrenden und ergötzenden Umgang, aber bin ganz deiner Meinung, dass ich ihn nicht zum Beichtvater möchte. Er ist ein Baumeister im grossen, dem aber die alltäglichen Handgriffe mangeln. Grosse Männer sind nicht für den Alltagsgebrauch, und die für das alltägliche Leben besten Menschen sind selten gross." (A letter of Schwarzenberg's to his aunt quoted in Cölestin Wolfsgruber, *Friedrich Kardinal Schwarzenberg* [Vienna: Carl Fromme, 1906], 1:232).
125. "Die Unordnung ist die wahre Ordnung" (quoted in Löwe, *Johann Emanuel Veith*, 108).
126. "Dies macht keinen anderen Eindruch auf mich, als dass ich streben werde, den göttlichen Willen in inneren Erkenntnis zu suchen." Ibid., 104–105.
127. Ibid., 97.
128. Leopold Graf Firmian (1766–1831) was in charge of the Vienna Archdiocese from 1822 until his death.
129. Löwe, *Johann Emanual Veith*, 117–118.
130. Ibid., 99–100.
131. J. E. Veith, *Vater Unser*, (Vienna: J. P. Solinger, 1831).
132. Löwe, *Johann Emanuel Veith*, 113–114.
133. Christian Kinsky (1777–1835) was a soldier and friend whom Veith often visited.
134. Löwe, *Johann Emanuel Veith*, 118–122.
135. The dates of his appointment vary. This date is the one recorded in the Vienna Archdiocesan Archive.
136. Löwe, *Johann Emanuel Veith*, 177.
137. J. E. Veith, *Austria's Trauer*, (Vienna: Mayer, 1835).
138. Löwe, *Johann Emanuel Veith*, 284.
139. Ibid., 184, 211–213.
140. Ibid., 190.
141. Ibid., 203–205.
142. Ibid., 210.
143. Bruno Schön, *Humoristische Pillen gegen üble Laune, Melancholie, und dergleichen Grillen*, 1–3 (Vienna: Prandl, 1856–58.
144. Löwe, *Johann Emanuel Veith*, 191–192.
145. Ibid., 314–19.
146. Homeopathic medicine was a technique whereby small doses of the disease virus were used to treat someone who already had the disease. It is a forerunner of vaccination but concentrated on those who already had the disease rather than on prevention.
147. Löwe, *Johann Emanuel Veith*, 180.
148. Ibid., 294.

Chapter 4. The World of Anton Günther

1. Peter Knoodt, *Anton Günther*, (Vienna: Braumüller, 1881), I, 104–105.
2. There is considerable debate about whether or not Johann Emanuel Veith was in fact a Güntherian. His works were investigated but not condemned by the Vatican. It is the contention of this author that Veith was indeed a Güntherian and his works were liable to the same censures as those of Günther.
3. J. Pritz, "Gedanken A. Günthers zur Union zwischen Katholiken und Protestanten" in *Theologische Praktische Quartalschrift* 110 (1962): 91–105.
4. Günther's collected works were reprinted by Minerva, Frankfurt am Main, in a nine-volume edition in 1968. The same publisher also reprinted the philosophical handbook *Lydia*, which was published from 1849 to 1854 by Günther and Veith, in a five-volume edition in 1963. The fundamental theology department of the theology faculty of the University of Vienna under the leadership of J. Reikersdorfer has begun to re-issue some of the more difficult to obtain works of Günther. To date, they have published one volume containing *Lentigos und Peregrins Briefwechsel* and *Anti-Savarese* (Vienna: Herold, 1978). J. Pritz has published a collection of Günther's writings with an introduction to his life and thought under the title *Glauben und Wissen bei Anton Günther, Wiener Beiträge zur Theologie*, (Vienna: Herder, 1963); the selection stresses the theological writings and Günther as a forerunner of Vatican Council II. Its weakness is that it is a bit too selective and does not give a flavor of the complete Günther. In spite of his negative conclusions about Günther's Roman Catholic orthodoxy, the best overall introduction to Günther and his thought remains Paul Wenzel's *Das wissenschaftliche Anliegen des Güntherianismus. Ein Beitrag zur Theologiegeschichte des 19. Jahrhunderts* (Essen: Luderus. 1961).
5. Günther's theory was fine; his practice was somewhat different. He had a particularly hard time accepting any criticism, even calling any who could not agree with him "apes" (E. Winter, *Die geistige Entwicklung Anton Günthers und seine Schule* [Paderborn: Schöningh, 1931], 158–60).
6. Knoodt, *Günther*, 2:150.
7. Jean Paul is the pseudonym for Johann Paul Friedrich Richter, a German writer who lived from 1763 to 1825. For Jean Paul, humor was the *ungekerte Erhabene, die angewandte Unendliche*.
8. G. McCool, *Catholic Theology in the 19th Century—The Quest for Unitary Method*, (New York: Seabury, 1977), 95.
9. E. Winter, *Geistige Entwicklung*, 255–66.
10. J. Pritz, "Zur Geschichte der philosophische-theologische Schule A. Günthers. Briefe A. Günthers an den Philosophen J. H. Löwe, 1841–1862" in *Festschrift F. Loidl*, ed. K. Flieder (Vienna: Brüder Hollinek, 1970), 1:241.
11. The common English translation for both *Begriff* and *Idee* is "idea." McCool (*Catholic Theology*, 92) and D. Dietrich ("German Idealism and the German Catholic Theological Response—Hermes, Möhler, Staudenmaier, and Günther—1815–1860" [Ph. D. diss., University of Minnesota; 1969], 338) translated *Begriff* as "concept" and *Idee* as "idea." In order to insure clarity, we shall continue to use the German words *Begriff* and *Idee*.
12. F. Lakner, "Die 'Idee' bei Anton Günther" in *Zeitschrift für Katholische Theologie* 59 (1935): 4.
13. E. Winter, "Anton Günther und die barock-romantische paternal-familiale Soziologie E. K. Winters" in *Theologische Quartalschrift* 111 (1930): 400.
14. Condemning all of philosophical and theological thought that had preceded him was one of Günther's least gracious and least explained assumptions. Günther himself did not treat this in any systematic fashion. However, L. Trebisch, in close

contact with Günther, wrote a history of Christian thought in which he systematically took to task all who had not seen the dualist insight. See L. Trebisch; *Die christliche Weltanschauung und ihre Bedeutung für Wissenschaft und Leben* (Vienna: Braumüller, 1852).

15. *Verstand* is usually translated as "understanding" or "common sense." Philosophically, it is understanding in terms of *Begriff*. It is not to be confused with *Vernunft*, which is also "understanding" but in the philosophical world, in the realm of *Idee*.

16. J. Pritz, *Glauben und Wissen*, 79.

17. McCool, *Catholic Theology*, 92.

18. The word "revealed" is consciously chosen here. For Günther there was no difference between faith and reason in this realm. Truly, one *believes* because there can be no direct sense-knowledge.

19. *Erscheinungen* is the German word. It is generally translated with the English word "appearances"—but this is not to be interpreted as unreal. Perhaps "manifestations" conveys a richer meaning, although it too suffers from an unreal quality in English.

20. Lakner, "Die 'Idee' bei Anton Günther," 52.

21. *Geist* is translated as "spirit" here. Dietrich translated the word as "soul" at times, "spirit" at others. He was then forced to translate *Seele* as "mind." McCool used the "spirit" translation of *Geist* and uses "soul" as the translation for *Seele*. To be a bit more precise, *Geist* is translated here as "spirit," but *Seele* is translated as "consciousness" since this seems to capture more of Günther's meaning.

22. J. Pritz, *Mensch als Mitte—Leben und Werk Carl Werners* (Vienna: Herder, 1968), 82.

23. A. Günther, *Vorschule zur Spekulativen Theologie des Positiven Christentums*, 2d. ed. (Vienna: Wallishaussen, 1848), 2:15.

24. A. Günther, *Lentigos und Peregrins Briefwechsel* (Vienna: Braumüller, 1857), 84.

25. Günther, *Vorschule*, 2:141.

26. Dietrich, "German Idealism," 411; Wenzel: *Das Wissenschaftliche Anglien*, 163–64; McCool, *Catholic Theology*, 103.

27. This relationship is a cognitive one. McCool (*Catholic Theology*, 102) introduced the relationship as a love relationship. There's no justification for this except perhaps to make Günther more palpable to the twentieth century and to the Roman Catholic audience he writes for.

28. E. Winter, *Das positive Vernunftkriterium in der Philosophie Anton Günthers* (Warnsdorf: Opitz, 1928), 13.

29. Günther, *Vorschule*, 2:360.

30. McCool, *Catholic Theology*, 104.

31. Pritz (*Mensch als Mitte*, 86) did not think Günther reached the unity he claims in the human. Pritz agreed with Günther's critics that Günther is out of step with the Council of Vienne which condemned Peter Olivi in 1311 and insisted that the human person is unified with the soul as the form of the body.

32. Günther, *Vorschule*, 2:360.

33. E. Winter, *Positives Vernunftkriterium*, 23.

34. Günther, *Lydia*, (1849), 184; *Vorschule*, 2:186; *Euristheus und Herakles—Metalogische Kritiken und Meditationen* (Vienna: Braumüller, 1843), 482.

35. Lakner, "Die 'Idee' bei Anton Günther," 236–37. Günther made little reference to Schleiermacher and was not directly influenced by him.

36. J. Pritz, "Offenbarung. Eine philosophisch-theologische Analyse nach A. Günther" in *Zeitschrift für katholische Theologie* 95 (1973): 252.

37. Günther, *Juste-Milieus*, 355–357.

38. A. Günther, *Janusköpe für Philosophie und Theologie* (Vienna: Wallishaussen, 1834), 257.
39. A. Günther, review of E. Reinhold's *Theorie des menschlichen Erkenntnisvermögens* in *Zeitschrift für Philosophie und katholische Theologie* 8 (1836): 146.
40. Günther, *Juste-Milieus*, 368.
41. Günther, *Vorschule*, 2:77. Günther presumed that conscience (not consciousness) is the voice of the divine left after the fall.
42. A. Günther, *Anti-Savarese*, ed. Peter Knoodt, (Vienna: Braumüller, 1883), 68.
43. Ibid., 76.
44. A. Günther, *Peregrins Gastmahl. Eine Idylle* (Vienna: Mechitaristen, 1830), 540.
45. Günther, *Vorschule*, 1.110.
46. Günther, *Vorschule*, 2:369.
47. Ibid., 536.
48. Ibid., 536–37.
49. Günther, *Lentigo*, 193.
50. Ibid., 189, Günther; *Janusköpfe*, 275.
51. McCool, *Catholic Theology*, 103; Pritz; "Offenbarung," 252–53; Wenzel; *Das wissenschaftliche Anglien*, 164–67; K. Beck; *Offenbarung und Glaube bei A Günther* (Vienna: Herder, 1967), 59–64.
52. Günther, *Lydia* (1849); 319.
53. Günther, *Euristheus*, 516.
54. Ibid., 511.
55. Günther found a *necessity of creation*—the Absolute Being finds expression in Trinity and in the *Nicht-ich* in an intrinsic sense. Pritz (*Mensch als Mitte*, 96) suggested that Günther was at variance with Roman Catholicism for the *Nicht-ich* is also dependent on the freedom of God.
56. Günther, *Vorschule*, 1:204.
57. Günther, *Lydia* (1849), 400.
58. Günther, *Juste-Milieus*, 361.
59. Günther, *Vorschule*, 1:30; *Peregrin*, 154; Dietrich; "German Idealism," 426.
60. Günther, *Euristheus*, 164; *Vorschule*, 2:68.
61. Günther, *Lydia* (1849), 241; (1851), 168.
62. Günther, *Antisavarese*, 74.
63. Günther, *Vorschule*, 1:117.
64. Günther, *Antisavarese*, 74 (*dreieinige Gott und* eindreiige Welt).
65. Günther, *Janusköpfe*, 111.
66. Günther; *Euristheus*, 367. E. Winter (*Positives Vernunftkriterium*, 55) saw the "error" of Günther in that he did not leave room for God to reveal himself except through his works, his creation. The present author disagrees with Winter's position, believing that although Günther's preferred direction is from this world—especially the human—to God, Günther also left room for revelation from above. This will be treated more thoroughly in the section on revelation and church.
67. Ernst Karl Winter ("Anton Günther: Ein Beitrag zur Romantikforschung" in *Zeitschrift für die gesamte Staatswissenschaft* 88 [1930], 290–91) recognized the tension and described Günther as rational Romantic or romantic Rationalist.
68. E. Winter, *Positives Vernunftkriterium*, 12.
69. Beck, *Offenbarung und Glaube*, 145–146; Pritz; *Glauben und Wissen*, 254–56.
70. McCool, *Catholic Theology*, 106.
71. A. Dempf, "Die letzte Vollanthropologie: Dem Andenken Anton Günthers" in *Wissenschaft und Weltbild*, 15 (1962), 188; Pritz ("Offenbarung," 254) insisted that Günther had not lost *Glaube* in *Vernunft*.
72. Ernst Karl Winter, "Anton Günther," 306. Winter also believed that Günther

only became a priest because of the momentary influence of Hofbauer and that he would have been much better off had he not followed that impulse.

73. Beck, *Offenbarung und Glaube*, introduction.
74. Günther, *Vorschule*, 2:34.
75. Ibid., 57.
76. H. Klinger, "Urzustand, Sündenfall und Erbsünde bei A. Günther" (Ph. D. diss., University of Vienna; 1964), 32; Günther; *Vorschule*, 2:160, 191, 287, 343, 345; and *Peregrin*, 358–59 and 474.
77. Dempf, "Die letzte Vollanthropologie," 189.
78. "Gott will die freien Geister nicht zwingen, weil er nicht kann, und er kann nicht, weil er nicht will. Er als ewige Liebe will nur Liebe, um in Liebe selig zu machen und erzwungene Liebe ist keine Liebe," wrote Günther in a review of L. A. Kähler's *Supernaturalismus und Rationalismus* in *Jahrbücher der Literatur* 10 (1820), 68.
79. A. Günther, *Süd-und Nordlichter am Horizonte spekulativer Theologie* (Vienna: Mechitaristen, 1832), 275; Beck; *Offenbarung und Glaube*, 156.
80. Günther, *Vorschule*, 2:cci, 327.
81. Ibid., 73–78, 87; *Peregrin*, 321; A. Günther; *Der Letzte Symboliker* (Vienna: Wallishauser, 1834), 28.
82. Günther, *Vorschule*, 2:51.
83. Günther, review of Kähler's *Supernaturalismus* in *Jahrbücher der Literatur* 9: 194.
84. Günther, *Vorschule*, 1:175, 179, 242; 2:57, 105, 128, 216, 238–40; P. Knoodt; *Günther*, 2:129.
85. A. Günther, review of A. Eschenmayer's *Religionsphilosophie* quoted in Pritz; *Glauben und Wissen*, 201; Pritz; *Mensch als Mitte*, 91.
86. Günther, *Vorschule*, 2:135, 162–63; *Letzte Symboliker*, 69, 308; *Süd-und Nordlichter*, 195, 213, 222, 226.
87. A. Günther, letter to J. N. Ehrlich, quoted in Pritz; *Glauben und Wissen*, 236.
88. A. Günther, *Thomas A Scrupulis. Zur Transfiguration der Persönlichkeits Pantheismen* (Vienna: Wallishauser, 1835), 216.
89. Pritz, *Mensch als Mitte*, 103.
90. J. Pabst, *Janusköpfe*, 96 (co-authored with Günther).
91. Beck, *Offenbarung und Glaube*, 149.
92. Pritz, "Offenbarung," 283–84.
93. Günther, *Thomas A Scrupulis*, 118.
94. Günther, *Vorschule*, 2:293–97.
95. A. Günther, review of J. S. Drey's *die Apologetik als wissenschaftliche Nachweisung der Göttlichkeit des Christentums* quoted in Pritz; *Glauben und Wissen*, 162.
96. Günther was sometimes accused of not believing that the human will of Christ *could* have sinned. Pritz countered these objections in *Glauben und Wissen*, 98.
97. J. Pritz, "Zur Lehre A. Günther's von der Kirche" in *Dienst an der Lehre. Studien zur heutigen Philosophie und Theologie. Festschrift für Kardinal Franz König*, Katholische Fakultät der Universität Wien *Wiener Beiträge zur Theologie* 10 (Vienna: Domverlag, 1965), 309.
98. Günther, *Peregrin*, 303.
99. Günther was rejecting Augustine here. See Pritz; "Lehre von der Kirche," 317.
100. R. Schnackenburg, *Gottes Herrschaft und Reich*, 4th ed. (Freiburg: Herder, 1965), introduction.
101. Günther, review of Kähler, 31.
102. Günther, *Letzte Symboliker*, 226.

Chapter 5. Johann Emanuel Veith as Güntherian and Preacher

1. On 9 September 1831, Veith combined his talents as priest and doctor and preached a sermon on the epidemic. He pictured the epidemic as an opportunity and suggested that God had let it happen to remind people of their humanness and to give them a chance to practice Christian love. It was a test of faith, our willingness to love God, and our willingness to love our neighbor. Veith also mentioned homeopathic medicine obliquely in the sermon (J. E. Veith, *Die Cholera im Lichte der Vorsehung* [Vienna: Mechitaristen Congregations Buchhandlung, 1831]).

2. When Veith taught, he took the usual professorial sitting position; but he spoke in a conversational tone. Unlike other professors who read elaborately prepared lectures, Veith lectured from brief notes which he wrapped around his finger and slowly unwound while he spoke (B. Schön, "Anhang als Schlüssel zum Verständnisse Veithischer Werke" in *Briefe über Geistesgestörte für Seelsorger, Ärzte, Richter, Eltern, Lehrer, Künstler, und alle Freunde der Menschenkunde* [Vienna: Hartleben, 1873], 102).

3. C. Wolfsgruber, *Friedrich Kardinal Schwarzenberg* (Vienna: Carl Fromme, 1906), 1:232.

4. T. W. Simons, Jr. ("Vienna's First Catholic Political Movement: The Güntherians 1848–1857" in *Catholic Historical Review* 55 [1969]: 182) quotes the Redemptorist Passarat, who wrote in a letter to his superiors: "Father Veith delivers the Lenten sermons with great profit for the soul and not a little applause; our church, which is not small, could scarcely hold all the people who thronged to it. Among the auditors were to be seen our bishop and persons of the Imperial Court, and even the Archdukes became curious to hear these sermons."

5. Veith delivered three sermons on 9, 10, and 11 April 1835. They praised the Habsburgs in general and Francis I in particular. Veith stressed the delivery from the fate of the French, viewing the French Revolution as a wild and lawless chaos. He stated with certitude that Francis I had received the crown of justice from the Judge of Rulers and Peoples (J. E. Veith, *Austria's Trauer* [Vienna: Mayer, 1835]).

6. Bruno Schön ("Anhang als Schlüssel," 124) recounts the following anecdote: "Hofrath Kiesewetter hatte einen Hausmeister, der jede Predigt von Veith besuchte. Da sagte ihm jener einmal: Du wirst was von Veith verstehen? Der ist für Dich zu gelehrt, zu hoch. Da erwiderte der Hausmeister: Alles versteh' ich, Euer Ganden, und woher hätte ich mein Bisl Gelehrsamkeit als von Veith?"

7. J. H. Löwe, *Johann Emanuel Veith. Eine Biographie* (Vienna: Braumüller, 1879), 173, reads: "Das Publikum, an das Veith seine Vorträge richtete, gehörte zum grossen Theile den höheren Ständen an, und—was nicht häufig vorzukommen pflegt—der weibliche Theil desselben wurde an Zahl bei weitem von dem männlichen überwogen, der zumeist aus Studierenden, Literaten, Beamten, Künstlern und Gelehrten sich zusammensetzte." O. Popelar ("J. E. Veith. Ein homiletischer Beitrag zur Aufklärung und Restauration" [Ph. D. diss., University of Vienna; 1969], 196), quoted Sebastian Brunner as observing that when Veith preached the congregation was "stets männlich überwiegend."

8. A. Innerkofler, *Der heilige Klemens Maria Hofbauer. Ein Österreichischer Reformator*, 2d ed. Regensburg and Rome: Pustet, 1913), 478.

9. C. Wolfsgruber, "Veith als Homilist" in H. Swoboda, *Erster Homiletischer Kurs in Wien* (Vienna: Kirsch, 1911), 130.

10. Wolfsgruber quoting L. Greif in *Schwarzenberg*, 1:190.

11. J. E. Veith, *Leidenswerkzeuge Christi* (Vienna: Ambruster, 1827) were the first of Veith's Lenten sermons preached and published. J. E. Veith, *Die Anfänge der Menschheit* (Vienna, Braumüller, 1865) were the final set preached and published.

12. Wolfsgruber, "Veith als Homilist," 130. Simons ("The Güntherians," 181) claims that Veith spoke to the head and *not* the heart. This is an oversimplfication and designed to fit into Simons's thesis that sees Veith as consciously interested in reaching out to the educated intellectuals of his time. See also H. Belovari, "Christlicher Demokratismus und christlicher Sozialismus im Jahre 1848 in Wien" Ph. D. diss., University of Vienna, 1960), 125–26.

13. J. H. Löwe, "Der hundertste Jahrestag der Geburt J. E. Veiths am 10. Juli 1887" in *Österreichisches Jahrbuch*, ed. J. Helfert, vol. 11 (1887), 178.

14. Ibid., 178. Wolfsgruber ("Veith als Homilist," 142) quotes Veith in an 1859 letter to Cardinal Schwarzenberg saying: "Die theologia speculativa führt Glatteis." Veith did in fact become disillusioned with speculative theology and tried to rid his sermons of it, but this did not occur until after the Günther controversy had begun. Those who read Veith's later works would question whether he was ever successful in abandoning speculative theology in his work.

15. Popelar, ("J. E. Veith," 209) quotes several sources, contemporary with Veith and later, friend and foe, who considered Veith to be *the* major speaker in the German world of his times.

16. Löwe, "Der hundertste Jahrestag," 183.

17. Wolfsgruber ("Veith als Homilist," 147) quotes Veith in a tongue-in-cheek passage about the need for preparation, but how it can be overdone and how the most important thing is the gospel and inspiration from above: "Ehedem galt es, die Füsse beschuken mit den Sandalen des Evangeliums, denn Kopf und Herz waren von oben erleuchtet. Jetzt müssen wir Geistliche studieren scholastisch, phantastisch, drastisch, aszetisch, apologetisch, synthetisch, analytisc, kritisch, ethisch, pathetisch, patristisch, allegorisch, historisch und endlich kommt gar wenig heraus mit den mühsam einstudierten Reden. Ohne himmlischen Zunder ist alles nur Plunder."

18. Löwe ("Der hundertste Jahrestag," 180) quoted Veith writing from Prague in April 1851: "Ich bin sehr faul dermalen und das schlimmste ist, dass ich aus dem Stegreife in der Kirche nicht reden kann noch mag. Ich höre mich gleich schwätzen, und das ist mir unerträglich." I. F. Castelli, *Memorien meines Lebens* (Munich: Müller, 1913), 1:29, did not remember how he met Veith but commented that he had never seen anyone who could compose and write down prose and poetry more quickly.

19. In his lifetime, Veith published close to fifty volumes of sermons and three prayer books. This is, of course, in addition to his many articles, short stories, plays, poems, etc. Wolfsgruber ("Veith als Homilist," 143) referred to sketches of Veith's sermons between 1825 and 1849 but does not mention where these were found. It is probable that, if these did exist, they were destroyed in the chaos of war. There is a large collection of sermons by Veith in the Archive of the City of Vienna. These were in the possession of Josef Bermann, a convert to Catholicism from Judaism and a Güntherian. These sermons, with several exceptions, are not in Veith's own hand but rather the work of someone who attended Veith's sermons (presumably Bermann himself) and wrote down their content. Most are in the same handwriting, but there are several in different handwritings, suggesting that at least several people recorded Veith. The manuscripts are valuable records of what Veith actually preached before it was reworked for publication. Popelar ("J. E. Veith") makes no mention of either the Wolfsgruber reference or the Bermann collection.

20. Popelar, "J. E. Veith," 191–93. Wolfsgruber ("Veith als Homilist," 137) speaks of Veith's sermons as "wohlgefügtes Ganzes in Geschlossenheit und Kraft. Einheit, das Grundgesetz alles Schönen, Guten, Wahren, ist ihr Gepräge. Klar und deutlich ist die Gliederung des Organismus, die Teile sind vollkommen gebildet, die Übergänge im besten Verhältnis zu den Teilen. Der Kanzelspruch ist das Allmachtswort,

das dem Gebilde den Odern des Lebens einhaucht. Es tönt durch die ganze Predigt hindurch und klingt aus in kurzen Worten des Segens oder einer Bitte als den wirklich zündenden Kurzschluss der Predigt." See also Wolfsgruber, "Veith als Homilist," 147.

21. J. E. Veith, *Homiletische Ährenlese. Auswahl von predigten und Gelegenheitsreden meist aus den Jahrn 1850*–1861 (Vienna: Braumüller, 1862), 156, 278.

22. J. E. Veith, *Homiletische Vorträge für Sonn und Festtage*, 3d ed. (Vienna: Mayer, 1854), 5:216.

23. Schön, ("Anhang als Schlüssel," 126), although writing in 1873, still treated Veith very much as a Güntherian. Popelar, the most recent scholar to do research on Veith, assumes that Veith was a Güntherian ("J. E. Veith"). On 46 and 131, Popelar claims that Veith would not have been in so much trouble had he not accepted Günther's ideas so uncritically. Popelar makes the claim that Veith never found a biblical God but got lost in Anton Günther, 178.

24. J. E. Veith, *Vater Unser*, 3d ed. (Vienna: Mayer, 1842). The first edition (1831) and the second edition (1833) were both published by J. P. Sollinger of Vienna. The third edition is a revised edition; but comparison with the first and second editions does not substantiate Popelar's claim that the third is not Güntherian (Popelar, "J. E. Veith," 46). After comparison, it would seem that little change was made. The third edition was used because it was more readily available.

25. Veith refers his readers directly to Günther on two occasions in *Vater Unser*, 31 and 326.

26. Ibid., 31.

27. This is an epistemology where human reason is very limited and a place where Güntherian confidence gives way to humble acceptance of our need for God. Although Günther was accused of semirationalism, Veith, in following Günther in spirit and conviction, was not to be accused of the same.

28. "Blue Monday" was a Viennese tradition of adding an extra holiday for the "Monday after," which allowed people to enjoy the full holiday without the thought of work the next day hanging over their heads. It was officially suppressed after the defeat of Napoleon, but the concept lingered on in the minds of workers (M. Brion, *Daily Life in the Vienna of Mozart and Schubert*, trans. Jean Stewart [London: Weidenfeld and Nicholson, 1961], 240).

29. Veith, *Vater Unser*, 23–24.

30. Ibid., 28. "Wenn aber diese absolute Macht der Urheber unsres Ichs ist, was ist sie dann selber? etwa die Seele der Welt, das verborgene innere Getriebe aller Kräfte und Bewegungen, selber blind und unpersönlich und bewusstlos? Wie dann, so wird in den Psalmen gefragt: 'der das Ohr gepflanzt hat, soll nicht hören? der das Auge geformt, wird derselbe nicht schauen? der den Menschen die Wissenschaft lehrt, soll der wohl ohne Wissenschaft sein?' d. h. der das Wesen des Ichs in uns erschaffen hat, soll kein Ich sein? der das Selbstbewusstsein in uns gelegt und geweckt hat, soll selber ohne Selbstbewusstsein gedacht werden?"

31. Ibid., 81. "Im Himmel bist Du, wir aber auf Erden; in Deinem ewigen Sein bist Du, wir aber in der Zeit und im Werden; in absoluter Seligkeit bist Du, wir aber im Stande des Schwankens, des Wählens, der Prüfung: und zu wem anders rufen wir, die wir auf Erden sind, als zu Dir, der Du bist im Himmel?"

32. Ibid., 90. ". . . Auf Dich hoffe ich, Dich bete ich an, Dich preise ich als meinen Gott, weil ich, meinerseits, gänzlich von Dir bedingt bin und von Dir abhänge, Du aber weder meiner selbst, noch meiner Güter bedarfst, denn herrlich und selig bist Du in Dir selbst, und kein Geschöpf vermag Dir, es sei innen oder aussen, etwas zu nehmen oder zu geben!"

33. Ibid., 144–45. "... Dein Wille, O Vater, geschehe in uns (durch uns) und an uns. In uns oder durch uns, indem wir den geoffenbarten göttlichen Gesetze, dem wir allerdings durch Ungehorsam widerstehen können, in freiem Gehorsam erfüllen. An uns, insofern der göttliche Wille in solchen Fügungen sich kund gibt, denen wir nicht widerstehen, wohl aber rebellisch widersprechen können."

34. Ibid., 175. "Und in Wahrheit, wenn wir aller der künstlichen und überkünstlichen Genüsse gedenken, die als Erfrischungen, Erquickungem, Erhitzungen Gaumenerlustigungen, bald glühend und dampfend, bald zu Eis gekühlt, gewürzt, candirt, garnirt, gesprudelt, geschäumt, in Gläsern, Tassen und Terrinen, in allen Gestalten und Farben, aus den Ritzen der Felsen, vom Strande des Meeres, vom Ganges und Mississippi, in tausendfachem Wechsel aufgetischt werden, und dann bei oder nach einer reich besetzten Tafel, etwa beim Dessert, uns nebenher der Bitte erinnern: unser tägliches Brod gib uns heute, so könnte uns wohl zu Muthe werden, als müssten wir uns einiger Massen schämen."

35. In Roman Catholicism there is a difference between preternatural, which is a quality assigned to the human before the fall but nonetheless properly human, and *supernatural*, which is beyond the nature of human before or after the fall. The German word *überwesentliches* could be translated either way. The word "supernatural" seems more appropriate because the chapter deals primarily with the Eucharist.

36. Veith, *Vater Unser*, 292.

37. Ibid., 293.

38. Ibid., 330.

39. Ibid., 306.

40. Perhaps Veith was unconsciously overstating his case. He left the Redemptorists at the end of this series of Lenten sermons. Oftentimes there is a strong stress on commitment, such as blind obedience represents, when difficulties are present.

41. Veith, *Vater Unser*, 338.

42. Ibid., 385.

43. J. E. Veith, *Die heiligen Berge* (Vienna: Sollinger, [1] 1833, [2] 1835). These were originally sermons but Veith, in the introduction, admitted to having lost the original outlines and spent his time "wandering on the holy mountains."

44. Ibid., 1:39–40. Veith calculated the flood as having happened in exactly 2344 B.C. and that Abraham was born 292 years later (ibid., 71). He was not convinced by Darwin in later years. His *Die Anfänge der Menschheit* (Vienna: Braumüller, 1865) is an attempt to reconcile science with the Bible. He claimed to embrace science and progress, but gave Scripture precedence.

45. Veith, *Die Heiligen Berge*, 1:234.

46. J. E. Veith, *Die Samariten* (Vienna: Mayer, 1840), 222–23.

47. Veith, *Samariten*, 122.

48. Veith, *Die Heiligen Berge*, 2:1–56.

49. Popelar, "J. E. Veith," 75, writes that Veith did not see man as the measure of creation but rather as the image of God. Most readers of Veith, including the present author, read Veith to say that man is the mirror image of God but also the measure of all things.

50. "Denn nichts kann verkehrter sein, als wenn das wesenhaft Freie dem wesenhaft Unfreien, der denkende Geist der träumerischen Natur sich zum Knecht hinghibt." Veith, *Samariten*, 67.

51. J. E. Veith, *Säulen der Kirche* (Vienna: Braumüller, 1849).

52. Veith, *Samariten*.

53. J. E. Veith, *Die Erweckung des Lazarus* (Vienna: Braumüller, 1842).

54. J. E. Veith, *Mater Dolorosa in zwölf Vorträgen* (Vienna: Mayer, 1844).

55. J. E. Veith, *Die Heilung des Blindgebornen in zwölf Vorträgen* (Vienna: Braumüller, 1846).
56. J. E. Veith, *Homilienkranz für das katholischer Kirchenjahr*, 1–5 (Vienna: Mayer, 1837–39).
57. J. E. Veith, *Erkenntnis und Liebe. Ein Gebetbuch* 1st ed. (Vienna: Franz Riedl, 1833), 40. ". . . Nicht ein Vater der Natur, nicht ein Vater der Berge, der Bäume, der Thiere, sondern ein Vater der Lichter, ein Vater der geistigen Geschöpfe: diesen allein hast Du die Freiheit des Willens, das Licht des Bewusstseins verliehen, damit sie von deiner Klarheit beseligt werden. O wie selig das Geschöpf welchem Du das Siegel Deiner Ebenbildlichkeit aufgedrücket hast, damit es als Vater Dich anrufen darf."

Chapter 6. 1848

1. ". . . An der Erlösung der Gattung zu arbeiten." Review by Günther of J. Salat's *Religionsphilosophie* in *Jahrbücher der Literatur* 18 (1824): 156.
2. Review by Günther of J. J. Wagner's *Religion, Wissenschaft, Kunst und Staat* in *Jahrbücher der Literatur* 17 (1822): 155 and 177.
3. Nikolaus Severinski, "Kirche und Staat bei A. Günther" (Ph. D. diss., University of Vienna, 1967), 86–93.
4. Ibid., 63–64. J. E. Veith, *Die Säulen der Kirche* (Vienna: Braumüller, 1849), 68–69. Cölestin Wolfsgruber, "Veith als Homilist" in *Erster Homiletischer Kurs in Wien,* eds. Heinrich Swoboda (Vienna: Heinrich Kirsch, 1911), 129.
5. J. E. Veith, *Die Heiligen Berge* (Vienna: Sollinger, 1835), 2:393.
6. Ibid., 298–302.
7. Severinski, "Kirche und Staat," 154–57.
8. Veith made frequent references to events in the United States of America. Without exception, these references are made with distaste. He was not impressed by the American experiment in democracy.
9. R. John Rath (*The Viennese Revolution of 1848* [Austin: University of Texas Press, 1957], 44) claimed that the Viennese were never able to blame Ferdinand.
10. The nineteenth-century liberal believed in the rights of individual to freedom of expression, religion, and private property. The nineteenth-century liberal favored government by consent of the adult male property holders of a society.
11. Rath, *Viennese Revolution*, vii.
12. Priscilla Robertson, *Revolutions of 1848: A Social History* (Princeton: Princeton University Press, 1952), 189–92.
13. Ibid., 194.
14. Robert Endres (*Revolution in Österreich* [Vienna: Danubia, 1947], 70) claimed that there were 2,719 students at the University of Vienna in 1846, mostly farm children from the provinces.
15. Rath, *Viennese Revolution*, 14.
16. Ibid., 118–19.
17. The government was placed in the hands of Pillersdorf, who was particularly ineffective. Ibid., 223.
18. Herbert Steiner (*Karl Marx in Wien: Arbeiterbewegung zwischen Revolution und Restauration 1848* [Vienna: Europaverlag, 1978]) traced Marx's stay in Vienna from 27 August through 7 September 1848.
19. The best English accounts of Vienna in 1848 remain the book by Rath (*Viennese Revolution*) and the section in Robertson (*Revolutions of 1848*). There is a brief and consequently superficial article by Stella Musulin entitled "Vienna in the Year of

Revolutions 1848" in *History Today* 28 (1978): 429–35. Robert Endres's work (*Revolution in Österreich*) remains a good German account. There are also some good accounts of the economic factors of the revolution in Wolfgang Häusler's *Von der Massenarmut zur Arbeiterbewegung: Demokratie und Soziale Frage in der Wiener Revolution 1848* (Vienna: Jugend and Volk, 1979); and Julius Marx's *Die Wirtschaftlichen Ursachen der Revolution von 1848 in Österreich* (Graz: Böhlau, 1965). The journalist Heinrich Drimmel's *Oktober Achtundvierzig: Die Wiener Revolution* (Vienna: Amalthea, 1978) is a day-by-day account of the time between the death of Latour (6 October 1848) and the end of the revolution; the work has no footnotes or bibliography, but is well written and there is little factual distortion.

20. Franz Loidl, *Geschichte des Erzbistums Wien* (Vienna: Herold, 1983), 231.

21. Loidl (*ibid.*, 227) only mentions three groups: the Josephinists, the ultramontanists, and the radicals. The Güntherians fall into the second group for Loidl. Eduard Winter's *Der Josephinismus und seine Geschichte: Beiträge zur Geistesgeschichte Österreichs 1740 bis 1848*, 2d ed. (Vienna: 1962), lists three groups as well: the German nationals, those for the rights of bishops and laity in relating to Rome, and those against centralization but for remaining with Rome.

22. H. Belovari, "Christlicher Demokratismus und christlicher Sozialismus im Jahre 1848 in Wien" (Ph. D. diss., University of Vienna; 1960), 60.

23. Donald Dietrich; "Anton Günther: Catholic Liberal in the Habsburg Empire" in *Journal of Church and State*, 23 (1981): 501.

24. Oskar Folkert; "Das Sturmjahr 1848 und die Kirche in Österreich" in *Wissenschaft und Weltbild*, 12 (1984): 170.

25. Bertram M. Gordon; "The Challenge of Industrialization: The Catholic Church and the Working Class in and around Vienna 1815–1848" in *Austrian History Yearbook* 9–10 (1973/74): 139.

26. When freedom of the press was granted by the state, Milde commented that it was an important but very dangerous *gift* (emphasis added). Milde is quoted in Gustav Otruba; "Katholischer Klerus und 'Kirche' im Spiegl der Flugschriftenliteratur des Revolutionsjahrs 1848" in Viktor Flieder, ed. *Festschrift Franz Loidl zum 65. Geburtstag* (Vienna: Hollinek, 1970), 2:278.

27. Beyond the sarcasm that the convinced democrat hears in the words of a preacher like Veith, there was also the deep and sincere conviction that was a part of this paternalistic approach. Such authority often genuinely *cared* for its people and honestly saw its role in society to be very important for the preservation of Truth. Its suggestions and criticisms were not meant to be self-seeking or malicious.

28. Thomas W. Simons, Jr., "Vienna's First Catholic Political Movement: The Güntherians 1848–1857" in *Catholic Historical Review* 55 (1970): 610.

29. Folkert, *Das Sturmjahr 1848*, 173.

30. There was one Viennese priest, Dr. Anton Füster, who was concerned about the working class and whose work found him alienated from both church and state. After the failure of the revolution, he fled to America. (Häusler, *Von der Massenarmut zur Arbeiterbewegung*, 344). For a fuller account of Füster, see Walter Sauer's "Anton Füster: Priester der Wiener Revolution 1848" in *Zeitgeschichte* 2 (1975): 249–56. Drimmel *Oktober Achtundvierzig*, 407–46) has an account of Füster's return to Vienna in old age. For more on the church and the workers, see Helmut Konrad's "Religiöser und sozialer Protest: Die frühe österreichishe Arbeiterbewegung und die Religionsgemeinschaften" in *Politik und Gesellschaft im alten und neuen Oesterreich: Festschrift Rudolf Neck*, ed. I. Ackerl (Vienna: Verlag für Geschichte und Politik, 1981), 195–213; and Erika Weinzierl-Fischer's "Österreichs Klerus und die Arbiterschaft: Ihr Verhältnis im 19 Jahrhundert nach der Quelle," in *Wort und Wahrheit* 12 (1957): 613–20.

31. L. W. Silberhorn, "Der Epilog eines Religiösen Reformers: Johannes Ronge 1813-1887—Ungedruckte Aufzeichnungen J. Ronges aus dem Londoner Exil" in *Zeitschrift für Religions-und Geistesgeschichte* 6 (1954): 114-38.

32. J. H. Löwe, *Johann Emanuel Veith* (Vienna, Braumüller, 1879), 215-16.

33. The grouping "Güntherian" runs into some difficulty when applied to the clergy active in 1848 because many would not have been particularly familiar with the thought of Anton Günther. Someone like Sebastian Brunner has been called a Güntherian by Joseph Alexander von Helfert (*Die Wiener Journalistik im Jahre 1848* [Vienna: Manz, 1877], 56) and Thomas W. Simons, Jr. "The Güntherians," 383-85); and other clerics active in the the revolution who were friends of Günther are often grouped with them, especially *after* the revolution. It would be more accurate to call those who were active in Vienna during 1848 the "Veithians" or the "Brunnerians" since these two played a more central role politically. Individuals and their connection to Günther are listed in the appendix of this work.

34. Dietrich, "Anton Günther," 500.

35. Simons, "The Güntherians," 379-81.

36. Belovari, "Christlicher Demokratismus," 175.

37. Brunner's paper was published three times weekly through 1873 (Friedrich Dragon; "Die Wiener Presse kirchlicher Tendenz von Revolutionsjahr 1848 bis zur Gründung der Reichspost 1894" [Ph. D. diss., University of Vienna, 1953], appendix. It is not clear what led Rath (*Viennese Revolution*, 223) to conclude that the paper ceased publication on 30 December 1848. Brunner's *Kirchenzeitung* is also treated in Rudolf Heilinger's "Die Wiener katholisch-konservativen und sozialdemokratischen Zeitschriften in der zweiten Hälfte des 19. Jahrhunderts" (Ph. D. diss., University of Vienna; 1974), 80-94.

38. Rudolf Till, *Hofbauer und sein Kreis* (Vienna: Herold, 1915), 99.

39. Simons, "The Güntherians," 381.

40. Cardinal Geissel of Cologne came to the conclusion that diocesan synods would take the sting out of the agitation of the lower clergy. Ibid., 611.

41. Eduard Winter, *Die geistige Entwicklung Anton Günthers und seine Schule* (Paderborn: Schöningh, 1931), 174-75.

42. Simons, "The Güntherians," 384. It would be a mistake to underestimate the intensity of the debate about clerical or religious dress. It has continued to be for many *the* measuring rod of true faithfulness to the vows. The experimentation with attire after Vatican Council II divided many religious communities into bitter camps, one side insisting that the religious habit or Roman collar was always to be worn, the other side insisting that it should not be worn at all. There was little compromise and little acceptance of the other position. So when Milde, upon receiving a messenger from a religious community, first asked him why he was dressed in secular clothing even though chaos reigned in the streets and the anticlericalism of the revolutionaries was well known, he was not simply being a cantankerous and fussy old man.

43. Till, *Hofbauer*, 97.

44. Schwarz was an Austrian by birth, a naturalized citizen of the United States, and a representative of the government of the United States of America in Vienna at the time.

45. Till, *Hofbauer*, 73.

46. Ibid., 108.

47. Peter Knoodt, *Anton Günther, Eine Biographie* (Vienna: Braumüller, 1881), 2:14.

48. Till, *Hofbauer*, 71.

49. Knoodt quoted Veith as claiming that he could have had *Aufwärts* reintroduced, but did not do so because he did not think it was worth the effort since there was so

little church support (*Günther*, 2:20). Knoodt also quoted a letter from Günther in which he talks of *Aufwärts* and the high cost in time and money that it was to Veith (ibid., 10).

50. Till, *Hofbauer*, 71.
51. Loidl, *Geschichte des Erbistums*, 229.
52. Karl Pleyer, "Johann Emanuel Veith und sein Kreis" (Ph. D. diss., University of Vienna, 1934), 51–54.
53. Otto Popelar, "J. E. Veith, Ein homiletischer Beitrag zur Aufklärung und Restauration" (Ph. D. diss., University of Vienna; 1969), 14.
54. Just exactly when this incident occurred is unclear. It could have been that Veith needed protection more than once. Löwe *Johann Emanuel Veith*, 215–16) mentions the incident during the August-September sermons against the German Catholics. Belovari "Christlicher Demokratismus," 128) cites Löwe. Eduard Hosp (*Kirche im Sturmjahr, Erinnerungen an Johann Michael Häusle* [Vienna: Herold, 1953], 41) quoted *Neue Sion*, 4 (1848): 244, in claiming that it occurred on 2 April and quotes from Veith's sermon of that day.
55. Löwe, *Johann Emanuel Veith*, 216, 221. It is interesting that, although Veith seems to have witnessed the violence against Latour from his window, it was Ludwig Croy (Knoodt, *Günther*, 2:19) who complained of the dangers of having been called to anoint Latour in the midst of the mob.
56. Löwe, *Johann Emanuel Veith*, 219.
57. Simons ("The Güntherians," 174) identified "liberal" with clerics entering into the political process. The examples of conservative clergy involved in politics before and after 1848 are too numerous not to be obvious. In fact, although there has always been clerical involvement in the affairs of this world, from both "liberal" and "conservative" clergy, the mere fact of becoming politically active does not make a clergyman "liberal."
58. The psalm that Veith called Psalm 50 has been renumbered in most Bibles and is now Psalm 51, but it is still the *Miserere*. For those who might not be familiar with it, it is quoted here from *The New American Bible* (New York: Collins, 1976), 661–62.

Have mercy on me, O God, in your goodness; in the greatness of your compassion wipe out my offense.
Thoroughly wash me from my guilt and of my sin cleanse me.
For I acknowledge my offense, and my sin is before me always:
Against you only have I sinned, and done what is evil in your sight,
That you may be justified in your sentence, vindicated when you condemn.
Indeed, in guilt was I born, and in sin my mother conceived me;
Behold, you are pleased with sincerity of heart, and in my inmost being you teach me wisdom.
Cleanse me of sin with hyssop, that I may be purified: wash me, and I shall be whiter than snow.
Let me hear the sounds of joy and gladness; the bones you have crushed shall rejoice.
Turn away your face from my sins, and blot out all my guilt.
A clean heart create for me, O God, and a steadfast spirit renew within me.
Cast me not out from your presence, and your holy spirit take not from me.
Give me back the joy of your salvation, and a willing spirit sustain in me.
I will teach transgressors your ways, and sinners shall return to you.
Free me from blood guilt, O God, my saving God; then shall my tongue revel in your justice.
O Lord, open my lips, and my mouth shall proclaim your praise.
For you are not pleased with sacrifices; should I offer a holocaust, you would not accept it.
My sacrifice, O God, is a contrite spirit; a heart contrite and humbled, O God, you will not spurn.
Be bountiful, O Lord, to Zion in your kindness by rebuilding the walls of Jerusalem.
Then shall you be pleased with due sacrifices, burnt offerings and holocausts; then shall they offer up bullocks on your altar.

59. J. E. Veith, *Misericordia, Zwölf Vorträge über den 50 Psalmen gehalten in der Minoritenkirche zu Prag während der Fasten 1852* (Vienna: Braumüller, 1853).

60. "Die Ereignisse jedoch, die zu jener Zeit in der Hauptstadt Wien sich drängten, führten eine so grosse Zerstreuung der Gemüther mit sich, und machten mitunter so viele Digressionen auf die Stimmungen und Irrungen des Tages nöthig, dass die Behandlung des Gegenstands selbst nicht mit der erforderlichten Gründlichkeit durchgeführt werden könnte." Ibid., iii.

61. The manuscripts are in the Vienna City Archives (Wiener Stadtsarchiv) in the Josef Bermann Collection, File IN68539, Numbers 102–113. There are twelve sermons and they will be referred to by their number in the Lenten series.

62. The sermon at the memorial service for Latour will be treated in the next chapter.

63. *Sermon 2*, 5.

64. Sie beschäftigen sich nur mit Baumwolle und_____, Eisen und Stahl, feldbau und manufacturen—kurz mit materiellen Angelegenheiten. Das ist aber rein Verleumdung; wir können uns alle Tage überzeugen, dass es anders ist: unsere Zeit ist mehr geistig bewegt, als irgend eine frühere, dann wann man immer nur reden hört von Nationalgeist und Volkgeist und_____geist; von Befreyung und Aberglauben und Befreyung von Joche der Zeit; vom gemeinsamen Reich und vom Fortschritte, so sind das lauter geistigen Ausdrücke. *Sermon 1*, 1.

65. *Sermon 3*, 1.
66. *Sermon 1*, 4.
67. *Sermon 2*, 3.
68. *Sermon 1*, 5.
69. *Sermon 3*, 1.
70. Ibid.
71. *Sermon 10*, 6.
72. *Sermon 12*, 4.
73. Ibid., 3.
74. Ibid.
75. Ibid., 4.
76. *Sermon 8*, 6.
77. *Sermon 3*, 5.
78. Ibid., 2.
79. *Sermon 9*, 6.

80. Leo XIII was the first of the popes to issue encyclicals on the dignity of the laborer.

81. *Sermon 3*, 6.
82. *Sermon 9*, 4. Veith had nothing to say about Galileo.
83. *Sermon 10*, 1.
84. *Sermon 4*, 4.
85. Ibid., 3.
86. Ibid., 3–4.
87. *Sermon 6*, 5.
88. *Sermon 8*, 2.
89. *Sermon 3*, 4–5.
90. *Sermon 7*, 2.
91. Ibid., 6.
92. *Sermon 9*, 7.
93. *Sermon 10*, 4.

94. Papal infallibility in matters proclaimed *ex cathedra* concerning faith and morals was first proclaimed at Vatican Council I in 1870. Until that time, Veith's position that only a council gathered together with the pope could declare "infallibly" was a

respected opinion in the Roman Church. When Pius IX proclaimed the doctrine of the Immaculate Conception on his own authority in 1854, it was in fact an innovation.

95. *Sermon 12*, 3.
96. Popelar, "J. E. Veith," 99–100.
97. *Aufwärts* 1 (1848): 80.
98. ". . . Ohne seine Übereinstimmung mit Petrus würde die Kirche selbst einen Paulus ihren Glauben versagen!" Ibid., 34.
99. Ibid., 49, 194.
100. Ibid., 197.
101. Rainer A. Dempf, "Die Staatsphilosophie Anton Günthers vom Jahre 1848" (Ph. D. diss., University of Vienna; 1948), 51–61; Nikolaus Severinski, "Kirche und Staat," 152.
102. Knoodt, *Günther*, 2:18–19.
103. Anton Günther, "Die doppelte Souveränität im Menschen und in der Menschheit" in *Aufwärts* 1 (1848): 54–57, 84–88, 132–134, 225–229, 233–237, 242–246.
104. *Aufwärts* (1848): 228.
105. Ibid., 227, 235.
106. Ibid., 56.
107. Ibid., 235.
108. Ibid., 243.
109. Ibid., 234.
110. Ibid., 246.
111. Ibid., 133.
112. Ibid., 84, 132.
113. Ibid., 133.
114. Ibid., 71.
115. Veith, *Sermon 10*, 2.
116. Veith, *Sermon 5*, 3.
117. Ibid., 6.
118. Veith, *Sermon 8*, 3.
119. Veith, *Sermon 12*, 6.
120. Löwe, *Johann Emanuel Veith*, 218.

Chapter 7. The Triumph of Infallibility

1. Johann Strauss the Elder was a conservative who supported the return of the monarchy. There were some contradictions in his conservative life, however. He was divorced in 1844 and lived with his mistress even before the divorce was final. There was also some controversy about the authorship of the Radetzky March. Philipp Fahrbach, a collaborator with the elder Strauss, claimed the composition as his own. Johann Strauss the Younger had broken with his father and since 1844 had worked in the elegant Dommeyer Casino near the gates of Schönbrunn. His political sympathies were more liberal.

2. William Timcheck, "The Struggle of Throne and Altar: Church against State in Austria 1848–1874" (Ph. D. diss., University of Wisconsin at Madison; 1974), 188. Timchek claims that Francis Joseph saw the declaration of papal infallibility as a threat to the religious policy promoted by the crown.

3. The Habsburg monarchy consisted of a conglomeration of peoples and languages accumulated by marriage and war through several centuries. The nineteenth-century

nationalism that swept European peoples made it increasingly difficult to govern these diverse elements. There were several theories of government–but the two major theories were the centralist and federalist. The centralist wanted to concentrate as much power in Vienna as possible, which then would balance one group against the other. Cardinal Rauscher became a supporter of this position. The federalist position wanted as much decentralization as possible. The Magyars were able to win this independence in 1867 when the Austrian became the Austro-Hungarian Empire. Slavic peoples in both the Austrian and the Hungarian parts of the empire were unable to achieve the same self-rule. Cardinal Schwarzenberg, after he moved to Prague, became a convinced federalist. Rudolf Till, *Hofbauer und sein Kreis* (Vienna: Herold, 1951), 138.

4. Timchek, "Throne and Altar," 22–23. Eduard Winter (*Die Geistige Entwicklung Anton Günthers und seine Schule* [Paderborn: Schöningh, 1934], 183) claimed that Josephinism continued after 1848 in the form of political liberalism.

5. A law published on December 31, 1852, (*Sylvesterpatent*) abolished the constitution and re-established absolutism.

6. On 5 June 1848 Schwarzenberg, then in Salzburg, met with all of his clergy. In September 1848 Schwarzenberg met with the bishops who were a part of the ecclesiastical province of Salzburg. Both meetings called for the government to grant freedom to the church. Milde was invited to attend the September meeting, but sent no response. In December of 1848 (after the revolution had been quelled) Milde joined with Bishop Ziegler of Linz and Bishop Buchmayer of St. Pölten in asking the government to preserve Roman Catholicism as the religion of state. See Eduard Hosp, *Kirche im Sturmjahr. Erinnerungen an Johann Michael Häusle* (Vienna: Herold, 1953), 58–60.

7. Timchek "Throne and Altar," 27–28) claimed that Rauscher and Schwarzbenberg worked together to convince Francis Joseph that further revolution could be prevented by giving freedom from temporal control to the church. Till (*Hofbauer*, 117) claimed that Archduchess Sophie and the new Minister of Education Thun wanted to move beyond Josephinism. Franz Loidl (*Geschichte des Erzbistums Wien* [Vienna: Herold, 1983], 231) stated simply that the minister of the interior called the meeting.

8. Loidl (*Geschichte des Erzbistums*, 235) claimed that Schwarzenberg and not Franz Joseph was the one who was influential in having Rauscher made a bishop.

9. Thomas W. Simons, Jr., "Vienna's First Catholic Political Movement: The Güntherians, 1848–1857" in *Catholic Historical Review* 55 (1970): 614.

10. Timchek, "Throne and Altar," 28.

11. Simons, "The Güntherians," 610–16.

12. Erika Weinzierl-Fischer, *Die Österreichischen Konkordate von 1855 und 1933* (Vienna: Verlag für Geschichte und Politik, 1960), chapter 1.

13. Friedrich Engel-Janosi, *Österreich und der Vatikan 1846–1918* (Vienna: Styria, 1958), 1:76. Pius IX apparently considered Milde a "scourge." It is also significant that Milde is one of the few archbishops of Vienna who never was made a cardinal; it is not certain whether the lack of initiative on this can be traced to Vienna or Rome.

14. Timcheck, *Throne and Altar*, 43.

15. Till, *Hofbauer*, 125. Oskar Folkert, "Das Sturmjahr 1848 und die Kirche in Österreich" in *Wissenschaft und Weltbild* 12 (1948), 168.

16. Loidl, *Geschichte des Erzbistums*, 241.

17. On his own authority as pope, Pius IX proclaimed the dogma of the Immaculate Conception (Mary, mother of Jesus, was herself conceived without stain of original sin) on 8 December 1854. The doctrine had been debated for centuries with impressive authorities on both sides. Sts. Bernard and Thomas Aquinas had not favored the doctrine. The Franciscans, notably Duns Scotus, had. The declaration in the nineteenth century was a part of the growing cult of the Virgin and the growing centralization

of church authority in the pope. The dogma was considered particularly offensive to Protestants for both reasons.

18. The best and most thorough accounts of the negotiations surrounding the concordat's making and unmaking are the works already cited by Timchek and Weinzierl-Fischer. Max Hussarek has also published extensive studies: "Die Verhandlungen des Konkordates von 18 August 1855" in *Archiv für Österreichische Geschichte* 109 (1922): 447–810; and "Die Krise und die Lösung des Konkordates vom 18 August 1855" in *Archiv für österreichische Geschichte* 112 (1932): 211–480.

19. G. Adrianyi, "Erzbishop Lajos Haynalds Mission in der österreichischen Konkordatsfrage" in *Donauraum* 16 (1971): 152–58.

20. Loidl, *Geschichte des Erzbistums*, 243.

21. Timchek, "Throne and Altar," 62.

22. Ibid., 177.

23. Loidl, *Geschichte des Erzbistums*, 247.

24. Timcheck, "Throne and Altar," 185.

25. Loidl, *Geschichte des Erzbistums*, 248.

26. Till, *Hofbauer*, 140. Christian Socialism was to be a strong movement in turn-of-the-century Vienna. It was politically conservative but included a recognition of the needs of the workers. Freiherr Karl von Vogelsang became the editor of the paper of the movement, *Das Vaterland*. Carl E. Schorske's *Fin-de-Siecle Vienna Politics and Culture* (New York: Random House–Vantage, 1981) has a good English summary.

27. Loidl, *Geschichte des Erzbistums*, 231.

28. Ibid., 241.

29. Simons, "The Güntherians," 618.

30. Till, *Hofbauer*, 118.

31. Simons ("The Güntherians," 625) claimed that Rauscher wrote off the middle class as unsalvageable.

32. Ibid., 611–18.

33. Ibid., 617–18.

34. *Österreichisher Volksfreund*, 3 (10 January 1849): 19–21.

35. Ibid., 5 (17 January 1849): 37–38.

36. Ibid., 14 (17 February 1849): 108–11.

37. Ibid., 18 (3 March 1849): 145–46. Since America was mission territory, each of the departing monks was given a mission cross.

38. Ibid., 4 (13 January 1849): 30.

39. Ibid., 3 (10 January 1849): 21–23.

40. Ibid., 2 (6 January 1849): 12–13.

41. Ibid., 25 (28 March 1849): 211–13.

42. Ibid., 38 (12 May 1849): 324–25.

43. Ibid., 46 (9 June 1849): 385–88.

44. Ibid., 15 (21 February 1849): 127.

45. Ibid., 20 (10 March 1849): 167–68.

46. Ibid., 42 (26 May 1849): 354–56.

47. Ibid., 16 (24 February 1849): 129–31.

48. Ibid., 4 (13 January 1849): 29–30.

49. Ibid., 52 (6 June 1849): 433–36.

50. Ibid., 32 (21 April 1849): 269–72.

51. Ibid., 24 (24 March 1849): 197–200.

52. Ibid., 2 (6 January 1849): 9–12.

53. Johann Emanuel Veith, "Das Werk der Sühnung. Rede vor dem Seelenamte für weiland Se. Excellenz des k.k. Kriegsministers und Feldzeugmeisters Theodor Grafen

Baillet de Latour," in *Politische Passionspredigten* (Vienna: Braumüller, 1849), 235–46.

54. Latour (1780–1848) was the minister of war during the revolutionary days. When the emperor and court fled Vienna, Latour remained behind to keep order. He was the focus of the hatred of those for whom the revolution moved too slowly. He was brutally murdered by mob violence on 6 October 1848. He became a martyr for those who saw democracy as a threat to public order and a villain to those who wished to do away with the monarchy.

55. Veith, *Politische Passionspredigten*, 146.

56. ". . . Dafür aber hat Gott ihn verherrlicht, also dass der Name Theodor Baillet de Latour im österreichischen Heere und Volke, unter allen christlichen Nationen, und in der Weltgeschichte leuchtet mit unverlöschlichem Glanze." Veith, Ibid., 236. Most preachers would cringe at such unabashed parallels between Latour and Christ.

57. "Der Wissenden und Eingeweihten waren wenige, der Getäuschten viele, fanatische Werkzeuge fanden sich in hinlänglicher Zahl; die Bestechung floss aus reicher Quelle, die Blendwerke waren zauberisch. Auf den Wegen des Verderbens geht es rasch, mit der beschleunigten Geschwindigkeit des Falles; so war in wenigen Monaten die Bethörung und Zerrüttung allgemein geworden, und es erfüllte sich der Ausspruch des berühmten Bayard, des Ritters ohne Furcht und Tadel: dass nichts gefährlicher sey, als Kühnheit und Macht mit der Unwissenheit im Bunde. Im Mitten dieser tollkühnen Unwissenheit, umgeben von einer oft bis zur Berserkerwuth aufgereizten Menge, und gegenüber einer Volksvertretung, in welcher die heillose Richtung überwiegend geworden, stand wie ein Fels in der Brandung, in unerschrockener Ruhe und heiterer Festigkeit, der Mann. . . .Die Führer und Handlanger der Zerstörung hatten diess auch bald erlauert; die Klapperschlangen und Vipern der Tagesblätter sprudelten gegen ihn ihr schärfftes Gift; die Worthelden der Linken erhoben gegen ihn ihr Wolfsgeheul; immer drohender zog der Sturm heran." Ibid., 237–38.

58. "Über die Werkführer der Anarchie war das Gericht besiegelt; die Rächer und Ordnunggebieter rüchten von allen Seiten heran, geführt von grossmüthigen Feldherren, die, bei all ihrer bewundernswerthen Langmuth und Milde, von schöngeistigen Flüchtlingen den Beinamen der 'Schrecklichen' hinnehmen mussten." Ibid., 140.

59. Ibid., 244. Veith is making reference to 1 Peter 2:17.

60. Veith, *Politische Passionspredigten*. These six sermons are also to be found in manuscript form, written by someone other than J. E. Veith, in the Vienna City Archives (Stadtarchiv), in the Berman Nachlass, IN 68539. The differences between printed text and manuscript are minimal.

61. "Wir haben ein ganz neues Heil gehofft und gesucht, und fürs erste nur Unheil gefunden. Dem Kreuze begegnen wir überall, wohin wir uns wenden, aber an diesem Kreuze fehlt uns Christus. Denn so bringen es politische Umwälzungen mit sich, dass die alten, treuen Gedanken des Glaubens, der Ehrerbietung, der Genügsamkeit, der Geduld und Selbstbeherrschung untergehen, und hingegen die Bestrebungen der Selbstsucht, der Eitelkeit, der Eigenmacht und der niedrigen Leidenschaften mit um so grössere Macht aus den Tiefen empor ringen." Ibid., 3.

62. Ibid., 34–36.
63. Ibid., 14, 24.
64. Ibid., 20.
65. Ibid., 32–33.
66. Ibid., 66.
67. Ibid., 93.
68. Ibid., 110. During the siege of Vienna, there were rumors that the city would be saved from the emperor's forces by Turkish armies.

69. Ibid., 214.
70. Ibid., 31, 222.
71. Ibid., 185.
72. Ibid., 199, 205.
73. Ibid., 47.
74. Ibid., 140.
75. Ibid., 134.
76. Ibid., 111.
77. Ibid., 141–42, 224, 226.
78. Ibid., 231.
79. Simons, "The Güntherians," 617–18. Cölestin Wolfsgruber (*Friedrich Kardinal Schwarzenberg* [Vienna: Mayer, 1916], 2:144) stated that Veith moved to Prague because of Milde's interference with the Catholic Union.
80. Till, *Hofbauer*, 120.
81. Loidl, *Geschichte des Erzbistums*, 229.
82. J. E. Veith, *Weltleben und Christenthum* (Vienna: Braumüller, 1851).
83. Ibid., 147.
84. Ibid., 7–8.
85. Veith, *Politische Passionspredigten*, 227–28.
86. Veith, *Weltleben und Christenthum*, 15. One cannot help but wonder if Veith had Milde in mind when he spoke of the "Eigenmacht, Verblendung, und sittlichen Verkehrtheit der Heuchler, Verräther und Baalspfaffen in ihrem eigenen Schosse."
87. Ibid., 40.
88. Ibid., 41.
89. Ibid., 20.
90. Ibid., 144–46.
91. Ibid., 163–64.
92. Ibid., 113–15.
93. Ibid., 171.
94. Veith preached at various churches in Prague and was particularly active with priests' retreats. Some of his works were later published—most importantly his reworking of the sermons on the psalm Misericordia which he had originally delivered in 1848 (*Misericordia* [Vienna: Braumüller, 1853]). The second *Misericordia* is not a political comment in any sense but rather is a totally different set of reflections. There is a strong defense of the right of the state to use capital punishment (162) and a strong statement of the rights of the church (344–49); but mostly Veith stays with personal sin and redemption.
95. Peter Knoodt, *Anton Günther* (Vienna: Braumüller, 1881), 1:409–10.
96. Ibid., 2:18–20, 43, 48, 55–56.
97. Ibid., 13.
98. E. Winter, *Geistige Entwicklung*, 182. The Güntherians who wrote for *Zeitschrift für die gesamte katholische Theologie* included Croy, Egerer, Ehrlich, Nickes, Werner, Zukrigl. Simons ("The Güntherians," 619) implies that Häusle, one of the founders of the periodical, was not a Güntherian when he blocked one of Croy's articles in 1851 and then that he was a Güntherian in his struggle over the Catholic nature of the university. At any rate, Simons' contention that the publication ceased to be open to Güntherians after the 1851 episode is contradicted by Günther's own article in the following year.
99. Anton Günther, "Ein Wort über den Vernunfthass auf katholischen Gebiet" in *Zeitschrift für die gesamte katholische Theologie*, 3 (1852): 53–64. E. Winter (*Geistige Entwicklung*, 182) identified Günther's pen in the pieces on pp. 235 and 253

of the 1851 issues of the same periodical. After the revolution, Günther also wrote an article that has not been recognized by scholars since. It is obviously Güntherian and is signed "AG." It is entitled "Die kirchliche und die Civil Ehe" and appeared in the *Österreichischer Volksfreund* (1850): 113–16, 121–24, 137–40, 146–48, 161–64.

100. *Lydia. Philosophisches Taschenbuch als Seitenstück zu A. Ruge's "Akademie"*, 1849–50, (reprinted, Frankfurt am Main: Minerva, 1973). The various volumes of *Lydia* found their way to America through Cardinal Wiseman whom both Veith and Günther hoped would be a help to their cause in Rome. Cf. Günther's letter to Veith from 1825, published in Erwin Mann, *Die Wiener theologische Schule A. Günthers im Urteil des 20. Jahrhunderts* (Vienna: Verband der wissenschaftlichen Gesellschaften Österreichs, 1979), 91.

101. E. Winter, *Geistige Entwicklung*, 181.

102. Donald Dietrich, "Anton Günther: Catholic Liberal in the Habsburg Empire" in *Journal of Church and State* 23 (1981): 512.

103. *Lydia* (1849), 181; (1850), 362; (1851), 170; (1852), 112, 328; (1854), 604.

104. *Lydia* (1849), 304–306, 328; (1852), 112.

105. Dietrich ("Anton Günther," 514–15) compares Günther and Leo XIII and claims that both encouraged the clergy to participate in politics, refused to accept the separation of church and state because they saw it as a subordination of church to state, and had misgivings about democracy but did not wholly condemn it. The comparison is strained.

106. *Lydia* (1850), 284.

107. Ibid., 268.

108. Ibid., 173. Actually, Günther only suggested that Trent, as any council, was an interim that needed to be continued.

109. Knoodt, *Günther*, 2:39.

110. See the appendix to this work for details on specific members.

111. Knoodt, *Günther*, 2:218.

112. See the appendix on Josefa von Hoffinger.

113. Thomas W. Simons, Jr., "The Prague Origins of the Güntherian Converts 1800–1850" in *Leo Baeck Institute Yearbook* 22 (1977): 245–56.

114. The entire story of the trial of Günther has yet to be told—and probably will not be told in its entirety because some of the materials remain unavailable to historians. The Vatican under Leo XIII opened the main archive to historians looking at least one hundred years in the past. That file contains some data in *Segr. Stato 1869 Rubrica 241* and *Archivio Particulare Pio IX*, which are basically reports from the nuncios in Vienna, Munich, and Cologne on issues surrounding the Güntherian question. There are also some of the writings of Geissel asking for clarifications and responses from Flir and Knoodt. The archives of the Congregation of the Index (changed to Congregation of the Faith after Vatican Council II) remain officially closed. Some of the documentation from the Congregation of the Index did find its way into the Jesuit library at the Gregorianum, and this material was used by Ladislao Orban (*Theologia Güntheriana et Concilium Vaticanum*, 2 vols. [Rome, 1949–50]). Most discussions of the trial of Günther come from sources other than the official Vatican proceedings. The most thorough accounts are in Knoodt (*Günther*, 2:84–399) and Wolfsgruber, (*Schwarzenberg*, 2:369–453). E. Winter's account (*Geistige Entwicklung*, 188–224) is based on Knoodt and Wolfsgruber. However, new archival material is used in Eduard Winter and Maria Winter, *Domprediger Johann Emmanuel Veith und Kardinal Friedrich Schwarzenberg. Der Güntherprozess in unveröffentlichten Briefen und Akten* (Vienna: Böhlau, 1972), 29–40.

115. Veith to Schwarzenberg, Ascension, 1853 (printed in Winter and Winter,

Domprediger Johann Emmanuel Veith und Kardinal Friedrich Schwarzenberg, 65). "Ganz in Unschuld kann er seine Hände nicht waschen, noch weniger in Tinte; er hat alle diese Feinde selber geschaffen und provociert."

116. E. Winter, *Geistige Entwicklung*, 158.

117. Ibid., 162; and Theo Schäfer, *Die Erkenntnistheoretische Kontroverse Kleutgen–Günther*, (Paderborn: Schöningh, 1961), 133–37.

118. Knoodt, *op.cit.*, I, 313.

119. E. Winter, *Geistige Entwicklung*, 150. When Drey's chair became vacant, it was offered first to Günther, who refused, then to Knoodt, who also refused, and finally to Zukriegl, who accepted. Drey himself had been more open to Günther's anti-Scholasticism. Möhler and Staudenmeier were more favorable to the Scholastics.

120. Thomas W. Simons, Jr., "Unveröffentliches über den Aufenthalt des Wiener Philosophen und Theologen A. Günther in Galizien" in *Wiener Geschichtsblätter* 30 (1975): 145–49. Another author, commenting on the trouble that Günther was having with the church, suggested that it would not have been nearly so much trouble if he had not become a priest (Ernst Karl Winter, "Anton Günther: Ein Beitrag zur Romantikforschung" in *Zeitschrift für die gesamte Staatswissenschaft* 88 [1930]: 294).

121. Knoodt, *Günther*, 2:76. Wolfsgruber (*Schwarzenberg*, 1:126) traced the antagonism of the Redemptorists for Günther's thought to their opposition to Pabst.

122. Roger Aubert, "Aufschwung und Niedergang des Güntherianismus" in Hubert Jedin, *Handbuch der Kirchengeschichte* (Vienna: Herder, 6/1), 454. E. Winter, *Geistige Entwicklung*, 163.

123. E. Winter, *Geistige Entwicklung*, 191.

124. Knoodt, *Günther*, 2:59.

125. E. Winter, *Geistige Entwicklung*, 164–65. The "passed over" were Clemens and Volkmuth, who were later to become bitter enemies of Güntherianism.

126. Georg Hermes (1775–1831) was a professor of theology at Bonn who was condemned by Rome in 1835. He was accused of semirationalism for accepting human reason as a norm for understanding supernatural truth. Hermes was responding to Kant.

127. Knoodt (*Günther*, 2:24) recounted how excited the young Kleutgen was about Günther's thought. E. Winter (*Geistige Entwicklung*, 203) traced Kleutgen's move to Rome in 1843 and his appointment as consultor to the Congregation of the Index in 1851. Schäfer (*Kontroverse*, 127–28) concluded that Kleutgen had indeed worked on the Günther trial and that Kleutgen's view of Günther's epistemology became the basis for Günther's condemnation.

128. Knoodt, *Günther*, 2:24. Winter and Winter, *Veith und Schwarzenberg*, 28–30. Peter Knoodt, a noted Güntherian, was a representative to the congress that met in Frankfurt. (Knoodt, *Günther*, 1:402, 413).

129. E. Winter (*Geistige Entwicklung*, 200) claimed that after 1846 the Herbartianer became the major thinkers in Austria. Schäfer (*Kontroverse*, 36) claimed that idealism and rationalism had passed their high point by 1850.

130. There has never been a systematic approach to investigation used by the Roman Curia. Most frequently, Rome responds to complaints—in the case of Günther, from Germans. The investigation is usually well advanced before the investigated thinker is aware of the process. Questions are raised; but the exact points of issue are not usually known to the defendant. He is expected to respond and place his thought within the tradition. Oftentimes this is done not by the individual himself (the defendant may no longer be living) but by someone within the investigation. Decrees of condemnation are usually short and pointed, and the one or ones condemned usually claim that they have been misunderstood.

131. Knoodt, *Günther*, 2:85, 104, 166–67) presumed that the Index Congregation was ready to pounce in 1851 but Pius IX held them off. Donald Dietrich ("German

Idealism and the German Catholic Theological Response—Hermes, Moeller, Staudenmaier, and Günther" [Ph. D. diss., University of Minnesota, 1969], 384–87) presumes that the trial began in 1852.

132. Knoodt, *Günther*, 2:139.
133. Ibid., 133–36.
134. E. Winter, *Geistige Entwicklung*, 184, 189. Hosp (*Kirche im Sturmjahr*, 69) quotes Rauscher commenting to Diepenbrock that the Güntherians were dangerous because they wanted a constitutional government of the church. That was in 1852.
135. Simons, "Vienna's First Catholic Political Movement," 622.
136. Knoodt, *Günther*, 2:164–65.
137. Ibid., 129.
138. Ibid., 102.
139. Ibid., 173, 186.
140. E. Winter, *Geistige Entwicklung*, 214.
141. Knoodt, Günther, 2:139.
142. Winter and Winter, *Veith und Schwarzenberg*, 50, 113.
143. Schäfer, *Kontroverse*, 36. The fact of the "unanimous decision" of the Index Congregation should not be surprising. The custom of the Vatican was to present as united a front as possible, and many voted with the majority or abstained in order to preserve this impression.
144. Joseph Pritz, "Anton Günther" in *Katholische Theologie Deutschlands im 19. Jahrhundert*, ed. Heinrich Fries (Munich: Kösel, 1975), 1:362.
145. Ibid.
146. Gerald A. McCool, *Catholic Theology in the Nineteenth Century* (New York: Seabury, 1977), 130–32. Schäfer, *Kontroverse*, 138–43.
147. Orban, *Theologia Güntheriana*, 2:197–204.
148. Hock to Schwarzenberg on 23 January 1857 quoted in Winter and Winter, *Veith und Schwarzenberg*, 124.
149. Ibid., 127.
150. Ibid., 132. Günther presented a docile image to the Cathoic world of his time. Lord Acton, writing in an essay entitled "Conflicts with Rome" noted that Günther was a model of how one should submit to the magisterium (*Essays on Freedom and Power*, ed. Gertrude Himmelfarb [New York: Meridian Books, 1948], 258).
151. Mann, *Die Wiener theologische Schule A. Günthers*, 100.
152. Ibid., 104.
153. Ibid., 105 (a letter from Anton Günther to Odilia Fabricius and Agnes Simrock in 1857).
154. Anton Günther, *Lentigo's und Peregrins Briefwechsel* (Vienna: Braumüller, 1857). There is a copy of this work in the Nationalbibliotek in Vienna. It has recently been republished under the editorship of Johann Reikerstorfer in the volume entitled *Anton Günther Späte Schriften* (Vienna: Herold, 1978).
155. Anton Günther, *Anti-Savarese*, edited with a forward by Peter Knoodt, (Vienna: Braumüller, 1883). This volume has been recently re-issued under the editorship of Johann Reikerstorfer in *Anton Günther Späte Schriften*.
156. Winter and Winter, *Veith und Schwarzenberg*, 69.
157. Anton Günther to J. E. Veith in 1852, printed in Mann, *Die Wiener theologische Schule A. Günthers*, 89.
158. Knoodt, *Günther*, 2:528–30.
159. Ibid., 1:255–56.
160. Ibid., 2:530–41.
161. Otto Popelar, "J. E. Veith. Ein homiletischer Beitrag zur Aufklärung und Restauration" (Ph. D. diss., University of Vienna; 1969), 206.

162. Rauscher to Schwarzenberg, cited in Winter and Winter, *Veith und Schwarzenberg*, 161. Other rumors about the process against Veith focused on possible complaints from Bishop Rudiger of Linz.

163. Wolfsgruber, *Schwarzenberg*, 2:453–67. The specific reference for this quote is on 463.

164. Johann Heinrich Löwe, *Johann Emanuel Veith* (Vienna: Braumüller, 1879), 288.

165. Constantin Vidmar, *Johann Emmanuel Veith. Ein Gedenkblatt zu seinem hundertsten Geburtstag* (Vienna: Mayer, 1887), 32.

166. J. E. Veith, *Die Anfänge der Menschheit*, (Vienna: Braumüller, 1865). The sermons are an attempt to reconcile the natural science of the time with the accounts of creation in Scripture.

167. Vidmar, *Veith, Ein Gedenkenblatt*, 30–31. There is one of Veith's pencil scribblings in the archives of the Nationalbibliotek in Vienna. It is illegible to any but the initiated.

168. Karl Pleyer, "Johann Emanuel Veith und sein Kreis" (Ph. D. diss., University of Vienna; 1934), 90.

169. E. Winter, *Geistige Entwicklung*, 230–33.

170. Winter and Winter, *Veith und Schwarzenberg*, 25.

171. Vidmar, *Veith, Ein Gedenkenblatt*, 37–38. Löwe, *Johann Emanuel Veith*, 307–11.

BIBLIOGRAPHY

Günther has certainly received more attention than Veith through the decades. His own works and then the investigation by Rome prompted attacks and defenses in large number. Even today that debate continues. Those in the neo-Thomist school maintain that Günther is a semirationalist with a faulty anthropology. Works by Orban, McCool, and Wenzel in the twentieth century build on the works of Clemens, Oischinger, Kleutgen in the last. Günther's defenders in the twentieth century have taken a different approach from those of the nineteenth. The main focus of defense came, paradoxically, from the fundamental theology department of the Catholic Theology faculty of the University of Vienna. Occupying the chair that Günther coveted but never attained, Joseph Pritz did much to revive interest in Günther. The numerous investigations of the Güntherians (including this one) were inspired by his enthusiasm for Günther as a precursor of Vatican Council II.

Neither denouncers nor defenders of Günther have been very good historians. Günther has generally been studied for his thought, taken out of the context of the time that gave that thought birth. Those who have studied Günther from a historical frame of reference (Eduard Winter, Folkert, Simons), have insisted that he and those who followed him were liberal, a point as difficult to make as that they were the prophets of Vatican II.

The historiography on Veith is thin, an occasional article or dissertation looking at his homiletic style or remembering a man who was active for his church, or commemorating a medical doctor and veterianarian. Those who have written about Veith's theology have insisted that Veith was not a Güntherian.

Works by Anton Günther

1. ARCHIVAL MATERIALS

Letters to J. N. Ehrlich, J. H. Löwe, V. Knauer, and an unknown person in the Archiv des Schottenstifften, Vienna.

Letters to Grillparzer, V. Knauer, and an unknown person, in the Stadtarchiv, Vienna.

Letter to Exner in the Nationalbibliotek, Vienna (in the Faszikel Hock).

Letters to P. Landes, S. J. in Archiv des Collegium Germanicum und Hungaricum, Rome (SI A 1841 Section EP Saeculum 19 no. 60).

Letters and Papers collected by Veith and delivered to Knoodt in the Archiv des Alt Katholischen Bistums, Bonn.

Three manuscripts, "Stabilität," "Über den Ursprung des Heidenthums," and "Über die Ebenbildlichkeit" in Bibliotek des Priesterseminars, Salzburg (Handschriften 603).

2. PRINTED COLLECTIONS OF SOURCES

Knoodt, Peter. *Anton Günther, eine Biographie*, vol. 1–2. Vienna: Braumüller, 1881.
  Ostensibly a biography of Günther but begins with Günther's autobiography and

continues with a series of loosely connected quotations from letters and papers of Günther and others.

Mann, E. "A. Günther und die Wiener Dichterin Josepha von Hoffinger" with an unpublished fragment of *Der Bart zum Platinaschlüssel* of A. Günther. In *Wiener Geschichtsblätter*, (1977), 206–215.

_____. *Die Wiener theologische Schule A. Günthers im Urteil des 20. Jahrhunderts*, with unpublished letters of A. Günther. Vienna: Verband der wissenschaflichen Gesellschaften Österreichs, 1979.

Pritz, J. *Glauben und Wissen bei Anton Günther, eine Einführung in sein Leben und Werk mit einer Auswahl aus seinen Schriften*. In *Wiener Beiträge zur Theologie*, no. 4. Vienna: Herder, 1963.

_____. *Wegweisung zur Theologie. Briefe A. Günthers an J. N. Ehrlich mit einer Einleitung*. In *Wiener Beiträge zur Theologie*, no. 37. Vienna: Domverlag, 1971.

_____. "Zur Geschichte der philosophtheologische Schule A. Günthers. Briefe A. Günthers an den Philosophen J. H. Löwe 1841–1862." In *Festschrift Franz Loidl* ed. Victor Flieder, 1:204–54. Vienna: Brüder Hollinek, 1970.

"Zwei unveröffentliche Briefe A. Günthers an einem Unbekannten. Vier unveröffentliche Briefe A. Günthers an V. Knauer 1859." in *Sacerdos et Pastor. Festschrift zum 40. jährigen Priesterjubilaeum Franz Loidl*, 105–23. Vienna: Domverlag, 1972.

3. BOOKS BY GÜNTHER

Anti-Savarese, ed. Peter Knoodt. Vienna: Braumüller, 1883. Also published in *Anton Günther Späte Schriften*, ed. Johann Reikerstorfer. Vienna: Herold, 1978. A collection of Günther fragments that say more of Knoodt than of Günther.

Euristheus und Herakles, Metalogische Kritiken und Meditationen. Vienna: Braumüller, 1843. Also a reprint of the 1882 edition. Frankfurt: Minerva, 1968. *Idee* (Herakles) frees itself from *Begriff* (Euristheus).

Januskōpfe für Philosophie und Theologie. Vienna: Wallishaussen, 1834. Also a reprint of the 1882 edition. Frankfurt: Minerva, 1968. An anti-Scholastic presentation of the Güntherian system.

Die Juste-Milieus in der deutschen Philosophie gegenwärtiger Zeit. Vienna: Beck, 1838. Also a reprint of the 1882 edition. Frankfurt: Minerva, 1968. A critique of the false attempt to mediate between unreconcilable opposites, especially freedom and necessity, and monism and creationism.

Lentigos und Peregrins Briefwechsel. Vienna: Braumüller, 1857. Also published in *Anton Günther Späte Schriften*, ed. Johann Reikerstorfer. Vienna: Herold, 1978. Günther's response to the critics, especially F. Michelis.

Der letzte Symboliker. Vienna: Wallishauser, 1834. Also a reprint of the 1882 edition. Frankfurt: Minerva, 1968. Günther's presentation of contemporary theology.

Lydia, philosophisches Jahrbuch, vol. 1–5 (1849–54), reprint. Frankfurt: Minerva, 1973. Edited and mostly written by Günther and Veith.

Peregrins Gastmahl, eine Idylle. Vienna: Mechitaristen, 1830. Also a reprint of the 1882 edition, Frankfurt: Minerva, 1968. Consciousness as the only starting point for philosophy, leading to creation and trinity.

Süd- und Nordlichter am Horizonte spekulativer Theologie. Vienna: Mechitaristen, 1832. Also a reprint of the 1882 edition. Frankfurt: Minerva, 1968. Discussion of soteriology and Christology.

Thomas A Scrupulis: Zur Transfiguration der Persönlichkeits Pantheismen neuster Zeit. Vienna: Wallishauser, 1835. Also a reprint of the 1882 edition. Frankfurt: Minerva, 1968. A response to the thought of I. H. Fichte and C. H. Weisse.

Vorschule zur spekulativen Theologie des positiven Christentums, vol 1–2, 2d ed. Vienna: Wallishaussen, 1846/47. Also a reprint of the 1882 edition. Frankfurt: Minerva, 1968. The fundamental exposition of Günther's system, first published in 1828/29. Volume 1 treats creation; volume 2, incarnation.

4. ARTICLES BY GÜNTHER

"Ansichten über den Zeitgeist." *Ölzweige* 2 (1820): 21–23.

"Auch ein Wort über die Lage der Philosophie in Deutschland." *Zeitschrift für Theologie* 17 (1847): 133–70; and 18 (1847): 209–72.

"Berichtigung der Ansichten über das christliche Fatum." *Wiener Modenzeitung und Zeitschrift für Kunst, schöne Literatur und Theater* 2 (1817): 305–10, 313–16.

"Die doppelte Souveränität im Menschen und in der Menschheit." *Aufwärts* 1 (1848): 54–57, 84–88, 132–34, 225–29, 233–37, 242–46.

"Gespräch zweier Kunstfreunde über das Trauerspiel Die Ahnfrau." *Wiener allgemeine Theaterzeitung* (1817): 137–39, 142–43.

"Die kirchliche und die civil Ehe." *Österreichischer Volksfreund* (1850): 113–16, 121–24, 137–40, 146–48, 161–64.

"Rezension: F. Bonterwerk, *Die Religion der Vernunft.*" *Jahrbücher der Literatur* 30 (1825): 277–336.

"Rezension: J. S. Drey, *Die Apologetik als wissenschaftliche Nachweisung der Göttlichkeit des Christentums.*" *Zeitschrift für Philosophie und spekulative Theologie* 2 (1838): 289–336; 4 (1839): 132–65; 5 (1840): 276–312; 6 (1840): 104–49.

"Rezension: A. Eschenmayer, *Religionsphilosophie*; W. Hindrichs, *Die Religion.*" *Jahrbücher der Literatur* 20 (1822): 29–91.

"Rezension: D. K. Hüllmann, *Geschichte des Ursprungs der Stände in Deutschland.*" *Literaturzeitung für katholische Religionslehrer* 10 (1819): 1, 97–128, 132–44, 148–60, 166–76, 183–92, 199–213.

"Rezension: L. A. Kähler, *Supernaturalismus und Rationalismus.*" *Jahrbücher der Literatur* 9 (1820): 163–97; and 10 (1820): 1–73.

"Rezension: F. Köppen, *Rechtslehre nach platonischen Grundsätzen.*" *Literaturzeitung für katholische Religionslehrer* 12 (1822): 2, 177–274.

"Rezension: J. P. Nöbe, *Erziehungsstufen der Religion.*" *Wiener Literaturzeitung* 4 (1816): 769–84.

"Rezension: E. Reinhold, *Theorie des menschlichen Erkenntnisvermögens.*" *Zeitschrift für Philosophie und katholische Theologie* 2, no. 5 (1833): 97–121; no. 6: 111–30; no. 7: 123–46; no. 8: 87–148.

"Rezension: Resonanzen, D. Schenkel, *Das neue Heidentum und das neue Judentum in der alten Kirche*; G. Baur, *Die biblische Darstellung des Sündenfalls.*" *Zeitschrift für die gesamte katholische Theologie* 2 (1851): 233–72.

"Rezension: Rust, *Philosophie und Christentum.*" *Katholische Literaturzeitung* 17, no. 3 (1826): 121–276.

"Rezension: J. Salat, *Religionsphilosophie.*" *Jahrbücher der Literatur* 18 (1822): 140–221.

"Rezension: R. Schluthess und J. K. Orelli, *Rationalismus, Supernaturalismus.*" *Jahrbücher der Literatur* 25 (1824): 26–70.

"Rezension: C. G. Schmid, *Religion und Theologie.*" *Jahrbücher der Literatur* 22 (1823): 150–79.

"Rezension: J. B. Schwetz, *Theologica dogmatica catholica.*" *Wiener Kirchenzeitung* 5 (1852): 102ff.

"Rezension: A. Stourdza, *Betrachtungen über die Lehre und den Geist der orthodoxen Kirche.*" *Literaturzeitung für katholische Religionslehrer* 9, no. 4 (1818): 3–13, 17–27, 49–63, 65–95, 97–104.

"Rezension: K. F. E. Trahndorff, *Wie kann der Supernaturalismus sein Recht gegen Hegels Religionsphilosophie behaupten.*" *Zeitschrift für Philosophie und spekulative Theologie*, New Series 4 (1841): 131–308.

"Rezension: G. G. Übelen, *Geist der neueren und neuesten Geschichte.*" *Wiener Literaturzeitung* 4 (1816): 1337–54.

"Rezension: J. J. Wagner, *Religion, Wissenschaft, Kunst und Staat.*" *Jahrbücher der Literatur* 17 (1822): 132–87.

"Rezension: J. Widmer, *Nachtrag zu Zimmers Biographie.*" *Jahrbücher der Literatur* 28 (1824): 87–168.

"Rezension: G. T. Ziegler, *Akademische Rede über die Verwerflichkeit des theologischen Rationalismus.*" *Jahrbücher der Literature* 15 (1821): 14–21.

"Stimmen aus der Gegenwart über die kirchlichen Wirren." *Zeitschrift für Philosophie und spekulative Theologie* 3 (1839): 312–31.

"Über den Atheismus in metaphysischen Systemen." *Zeitschrift für Philosophie und spekulative Theologie* 3 (1839): 312–31.

"Über die Inkarnationslehre aus der Gegenwart für die Gegenwart." *Zeitschrift für die gesamte katholische Theologie* 8 (1860): 59–92.

"Ein Wort über den Vernunfthass auf katholischem Gebiet." *Zeitschrift für die gesamte katholische Theologie* 3 (1852): 53–64.

Works by Johann Emanuel Veith

1. ARCHIVAL MATERIALS

Considerable materials available in the Stadtarchiv, Vienna under Veith (his own sermon notes, letters to and from Veith, and poems) and under Bermann (Veith's sermons from 1824 to 1856 transcribed by a listener).

Sermon for the third Rogation day of 1843 and letters to Castelli, Arnoldi, Flora Fries, and Leopoldine Himany, as well as an illegibile scratching from his blind years in the Handschriftensammlung of the Nationalbibliotek, Vienna.

Fragments of notes and letters about Veith in the Erzbischöfliches Diözesanarchiv, Vienna.

2. PRINTED COLLECTIONS OF SOURCES AND NEWSPAPERS

"Schreiben zum Nachweis der Rechtgläubigkeit seines (Günthers) Systems zur Vorlage bei der Indexkongregation." In Ladislao Orban, *Theologica Güntheriana et Concilium Vaticanum*, vol. 2: 197–204. Rome: 1949.

"Das dreifache Mysterium der Epiphanie, Trauungsrede für Johann Elias Veith, 6

Januar 1824," in C. Vidmar, *Johann Emanuel Veith. Ein Gedenkblatt zu seinem hundertsten Geburtstag*, 57–65. Vienna: Mayer, 1887.

Letters and papers of Veith in Eduard Winter and Maria Winter, *Domprediger Johann Emanuel Veith und Kardinal Schwarzenberg, Der Güntherprozess in unveröffentlichten Briefen und Akten, Veröffentlichungen der Kommission für Geschichte der Erziehung und des Unterrichts 13*. Vienna: Böhlau Nachfolger, 1972.

Aufwärts.

Friedensblätter.

Ölzweige.

Der österreichische Volksfreund.

3. BOOKS BY VEITH.

Die Anfänge der Menschheit. Apologetische Vorträge über Genesis 1–11 gehalten in der Capuzinerkirche im Frühjahr 1863. Vienna, Braumüller, 1865.

Ein Aufblick zum guten Hirten. Anrede an die Mitglieder des Frauen Wohltätigkeitsvereins der innern State Wien bei Gelegenheit der am 6. April 1856 veranstalteten jährlichen Hauptversammlung. Vienna: Carl Überreuter, 1856. Cites several women who were courageous when the men failed.

Austrias Trauer. Drei Reden gehalten bei den feierlichen Exequien für Weiland se. Majestäi den allerdurchlauchtigsten Kaiser Franz I. in der Metropolitankirche S. Stephan 9.10.11. April 1835. Vienna: Mayer, 1835.

Balsaminen. Vienna: Volke, 1823. Poetry.

Beherzigungen des Wissenwürdigsten vom Ablass und Jubilaum. Vienna, Wallishasser, 1926. Roman Catholic understanding of sin, confession, and indulgences.

Charitas. Neun Kanzelvorträge gehalten während der Faste des Jahres 1851 mehrentheils in der Hauptkirche St. Nicolaus in Prag. Vienna: Braumüller, 1851.

Die Cholera im Lichte der Vorsehung. Ein Kanzelvortrag gehaltem am Schlusse der öffentlichen Bittgänge in der Metropolitankirche S. Stephan 9 September 1831. Vienna: Mechitaristen, 1831.

Christus Gestern, Heute, Ewig. Gebet und Erbauungsbuch für Gebildete. Vienna: Braumüller, 1876.

Denkbüchlein vom Leiden Christi: für die Tage der sieben Fastenwochen. Vienna: Sollinger, 1823.

Dikaiosyne. Die Epistelreihe des Kirchenjahres in ihrem Verhältnisse zu den Evangelien. Vienna: Braumüller, 1874.

Dodecatheon. Zwölf Vorträge gehalted während der Fastenzeit der Jahre 1857 und 1858 in der Pfarrkirche zu den neuen Chören der Engel in Wien. Vienna: Braumüller, 1859.

Erkenntnis und Liebe. Ein Gebetbuch. Vienna: Franz Riedl, 1833. (2nd ed., Vienna: Lienhart, 1860).

Die Erweckung des Lazarus. Fastenpredigten 1841 in Dom. Vienna: Braumüller, 1842.

Erzählungen und Humoresken. 2d ed., vol. 1–3. Vienna: Braumüller und Seidel, 1842. Fiction and poetry.

Erzählungen und kleine Schriften, vol. 1–2. Vienna: Sollinger, 1831. Fiction, prayers, and poetry.

Eucharistia. Zwölf Vorträge über das heilige Messopfer. Fastenpredigten 1846 Kirche am Hof. Vienna: Braumüller, 1847.

Festpredigen zumeist in einer Doppelreihe, vol. 1–2. Vienna: Braumüller und Seidel, 1844.

Fest- und Feiertags Predigten. Vienna: Mayer, 1838.

Die Feyer der Grundsteinlegung des neuerbauten Hauses der Barmherzigen Schwestern in Wien am 5 November 1834. Vienna: Aus der theolog. Zeitschrift zum Vortheile der Barmherzigen Schwestern besonders abgedruckt, 1834.

Das Friedensopfer in einer Folgereihe katholischer Darstellung. Fastenpredigtzyklus in der Redemptoristenkirche 1828. Vienna: Armbruster, 1828.

Die geistige Rose. Vienna: Mayer, 1844. The fifteen mysteries of the rosary explained by Veith and illustrated by Joseph Führich.

Die heiligen Berge. Fastenpredigten 1831 in der Pfarrkirche am Hof, vol. 1–2. Vienna: Sollinger, 1833, 1835. Not the original sermons, which were lost, but rather imaginative reconstructions of various holy mountains Veith never visited.

Die Heilung des Blindgebornen in zwölf Vortragen. Fastenpredigten 1844 im Dom. Vienna: Braumüller, 1846.

Die himmlische Fürsprecherin. Predigt in der Pfarrkirche zu Maria-Hietzing am 15 August 1859. Vienna: Carl Gerolds Sohn, 1859.

Homilienkranz für das katholische Kirchenjahr, vol. 1–5. Vienna: Mayer, 1837–39.

Homiletische Ährenlese. Auswahl von Predigten und Gelegenheitsreden meist aus den Jahren 1850–1861. Vienna: Braumüller, 1862.

Homiletische Vorträge für Sonn und Festtage, vol. 1–7. Vienna: Mayer, 1846–55.

Homiletische Werke, 16 vols. Vienna: Braumüller, 1855–77.

Hundert Psalmen übersetzt und mit Erklärungen begleitet. Vienna: Braumüller, 1868.

Jesus meine Liebe. Ein Gebetbuck für gebildeten Katholiken. Vienna: Riedl, 1827.

Klosterfrau und Meisterin. Predigt beim Beschlusse der dreihunderjährigen Jubelfeier des Ordens der wohlehrwürdigen Frauen St. Ursula am letzten Sonntage nach Pfingsten 1837. Vienna: Mechitaristen, 1837.

Koheleth und Hoheslied übersetzt und erklärt. Vienna: Braumüller, 1878.

Lebensbilder aus der Passionsgeschichte. Fastenpredigten 1829 in der Redemptoristenkirche. 2d ed. Vienna: Mayer, 1836.

Leid und Mitleid. Ein Kangelvortrag gehalten am Gedächtnisstage aller verstorbenen Christgläubigen in der Metropolitankirche zu S. Stephan. Vienna: Mechitaristen, 1831.

Der Leidensweg des Herrn. Sechsundvierzig Meditationen für alle Tage der Fastenzeit. Vienna: Braumüller, 1869.

Die Leidenswerkzeuge Christi. Quadragesima Vorträgen, Maria am Gestade 1826. Vienna: Armbruster, 1827.

Lesefrüchte aus dessen homiletischen Werken des hochwürdigsten Canonicus Dr. Johann Em Veith. Vienna: Mayer, 1870.

Mater Dolorosa in zwölf Vorträgen. Fastenpredigten 1843 in Dom. Vienna: Mayer, 1844.

Misericordia. Zwölf Vorträge über den 50. Psalmen gehalten in der Minoritenkirche zu Prag während der Fasten 1852. Vienna: Braumüller, 1853.

Mutter und Magd des Herrn. Ein Kanzelvortrag gehalten am Feste der unbefleckten Empfängnis Maria 1857 aus Sekundizfeier des hochwürdigen P. Petrus Becker Exprovinzial und Definitor der Capistraner Provinz in der Ordenskirche zum heiligen Hieronymus in Wien. Vienna: Mechitaristen, 1858.

Politische Passionspredigten. Fastenpredigten 1849 in Kirche am Hof nebst der Rede zum Seelenamt des k.k. F. Z. M. Baillet de Latour. Vienna: Braumüller, 1849.

Predigt zur Primizfeier des hochwürdigsten hochgebornen Herrn Friedrich Fürsten zu Schwarzenberg, Herzogs von Kruman. Vienna: Mechitaristen, 1833.

Prophetie und Glaube. Fastenpredigten 1855 zu S. Peter. Vienna: Braumüller, 1866.

Die Rückfahrt des Kaisers. Ein Singspiel. Vienna: Für das k.k. privat Theater Wien, 1814.

Die Säulen der Kirche. Zwölf Vorträge über die Apostelgechichte. Fastenpredigten 1847 Kirche am Hof. Vienna: Braumüller, 1849. Deals mostly with Paul.

Die Samariten. Fastenpredigten 1832 in Dom. Vienna: Mayer, 1840.

Stechpalmen. Erzählungen, Novellen, und vermischte Aufsätze. Vienna: Braumüller, 1871.

Vaterschaft und Familie. Acht Predigten gehalten zur 700-jähr Jubelfeier des Benedictinerstiftes zu den Schotten in Wien vom 1. bis 8. Mai 1858. Vienna: Überreuter, 1858.

Vater Unser. Fastenpredigten 1830 in der Redemptoristenkirche. 3d ed. Vienna: Mayer, 1842.

Der verlorene Sohn. Fastenpredigten 1832 in Dom. Vienna: Mayer, 1838.

Der Weg, die Wahrheit und das Leben. Zwölf Vorträge gehalten während der Fasten des Jahres 1854 in der Pfarrkirche auf der Landstrasse in Wien. Vienna: Braumüller, 1856.

Weltleben und Christenthum. Sechs Vorträge gehalten in der Fasten des Jahres 1850 in der Pfarrkirche am Hof. Nebst einigen Zugaben. Vienna: Braumüller, 1851.

Wintergrün. Gedichte, Geschichten und Reime. Vienna: Braumüller, 1874.

Die Worte der Feinde Christi. Fastenpredigten gehalten 1827 in der Redemptoristenkirche. 3d ed. Vienna: Mayer, 1851.

Zwölf Stufenpsalmen in eben so vielen Vorträgen. Fastenpredigtzyklus 1862 bei den Kapuzinern in Wien. Vienna: Braumüller, 1863.

Veith and J. P. Silbert. *Der Bote von Jericho.* Vienna: Armbruster, 1828.

Works by Contemporaries of Günther and Veith

1. BOOKS

Baltzer, Johann Baptist. *Neue theologische Briefe an Dr. Anton Günther. Ein Gericht für seiner Ankläger.* Breslau: Georg Philipp Aderholz, 1853. A defense of Günther by a former Hermesian.

Beidtel, Ignaz. *Untersuchungen über die kirchlichen Zustände in der kaiserliche österreichischen Staaten und die Art ihre Entstehung und die in Ansehung dieser Zustände wünschenswerten Reformen.* Vienna: Gerold, 1849.

Brunner, Sebastian. *Bremsen für den Freimüthigen in Sachen des neuen Wiener-Apostels Herrn Mahler und des alten Wiener-Apostels Dr. Veith.* Vienna: Mayer, 1848.

———. *Clemens Maria Hofbauer und seine Zeit. Minaturen zur Kirchengeschichte von 1780–1820.* Vienna: Braumüller, 1858.

———. *Denk-Pfennige zur Erinnerung an Personen, Zustände und Erlebniss vor, in, und nach dem Explosionsjahr 1848.* Vienna and Würzburg: Wörl, 1886.

———. *Einleitung zur Homiletik der Neuzeit.* Regensburg: Manz, 1849.

———. *Kanzel und Politik. für Dr. Veiths Freunde und Feinde.* Vienna: Mayer, 1850.

———. *Woher? Wohin? Geschichte, Gedanken, Bilder, und Leute aus meinem Leben.* 2d ed., vol. 1–3. Regensburg: Manz, 1865/66.

Castelli, Ignaz Franz. *Memorien meines Lebens.* Reprint, vol. 1–2. Munich: Georg Müller, 1913.

Clemens, Franz Jacob. *Offene Darlegung des Widerspruchs der Güntherischen Speculation mit der katholische Kirchenlehre durch Herrn Professor Doktor Knoodt in seiner Schrift "Günther und Clemens." Eine Replik.* Cologne: Lachem, 1853.

———. *Die spekulative Theologie A. Günthers und die katholische Kirchenlehrer.* Cologne: Bachem, 1853.

Flegel, J. *Anton Günthers Dualism von Geist und Natur.* Breslau: Gosohosch, 1880.

Haringer, Michael. *Einige Gebete des Dieners Gottes Clemens Maria Hofbauer.* 4th ed. Vienna: Sartori, 1865.

———. *Leben des ehrwürdigen Dieners Gottes Clemens Maria Hofbauer.* Vienna: Verlag der Redemptoristen, 1864.

Hoffinger, Dr. Johann von. *Dr. J. N. Ehrlich, eine Skizze seines Lebens.* Prague: k. böhmische Gesellschaft der Wissenschaften, 1866.

Hungari, A. *Musterpredigten der katholischen Kanzel-Beredsamkeit Deutschlands aus neuer und neuester Zeit,* vol. 1–5. Frankfurt: 1846.

Kehrein, Josef. *Geschichte der katholischen Kanzelberedsamkeit der Deutschen von der ältesten bis zur neuesten Zeit,* vol. 1–2. Regensburg: Manz, 1843.

Kleutgen, Joseph, S. J. *Theologie der Vorzeit verteidigt,* vol. vol. 1–3. Münster: Theissing, 1867–74.

Knoodt, Peter. *Anton Günther,* vol. 1–2. Vienna: Braumüller, 1881.

———. *Günther und Clemens, offene Breife,* vol. 1–3. Vienna: Braumüller, 1853–54.

Löwe, Johann Heinrich. *Johann Emanuel Veith. Eine Biographie.* Vienna: Braumüller, 1879.

Mader, Carl, C.S.S.R. *Die Congregation des allerheiligsten Erlösers in Österreich.* Vienna: St. Norbertus Buch und Kunstdruckerei, 1887.

Oischinger, Johann Nepomuk Paml. *Die Günthersche Philosophie mit Rücksicht auf die Geschichte und das System der Philosophie so wie auf die christliche religion dargestellt und gewürdigt.* Schaffhausen: Hurter, 1852.

Rosenthal, David August. *Convertitenbilder aus dem 19. Jahrhundert,* vol. 1–3. Shaffhausen: Hurter, 1865–70.

Schön, Bruno OFMConv. *Briefe über Geistesgestörte. Nebst einem Anhang als Schlüssel zum Verständnisse der Schriften von Dr. J. E. Veith.* 2 ed. Vienna: Hartleben, 1873.

———. *Humoristische Pillen gegen üble Laune, Melancholie, und dergleichen Grillen,* vol. 1–3. Vienna: Prandl, 1856–58.

Sorg, Ildefons. *Die Unhaltbarkeit des spekulativen Systems der Güntherianer, nachgewiesen vom kirchlichdogmatischen Standpunkte aus.* Graz: Tanzer, 1851.

Trebisch, Leopold. *Die Christliche Weltanschauung und ihrer Bedeutung für wissenschaft und Leben.* Vienna: Braumüller, 1852.

Weiss, Karl. *Geschichte der Stadt Wien.* Vienna: Rudolf Lechner, 1872.

Wolf, Gerson. *Geschichte der Juden in Wien 1776–1876.* Vienna: Hölder, 1876.

2. ARTICLES

Acton, John Emerich Edward Dalberg Lord. "Conflicts with Rome." *Essays on Freedom and Power*, ed. Gertrude Himmelfarb. New York: Meridian Books, 1962.

Brunner, Sebastian. "J. E. Veith. Eine Lebens- und Charakterskizze." *Deutscher Hausschatz* 3 (1877–78): 260–63, 275–78, 298–301.

Ehrlich, J. N. "Günther und Oischinger." *Wiener Kirchenzeitung* 6 (1853): 4–5.

Hoffinger, J. B. "Die Revolution und die Religion." *Das monarchisch-constitutionelle Österreich* no. 5 (17 December 1848): 17–18.

Knoodt, Peter. "Anton Günther." *Allgemeine Deutscher Biographie*, 10: 146–67. Leipzig: Duncker und Humblot, 1879.

_____. "Anton Günther und seine Lehre." *Brockhausischen Jahrbuch zum Conversationslexicon "Unsere Zeit,"* 1: 609–32. Leipzig: Brockhaus, 1857.

Löwe, Johann Heinrich. "Der hundertste Jahrestag der Geburt J. E. Veiths am 10 Juli 1887." *Österreichisches Jahrbuch*, ed. J. Helfert, 11 (1887): 171–84.

Secondary Sources

1. BOOKS

Aubert, Roger, et al. *The Church between Revolution and Restoration.* Vol. 7, *The History of the Church.* Edited by Hubert Jedin and John Dolan. Translated by Peter Becker. New York: Crossroads, 1981.

_____. *The Church in the Age of Liberalism.* Vol. 8, *History of the Church*, Edited by Hubert Jedin and John Dolan. Translated by Peter Becker. New York: Crossroads, 1981.

Bach, Maximilian. *Geschichte de Wiener Revolution im Jahr 1848.* Vienna: Wiener Volksbuchhandlung Ignaz Brand, 1898.

Bammer, Winfried, "Beiträge zur Sozialstruktur der Bevölkerung Wiens auf Grund der Verlassenschaftakten des Jahres 1830." Ph. D. University of Vienna, 1968.

Barea, Ilsa. *Vienna.* New York: Knopf, 1966.

Barton, Peter, ed., *Im Lichte der Toleranz. Aufsätze zur Torleranzgesetzgebung des 18. Jahrhunderts in den Reichen Josephs II., ihren Voraussetzungen und ihren Folgen.* Vol. 1–2. Vienna: Institut für protestantische Kirchengeschichte, 1981.

Bartoski, J. "Universalgeschichtliche Sicht der Kirche. Zu einem Vergleich der Ekklesiologie A. Günthers mit "Lumen Gentium" des II. Vaticanums." Dipl., University of Vienna, 1978. A short and strained account.

Bastgen, H. *Forschungen und Quellen zur Kirchenpolitik Gregors XVI.* Paderborn: Schöningh, 1929. Deals mostly with Prussia but some references to Austria. Long section on Hermes.

Bauer, Roger. *Idealismus und seine Gegner in Österriech.* Heidelberg: Carl Winter, 1966. A survey with short sections on Günther, Schlegel, and Müller.

Bauernfeld, Eduard. *Wiener Biedermeier.* Vienna: Bergland, 1960. Introduction defines difference between Biedermeier (culture) and Vormärz (politics).

Beck, Karl. *Offenbarung und Glaube bei A. Günther*. In *Wiener Beträge zur Theologie*, no. 17. Vienna: Herder, 1967.

Belovari, H. "Christlicher Demokratismus und christlicher Sozialismus im Jahre 1848 in Wien." Ph. D. diss., University of Vienna, 1960.

Bernard, Paul. *Jesuits and Jacobins. Enlightenment and Enlightened Despotism in Austria*. Urbana: University of Illinois Press, 1971.

———. *The Origins of Josephinism*. In *Colorado Studies*, no. 7. Colorado Springs: The Research Committee, 1964.

Blum, Jerome. *Nobel Landowner and Agriculture in Austria 1815-1848*. Baltimore: Johns Hopkins University Press, 1948.

Blunk, Laura A. "To Consider the Needs of Men: Viennese Workers in the 1848 Revolution." Ph. D. diss., Kent State University, 1981. An excellent study of the issues the workers faced.

Böhmer, Günther. *Die Welt des Biedermeier*. Munich: Desch, 1968. The best of the picture books.

Bradler-Rottman, Elisabeth. *Die Reformen Kaiser Josephs II*. In *Göppinger Akademische Beiträge*, no. 67. Göppingen: Alfred Kümmerle, 1973. Pages 144–65 treat religious politics.

Brenner, Franz. "Sebastian Brunners Verdienste um die Anfänge der katholischen Presse." Dipl., University of Vienna, 1976.

Brenner, Wilfried. "Die Arbeiterfrage im Vormärz. Ideale Grundlagen und geschichtliche Folgen." Ph. D. diss., University of Vienna, 1955. Sees the problems of the time related to the decline of traditional religious and family values.

Brion, Marcel. *Daily Life in the Vienna of Mozart and Schubert*. Translated by Jean Stewart. London: Weidenfeld and Nicolson, 1961. Distinguishes Austrian from German Romanticism.

Brück, H. *Geschichte der katholischen Kirche in Deutschland im 19. Jahrhundert*. Vol. 1–3. Mainz: Franz Kirchheim, 1887–91. Austria included in the broader German picture.

Brühl. Moritz. *Geschichte der katholischen Literatur Deutschlands*. Vienna: Manz, 1861. Veith receives considerable coverage.

Chadwick, Owen. *The Popes and European Revolution*. Oxford: Oxford University Press, 1981. A tour de force.

Chadwick, Owen. *The Secularization of the European Mind in the Nineteenth Century*. Cambridge: Cambridge University Press, 1975.

Collins, James. *Interpreting Modern Philosophy*. Princeton: Princeton University Press, 1972.

Coreth, Anna. *Pietas Austriaca: österreichische Frömmigkeit im Barock*. 2d. rev. ed. Vienna: Verlag für Geschichte und Politik, 1982. Considers the pious practices of individual Habsburgs.

Corti, Egon Caesar Conte. *Metternich und die Frauen*. Vienna: Kremayr und Scherian, 1977. Based on letters between Metternich and Katharina Bagration, Caroline Murat-Bonaparte, Wilhelmine von Sagan, and Dorothee Lieven. Mostly gossip.

Czeike, Felix. *Geschichte der Stadt Wien*. Vienna: Fritz Molden, 1981.

Dempf, Alois. *Weltordung und Heilsgeschichte*. Einsiedeln: Johannes Verlag, 1958. Pages 111–27 provide a treatment of Günther as philosopher.

Dempf, Rainer A. "Die Staatsphilosophie Anton Günthers vom Jahre 1848." Ph. D. diss., University of Vienna, 1948.

Dietrich, Donald. "German Idealism and the German Catholic Theological Response —Hermes, Möhler, Staudenmaier, and Günther." Ph. D. diss., University of Minnesota, 1969. The most thorough account of Günther's thought in English.

Dollinger, J. "Vergleich der Ehelehre in den deutschsprachigen Gesamtdarstellungen der katholische Moraltheologie des 19. Jahrhunderts mit der C. Werners." Ph. D. diss., University of Vienna, 1974.

Dragon, Friedrich. "Die Wiener Presse kirchlicher Tendenz vom Revolutionsjahr 1848 bis zur Gründung der Reichspost (1894)." Ph. D. diss., University of Vienna, 1953. Strongly anti-semitic. Valuable listing of the vairous periodicals, which makes up majority of the ninety-four page work.

Drimmel, Heinrich. *Oktober Achtundvierzig. Die Wiener Revolution*. Vienna: Amalthea, 1978.

Ehrensperger, Alfred. *Die Theorie des Gottesdienstes in der späten deutschen Aufklärung (1770–1815)*. In *Studien zur Dogmengeschichte und systematischen Theologie*, no. 30. Zurich: Theologischer Verlag, 1971. Concentrates on eighteenth century and on Germany, but good background.

Emrich, Berthold, "Jean Pauls Wirkung in Biedermeier." Ph. D. diss., University of Tübingen, 1948.

Endler, Franz. *Wien in Barock*. Vienna: Überreuter, 1979.

———. *Wien im Biedermeier*. Vienna: Überreuter, 1978.

Endres, Robert. *Revolution in Österreich 1848*. Vienna: Danubia, 1947. A summary of Bach.

Engel-Janosi, Friedrich, *Österreich und der Vatikan 1846–1918*. Vol. 1–2. Vienna: Styria, 1958.

Engel-Janosi, Friedrich, et al. *Die politische Korrespondenz der Päpste mit den österreichischen Klerus 1804–1918*. Vienna: Herold, 1964.

Eulner, F. K. *St. Clemens Maria Hofbauer, der Apostel von Wien*. Vorarlberg: Höchst, 1948. A short and very pious account.

Fischer, Josef Michael. *Volksnahe Verkündigung Alfons von Liguori und sein Einfluss auf die Predigt in Österreich*. In *Veröffentlichungen des Kirchenhistorischen Institutus der katholischen Fakultät der Universität Wien*, no. 7. Vienna: Domverlag, 1974. Contains a significant section on Veith.

Flinterhoff, Fritz. *Das Literaturapostolat eines Heiligen. Verdienste des Hl. Kl. M. Hofbauer um die katholische Literatur*. Paderborn: Bonifacius, 1912. Short biographies of the literati of the Hofbauer Circle, including Veith.

Foucault, Michael. *The Order of Things: An Archeology of the Human Science*. New York: Pantheon, 1970.

———. *Power/Knowledge, Selected Interviews and Other Writings 1972–1977*. Edited by Colin Gordon. New York: Pantheon, 1980.

Frieben, Birgit. "Die Sozialstruktur Wiens am Anfang des Vormärz." Ph. D. diss., University of Vienna, 1966.

Ganzer, Karl Richard. *Der heilige Hofbauer, Träger der Gegenreformation im 19. Jahrhundert.* Hamburg: Hanseat, 1939. Nazi propaganda.

Gierach, E., ed., *Sudetendeutsche Lebensbilder.* Vol. 1–2. Reichenberg: 1930. Sketches of Hofbauer, Bolzano, Günther, Veith, and Ehrlich by E. Winter.

Götze, Karl-Heinz. *Grundpositionen der Literaturgeschichtsschreibung im Vormärz.* Frankfurt: Lang, 1980.

Goldenits, Walter. "Das höhere Priesterbildungs-institut für Weltpriester zum hl. Augustin in Wien oder 'Das Frintaneum' bzw. 'Das Augustineum'." Ph. D. diss., University of Vienna, 1969.

Gordon, Bertram M. "Catholic Social Thought in Austria 1815–1848." Ph. D. diss., Rutgers University, 1969. Good description of how the churchmen did not recognize what was happening.

Gottschall, Klaus. *Dokumente zum Wandel im religiösen Leben Wiens während des Josephinismus.* Vienna: Institut für Volkskunde der Universität, 1979. The first part is his 1974 Dissertation.

Goyau, Georges. *L'Allemagne religieuse. Le Catholicisme 1880–1848.* Vol. 1–2. Paris: Librairie Academique Perrin, 1910. Lengthy treatment of Günther based on the biography of Knoodt.

Greifender, Justinus. "Elemente einer Theologie der Geschichte bei A. Günther." Dipl., University of Vienna, 1975. Too short to be thorough.

Gröner, Richard. *Wien wie es war. Ein Nachschlagewerk für Freunde des alten und neuen Wien, vollständig neu bearbeitet und erweitert von Dr. Felix Czeike.* 5th ed. Vienna: Fritz Molden, 1965.

Güttenberger, Heinrich. *Klemens Maria Hofbauer, der Heilige der Romantik.* Vienna: Reinhold, 1927. Treats Hofbauer and his circle.

Guggenberger, Siegmund. *Kirche und Staat in Österreich.* Vienna: Volksbundverlage, 1922.

Haberzettl, Hermann. *Die Stellung der Exjesuiten in Politik und Kulturleben Österreichs zu Ende des 18. Jahrhunderts.* Vienna: Verlage der Wissenschaftlichen Gesellschaften Österreichs, 1973. Most joined the bureaucracy as librarians and teachers.

Häusler, Wolfgang. *Das Judentum im Revolutionsjahr 1848.* Vienna: Herold, 1974. A collection of documents with an introductory essay on confessional issues of 1848.

———. *Von der Massenarmut zur Arbeiterbewegung. Demokratie und soziale Frage in der Wiener Revolution 1848.* Vienna: Jugend und Volk, 1979. The Catholic Church was afraid of the proletariat.

Hansen, Johann Jakob. *Lebensbilder hervorragender Katholiken des 19. Jahrhunderts.* Paderborn: Bonifacius, 1901. Treats the conservative circle around Karl Ernst Jarcke.

Hantsch, Hugo. *Die Geschichte Österreichs.* 4th ed. Vol. 1–2. Vienna: Styria, 1968. Volume 1 contains Hantsch's treatment of Biedermeier Vienna and 1848.

Hartley, Thomas J. A. *Thomistic Revival and the Modernist Era.* Toronto: St. Michael's Institute of Christian Thought, 1971. Concentrates on end of nineteenth century but does treat Kleutgen.

Heilinger, Rudolf. "Die Wiener katholisch-konservativen und sozialdemokratischen Zeitschriften in der zweiten Hälfte des 19. Jahrhunderts." Ph. D. diss., University of Vienna, 1974. Treats Brunner's Kirchenzeitung.

Helfert, Joseph Alexander Freiherr von, *Geschichte der österreichischen Revolution in Zusammenhang mit der mitteleuropäischen Bewegung der Jahre 1848–1849*, Vol. 1–2. Freiburg: Herder, 1907.

———. *Johann baptist Ritter von Hoffinger. Ein Lebens- und Charakter- und auch ein Zeitbild.* Vienna: Sonderdruck aus dem österreichischen Jahrbuch, 1881.

———. *Die konfessionelle Frage in Österreich 1848. Zugleich ein Beitrag zur Tages und Flugschriften Literatur jener Zeit.* Vol. 6–13 of *Österreichisches Jahrbuch.* Vienna: Verlag des österreichischen Volksschriften Vereines, 1882–89.

———. *Die Wiener Journalistik im Jahre 1848.* Vienna: Manz, 1877. Treats *Aufwärts, Österreichischer Volksfreund,* and Sebastian Brunner.

Hocedez, E. *Histoire de la theologie au xix. siecle,* Vol. 1–3. Paris: Desclee de Brouwer, 1947–52.

Hofer, Johannes, C.S.S.R. *Der Heilige Klemens Maria Hofbauer.* Freiburg: Herder, 1921.

Hollerweger, Hans. *Die Reform des Gottesdienstes zur Zeit des Josephinismus in Österreich.* In *Studien zur Pastoralliturgie,* no. 1. Regensburg: Friedrich Pustet, 1976.

Holzknecht, Georgine. *Ursprung und Herkunft der Reformideen Kaiser Josephs auf kirchlichem Gebiete.* Innsbruck: Verlag der Wagner'schen k.k. Universitätsbuchhandlung, 1914.

Honek, Klemens, *Johann Emanuel Veith 1787–1876. Vom Direktor des tierarzneiinstitutes zum bedeutenden Homileten des 19. Jahrhunderts.* In *Miscellanea, Neue Reihe, Wiener Katholische Akademic,* no. 143. Vienna: Katholische Akademie, 1983. A short address delivered to the academy, building on early works.

Hosp, Eduard. *Bischof Gregorius Thomas Ziegler. Ein Vorkämpfer gegen den Josephinismus.* Linz: Oberösterreichischer Landesverlag, 1956.

———. *Erbe des H. Klemens Maria Hofbauer. Redemptoristen in Österreich 1820–1951.* Vienna: Verlag Prokuratur der Redemptoristen, 1953.

Der heilige Klemens Maria Hofbauer 1751–1820. Vienna: Seelsorge Verlag, 1951.

———. *Kirche im Sturmjahr. Erinnerungen an Johann Michael Häusle. Beiträge zur neueren Geschichte des christlichen Österreichs II.* Vienna: Herold, 1953.

———. *Kirche Österreichs im Vormärz 1815–1850.* Vienna: Herold, 1971. A history of each diocese.

———. *Zeugnisse aus bedrängter Zeit. der heilige Klemens Maria Hofbauer in Briefen und weiteren Schriften.* In *Miscellanea, Neue Reihe, Wiener Katholische Akademie,* no. 67. Vienna: Katholische Akademie, 1982.

Hudal, Alois. *Die österreichische Vatikanbotschaft 1806–1918.* Munich: Pohl, 1952.

Hugelmann, Karl. *Historisch-politische Studien: Das politische Vereinsleben des Jahres 1848 in Österreich.* Vienna: Josef Roller, 1915.

Innerkofler, Adolf. *Der Hl. Klemens Maria Hofbauer. Ein österreichischer Reformator.* 2d ed. Regensburg: Pustet, 1913.

Kann, Robert A. *A Study in Austrian Intellectual History from Late Barogue to Romanticism.* New York: Praeger, 1960.

Kapner, Gerhard. *Barocker Heiligenkult in Wien und seine Träger.* Munich: Oldenbourg, 1978.

Kaufmann, Paul. *Brauchtum in Österreich. Feste, Sitten, Glaube.* Vienna: Paul Zsolnay, 1982.

Kleinberg, Alfred. *Die Zensur im Vormärz.* Vienna: Schulwissenschaft Verlag, 1917.

Klinger, Hans, "Urzustand, Sündenfall und Erbsünde bei A. Günther." Ph. D. diss., University of Vienna, 1964.

Köhler, Benedikt. *Ästhetik der Politik. Adam Müller und die politische Romantik.* Stuttgart: Klett-Cotta, 1980.

Koller, Franz. "Jesus Christus—Gottmensch und zweiter Adam. Darlegung zur Christologie A. Günthers." Dipl., University of Vienna, 1974.

Kovacs, Elisabeth, ed. *Katholische Aufklärung und Josephinismus.* Munich: Oldenbourg, 1979.

Kovacs, Elisabeth, *Ultramontanism und Staats-kirchentum im theresianisch-josephinischen Staat. Der Kampf der Kardinäle Mizazzi und Frankenberg gegen den Wiener Professor der Kirchengeschichte Ferdinand Stöger.* In *Wiener Beiträge zur Theologie,* no. 51. Vienna: Domverlag, 1975.

Kummer, Gertrude. *Die Leopoldinenstiftung 1829–1914. Der älteste österreichische Missionsverein.* In *Veröffentlichungen des Kirchenhistorischen Instituts der kath.-theol. Fakultät Wien,* no. I. Vienna: Domverlag, 1966.

Lesky, Erna. *Meilensteine der Wiener Medizin. Grosse Ärzte Österreichs in drei Jahrhunderten.* Vienna: Wilhelm Maudrich, 1981.

———. *Die Wiener medizinische Schule im 19. Jahrhundert.* 2d ed. Vienna: Böhlaus, 1978.

Link, Edith M. *The Emancipation of the Austrian Peasant 1740–1798.* New York: Columbia University Press, 1949.

Linsmaier, Monika. "Die katholische Publizistik. Ein Beitrag zur Wiener Pressegeschichte der zweiten Hälfte des 19. Jahrhunderts." Ph. D. diss., University of Vienna, 1979. Begins after 1848.

Loidl, Franz. *Geschichte des Erzbistums Wien.* Vienna: Herold, 1983. A tightly-written and thorough work.

Maass, Ferdinand. *Der Josefinismus. Quellen zu seiner Geschichte in Österreich 1760–1790,* Vol. 1–5. Vienna: Herold, 1951. Documents collected to support his theory of Josephinism as the establishment of a state church.

Mann, Christine. "Der Philosophie Historiker Vinzenz A. Knauer 1828–1894." Ph. D. diss., University of Vienna, 1973.

Mann, Erwin, ed. *Erbe als Auftrag. Zur Theologie und Geistesgeschichte des 19. Jahrhunderts. J. Pritz zum 60. Geburtstag.* In *Wiener Beiträge zur Theologie,* no. 40. Vienna: Domverlag, 1973.

Mann, Erwin. *Idee und Wirklichkeit der Offenbarung. Methode und Aufbau der Fundamentaltheologie des Güntherianers J. N. Ehrlich.* Vienna: Verband der wissenschaftlichen Gesellschaften Österreichs, 1977.

———. *Die Wiener theologische Schule A. Günthers im Urteil des 20. Jahrhunderts. Nebst ein Anhang: Unbekannte Briefe A. Günthers.* Vienna: Verband der wissenschaftlichen Gesellschaften Österreichs, 1979.

———. *Das "Zweite Ich" A. Günthers: J. H. Pabst.* In *Wiener Beiträge zur Theologie,* no. 27. Vienna: Domverlag, 1970.

Marx, Julius. *Die österreichishe Zensur im Vormärz.* Vienna: Verlag für Geschichte und Politik, 1959. Attempts to say that it was not so bad.

———. *Die wirtschaftlichen Ursachen der Revolution von 1848 in Österreich.* Graz: Böhlau, 1965.

Mayer, Hermann. "Anton Günther: Peregrins Gastmahl." Ph. D. diss., University of Vienna, 1951. A good summary of Günther's use of humor.

Mayer, Sigmund. *Die Wiener Juden 1700–1900. Kommerz, Kultur, Politik.* Vienna: Löurt, 1917. Anti-semitic and praises Veith for turning on Judaism.

McCool, Gerald A. *Catholic Theology in the Nineteenth Century. The Quest for Unitary Method.* New York: Seabury, 1977. An erudite account slanted towards neo-Thomism.

Musulin, Stella. *Vienna in the Age of Metternich from Napoleon to Revolution 1805–1848.* London: Faber and Faber, 1975.

Neill, Thomas P. *The Rise and Decline of Liberalism.* Milwaukee: Bruce, 1953.

Neuburger, Max. *Die Wiener medizinische Schule in Vormärz.* Vienna: Rikola, 1921.

Obrovski, Herta. "Das Wiener Vereinswesen im Vormärz." Ph. D. diss., University of Vienna, 1970.

O'Meara, Thomas F., O.P. *Romantic Idealism and Roman Catholicism: Schelling and the Theologians.* Notre Dame: University of Notre Dame Press, 1982.

Orban, Ladislao, *Theologia Güntheriana et Concilium Vaticanum.* Vol. 1–2. Rome, 1949–50. Anti-Günther account based on Index documents in the Gregorianum and background papers for discussion in Vatican Council I.

Pannagl, Franz. "Der Irrenhausseelsorger P. Bruno Schön 1809–1881." Dip., University of Vienna, 1977.

Pleyer, Karl. "Johann Emanuel Veith und sein Kreis." Ph. D. diss., University of Vienna, 1934.

Popelar, Otto. "J. E. Veith. Ein homiletischer Beitrag zur Aufklärung und Restauration." Ph. D. diss., University of Vienna, 1969.

Pritz, Joseph. *Franz Werner. Ein Leben für Wahrheit in Freiheit.* Vienna: Herder, 1957.

———. *Glauben und Wissen bei Anton Günther.* In *Wiener Beiträge zur Theologie*, no. 4. Vienna: Herder, 1963.

———. *Mensch als Mitte: Leben und Werk Carl Werners.* Vienna: Herder, 1968.

———. *Wegweisung zur Theologie. Briefe A. Günthers an J. N. Ehrlich mit einer Einleitung.* In *Wiener Beiträge zur Theologie*, no. 37. Vienna: Domverlag, 1971.

Rachholz, Elisabeth. "Zur Armenfürsorge der Stadt Wien von 1740–1904. Von der privaten zur städtischen Fürsorge." Ph. D. diss., University of Vienna, 1970.

Rath, Reuben John. *The Viennese Revolution of 1848.* Austin: University of Texas Press, 1957.

Reikerstorfer, J. "Kritik der Offenbarung. Die 'Idee' als System-theoretisches Grundprinzip einer Offenbarungstheologie: A. Günther in Begegnung mit J. S. v. Drey." Vol. 1–2. Inaug. diss., University of Vienna, 1977.

———. *Offener Ursprung. Eine Interpretation der Anthropologie C. Werners.* In *Wiener Beiträge zur Theologie*, no. 32. Vienna: Herder, 1971.

———. "Die zweite Reflexion über den Begriff der Philosophie A. Günthers." Ph. D. diss., University of Vienna, 1975.

Reinerman, Alan J. *Austria and the Papacy in the Age of Metternich.* Vol. 1: *The Union of Throne and Altar 1809–1830.* Washington D.C.: Catholic University of America Press, 1979.

Reiser, Herbert. *Der Geist des Josephinismus und sein Fortleben. Der Kampf der Kirche um ihre Freiheit*. Vienna: Herder, 1963. Josephinism viewed as attempt to establish a state church.

Reschauer, Heinrich. *Das Jahr 1848. Geschichte der Wiener Revolution*. Vol. 1–2. Vienna: Waldheim, 1872.

Ritzen, Renatus, O.F.M. *Der junge Sebastian Brunner in seinem Verhältnis zu Jean Paul, Anton Günther, und Fürst Metternich*. Aichach: Schütte, 1927.

Robertson, Priscilla. *Revolutions of 1848. A Social History*. Princeton: University Press, 1952.

Sauer, Wolfgang. *Katholisches Vereinswesen in Wien. Zur Geschichte des christlichsozialkonservativen Lagers vor 1914*. In *Geschichte und Sozialkunde Forschungen*, no. 5. Salzburg: Neugebauer, 1980.

Schäfer, Theo. *Die Erkenntnistheoretische Kontroverse Kleutgen–Günther. Ein Beitrag zur Entstehungsgeschichte der Neuscholastik*. Paderborn: Schöningh, 1961.

Schnackenburg, Rudolf. *Gottes Herrschaft und Reich*. 2d ed. Freiburg: Herder, 1965.

Scheffczyk, Leo, ed. *Theologie im Aufbruch und Widerstreit. Die deutsche katholische Theologie im 19. Jahrhundert*. Bremen: Schünemann, 1965.

Scheincher, J. *Sebastian Brunner. Ein Lebensbild, zugleich ein Stück Zeit- und Kirchengeschichte*. Vienna: Wörl, 1888.

Schmidt, Erwin, *Wiener Stadtgeschichte*. 3d ed. Vienna: Jugend und Volk, 1978.

Severinski, Nikolaus. "Kirche und Staat bei A. Günther." Ph. D. diss., University of Vienna, 1967.

Silber, Erika. "Beiträge zur Sozialstruktur Wiens im Vormärz. Eine sozial- und wirtschaftsgeschichtliche Arbeit auf Grund der magistratischen Verlassenschaftsakten des Jahrens 1840." Vol. 1–2. Ph. D. diss., University of Vienna, 1977. The tables in volume 2 are most valuable.

Silberbauer, Gerhard. *Österreichs Katholiken und die Arbeiterfrage*. Graz: Styria, 1966. The Catholic Church did not recognize the problem.

Silbernagl, Isidor. *Die kirchenpolitischen und religiöse Zustände im 19. Jahrhundert. Ein Kulturbild*. Landshut: Krüll'schen Universitätsbuchhandlung, 1901.

Simon, Elisabeth. "Das Wiener Schulwesen im Vormärz." Ph. D. diss., University of Vienna, 1949.

Simonis, Walter. *Trinität und Vernunft*. Frankfurt: Kneckt, 1972.

Singer, Peter. *Hegel*. Oxford: Oxford University Press, 1983.

Stein, Peter. *Epochenproblem "Vormärz" 1815–1848*. Stuttgart: Metzlersche Verlagsbuchhandlung, 1974.

Steiner, Herbert. *Karl Marx in Wien—Arbeiterbewegung zwischen Revolution and Restauration 1848*. Vienna: Europaverlag, 1978.

Stekl, Hannes. *Österreichs Aristokratie im Vormärz*. Vienna: Verlag für Geschichte und Politik, 1973.

Stingeder, Franz. *Geschichte der Schriftpredigt*. Vol. 2 Paderborn: Schöningh, 1920.

Stout, Jeffrey. *The Flight from Authority: Religion, Morality, and the Quest for Autonomy*. Notre Dame: University of Notre Dame Press, 1981.

Swidler, Leonard. *Aufklärung Catholicism 1780–1850. Liturgical and Other Reforms in the Catholic Aufklärung*. Missoula, Mont. Scholars Press, 1978.

Thauren, Johannes, S.V.D. *Die Leopoldinen-Stiftung zur Unterstützung der amerikanischen Mission. Ihr Werden und Wirken.* Vienna: Missionsdurckerei St. Gabriel, 1940.

Till, Rudolf. *Hofbauer und sein Kreis.* Vienna: Herold, 1951.

Timchek, William. "The Struggle of Throne and Altar: Church against State in Austria 1848-1874." Ph. D. diss. University of Wisconsin at Madison, 1974.

Tomek, Ernst. *Kirchengeschichte Österreichs.* Vol. 1-3. Vienna: Tyrolia, 1959.

Valjavec, Fritz. *Der Josephinismus: Zur geistigen Entwicklung Österreichs im 18. und 19. Jahrhundert.* 2d ed. Munich: Oldenbourg, 1945.

Veith, Andreas Ludwig, and Ludwig Lenhart, *Kirche und Volksfrömmigkeit in Zeitalter des Barocks.* Freiburg: Herder, 1956. German piety in general.

Vidmar, Constantin. *Johann Emanuel Veith. Ein Gedenkblatt zu seinem hundertsten Geburtstag.* Vienna: Mayer, 1887. A summary of Löwe.

Weinzierl-Fischer, Erika. *Die österreichischen Konkordate von 1855 und 1933.* Vienna: Verlag für Geschichte und Politik, 1960.

_____. *Politische Korrespondence der Päpste mit dem österreichischen Kaisern 1804-1918.* Vienna: Herold, 1964.

Welch, Claude. *Protestant Thought in the Nineteenth Century.* Volume 1: *1799-1870.* New Haven: Yale University Press, 1972.

Wenzel, Paul. *Der Freundeskreis um Anton Günther und die Gründung Beurons. Ein Beitrag zur Geschichte des deutschen Katholizismus in 19. Jahrhundert.* Essen: Ludgerus, 1965.

_____. *Das wissenschaftliche Anliegen des Güntherianismus. Ein Beitrag zur Theologiegeschichte des 19. Jahrhunderts.* Essen: Ludgerus, 1961.

Weyrich, Isabel. "Die Zensur als Mittel der Unterdrückung von liberalen Bestrebungen im österreichischen Vormärz 1830-1848." Ph. D. diss., University of Vienna, 1976.

Widmann, Ernst. *Die religiöse Ansichten des Fürsten Metternich.* Darmstadt: Winter, 1914.

Winner, Gerhard. *Die Klosteraufhebungen in Niederösterreich und Wien.* Vienna: Herold, 1967.

Winckler, Rupert. *Der Zustand der Klöster in der Wiener Erzdiözese um 1828 nach den Visitationsberichten des Wiener Erzbischofs Leopold Maximilian Graf Firmian.* In *Miscellanea aus dem Kirchenhistorischen Instituts der katholisch-theologischen Fakultät Wien,* no. 22. University of Vienna: Institut für Kirchengeschichte, 1972.

Winter, Eduard. *Barock, Absolutismus und Aufklärung in der Donaumonarchie.* Vienna: Europe, 1971.

_____. *Frühliberalismus in der Donaumonarchie: Religiöse, nationale und wissenschaftliche Strömungen von 1790-1868.* Berlin: Akademie Verlag, 1968. Also published as *Romanticismus, Restauration, und Frühliberalismus im österreichischen Vormärz.* Vienna: Europa, 1968.

_____. *Die Geistige Entwicklung Anton Günthers und seine Schule.* Paderborn: Schöningh, 1831.

_____. *Josef II. Von den geistigen Quellen und letzten Beweggründen seiner Reformideen.* Vienna: Bindenschild, 1946.

———. *Der Josephinismus und seine Geschichte: Beiträge zur Geistesgeschichte Österreichs 1740–1848.* 2nd ed., Vienna: Rohrer, 1962.

———. *Das positive Vernunftkriterium in der Philosophie A. Günthers.* Warnsdorf: Opitz, 1928.

———. *Revolution, Neoabsolutismus und Liberalismus in der Donaumonarchie.* Vienna: Europa, 1969.

———. *Tausend Jahre Geisteskampf in Sudetenraum. Das religiöse Ringen zweier Völker.* Salzburg: Otto Müller, 1938.

Winter, Eduard, and Maria Winter. *Domprediger Johann Emanuel Veith und Kardinal Friedrich Schwarzenberg. Der Güntherprozess in unveröffentlichen Briefen und Akten.* Vienna: Böhlau Nachfolger, 1972.

Wisshaupt, Erhard. "Die wirtschaftliche und soziale Lage in Österreich von 1830 bis 1839 nach amtlichen Berichten," Ph. D. diss., University of Vienna, 1952.

Wodka, Josef. *Kirche in Österreich, Wegweiser durch ihre Geschichte.* Vienna: Herder, 1959.

Wolfsgruber, Cölestin. *Friedrich Kardinal Schwarzenberg.* Vol. 1–3. Vienna: Carl Fromme, 1906-17.

———. *Joseh Othmar Cardinal Rauscher.* Freiburg: Herder, 1888.

———. *Kirchengeschichte Österreich-Ungarns.* Vienna: Heinrich Kirsch, 1909.

Zenker, Ernst Viktor. *Geschichte der Wiener Journalistik von Anfängen bis zum Jahre 1848.* Vienna: Braumüller, 1892. Does not include the revolution.

Zöllner, Erich. *Geschicht Österreichs* Munich: Oldenbourg, 1979.

2. ARTICLES

Adrianyi, G, "Erzbischof Lajos Haynalds Mission in der österreichischen Konkordatsfrage." *Donauraum* 16 (1971): 152–58.

Banik-Schweitzer, Renate, and Wolfgang, Pircher. "Zur Wohnsituation der Massen im Wien des Vormärz." In *Wien im Vormärz*, edited by Felix Czeike, 133–74. Vienna: Verein für Geschichte der Stadt Wien Kommisionsverlag Jugend und Volk, 1980.

Bauer, Roger. "Le Josephinisme." *Critique* 134 (1958): 622–39.

Beer, Adolf. "Kirchliche Angelegenheiten in Österreich 1816–1842." *Mitteilung des Instituts für österreichische Geschichtsforschung* 18 (1897): 493–581.

Benda, Kalman. "Probleme des Josephinismus und des Jakobinertums in der Habsburgischen Monarchie." *Südost-Forschungen* 15 (1966): 38–71.

Benna, Anna Hedwig. "Das Kaisertum Österreich und die römische Liturgie." *Mitteilungen des österreichischen Staatsarchivs* 9 (1956): 118–36.

Bernard, Paul. "Joseph II and the Jews: Origins of the Toleration Patent of 1782." *Austrian History Yearbook* 4/5 (1968–69): 101–19.

Beumer, J. "Konrad Martin, Bischof von Paderborn und seine Haltung gegenüber dem Güntherianismus." *Theologie und Glaube* 67 (1977): 83–91.

Braudel, Manfred. "Theologie im österreichischen Vormärz." In *Kirchen und Liberalismus im 19. Jahrhundert,* edited by M. Schmidt and G. Schwaisger, 126–42. Göttingen: Vandenhöck and Ruprecht, 1976. Sees Veith as an anti-liberal, especially in his *Meisterlosigkeit.*

Brinton, Crane. "Romanticism." In *The Encyclopedia of Philosophy* 7: 206–09. New York: Macmillan, 1967.

Coreth, Anna. 'Pietas Austriaca: Wesen und Bedeutung habsurgischer Frömmigkeit in der Barockzeit." *Mitteilungen des österreichischen Staatsarchivs* 7 (1954): 90–119.

Dempf, Alois. "Erneuerung und Neubildung des Cartesianismus in der christlichen Philosophie des 19. Jahrhunderts." In *Cartesio. Revista di Filosofit Neo-Scholastica. Supplemento speciale al Volume XXIX*, 285–92. Milan: Publicatione a cura della Facolta di Filosofia dell'Universita Cattolica del sacro cuore Societa Editrice Vita e Pensiero, July 1937.

———. "Die erste Wiener philosophische Schule." *Wiener Zeitschrift für Philosophie, Psychologie und Pädagogik* 1, no. 1 (1947): 1–12.

———. "Die letzte Vollanthropologie: Dem Andenken Anton Günthers +1863." *Wissenschaft und Weltbild* 15 (1962): 184–92.

Dietrich, Donald. "Anton Günther: Catholic Liberal in the Habsburg Empire." *Journal of Church and State* 23, no. 3 (1981): 497–517.

Eckhardt, Johann. "Clemens M. Hofbauer und die Wiener Romantikerkreise am Beginn des 19. Jahrhunderts." *Hochland* 8 (1910/1911): 17–27, 182–92, 341–50.

Engel-Janosi, Friedrich. "The Church and the Nationalities in the Habsburg Monarchy." *Austrian History Yearbook* 3, no. 3 (1967): 67–82.

———. "Über die Entwicklung der sozialen und volkswirtschaftlichen Verhältnisse im deutschen Österreich 1815-1848." *Vierteljahrschrift für Sozial- und Wirschaftsgeschichte* 18 (1924): 95–108. Somewhat outdated.

Engelmann, Ursmar. "Anton Günther und Beuron," *Erbe und Auftrag* 42 (1966): 240–45. A positive review of Wenzel's book on the subject.

Feldbauer, Peter, and Hannes Stekl. "Wiens Armenwesen im Vormärz." In *Wien im Vormärz*, edited by Felix Czeike, 175–201. Vienna: Verein für Geschichte der Stadt Wien Kommissionsverlag Jugend und Volk, 1980.

Felderer, Josef, S.J. "Kirchenbegriff in Flugschriften des josephinische Jahrzehnts." *Zeitschrift für katholische Theologie* 75 (1953): 257–330.

Fichtner, Paula Sutter. "History, Religion, and Politics in the Austrian Vormärz." *History and Theory* 10 (1971): 22–48. History as a discipline was threatening to the Austrians.

Fischer, I. "Beiträge zur medizinischen Kulturgeschichte: Johann Emanuel Veith." *Wiener klinische Wochenschrift* 36 (1923): 112–14.

Folkert, Oskar. "Das Sturmjahr 1848 und die Kirche in Österreich." *Wissenschaft und Weltbild* 12 (1948): 165–74. Considers Günther and Veith to be liberals.

Glossy, Karl. "Kaiser Franz' Reise nach Italien im Jahre 1819." *Jahrbuch der Grillparzergesellschaft* 14 (1904): 149–69.

Gordon, Bertram M. "The Challenge of Industrialization: The Catholic Church and the Working Class in and around Vienna 1815-1848." *Austrian History Yearbook* 9/10 (1973–74): 123–43.

Goyau, Georges. "Les Origines du Culturkampf Allemand." *Revue des deux Mondes* 44 (1908): 276–311. Treats Güntherians on 278–87.

Gross, N. T., "The Habsburg Monarchy 1750–1914." In *The Emergence of Industrial Societies*, ed. Carlo M. Cipolla. *Part I. Fontana Economic History of Europe*, 4: 228–78. New York: Barnes and Noble, 1976.

Günther, Gustav. "Johann Emanuel und Johann Elias Veith. Das Dioskurenpaar der Wiener Schule." *Deutschösterreichische tierärztliche Wochenschrift* 8 (1926): 115–17. Claims that Johann Emanuel Veith became a priest because he was disappointed in love.

Güttenberger, Heinrich. "Besuch im Kreise Hofbauers." *Reichspost*, no. 88 (22 March 1921): 1–2. A sentimenal look at the followers of Hofbauer buried in the cemetery at Maria Enzersdorf.

Guggenberger, Siegmund. "Die Anfänge der katholischen Volksbewegung in Österreich." *Volkswohl, christlich-soziale Monatschrift* 13 (1920): 165–70. A nostalgic look at the medieval guilds and third orders destroyed by Josephinism.

Guglia, Eugen. "Religiöses Leben in Wien 1815–1830." *Allgemeine Zeitung* (Munich). Suppl. 128–29 (5–6 June 1891): 1–6.

Hantsch, Hugo. "Der geistige Gehalt der Barockzeit." *Christliche Kunstblätter* 97 (1959): 1–5.

Hoffmann, Alfred. "Bürokratie insbesondere in Österreich." In *Beiträge zur neueren Geschichte Österreichs*, edited by Heinrich Fichtenau and Erich Zöllner, 12–31. Vienna: Böhlaus Nachfolger, 1974.

Holböck, Ferdinand. "Anton Günther und seine Freunde." *Österreichisches Klerusblatt* 95 (1962): 52–54. A letter from Peter Knoodt.

Hollerweger, Hans. "Die Reform des Gottesdienstes zur Zeit des Josephinismus in Österreich." *Beiträge zur Wiener Diözesangeschichte* 19, no. 3 (1978): 35.

―――. "Tendenzen der liturgischen Reformen unter Maria Theresia und Joseph II." In *Katholische Aufklärung und Josephinismus*, edited by Elisabeth Kovacs, 295–306. Vienna: Verlag für Geschichte und Politik, 1979.

―――. "Zwischen Kaiser und Volk. Bemerkungen zur Situation des Priesters in der josephinischen Zeit." In *Priesterbild im Wandel. Linzer Theologische Reihe I. Festschrift Alois Gruber 70. Geburtstag*, edited by Professoren de Philosophisch-Theologischen Hochschule Linz, 87–104. Linz: Oberösterreichischer Landesverlag, 1972.

Hosp, Eduard. "St. Klemens und der Stifter." *Spicilegium Historicum* 2 (1954): 432–50.

―――. "Leben des Pater Josef Prost 1804–1884 nach seinem eigenen Aufzeichnungen." *Spicilegium Historicum* II (1963): 374-432.

―――. "P. Dr. Johannes Madlener, Philosoph und Homilet der Hofbauerkreis." *Spicilegium Historicum* 5 (1957): 353–403.

―――. "Die theologischen Lehrbücher der josephinischen Zeit in Österreich." *Theologisch-praktischen Quartalschrift* 105 (1957): 195–214. Also appeared as typed manuscript, *Miscellanea VIII*. Vienna: Wiener Katholische Akademie, 1976.

―――. "Veith." In *Lexikon für Theologie und Kirche*, 2d ed. Edited by Joseph Höfer and Karl Rahner, 10: 653. Freiburg: Herder, 1965.

Hussarek, Max. "Die Krise und die Lösung des Konkordates vom 18 August 1855." *Archiv für österreichische Geschichte* 112 (1932): 211–480.

―――. "Die Verhandlungen des Konkordates vom 18. August 1855. Ein Beitrag zur Geschichte des österreichischen Staatskirchenrechtes." *Archiv für österreichische Geschichte* 109, no. 2 (1922): 447–810.

Innerkofler, Adolf. "Der hl. Klemens Maria Hofbauer als Prediger." In Swoboda, Heinrich, *Erster homiletischer Kurs in Wien*, edited by Heinrich Swoboda, 116–29. Vienna: Heinrich Kirsch, 1911.

Katann, Oskar. "Fragen des Katholischen Geisteslebens. Die seinerzeitigen Kämpfe Anton Günther und seine Schule." *Schönere Zukunft* 7 (1932): 717-19.

———. "Kl. M. Hofbauer und die katholischer Literatur." *Das neue Reich* 2, no. 25-26 (21 March and 26 March, 1920): 394-95, 411-13.

Klinger, Hans. "A. Günther und die Beuroner Gründer Äbte." *Seckauer Hefte* 26 (1963): 27-32.

———. "Sündenfall und Erbsünde bei Anton Günther." In *Erbe als Auftrag. Joseph Pritz zum 60. Geburtstag*, edited by Erwin Mann, 119-67. Vienna: Domverlag, 1973.

Konrad, Helmut. "Religiöser und sozialer Protest: Die frühe österreichische Arbeiterbewegung und die Religionsgemeinschaften." In *Politik und Gesellschaft im alten und neuen Österreich. Festschrift Rudolf Neck*, edited by I. Ackerl et al., 195-213. Vienna: Verlag für Geschichte und Politik, 1981. It was not as simple as church and capitalism versus worker in the early nineteenth century in Austria.

Kovacs, Elisabeth. "Die Bedenken des Kardinals Joseph Othmar von Rauscher, Fürsterzbischof von Wien 1853-1875, zur Dogmatisierung der päpstlichen Unfehlbarkeit während des Ersten Vaticanums 1869-1870." In *Festschrift Franz Loidl zum 65. Geburtstag*, edited by Elisabeth Kovacs, 3: 94-121. Vienna: Brüder Hollinek, 1971.

———. "Die Diözesanregulierung unter Joseph II 1782-1789." In *Österreich zur Zeit Kaiser Josephs II*, Katalog der Niederösterreichischen Landesausstellung, Stift Melk (29 March-2 November 1980): 176-80.

———. "Ultramontanismus und Staatskirchentum. Der Kampf der Kardinäle Migazzi und Franckenberg gegen den Wiener Professoren der Kirchengeschichte Ferdinand Stöger." *Beiträge zur Wiener Diözesangeschicht* 18, no. 1 (1977): 4.

———. "Die Hofpredigerkonkurrenz des Jahres 1845 in der kaiserlichen Berg zu Wien." In *Sacerdos et Pastor semper et ubique. Festschrift zum 40. järigen Priesterjubiläum Prälat Univ.-professor Dr. Franz Loidls*, 325-32. Vienna: Veröffentlichungen des Kirchenhistorischen Instituts der katholisch-theologischen Fakultät der Universität Wien 13, 1972.

Lakner, Franz. "Die 'Idee' bei Anton Günther." *Zeitschrift für katholischer Theologie* 59 (1935): 1-56, 197-245. Compares Günther with Hermes.

———. "Kleutgen und die kirchliche Wissenschaft Deutschlands im 19. Jahrhundert." *Zeitschrift für katholische Theologie* 57 (1933): 161-214.

Lauchert, Friedrich. "Anton Günther." In *The Catholic Encyclopedia*, 7: 85-88. New York: Robert Appleton, 1910.

Loidl, Franz. "Pfarrer Johann Michael Korn, Hofbauer Jünger 1788-1825." *Jahrbuch für Landeskunde von Niederösterreich*, Neue Serie 34 (1964): 543-59.

———. "Der Wiener Beicht Vater Klemens Maria Hofbauers: Franz Seraph Schmid." *Beiträge zur Wiener Diözesangeschichte* 10, nos. 5-6 (1969): 33-39, 41-44.

Lovejoy, Arthur O. "The Meaning of Romanticism for the Historian of Ideas." *Journal of the History of Ideas* 3 (June 1941): 257-78.

Mann, Christine. "Der Philosophiehistoriker Vinzenz Knauer in seinem Verhältnis zu Anton Günther." In *Erbe als Auftrag. Josef Pritz zum 60. Geburtstag*, edited by Erwin Mann, 168-85. Vienna: Domverlag, 1973.

Mann, Erwin. "A. Günther und die Benediktiner von St. Paul in Kärnten." In *Sacerdos et Pastor. Festschrift zum 40. järigen Priesterjubiläum Franz Loidl*, Herausgegeben von seinen Freunden, Mitarbeitern, und Schülern, 91-103. Vienna: Domverlag, 1972.

———. "A. Günther und die Wiener Dichterin Josepha von Hoffinger." *Wiener Geschictsblätter* 2, no. 3 (1977): 206–15.

———. "Kirche vor der Kirche." *Zeitschrift für katholische Theologie* 95 (1973): 200–210.

———. "Offenbarung als göttliche Erziehung." In *Erbe als Auftrag. Zur Theologie und Geistesgeschichte des 19. Jahrhunderts. J. Pritz zum 60. Geburtstag*, edited by Erwin Mann, 186–204. Wiener Beiträge zur Theologie 40. Vienna: Domverlag, 1973.

———. "Die philosophisch-theologische Schule A. Günthers: Der Literat, Philosoph und nationalökonom C. F. Hock." In *Festschrift F. Loidl*. edited by V. Flieder, 228–57. Vienna: Brüder Hollinek, 1970.

———. "Die Wiener theologische Schule A. Günthers." *Beiträge zur Wiener Diözesangeschichte*, 20, no. 2 (1979): 17–18.

———. "Zur Günther Forschung." *Theologisch-praktische Quartalschrift*, 127 (1979): 168–71.

März, Eduard. "Comments to Richard Rudolph. 'The Pattern of Austrian Industrial Growth from the 18th to the early 20th Century'." *Austrian History Yearbook*, II (1975): 26–32.

Matis, Herbert. "Comments on Richard Rudolph 'The Pattern of Austrian Industrial Growth for the 18th to the early 20th Century'." *Austrian History Yearbook* II (1975): 33–36.

Mraz, Gottfried. "Kirche und Verkündigung im aufgeklärten Staat. Anmerkungen zur katholischen Pastoraltheologie im josephinischen Österreich." In *Formen der europäischen Aufklärung*, edited by Friedrich Engel-Janosi, et al., 81–95. Vienna: Verlage für Geschichte und Politik, 1976.

Müller, Dr. Ernst. "Der kirchliche Gehorsam und Günther." *Theologisch-praktische Quartalschrift* 30 (1877): 1–15. Günther's humility is praised as an example to others.

Musulin, Stella. "Vienna in the Year of Revolutions 1848." *History Today* 28, no. 7 (1978): 429–35.

Opel, Ferdinand. "Studien zur Versorgung Wiens mit Gütern des täglichen Bedarfs in der ersten Hälfte des 19. Jahrhunderts." In *Studien zur Wiener Geschicthe*, edited by Peter Csendes, 50–87. Vienna: Selbstverlag des Vereins für Geschichte der Stadt Wien, 1981.

Otruba, Gustav. "Katholischer Klerus und 'Kirche' im Spiegel der Flugschriftenliteratur des Revolutionsjahrs 1848." In *Festschrit Franz Loidl zum 65. Geburtstag*, edited by Viktor Flieder, 2: 265–313. Vienna: Brüder Hollinek, 1970.

Pircher, Wolfgang. "Mutmassungen über den Vormärz." In *Wien im Vormärz*, edited by Felix Czeike, 3–8. Vienna: Verein für Geschichte der Stadt Wien Kommissionsverlag Jugend und Volk, 1980.

Pircher, Wolfgang, and Andreas Priberski. "Die Gesundheit, die Polizei und die Cholera." In *Wien im Vormärz*, edited by Felix Czeike, 202–14. Vienna: Verein für Geschichte der Stadt Wien Kommissionsverlag Jugend und Volk, 1980.

Pleyer, Karl. "Leben und Bedeutung Johann Emanuel Veiths." *Wiener Tierärztliche Monatschrift* 39 (1952): 129–34. Also appeared as a Sonderdruck (Vienna: Urban und Schwarzenberg, 1952).

Posch, Andreas. "Kirchenpolitische Einstellung Metternichs." *Religion, Wissenschaft und Kultur* 13 (1962): 119–27.

Pritz, Joseph. "Anton Günther." In *Katholische Theologie Deutschlands im 19. Jahrhundert*, edited by Heinrich Fries and Georg Schwaiger, 1: 348-75. Munich: Kösel, 1975.

———. "Anton Günther." In *Tausend Jahre Österreich*, edited by Walter Pollak, 2: 26-31. Vienna: Jugend und Volk, 1973.

———. "Die Aufassung von Tradition und Schrift bei Anton Günther." *Zeitschrift für katholische Theologie* 84 (1962): 323-58.

———. "Carl Werner." In *Katholische Theologie Deutschlands im 19. Jahrhundert*, edited by Heinrich Fries and Georg Schwaiger, 3: 145-68. Munich: Kösel, 1975.

———. "Gedanken A. Günthers zur Union zwischen Katholiken und Protestanten." *Theologisch-praktische Quartalschrift* 110 (1962): 91-105.

———. "Glauben und Wissen. Ein Versuch zur Lösung des Problems nach A. Günthers." *Zeitschrift für katholische Theologie* 97 (1975): 253-81.

———. "Offenbarung. Eine philosophisch-theologische Analyse nach A. Günther." *Zeitschrift für katholische Theologie* 95 (1973): 249-85.

———. "Zur Geschichte der philosophisch-theologische Schule A. Günthers. Briefe A. Günthers an den Philsophen J. H. Löwe 1841-1862." In *Festschrift F. Loidl zum 65. Geburtstag*, edited by Victor Flieder, 1:204-254. Vienna: Brüder Hollinek, 1970.

———. "Zur Lehre A. Günthers von der Kirche." In *Dienst an der Lehre. Studien zur heutigen Philosophie und Theologie. Festschrift Franz König*, 275-335. Vienna: Katholische Fakultät der Universität Wien, 1965.

———. "Zur Literarischen Form des Schrifttums Anton Günthers." In *Anton Günther. Späte Schriften*, edited by Johann Reikerstorfer, 197-222. Vienna: Herold, 1978.

———. "Zwei unveröffentlichte Briefe A. Günthers an einem Unbekannten. Vier unveröffentlichte Breife A. Günthers an V. Knauer 1859." In *Sacerdos et Pastor. Festschrift zum 40. jährigen Priesterjubiläum Franz Loidls*, 105-23. Vienna: Domverlag, 1972.

Reikerstorfer, Johann. "Das Dilemma der historischen Theologie. Zur Aufgabenstellung einer kritischen Fundamentaltheologie." *Theologie und Glaube* (1975): 321-36.

———. "Zum Offenbarungsbegriff A. Günthers." In *Sacerdos et Pastor. Festschrift zum 40. jährigen Priesterjubiläum Franz Loidls*, 125-37. Vienna: Domverlag, 1972.

———. "Zur Frage nach dem Motiv der Schöpfung bei Anton Günther." In *Erbe als Auftrag. J. Pritz zum 60 Geburtstag*, edited by Erwin Mann, 205-43. Vienna: Domverlag, 1973.

Reimann, Augustine, C.S.S.R. "Der heilige Klemens Maria Hofbauer als Milieuseelsorger." *Der Seelsorger* 28 (1957-58): 124-27.

Reinermann, Alan. "The Return of the Jesuits to the Austrian Empire and the Decline of Josephinism 1820-1822." *Catholic Historical Review* 52 (1966): 372-90.

Reingrabner, Gustav. "Zur rechtlichen Lage der evangelischen Kirche in den österreichischen Erbländer nach 1781." *Österreich in Geschichte und Literatur* 10 (1966): 525-39.

Rösler, Augustin. "Die kulturgeschichtliche Bedeutung von Zacharias Werners Entwicklungsgang." *Die Kultur* 3 (1901): 19-35.

Rudolph, Richard. "The Pattern of Austrian Industrial Growth from the 18th to the Early 20th Century." *Austrian History Yearbook* 11 (1975): 3-25.

Sandgruber, Roman. "Indikationen des Lebenstandards in Wien in der ersten

Hälfte des 19. Jahrhunderts." In *Wien im Vormärz*, edited by Felix Czeike, 57–74. Vienna: Verrein für Geschichte der Stadt Wien, Kommissionsverlag Jugend und Volk, 1980.

Schapirnik, Alfred. "Geschichte der Juden in Kuttenplan und Umgebung." In *Die Juden und Judengemeinde Böhmens in Vergangenheit und Gegenwart*, edited by Hugo Gold, 335–41. Brünn: Jüdischer Buch und Kunst Verlag, 1934.

Scheffczyk, Leo. "Der Weg der deutschen katholischen Theologie im 19. Jahrhundert." *Tübinger Theologische Quartalschrift* 145 (1965): 273–306.

Schreiber, Josef. "Johann Emanuel Veith und die Wiener tierärztliche Schule." *Wiener Tierärztliche Monatschrift* 39 (1952): 134–43.

Schwaiger, Georg. "A. Günther und der Güntherianismus." *Münchener Theologische Zeitschrift* 13 (1962): 297–300.

Schweitzer, M. Baptist (Walburga). "Kirchliche Romantik. Einwirkung des hl. Kl. M. Hofbauer auf das Geistesleben in Wien." *Historisches Jahrbuch der Görresgesellschaft* 48 (1928): 388–460.

Seton-Watson, R. W. "Metternich and Internal Austrian Policy." *Slavonic and East European Review* 17 (1939): 539–55; and 18 (1940): 129–41.

Simons, Thomas W. Jr. "The Prague Origins of the Güntherian Converts 1800–1850." *Leo Baeck Institute Yearbook* 22 (1977): 245–56.

———. "Unveröffentliches über den Aufenthalt des Wiener Philosophen und Theologen A. Günther in Galizien." *Wiener Geschichtsblätter* 30 (1975): 145–49.

———. "Vienna's First Catholic Political Movement: The Güntherians 1848–1857." *Catholic Historical Review* 50 (1969–70): 173–94, 377–93, 610–26.

Sissulak, Franz, S.J. "Das Christentum des Josephinismus. Die josephinische Pastoralliturgie in dogmatischer Sicht." *Zeitschrift für katholische Theologie* 71 (1949): 54–89.

Söhngen, G., et. al. "Das Erbe des 19. Jahrhunderts." *Bonner Zeitschrift für Theologie und Seelsorge* 6 (1929): 81–87.

Spahn, Martin. "Clemens Maria Hofbauer. Aus Anlass seiner heiligsprechung am 20 Mai 1909." *Hochland* 6, no. 2 (1909): 299–313.

Stein, G. "Die Beziehungen von Joseph von Görres zu Wien nebst zwei Briefen von Görress an Anton Günther." *Philosophisches Jahrbuch der Görresgesellschaft* 73 (1953): 142–52.

Till, Rudolf. "Die Anfänge der christlichen Volksbewegung in Österreich." *Jahrbuch der österreichischen Leo Gesellschaft* (1937): 56–103.

———. "Hofbauer und der Frömmigkeitsstil Wiens im 19. Jahrhundert. Ein Rückblick zum 150. Todestag des Wiener Stadtpatrons." *Unsere Heimat* 41. (1970): 1–5.

———. "Kardinal Josef Othmar Rauscher 1791–1875. In *Gestalter der Geschichte Österreichs*, edited by Hugo Hantsch, 397–406. Vienna: Tyrolia, 1962.

———. "Theologen in der Wiener Stadtverwaltung." *Jahrbuch des Vereins für die Geschichte der Stadt Wien* 13 (1957–58): 203–27. On Ignaz Bondi.

Triebl, Johann. "Die Ölzweige." *Reichspost* 30, no. 341 (14 December 1923): 1–2.

Walter, Friedrich. "Die Ursachen des Scheiterns der madjarischen Waffenhelft für die Wiener Oktober Revolutionaere 1848." *Südostforschungen* 22 (1963): 377–400.

Wagner, Hans. "Der Einfluss von Gallikanismus und Jansenismus auf die Kirche und Staat der Aufklärung in Österreich." *Österreich in Geschichte und Literatur* 11 (1967): 521–34.

Wandruska, Adam. "Geheimprotestantismus, Josephinismus und Volksliturgie in Österreich." *Zeitschrift für Kirchengeschichte*, Vierte Folge 78 (1967): 94–101.

Weinzierl-Fischer, Erika. "Die Kirchenfrage auf den österreichischen Reichstag 1848/49." *Mitteilungen des österreichischen Staatsarchivs* 8 (1955): 160–90.

———. "Klemens Maria Hofbauer." In *Tausend Jahre Österreich*, edited by Walter Pollak, 397–402. Vienna: Jugend und Volk, 1973.

———. "Österreichs Klerus und die Arbeiterschaft. Ihr Verhältnis im 19. Jahrhundert nach den Quellen." *Wort und Wahrheit* 12, no. 8 (1957): 613–20.

Wenzel, Paul. "Anton Günther." In *Lexikon für Theologie und Kirche*, edited by Josef Höfer and Karl Rahner, 4: 1276–78. Freiburg: Herder, 1960.

———. "Rezension: Pritz, *Glauben und Wissen bei Anton Günther*." *Theologische Revue* 62, no. 2 (1966): 107–9. Unfavorable.

Wiedemann, Theodor. "Die kirchliche Bücherzensur in der Erzdiözese Wien." *Archiv für österreichische Geschichte* 50 (1873): 213–520.

Winckler, Rupert. "Aus den Visitationsberichten Firmian 1822–1831." *Beiträge zur Wiener Diözesangeschichte* 12, No. 6 (1971): 47–48; 13, no. 1 (1972): 7–8; 13, no. 2 (1972): 12–16; 14, no. 3 (1973): 23–24.

Winter, Eduard, "Anton Günther und die barock-romantische paternal-familiale Soziologie E. K. Winters." *Theologische Quartalschrift* 3 (1930): 399–411.

———. "Differenzierungen in der katholischen Restauration in Österreich. Eine Skizze." *Historisches Jahrbuch* 52 (1932): 442–50.

———. "Early Liberalism in the Habsburg Monarchy: Religious and National Thought Particularly of the Austrian Slavs." *East Central Europe* 1 no. 1 (1974): 1–11.

———. "Der Einfluss einer Theologie auf das Geistesleben der Nation: A Günther." *Hochland* 29 (2 June 1932): 243–49.

———. "Die katholische Restauration in Österreich 1808–1820. Ihre Entwicklung und Auswirkung." In *Katholischer Glaube und deutsches Volkstum in Österreich*, 149–59. Salzburg: Pustet, 1933.

———. "Die Wiener theologische Schule Anton Günthers in seinen und Franz Egerers Briefen an K. Werner." *Jahrbuch der österreichischen Leogesellschaft* (1929): 243–90.

Winter, Ernst Karl. "Anton Günther: Ein Beitrag zur Romantikforschung." *Zeitschrift für die gesamte Staatswissenschaft* 88 (1930): 281–333.

Wodka, Josef. "Die Kirche und die Aufklärung." *Österreich in Geschichte und Literatur* 10 (1966): 223–31.

Wolfsgruber, Cölestin. "Die Haltung des Wiener Klerus in den Märztagen 1848." *Jahrbuch für Landeskunde von Niederösterreich*, Neue Folge 13/14 (1914–15): 483–94.

———. "Veith als Homilist." In *Erster homiletischer Kurs in Wien*, edited by Heinrich Swoboda, 129–48. Vienna: Heinrich Kirsch, 1911.

Zabel, Johann. "Ein lebendiges Bild des hl. Klemens Maria Hofbauer." *Beiträge zur Wiener Diözesangeschichte* 16, no. 3 (1975): 17.

Zöllner, Erich. "Bemerkungen zum Problem der Beziehung zwischen Aufklärung und Josephinismus." in *Österreich und Europa. Festgabe für Hugo Hantsch zum 70. Geburtstag*, 203–19. Vienna: Styria, 1965.

INDEX

Acton, Lord, 207 n.150
Aeterni Patris, 160
Aristotle, 15–19, 77–78
Arnoldi, Wilhelm, 153, 163, 167
Aufwärts, 127, 134–36, 197 n.49
Augustine of Hippo, 15–17, 72–73, 87, 99, 112, 190 n.99
Authority, 10, 16–19, 49, 89, 92, 116

Baader, Franz von, 55, 166, 181 n.34
Baltzer, Johann Baptist, 163–64, 166–67
Baptism, 18, 43, 91, 110, 117
Begriff, 76–79, 81–82, 84, 87–88, 101, 104–5, 114, 136, 188 n.15
Bermann, Moritz, 163
Biedermeier Era, 31, 33–35, 42–44, 50–51, 96–98, 100, 119, 139, 161, 172 n.1
Blue Monday, 103, 193 n.28
Bolzano, Bernard, 54, 64, 180 n.19
Bondi, Ignaz, 145, 163
Braun, Johann Wilhelm Joseph, 163
Brentano, Clemens, 48, 177 n.60
Bretzenheim-Regetz, Ferdinand, 55, 57, 153
Brüggemann, Th., 163
Brunner, Sebastian, 124–25, 137, 145, 163–64, 166, 197 n.33

Catergian, J., 164
Catholic Union (*Katholikenverein*), 126–27, 130, 145, 147, 149–50, 152–53, 163, 166
Censorship, 27, 116, 120, 129, 151–53, 167
Communism, 22, 100, 131, 133, 145, 147–50, 152
Concordat, 26, 42, 51, 123, 139–45, 157, 202 n.18
Congregation of the Index, 27, 156–58, 164, 167–68, 205 n.114, 206 nn. 127, 130, and 131, 207 n.143
Conscience (*Gewissen*), 30, 89–90, 114, 117, 129, 136, 147, 157

Consciousness, 32, 79–84, 91–92, 114–15, 126, 188 n.21
Constitution, 26, 116, 120–21, 123, 126–27, 130–34, 137, 140–41, 145–47, 152, 163
Croy, Ludwig, 135, 155, 164, 166, 204 n.98

Darwin, Charles, 100, 194 n.44
Democracy, 10, 26, 94, 101, 117, 122–24, 133, 135, 145–48, 152, 155, 195 n.8, 203 n.54, 205 n.105
Descartes, René, 19, 76, 80, 82, 167
Dialectic, 30, 75, 82
Diepenbrock, Melchior von, 153, 155, 164
Drey, J. S., 154, 206 n.119
Dualism, 71, 75–77, 94, 114, 116, 135, 152, 154, 156

Egerer, Franz, 164, 166, 204 n.98
Egger, A., 164
Ehrlich, J. N., 155, 164, 166, 204 n.98
Elvenich, J. P., 164
Enlightenment, 19–21, 24, 28–29, 37, 42, 46–47, 61, 63, 73–74, 86, 100, 110, 128, 146
Eucharist, 24, 36, 39, 93, 108, 174 n.18, 194 n.35

Faith (*Glaube*), 29, 76, 86–88, 114, 133, 135, 148
Febronianism, 25, 148
Ferdinand I, 41, 118–21, 131, 158
Feuerbach, Ludwig, 30, 83
Firmian, Leopold, 42, 68, 186 n.128
Flir, Alois, 153, 205 n.114
Förster, Heinrich, 153, 164
Francis I, 41–44, 50, 53, 96, 176 n.50, 191 n.5
Francis Joseph I, 51, 119, 121, 123, 139–41, 143–44, 158, 178 n.68, 200 n.7
Frank, Jacob, 63, 163, 184 n.92

Freedom, 20, 29, 49, 83, 106, 110–11, 114, 116, 120–22, 124, 126, 130, 132, 134–40, 151, 178 n.65; of conscience, 30, 124; free will, 105, 115, 151; of press, 22, 26, 44, 120–22, 124, 129–30, 133, 139, 151, 196 n.26; of religion, 22, 120–22, 124, 126, 130, 133, 140, 151, 195 n.10
French Revolution, 20, 23–25, 41, 137
Führich, Josef, 164

Gallicanism, 25
Gangauf, Theodor, 165
Gärtner, Wilhelm, 124, 164–65
Gasser, Vinzenz, 165
Geissel, Johann von, 155–56, 205 n.114
Gerkrath, L., 165
German Catholicism, 123, 198 n.54
Glücker, Michael, 58, 71, 165
Glücker, Notburga Piuma, 58, 71, 165
Goethe, Johann Wolfgang von, 28, 99, 134
Greif, Laurenz, 48, 56–57, 71, 135, 153, 156–59, 165, 177 n.61
Grillparzer, Franz, 157
Gruscha, Anton, 144
Günther, Anton, 10, 31, 40, 52, 57, 72, 145, 151–53, 163–69, 179 n.4, 182 n.56; anthropology of, 73, 81–83, 89–91, 135; as censor, 42, 59; Christology of, 89–94; contrapositional dualism of, 71, 75–77, 81, 85, 94, 135; creation theory of, 84–86; early years, 53–58; ecclesiology of, 92–94; faith and reason, 86–88; historical criticism of, 73–74, 88–89, 92; Hofbauer and, 48, 50–52, 177 nn. 61–62, 64, and 68, 179 nn. 74 and 80; Jesuits and, 57–58, 68, 157; as liberal, 118, 128, 136–38, 198 n.57; revelation theory of, 85–88; Revolution of 1848 and, 116–19, 126, 135–36; theory of God and, 81–85; trial and condemnation, 72, 113, 138, 153–58, 160–61, 205 n.114, 206 nn. 120–21; two realms theory (*Natur* and *Geist*) of, 76–81; Veith and, 63, 65, 68, 70–71, 99–107, 111, 113–14; Vienna and, 58–60, 182 n.57; writing style of, 74–76

Haskalah, 183 n.84
Häusle, Johann Michael, 145, 149, 152, 165, 167, 204 n.98
Hegel, Georg Wilhelm Friedrich, 29–30, 51, 75, 77–78, 80, 82, 135
Herder, Johann Gottfried, 28
Hermes, Georg, 155, 163, 206 n.126
Hilgers, J., 165
Hock, Carl Ferdinand von, 145, 149, 156, 164
Hofbauer, Clement, 44–52, 56, 65–66, 68, 72–73, 87, 96, 100–101, 116, 119–20, 122–23, 130, 137, 141, 147, 159, 176 n.53, 177 n.63, 181 n.38, 190 n.72
Hoffinger, Anna von, 159, 165
Hoffinger, Johann Baptist von, 166
Hoffinger, Josefa von, 166
Hohenlohe, Gustav Adolph, 153, 155, 165–66
Hohenwart, Archbishop (of Vienna), 42, 45
Hönig, Antonie, 159
Hörfarter, M., 165
Horny, Leopold, 48, 177 n.62
Hubner, J. N., 157

Idealism, 54, 74, 76, 86, 154–55, 206 n.129
Idee, 76–79, 81–90, 101, 103–5, 109, 114, 136, 188 n.15
Immaculate Conception, 27, 60, 112, 142, 164, 199 n.94, 201 n.17
Industrial Revolution, 10, 34, 119, 144
Infallibility, 27, 92–93, 139, 143–44, 157, 159–60, 179 nn. 4 and 79
Isfordink, Johann Nepomuk, 166

Jansenism, 19, 23–24, 27, 38–39
Jean Paul. *See* Richter, Paul Friedrich
Jesuits, 19, 23, 25, 27, 29, 36, 38, 45, 57–58, 65, 69–70, 154, 166, 176 nn. 48 and 50, 182 n.54
Josephinism, 35–39, 41–42, 44–46, 49–51, 57, 95, 100, 116, 122, 124, 130, 133, 137, 141–42, 144, 147, 149, 153, 173 n.16, 196 n.21, 201 nn. 4 and 7
Joseph II, 33, 35–43, 45, 53, 61, 118, 143, 174 n.23, 183 n.84, 184 n.95

Kalmus, Franz, 166
Kant, Immanuel, 10, 19–21, 23, 26, 29–30, 77–78, 80, 161, 163, 206 n.126
Katholikentag, 144
Kaulich, W., 166
Kayser, J. B., 166
Kingdom of God/Christ, 106, 130, 150
Kinsky, Christian, 69, 186 nn. 122 and 133
Kleutgen, Joseph, 155, 160, 168–69, 206 n.127
Klinkowström, Friedrich August, 48, 177 n.63
Knauer, Vinzenz, 166
Knoodt, Peter, 135, 155, 157, 163–67, 206 nn. 119 and 128
Korn, Michael, 55–57, 59

Landes, Pater, 57–58, 182 n.52
Lasaulx, Ernst von, 166
Latour, Theodor Baillet de, 121, 127–28, 146, 198 n.55, 202 n.53, 203 n.54
Leopoldinenstiftung, 44
Leo XIII, 131, 160–61, 199 n.80, 205 nn. 105 and 114
Lewisch, J. C., 166
Liberalism, 22, 25, 118, 128, 130, 134, 137, 140–43, 160, 198 n.57, 201 n.4
Liguori, Alphonsus, 25, 46
Löwe, Johann Heinrich, 166
Löwe, Josef, 167
Lydia, 152, 203 n.100

Madlener, Johann, 48, 178 n.64
Maria Theresa, 28, 33, 35, 37–41, 45–46, 118, 172 n.2, 174 n.17, 184 n.95
Marx, J., 167
Marx, Karl, 30, 34, 119–21, 161
Mayer, Georg Karl, 167
Melzer, Ernst, 167
Mensch, 81–85, 89–91, 103–5, 107, 111–12, 114, 116, 123, 126, 128–29, 133, 136, 151
Merten, Jacob, 167
Messenhauser, Wenzel, 127
Metternich, Clement Lothar, 34, 41–42, 44, 49, 51, 53, 55, 71, 118–19, 176 n.50
Milde, Vinzenz Eduard, 42, 120, 122, 124–25, 127, 140–41, 145–47, 149–50, 153, 155, 196 n.26, 201 n.6, 204 n.86

Monarchy, 22–23, 33, 37, 44, 116–18, 123, 127, 133–34, 136, 141, 143, 147, 149, 152, 203 n.54
Müller, Adam, 48, 51, 55–56, 64, 178 n.65
Müller, Georg, 153, 167
Munich Theological Faculty, 29, 181 n.34, 182 n.56

Napoleon Bonaparte, 10, 19–21, 23–29, 32–33, 35, 41, 44–46, 55, 96, 160–61
Nationalism, 28, 133–34, 139, 148, 200 n.3
Nature (*Natur*), 19, 22, 79–81, 83, 85, 89, 91–92, 101, 103–4, 106–8, 111, 114–16, 135–36, 148, 152
Nickes, Johann Peter, 167, 204 n.98
Noumena, 20, 75, 80

Obedience, 30, 68, 111, 134–35, 137
Old Catholics, 123, 157, 159–60, 163–67, 169
Ölzweige, 178 n.66
Opinio, 9, 16–21, 30, 161
Österreichische Volksfreund, Der, 127, 145, 149–50

Pabst, Johann Heinrich, 76, 163, 167, 206 n. 121
Pantheism, 30, 51, 60, 74–82, 85, 100, 103–4, 108, 110, 128, 135, 138, 153–54
Pappalettere, Simplicio, 153, 167
Passy, Georg, 48, 178 n.66, 185 n.102
Passy, Johann, 48, 178 n.66
Pastoral theology, 24, 38, 58, 124, 174 n.23
Penckler, Joseph von, 46–47, 177 n.55
Piarists, 53, 164, 166
Pichler, Caroline, 47, 177 n.57
Pilat, Josef Anton von, 48, 118 n.67, 177 n.63
Pius IX, 29, 141, 143, 154–57, 166, 205 n.114, 206 n.131
Pius VII, 23, 25, 57
Pius VI, 23, 37
Piusverein, 126
Plato, 18–19, 77–78, 80
Pogazar, Johann Chrysostom, 167

Index

Pope/Papacy, 16–18, 21, 23, 25–26, 36, 38, 42, 44–45, 49–50, 94, 117, 123, 133, 137, 139–43, 150–51, 161, 169, 200 n.3

Priesthood, 46, 57, 65–66, 93, 106, 117, 133, 158

Private property, 22, 145, 148, 152

Rationalism (Semi-rationalism), 30, 114, 155–56, 160, 206 nn. 126 and 129, 178 n.64, 193 n.27

Rauscher, Joseph Othmar von, 48, 51, 123, 140–44, 150, 153, 155–56, 158, 178 n.68, 200 n.3, 201 n.7, 202 n.31, 207 n.134

Reason, 19, 29, 54, 76, 86–88, 193 n.27

Redemptorists, 45–47, 50–51, 57–58, 66–71, 95–97, 120, 123, 128, 155, 177 n.54, 178 nn. 64, 66–70, and 72, 179 n.73, 182 nn. 45 and 54, 206 n.121

Reinkens, Joseph Herbert, 164, 167, 169

Reinkens, Wilhelm, 167

Republicanism, 26, 118, 131, 133, 145

Revelation, 29, 47, 56, 76, 78, 85–89, 91–92, 111, 114, 122, 130, 188 n.18

Revolution of 1848, 22, 27, 35, 94, 96, 118–34, 144–47, 152, 160, 203 n.68

Richter, Paul Friedrich (Jean Paul), 74, 100, 187 n.7

Roman Catholic revival, 47–48

Romanticism, 21, 23, 28–29, 42, 45, 55, 63, 72–75, 79, 86, 100

Rudiger, Bishop (of Linz), 208 n.162

Scheiner, Josef, 152, 165, 167

Schlegel, Dorothea von, 47, 177 n.58

Schlegel, Friedrich von, 47, 51, 56, 64, 177 n.58, 178 n.65

Schleiermacher, Friedrich, 66, 185 n.115, 188 n.35

Schlör, A., 168

Schlüter, C. B., 168

Schmid, Francis Xavier, 168

Scholasticism (Neo-scholasticism, Thomists), 27, 73–74, 82, 86, 91, 152, 154–56, 160, 166, 169

Schön, Bruno, 70, 153, 168, 186 n.143

Schülter, Bernhard, 168

Schwarz, I. G., 126, 194 n.44

Schwarzenberg, Ferdinand, 56, 59, 113, 126, 140, 144, 149, 151, 153–59, 168, 178 n.68, 186 n.124, 200 n.3, 201 nn. 7–8

Schwingenschlögl, Julius, 168

Scientia (science), 9, 16–21, 30, 76, 86–88, 131, 135, 146, 157, 161, 194 n.44; scientific revolution, 10, 73; *Wissenschaft*, 54–56, 59, 86, 103, 108, 114, 152, 154, 165

Secularization, 23, 26, 144

Separation of church and state, 26, 116, 135–36, 205 n.105

Sermon methods, 24–25, 39, 43–44; Hofbauer's, 47–49; Veith's, 68–69, 95–102, 129, 131–32

Severinusverein. See Catholic Union

Silbert, Johann Peter, 48, 178 n.69

Sin, 90, 106–11, 114, 116, 129–31, 134, 151, 181 n.39, 198 n.58

Smith, Berhard, 168

Socialism, 22, 131, 133, 146, 148

Spirit (*Geist*), 79–85, 87, 89, 91–93, 101–4, 106–8, 111, 114, 116, 132, 135–36, 148, 152, 188 n.21

Spörlein, Johannes, 168

Springer, Franz, 48, 178 n.70

Staudenmaier, Franz, 48

Steinringer, F., 168

Strobelhofgesellschaft, 64, 185 n.102

Syllabus of Errors, 156

Szechenyi, Franz, 48, 178 n.71

Tarnoczy, Archbishop (of Salzburg), 153, 165, 169

Theil, Andreas, 169

Thomas Aquinas, 9–10, 15, 19, 51, 78, 99, 152, 154, 160–62, 169, 201 n.17

Tolerance/Toleration, 19, 26, 36, 39, 43, 49, 143, 183 n.84

Tradition, 32, 47, 73, 93

Trebisch, Leopold, 164, 169, 187 n.14

Trent, Council of, 23, 112, 152, 205 n.108

Trinity, 30, 81, 83, 85, 104

Trütschel, Maximilian, 169

Tübingen Theological Faculty, 29, 51, 154, 179 n.1, 182 n.56

Ultramontanism, 26, 44, 51, 122, 178 n.65, 196 n.21

Vaterland, Das, 144
Vatican Council I, 123, 159, 163, 199 n.94
Veith, J. E., 10, 31, 41, 48, 50–52, 54, 56, 59–61, 66, 158–61, 163–69, 178 nn. 66 and 68–69, 179 nn.73 and 80, 181 n.38; in Catholic Union, 126–27, 134; as doctor, 63–64, 67, 70, 95; early years, 61–71; and Günther, 72, 88, 94, 101–4; as Güntherian 100–107, 111, 113–15, 128–29, 138; at Günther's trial, 152–54, 156–58; and Judaism, 61–62, 64–65, 151, 183 n.83, 184 n.93; as a liberal, 118, 128, 130, 136–38, 198 n.57; in Prague, 144–51; as preacher, 68–70, 95–102, 129, 131–32; as Redemptorist, 66–69; and Revolution of 1848, 116–19, 123, 128–33; as teacher, 95, 191 n.2; *Vater Unser*, 101–13
Vernunft (reason), 29, 54, 78, 80, 86–88, 152, 188 n.15

Verstand (understanding), 29, 78–80, 103, 188 n.15
Vogelsang, Karl von, 144, 202 n.26

Watterich, Johannes M., 169
Weber, Theodor, 169
Werner, Carl, 164, 168–69
Werner, Franz, 169, 204 n.98
Werner, Zacharias, 48, 178 n.72
Wolter, Ernst, 169
Wolter, Gustav Rudolf, 169

Zängerle, Roman, 48, 179 n.73
Zelanti, 25–26
Zenner, F. X., 48, 179 n.74
Zeitschrift für die gesamte katholische Theologie, 152, 165, 167, 204 n.98
Ziegler, Gregory Thomas, 48, 179 n.75, 200 n.6